THE
GOOD NEWS
ABOUT
DEPRESSION

THE GOOD NEWS ABOUT DEPRESSION

Cures and Treatments in the New Age of Psychiatry

REVISED EDITION

MARK S. GOLD, M.D.

with Lois B. Morris

BANTAM BOOKS

NEW YORK   TORONTO   LONDON   SYDNEY   AUCKLAND

THE GOOD NEWS ABOUT DEPRESSION, REVISED EDITION

A Bantam Book / July 1995
PUBLISHING HISTORY
Villard edition published February 1987

Library of Congress Cataloging-in-Publication Data
Gold, Mark S.
  The good news about depression / Mark S. Gold. — Rev. ed.
  p.   cm.
  Includes bibliographical references and index.
  ISBN 0-553-37214-9
  1. Depression, Mental—Popular works.   2. Biological psychiatry.
I. Title.
RC537.G64   1995
616.85'27—dc20   95-1691
                                                                       CIP

Published simultaneously in the United States and Canada

PRINTED IN THE UNITED STATES OF AMERICA

BVG   10   9   8   7   6

CONTENTS

The New Good News

You couldn't have picked a better time in human history to feel miserable.

In 1986, when the first edition of this book was published, there were some effective treatments and cures for depression. Back then, the good news was that we had begun to differentiate clearly between a disease called depression and a condition that is a symptom of other diseases, only appearing to be depression. This breakthrough was the result of tests and diagnostic instruments developed and implemented by a handful of psychiatrists and neuroscientists who worked tirelessly, and often without recognition, to bring a new science to the practice of psychiatry and the relief of mental suffering.

We who worked in this new field called our science biopsychiatry, the new medicine of the mind. At that time, few psychiatrists called themselves biopsychiatrists. Today, few would mind that title. Our approach, so controversial in the old days, is now the norm.

But now there's *new* good news. For one thing, we now have greater knowledge about how the brain works and what probably is at the root of depression. Just as important, today we have a new generation of medicines that are so effective in the treatment of depression that our diagnostic techniques are even better. The medications you'll read about have changed the way we diagnose depression—and may even change the way we define it. Biopsychiatry has ushered in a new age of optimism in psychiatry and psychotherapy after years of treatments—from talking to taking pills—that didn't work, or didn't last.

If you have ever sought help from a psychiatrist, your doctor, a psychologist, a social worker, a nurse, or a minister because you're depressed and can't seem to shake it, you will see as you read this book just how different, how straightforward, the biopsychiatric approach to your pain is. Biopsychiatry, or more simply *medical psychiatry,* returns psychiatry to the medical model. In doing so it incorporates all the latest advances in scientific research and, for the first time in history, provides a systematic method of diagnosis, treatment, cure, and even prevention of depression.

Mental illness has a tremendous impact on our whole society. Up to 50 million of the 252 million U.S. citizens will experience some form of mental disorder at some point in their lives. Yet many psychiatric disorders go untreated; only about 10 to 20 percent of those people who would benefit from medication actually receive the treatment they need. According to recent U.S. government figures, one-third of the homeless suffer from untreated severe mental illness.

Of the many forms of mental illness, depression is the most common. In fact, depression is sometimes called the common cold of psychiatry, because it is the condition for which more people seek medical attention than any other, including viral infections, high blood pressure, headaches—and, for that matter, the common cold. Throughout the world, over one hundred million people are estimated to be suffering from severe depression requiring (but not necessarily receiving) a doctor's care. In the United States alone, the number of people experiencing depression at any given time may be as high as sixteen million. Hundreds of thousands of others may suffer from masked depression, in which physical aches and pains are actually unrecognized symptoms of depression. Whatever its form, this serious illness can devastate entire families. Suicide is a frequent outcome of depression. In 1991, thirty thousand people in the United States committed suicide, and over half a million attempted it. Put another way, in a two-year period, as many Americans kill themselves as were killed in the entire Vietnam War. Many of these suicides are a direct consequence of the hopelessness and helplessness that arise from severe depression.

It is well known that America spends more on health care than any other country, over $600 billion a year. For years, mental health care accounted for about 10 percent of this cost, but from 1987 to 1992, the cost to employers for mental health care of employees rose by 300 percent. Much of this increase is due to late identification of mental health problems, failure to seek timely treatment due to the stigma attached to mental disorders, and the costs of dealing with substance abuse, which in many cases results when people try to self-treat their illness through use of illicit drugs or alcohol.

In this book I'll use depression as a kind of lens to show you how biopsychiatry works and what practitioners such as myself can offer those who suffer from the mental—and physical—agony of the disease. By comparison, you'll see how and why traditional psychiatric and psychological approaches still do not—and indeed, cannot—work.

What is depression and why is it so common? It is the first priority for study by biopsychiatrists in research and laboratory settings, in hospitals and clinics. Through continuing intensive efforts, we have amassed an impressive amount of theoretical and practical knowledge, so that today we know more about depression than any other psychiatric affliction. To learn about the disorder, we as scientists had to ask ourselves countless questions. Not only did we have to learn what depression *is,* we also had to find out what it *isn't.* How does it work in the body? Which parts of the brain are involved? What's "body"? What's "mind"? What are the psychological and physiological causes? What is the relationship, if any, between the symptoms of depression and its cause (or causes)? Do animals get depressed? If so, why, and what can we learn by studying their behavior? Is there an evolutionary advantage to depression?

Are there biochemical, behavioral, or genetic traits that can indicate who is or will be subject to depression? What happens to brain cells during depression? Which body chemicals are involved? Which genes? Which glands? Why do depressed people have bodily symptoms? How many kinds of depression are there, and what are the different criteria of each? Are there types of depression that are not physiological, and if so, how can we tell?

What is the relationship between stress and depression? What makes some people subject to depression and others not? Is there a relationship between depression and personality? Is depression related to other emotional problems, such as eating disorders, school phobia, impulsiveness? Are people who commit suicide physiologically and/or psychologically different from other depressed people or the population at large?

Can we develop new and better laboratory tests to diagnose depression and to follow the progress of treatment?

Does depression have a lasting effect on the body? On behavior? How can we treat the symptoms of depression? How can we cure it? Better yet, how can we prevent it?

Question after question led us into some of the most incredible medical research ever done in the 1980s and early 1990s. Some of the leading minds in all areas of the life sciences have probed the frontiers of science and human understanding, wherein lie the ultimate comprehension and cure of all mental illness.

Biopsychiatry is closing the gap between body and mind. Our understanding has penetrated the actual cells of key brain areas, giving us knowledge of the submicroscopic spaces between nerve cells and structures on the cells, the chemicals that are synthesized in tiny amounts, the cell walls, the ions that penetrate them.

We now have a working knowledge of the anatomy of mood. We know which of the brain's chemical messengers and hormonal systems regulate our good and bad moods. Using the most advanced laboratory technology, we've developed tests to diagnose, monitor, and predict the course of depression. We now have tests to identify subtypes of depression in order to choose the appropriate treatment or blend of treatments. When medication is required, other tests can identify the correct dosage for each individual, and still others can tell when the medication is working.

Incredibly, we have even made significant progress identifying chemical and genetic traits in children and relatives of depressed people, so we can let them know who will be at risk of severe depressive disease during their lifetimes. This means that someday soon, as we develop appropriate precautions for the at-risk population, we will be able to prevent depression from taking its deadly toll. By identifying certain chemicals in the blood, we may even be able to predict who is at risk of suicide.

Some of the tools we use to treat depression are newly developed (including light therapy and tinted glasses for seasonal emotional disorders); some, such as medication and psychotherapy, are more traditional. But the difference today is that we use these treatments in a much more systematic and creative way, determining which patient requires which specific medication or medications, which type of psychotherapy, how much and for how long, and who's likely to get better without any major intervention.

BETTER NEWS ABOUT PSYCHIATRISTS

A decade ago I viewed the medical profession—including psychiatrists, internists, psychologists, and social workers—as one of the main reasons depression often went untreated. Many of these caregivers simply were unable or unwilling to accept the emerging advances in biopsychiatry.

Over the years, however, this has changed. One reason is that we psychiatrists have now aired some of the uncomfortable truths about our profession, and there has been real, significant change.

Today, biopsychiatry has become the only viable form of psychiatry, and it will remain so in the future. Many, many psychiatrists have returned to *being* doctors and to *thinking* like doctors. A decade ago most psychiatrists practiced psychiatry, but not medicine. They didn't carry a physician's black bag, perform a complete physical exam with blood and urine tests, or even take a complete medical history. But that's changing, and that's why the news about psychiatrists is getting better.

Medicine, as the saying goes, is as much art as science. Psychiatrists have long practiced their art without the science to back it up and make it work. In part, this is because, until this last decade, relatively little was known about the interactions of the brain, the body, and behavior. I'm not against psychotherapy (the "talking cure"); on the contrary, when it comes to problems of living and being, the psychotherapist's art is *de rigueur* in helping you get your life on track and achieve a larger measure of gratification and effectiveness. Depression, however, is not always the kind of problem for which talking to someone can help you.

Depression can be a biological illness for which you need a doctor. It can be the first sign of a developing physical illness—perhaps even a deadly illness. Depression can be a side effect of virtually any prescription or illegal drug, or a symptom of another physical illness. In any of these cases, traditional psychotherapy in the absence of appropriate medical diagnosis and care will not help you and may even hurt you. One recent study shows, for example, that the longer the delay in receiving appropriate medical care for major (biological) depression, the more likely it is that the condition will become chronic and possibly untreatable. Different types of depression share the same constellation of symptoms. You cannot know what kind of depression you have unless you consult a specialist in the differential diagnosis of depression: a biopsychiatrist. Today, most of us recognize that this is the type of psychiatry that gets the best results.

Society has conferred a particular mandate on physicians: to heal the sick. Of all the mental health professionals who practice in this country, only psychiatrists are M.D.s. Having been trained to fulfill this mandate, psychiatrists have the moral and ethical responsibility to return to the medical practice of their specialty. At present, many psychiatrists routinely fail to recognize medical diseases in their patients. Study after study reveals that many diagnoses of depression are in fact misdiagnosed physical illnesses of which depression is a symptom.

You may feel and act like you're miserably depressed, and your psychiatrist or other therapist may well agree with you. Actually, though, your emotional symptoms may be an early indication of thyroid disease, heart disease, alcoholism, Alzheimer's disease, diabetes, mononucleosis, nutritional deficiencies, or even (and not unusually) cancer. There are at least seventy-five diseases that first appear with emotional symptoms. Biopsychiatrists, with their medical approach, look for and rule out these diseases *before* beginning to treat you for depression.

Once the diagnostic process has ruled out physical disease as a cause of primary depression, the next step for the biopsychiatric physician is to identify which type of depression you are suffering from. Research has identified many types and subtypes of depression, from normal feelings of sadness, which affect every human being in the course of a lifetime—for example, after a death or job loss—and which always go away, to types of recurring depression that depend on the supply of chemicals deep inside key areas of your brain.

Effective, lasting treatment of depression depends entirely on matching the treatment to the kind of depression you have. Again, a psychologist or a traditional psychiatrist, including one who dispenses drugs, does not always make these essential distinctions. That is another of many reasons why the treatment you or a family member has received for depression may not have worked.

EVERYBODY'S DOING SOMETHING WRONG

Why do so many cases of depression go undiagnosed and thus untreated? Even when treatment is applied, why does it so often fail? The roots of the problem are tangled, and they run deep.

One major concern is that the task of recognizing depression is handled by a wide range of health care professionals—not just psychiatrists but primary-care physicians, and not just doctors but psychologists and social workers who do not have medical training. It's a striking fact that, in this country, primary-care physicians (family doctors, internists, and so on) write most of the prescriptions for antidepressants. Unfortunately, studies reveal that many of these physicians have a poor record of diagnosing depression correctly or treating it properly. And there are more psychologists (Ph.D.s) and social workers (M.S.W.s) in the field of mental health than there are psychiatrists. As skilled as these practitioners may be, they simply do not have the medical education to recognize and distinguish among the diseases that so often masquerade as depression. You wouldn't dream of going to a social worker seeking treatment for the flu, yet many people wouldn't think twice about seeing a counselor for depression.

What's more, caregivers who do not have medical degrees are not allowed to prescribe medication, and so may not be able to offer the treatment that might have the best chance of working. Too often, turf wars erupt over the need to hold on to patients (and their payments). This fosters competitiveness and a lack of cooperation among the different professions. To secure their positions, nonmedical therapists may promote certain myths: that use of medication is a crutch, that it is addicting, that it interferes with therapy.

Some doctors contribute to the situation by believing, against the evidence, that depression is "all in your head." This is a typical response women hear, especially those who experience mood swings during their menstrual cycles, after giving birth, or around the time of menopause. In fact, though, our moods are governed to a large extent by changes in our hormones. That biological fact is one reason why women experience depression at twice the rate of men.

Another problem is that most people don't know how to recognize depression. One tragic reflection of this is the high incidence of suicides among adolescents. Parents and teachers often claim they had no idea the child was so unhappy. But if they had been taught that depression can strike even young children, and if they had learned to spot the warning signs, they might have prevented disaster.

Contrary to common belief, the elderly are not more likely to become depressed than younger people. Often, though, relatives and caregivers assume that their symptoms of depression are the result of senility or dementia. And the elderly often have ailments, such as cancer, that may masquerade as depression. Too often doctors dismiss these people as grouchy time-wasters, and so refuse to look carefully for the source of their trouble, when the fact is that depression, even in the elderly, is reversible.

And what about you? Like nine out of ten people with depression, you may be contributing to the problem by trying to treat it yourself. Often that means using tranquilizers, painkillers, illicit drugs, or alcohol. These substances may lift your mood for a while, but over time they can actually make depression worse. People refuse to see doctors for any number of reasons: they are ashamed; they believe nothing can be done; they may have had bad experiences with treatment in the past. Sometimes they may not even know they're depressed; they've felt bad for so long that they think it's normal.

For you and others like you, there's good news: Plenty of help for depression is available. In the past few years, people like you have demanded better answers and better results. As a result, our body of knowledge is growing and the quality of care is improving. Today biopsychiatry has become the accepted approach to treatment.

You'll be learning a lot of inside information in these pages: how psychotherapists and doctors think, how they arrive at their conclusions, and how and why they treat you the way they do. If you are well informed, you can demand better treatment when mental illness strikes you or your family. You can ask questions of your therapist to see how educated he or she is in the biological aspects of depression. You can seek help among those practitioners who are up to date in diagnosis and treatment. You can evaluate the treatment you're getting before it's too late. And—this is no small point—you can know what is expected of you in order to achieve fully successful treatment.

The ultimate aims of biopsychiatry are identical to those of all the mental health professions: to remove or lessen the obstacles that stand in the way of living a healthy and productive life. Once depression is cured, you can pursue and experience happiness.

Critics accuse biopsychiatrists of disregarding psychology in favor of biology because we insist on additional medical training (especially in neurology and endocrinology) and a medical approach. But biopsychiatry is the first science of the mind to include *all* of you. Science will no longer allow us to separate the mind from the body. Ongoing research reveals more and more the complex, exquisite interrelationships between physical illness and behavior, between the state of your mind and the state of your body.

Psychiatry has had to wait a long time, longer than other medical specialties, for knowledge and technology to advance sufficiently to penetrate the inner workings of the brain. Now we are doing so, and at long last we are beginning to comprehend the biology, the etiology, the physiology of mental illness, and to develop treatments corresponding to our new knowledge. Today, with new and effective medications being approved for depression at a breakneck pace, we are learning to apply this knowledge to bring relief to millions of people. And that's really the good news.

PART I

WHAT IS A PSYCHIATRIST?

CHAPTER 1

The Case of the Famous Actor Who Couldn't Go On

He was a Hollywood legend, one of the most well known and beloved stars of all time. He had come to see me as a last resort, and now we had to tell him what we'd found. We had to tell him he had cancer. *It was the best news he had heard in years.*

Fortunately, we don't often have to deliver a diagnosis of cancer. Still, this case was not unusual for us. Psychiatrists in private practice or at other psychiatric hospitals often refer their "nonresponders"—their hopeless cases—to us for evaluation. Or people call us saying they've been treated for depression for umpteen years and they're not getting any better. Their friends and families and even their doctors urge them to *learn to live with it;* this misery is part of who they are. Is there anything we can do for them? They're at the end of their ropes, a lot of them.

So often what we find is that their misery results from a *disease* they have. Sometimes that disease is the brain dysfunction we call major depression. Sometimes that disease is drug toxicity. Or it is an overactive thyroid or ovarian cysts or pancreatitis or a dietary deficiency or diabetes or heart disease or Parkinson's disease . . . or cancer.

PROLOGUE: THE ACTOR'S ENTRANCE

This very famous actor—let's call him FA—had been treated for depression without success for three and a half tormented years. Famous and wealthy as he was, he was able to consult some of the best-reputed and most expensive psychiatrists in New York, and to afford any treatment they recommended. Still, in this day of "miracle cures" for depression, instead of getting better, FA grew worse. His personality seemed to change

3

and, beloved though he had been to friends and fans alike, he had become distinctly unlikable. His doctors washed their hands of him and turned him over to us.

Well-known people are not unusual among patients I've treated; my staff doesn't often blink an eye at celebrities. But anticipating the arrival of this man, this star of some of the finest classic movies, this heartthrob and role model, still so virile in his early sixties, silver hair matched by a softly curving silver mustache, with steel-gray eyes and rugged features—well, we were all rather weak in the knees!

When he checked in, however, he barely resembled that familiar face and sinewy body. His skin was pale, his eyebrows were knitted, and his whole face drooped. He looked as if he hadn't been eating or sleeping. His gait was ponderous; he walked like an old man.

And was he in a rotten mood! It was his first day on our evaluation unit, and he lashed out when anyone approached him. At a psychiatric hospital, the staff doesn't take a patient's angry outbursts personally. Patients come here because of their behavioral difficulties; if they acted normally, we'd wonder what they were doing here. But with FA, who had been known so long for his gentle manner, the hostile, angry behavior was disconcerting. As far as he was concerned, we couldn't do anything right, and he was sure to let us know about it.

It all started when the nurse asked him to take off all his clothes and put on a hospital gown. She handed him the white gown, and he let her have it: "What the hell kind of place am I in? Who the hell do you think you are? Look, miss, or is it Ms.," he said with a sneer, "I'm in this nuthouse with a bunch of lunatics because I've been stinking depressed for years. Get it? I say that to that doctor out there and it's like he hasn't heard me. He just smiles and says, 'Pee in this jug, please.' Now I've got to strip. I've already *had* a physical—I've had *two* physicals! I've come here for my head, get it?" He drew his finger across his neck in an off-with-his-head gesture that conveyed all too well how desperate he was feeling.

FA was behaving badly, but who wouldn't, after all he had been through? For the past three and a half years he'd suffered progressively worsening symptoms despite the ministrations of well-meaning doctors. Each of them had diagnosed his condition as depression. His symptoms ran the gamut from hopelessness and lack of self-esteem to loss of energy and appetite, sleeplessness, an inability to concentrate, and the disappearance of all interest in sex. From this list of rather typical symptoms, there was no reason to think that he didn't have major depression. However—and here's the secret to the approach my colleagues and I use—*neither was there any reason to suspect that he did.*

THE ACTOR'S DOWNFALL

The beginning of FA's suffering had coincided with his return to Broadway after nearly forty years. The dramatic role he was playing was demanding. He had worked harder at it than he had in a long time, for which he was rewarded with good reviews. He remembers beginning to feel exhausted and low after the third or fourth week of performances. "I'd be onstage, involved completely in my role, then all of a sudden I'd feel like calling it quits. I'd looked forward to my return to Broadway as coming full circle in my life. But now that I was here I felt that my life had no meaning, that it had *never* had meaning."

It wasn't the first time that FA had suffered a down mood. "I was a stage actor originally," he says, "and every young actor who comes to New York fully prepared to triumph gets hit with a painful dose of reality. I was no different from anyone else, although I thought, of course, that because I had been in summer stock for three seasons I was extraordinarily superior to all the other actors and actresses in New York who were waiting tables while waiting for their big break." He smiles that soft, familiar smile known so well to generations of moviegoers.

"I couldn't even get an audition," he remembers woefully, "and when I did, it seemed an exercise in humiliation. They would cut me off after two sentences and sometimes call out the next name without even acknowledging I'd been there. I'd go back to my rented room and feel like hell." FA groaned in reminiscence. "But I had to be an actor, I had to make it, because there wasn't anything else I could do. I couldn't even wait tables without dropping something."

Paradoxically, FA's down mood strengthened his resolve and dedication. It took him two and a half years to land a decent role on Broadway. When he did, critics and audiences loved him. From that point on, he seemed blessed. He went straight to Hollywood for forty years of uninterrupted stardom.

But this depressed mood, four decades later, had taken everything out of him. His guardian angel had deserted him. He didn't enjoy his work. He didn't enjoy anything. He couldn't sleep, but he was so tired he couldn't get up. And for the first time in his adult life he wasn't at all interested in sex. It took him a while to admit this, even to himself. He'd been married only a few months to a woman who was twenty-five years younger. After several nights of excuses, which he blamed on exhaustion from eight performances a week, he would push her away angrily when she approached him. His wife began to think it must be her fault. She tried to talk to FA about it, but he didn't want to discuss it. His angry outbursts became more frequent. Afterward he felt guilty and disgusted with himself. But he couldn't tell her—this young, beautiful, sexual woman with whom he had hoped to spend the rest of his life—that he believed in the depths of his heart that age had caught up with him. From now on, he knew, it was all over for him. He allowed her to leave him rather than tell her what he was so sure was the truth.

His wife was the first to seek psychiatric help. Her psychiatrist suggested that it was FA who needed the help.

Mr. Famous Actor remained in touch with his estranged wife, but he was reluctant to consult a psychiatrist. He wasn't the type to seek help; he would tough it out as best he could. Then the night came when he faced the audience and knew, despite a contract obligating him to four more months of performances, that he could no longer go on. He broke his contract, and his life seemed to collapse around him. He lay in bed for days, hating himself, regretting his lost youth, knowing he had no more future.

Then one day, weeks later, he got up and went outside. It was a clear, sharp late-winter day that promised the arrival of spring to those who could hold out just a bit longer. FA went for a walk in Central Park. He sat down on a bench and watched the joggers and the bike riders and the nannies with their tiny charges. It became clear that it was time to take action. He went back to his hotel and made an appointment with a psychoanalyst.

Successful Actor/Treatment Failure

Dr. Pierce, we'll call him, had been recommended to FA by his director as being "brilliant" with creative people. He was a psychiatrist who had undergone Freudian analytic training and used that technique with his patients. He worked with FA for two years, four days a week. At first they discussed FA's immediate symptoms, the onset of his depression at that particular time in his life, and its consequences, such as the shattered relationship with his new, young wife and his abandoned Broadway role.

Mr. Famous Actor learned a great deal about himself in his two years with Dr. Pierce, but his depression did not improve. Sometimes the symptoms would lift, only to return. Slowly but surely, things got worse. During bad times FA found it difficult to concentrate; he lost his ability to have an erection, he became angry and withdrawn, and he hated himself. He couldn't get himself to look at scripts or to talk about working again.

Gossip columns were full of items about his "changed personality." Though never directly stated, it was implied that FA was an alcoholic.

A concerned friend who knew the truth of FA's erratic behavior, and who had suffered a bout of depression himself a few years before, told FA how much he had been helped by antidepressant medication. He was surprised to find out that Dr. Pierce—who was, after all, a physician—had never recommended a trial of medication. FA mentioned this conversation to the doctor, who wondered why, after two years of therapy, FA would now be bringing this up. His implication was that FA's question was a wish to escape the work of the analysis, and that this in itself should be explored. Dr. Pierce was a psychoanalyst of the old school and would not under any circumstances prescribe medication.

FA could bear his symptoms and the vicious gossip no longer. Now that he knew there were other approaches to his depression, he felt he owed it to himself to try them. He parted from his analyst and made an appointment with his friend's psychiatrist.

The first session was a great relief for FA. The doctor listened to his symptoms and agreed that FA was certainly depressed. He reassured him that medication was available, and that from his symptoms it sounded as if FA would be a good candidate for drug treatment. Before he would prescribe anything, however, he wanted FA first to undergo a physical exam. He wanted to make sure, he said, that FA would be able to tolerate the potential side effects of the medication. Mr. Famous Actor went to the internist that the psychiatrist had recommended. The exam lasted twenty minutes, and was followed by an electrocardiogram. The internist told him his heart was sound and in his opinion there was no reason why FA should not take antidepressants.

FA returned to the psychiatrist, who reached for his prescription pad. "What about the reasons why I'm depressed?" asked FA. "We've plenty of time to talk about that, if we need to," replied the doctor, and he wrote a prescription for Elavil. He explained that he would slowly build up to the proper dosage, and that the pills would require anywhere from days to weeks before they achieved their desired effect. He told him, too, that he might experience some possibly disconcerting side effects, such as exhaustion, dry mouth, palpitations, constipation, and confusion. These, he said reassuringly, would probably disappear in time. He also explained that this initial choice of antidepressant medication might prove ineffective, and that they wouldn't know until at least six weeks after they had built up to the proper dosage. If needed, they would then try another type of medication. There was no lack of pills to try, he said, urging FA to have patience.

Mr. Famous Actor took the pills as prescribed, and he had a rough go with them. He had heart palpitations; he was anxious and restless and couldn't concentrate; he was dizzy; he sucked hard candies constantly because his mouth was painfully dry; he was constipated and occasionally nauseated. He stuck it out for two months because he believed this was finally going to work for him. The side effects lessened. The depression didn't. Still, the psychiatrist reassured him that, given time, they would find a medication that would work for him.

They didn't. Two changes of prescription and almost five months later, FA was even worse off than he had been before, and he felt that he was getting to the end of his rope. The doctor admitted him to the psychiatric unit of a famous teaching hospital. There the resident gave him another brief physical exam, in which he found nothing unusual. He prescribed various drugs and then more innovative combinations of medications for close to five months, during which time FA's behavior deteriorated. He was angry, impatient, belligerent, and often downright rude to the staff, who expected him to be his Famous Actor self, no matter what he was suffering from.

When FA refused shock treatments, the staff gave up and called me. "Treatment failure," said the psychiatrist in charge of his case. "The guy's an old crock," he added.

ENTER THE BIOPSYCHIATRISTS

Nobody likes to fail. When doctors fail, why not blame the patient? I can't tell you how often I hear the words *nonresponder* or *treatment failure* coupled with a negative view of the patient. Here all these doctors had spent so much time and energy on Mr. Famous Actor. Because he was who he was, they might even have worked harder with him than with a more "ordinary" patient. Yet he had the temerity not to get better! To add insult to injury, he did not seem grateful to them for their failed efforts.

To be sure, he was difficult. The disease he was suffering from, which everybody took to be depression because it looked and sounded like it, had changed him. So had the frustration of trying to find help. I doubt there's a psychiatrist in this country who wouldn't claim that he or she could offer a depressed patient significant help. Mr. Famous Actor had believed his doctors' claims. And still . . .

To him, my colleagues and I were yet another stop on the train to nowhere. So if he took extreme offense at us for making him undress in order for us to examine every nook and cranny of his body, well, so what?

It was the urological exam that made him angriest. "I want a goddamn psychiatrist," he growled. The doctor, now examining his testicles, looked up and said calmly, "I am a psychiatrist."

There was a moment of silence. FA sighed. "I give up," he said. "Almost four years of headshrinkers and I haven't the vaguest idea what a psychiatrist does—what a psychiatrist *is*." He was quiet for the remainder of the physical-examination portion of the evaluation.

A complete medical history and evaluation always come first in our evaluation of each new psychiatric patient. For many of our patients, it is the most thorough physical they have ever had. If nothing abnormal shows up that could explain the patient's psychiatric symptoms, we then proceed to an equally thorough diagnosis of the psychiatric condition. If patients are surprised at the physicals, they're doubly so when we start taking blood and urine specimens for laboratory analysis, to confirm, first, the existence of depression, then the type of depression, then blood levels of medication, and then physiological responses to it. Usually, they're pleased. Here we are, psychiatrists, getting up from our consulting chairs and aggressively and energetically taking their problems as seriously as if they'd told us they had chest pain.

As it happened, we did not have to go on to test FA specifically for depression. The examining physicians, the lab work, and a biopsy all confirmed that Mr. Famous Actor was suffering from a disease that would account for all his symptoms: low-grade seminoma, a form of testicular cancer. Despite his symptoms, depression turned out to be a misdiagnosis. Thus, all the treatments he had undergone were incorrect. His symptoms arose out of his medical condition and would disappear only when the cancer was treated.

We referred FA to the appropriate specialists for treatment of his illness. He was hardly cheered when he heard that he had cancer. This time he got depressed for real, a normal reaction to what he was at first convinced was the worst news he'd ever heard. But when we told him that we had caught the disease in time and that the likelihood of a complete cure was 95 percent, he began to cheer up.

He asked the logical question: "Why didn't any of the other doctors pick it up?"

There are several answers to his question. One is that no one was looking for this illness—or for any illness at all. He was a psychiatric patient, and to most internists and psychiatrists, that means the problem is located somewhere above the neck. The last thing they consider, despite indisputable evidence to the contrary, is that emotional symptoms can often be the first—sometimes the only—signs of serious physical illness. By the time the distressing physical symptoms suddenly appear and the diagnosis is made, it is often too late for a cure.

THE HAPPY ENDING

Our diagnosis, even though it was cancer, truly was the best news he had had in three and a half years. We identified what FA really was suffering from, so that at long last he could receive the proper treatment. That's what it took for Mr. Famous Actor's "depression" to go away, along with his cancer.

Biopsychiatrists save lives. Any more treatment for depression and our famous patient might have died.

Surgeons removed the malignancy; afterward he underwent a course of radiation therapy. Chemotherapy was not considered necessary. FA has had no recurrence of cancer or depression.

Mr. Famous Actor is back in front of the cameras. He is thinking of returning to Broadway in a revival of his original success forty-plus years ago. He and his wife have reunited, their sex life is great, and he is his former self again, almost. Unfortunately but not surprisingly, his years-long experience of trying to get help has left a scar: a deep-rooted bitterness toward psychiatrists.

WHAT EVERYBODY DID WRONG

FA's psychoanalyst was trained as a psychiatric physician, but he had abjured his medical training. He made no effort to diagnose the cause of his patient's depression. He assumed the symptoms arose from FA's psyche and that they could be explained by FA's life experiences. He might have been right. Any biopsychiatrist can tell you there are a number of reasons why a person will exhibit symptoms of depression; some, indeed, may be embedded in an individual's personality.

But Dr. Pierce made no attempt to verify his assumptions by ruling out any of the many other diseases or conditions that could just as well explain his patient's suffering. And since he never prescribed medication for his patients, he apparently did not believe that depression can in itself be a biological illness, much less a symptom of a medical illness. Doctor though he may be, he has not remained in touch with current medical knowledge.

The psychiatrist who prescribed medication for FA made the same initial error: diagnosis by description of symptoms. Unlike his predecessor, however, he did request a medical consultation, but only to make certain his patient could tolerate the side effects of the pills, and probably to protect himself in the event of a malpractice suit. If he was willing to prescribe medication, he obviously accepted the notion of depressive illness, but despite the increasing number of examinations and tests available to psychiatrists, he did nothing to prove or disprove that FA was an appropriate candidate for medication. (In fact, he should have realized that with each treatment that *should have* succeeded and did not, the chance of misdiagnosis rose.) Neither did he use any of the available laboratory techniques to identify the medication most likely to be effective; to estimate the dosage, which varies from individual to individual; or to follow the course of treatment. His treatment of his patient was nothing more than trial and error, which prolonged the suffering of his patient and, since he was working from an incorrect diagnosis, was doomed to fail.

Let's not forget the internist whom FA visited. Because his patient had been referred by a psychiatrist, he apparently assumed that all FA's problems were in his head, and thus he performed only a perfunctory examination. He probably was uncomfortable dealing with psychiatric patients. Yet he must have known that psychiatric symptoms are frequently caused by any one of an extraordinary number of physical illnesses.

In terms of both physical examination of the patient and differential diagnosis of his condition, the doctors at the hospital were no better. Even in a hospital setting, they made no use of formal evaluation, comprehensive examination, or laboratory technology. Their contribution was to try the patient on newer, more innovative combinations of medications. Throwing pills at people can be very effective for the treatment-resistant patient, but only if depression is the problem. Which it wasn't.

Our famous actor friend made his own mistakes, not that he could be held accountable. He too operated on assumptions: that a psychiatrist is a psychiatrist is a psychiatrist; that they all have the same training and the same point of view; that they are all equally capable of recognizing what lurks behind psychiatric symptoms; and that they'll provide similar treatment for it. Not until he looked down and found a psychiatrist squeezing his testicles did FA ask himself an essential question: What is a psychiatrist? If Mr. Famous Actor thought he was confused about the definition of a psychiatrist, he should only have known how confused psychiatry is itself.

Is a psychiatrist:

- a psychotherapist, who uses verbal therapeutic techniques to treat all patients, regardless of their complaints?
- a drug therapist, who believes that medication can help most patients who complain of psychiatric symptoms?
- a professional spokesperson for social causes?
- a consultant to defense and prosecuting attorneys?
- a specialist who believes that normal behavior is a matter of relearning more appropriate actions or thoughts?
- an allergist?
- a kind of counselor who assists essentially normal people to achieve more fulfilled existences?

The answer is yes to any of these definitions of psychiatry. Each psychiatrist has his or her own "thing." Each will claim an interpretation of, and a therapy for, depression. Analytic-style psychiatrists, for example, will investigate early loss, rage, and self-esteem issues. Cognitive doctors will say you learned your depression and you can unlearn it. Feminist therapists may find sufficient explanation for a woman's depression in the dependent position into which women are forced, and by way of cure help the woman to assert her rightful place in society. A family therapist will find the roots of a family member's depression within the functioning of the family as a whole. Psychopharmacologists are likely to explain that depression is the result of a chemical deficiency, and recommend medication . . . and on and on and on.

None of these approaches is necessarily wrong, but who says which one is right for you? Too often the burden falls on the patient, as it did on Mr. Famous Actor, to know what the problem really is in order to get help for it. What if you were having a heart attack and the cardiologists in your city each had a different cure? Whom would you consult? How would you know which one had the right treatment for you? Relying on trial and error could kill you. Fortunately, cardiology and most of the other medical specialties have come a long way since those days, not so long ago, when diagnosis and treatment might depend on the beliefs or idiosyncrasies of a particular practitioner. Cardiology consists of a body of knowledge and procedures that are universally applied. The only variable in treatment is the competence of the particular physician using these procedures, which is why most people rely on referrals from doctors they trust.

As a subspecialty of medicine, psychiatry espouses no such consistency. Disagreements are often based on theory and are not resolved through research. Psychiatrists are notoriously contentious and frequently view other approaches with contempt rather than with an interest in learning from one another and in unifying the field within itself and within medicine.

The identity confusion in psychiatry reaches to the deepest roots of the profession. Biopsychiatry has appeared on its white charger, in effect, to rescue the profession and its patients. What is a biopsychiatrist? Simply put, he or she is a specialist in all problems affecting human behavior, is trained to perform a differential diagnosis assisted by all available technology, and is able then to choose the most effective treatment for the patient based on the diagnosis. *Biopsychiatrist* and *psychiatrist* ought to be synonymous terms.

CHAPTER 2

Why I Still Am a (Bio)Psychiatrist

It was my senior year in medical school. My professors thought I was going off the deep end. They tried desperately to stop me.

"Psychiatry?" exclaimed the neurology department chairman. "How could you throw away your career?"

My neurosurgery professor talked about my love for pure science. He recalled the years I had spent in labs working on special research projects, my dedication to medicine. It sounded like a eulogy. He called psychiatry my "death wish."

These two men were my mentors, and it was difficult not to have their support. I understood their objections, of course. At that very moment in the mid-1970s, while the rest of medicine was reveling in a new era of scientific discovery and advances, psychiatrists were expending their energy in backbiting and attacking each other's competing approaches. The psychodynamic psychiatrists fought the biological psychiatrists, who fought the social psychiatrists, who attacked the behavioral psychiatrists. . . . Pity the poor patients who were trapped in between. Psychiatry had lost its focus.

Fortunately, the dean of the medical school and its dean of students recognized my mission. As they put it, what psychiatry needed above all was individuals to make it important again and relevant to the rest of medicine without sacrificing the advances that had been made in our understanding of the mind. It would take scientists, pioneers, individuals with a steadfast and single-minded vision to attach the body to the mind, the mind to the body, once and for all.

That thought struck me. No doubt the discoveries of the extraordinary complexities of the mind and the corresponding development of psychology have been giant steps forward. But the insistence on separating the head from its own corporeal existence is an even larger step backward, toward some of the least-enlightened times in our history.

FROM THE PHARAOHS TO FREUD

Some four thousand years ago, the ancient Egyptians did not differentiate between mental and physical illnesses; they believed that despite their manifestations, all diseases had physical causes. They thought the heart was responsible for mental symptoms. Hippocrates and the early Greeks believed as well that all illness resulted from an imbalance of bodily fluids, or *humors;* depression, for example, arose from an excess of "black bile."

The ancients may have been off the mark as to specific causes, but their nonpejorative view of mental suffering and their search for medical causes were right on track. As history progressed, however, the "mind" view of mental illness came to predominate, and with it the conviction that the victim was to blame. Possession by evil spirits, moral weakness, and other such explanations made a stigma of mental illness and placed the responsibility for a cure on the resulting outcasts themselves. The most apparently ill were chained to walls in institutions such as the infamous Bedlam, where the rest of society could forget they existed.

In our supposedly more humane era, we have freed the mentally ill from institutions and, instead of providing continuing care, have left them to fend for themselves. Forced to be aware of them, we disdain the "crazies" out there and wish they would get it together and behave themselves; down deep, we really believe that if they had the strength of character, they would straighten out.

The stigma of illness of the mind is all-pervasive. If we or members of our families experience mental illness, the shame may prevent us from seeking available help or even from following the doctor's advice. Psychiatrists often fail at effecting a cure because patients resist taking the prescribed medication.

I had a patient not long ago, a woman named Julie, who at age thirty-eight had earned a top executive position at a major manufacturing company. She had been referred to me by her family physician because she suffered severe, recurrent depressions. Lately she had found herself contemplating suicide, and her fear of what she might do forced her for the first time to reveal a history of desperate anguish on and off for almost twenty years. It was her "secret shame."

Julie appeared extraordinarily well put together in her dark suit, off-white high-necked blouse, and colorful little bow tie. Her medium-length auburn hair was conservatively cut and carefully combed. Her makeup was perfect. It took much of her strength to maintain this facade, behind which she hid her true feelings. No wonder she seemed so aloof and chilly.

We were able to determine that Julie was biologically depressed, and our lab quickly identified the type of antidepressant that she would respond to. We worked to get the concentration of medication in her blood up to the optimum level. Results were dramatic. For the first time in years her mood range was normal. Her facial expression had lost its disdainful severity, and she smiled warmly and often.

Yet we weren't able to maintain Julie at an effective medication level, because every time she had to go out of town on business, which was about twice a month for a week each time, she'd manage to "forget" her pills. After protesting that she really had forgotten them, she finally confessed that she was terrified one of her customers or colleagues would find out what she was taking and why, and that would be the end of their respect for her and, what she most feared, the end of her rapid progress in her corporate career.

She could imagine them buzzing behind her back that her depression was so bad she had to take pills for it. I pointed out that she regularly took pain medication for a jogging injury. "That's not the same thing," she insisted. "In fact, that's something to be proud of—it makes me one of the guys. But depression," she said, her voice rising in self-disgust, "that makes it seem like I can't control my own emotions, like the stereotypical, weak, afflicted, helpless woman."

I told her that she didn't seem to understand what depressive illness was; her tests clearly showed her to be suffering from a biological disease that afflicted even male presidents of corporations. She waved away my explanation with a hint of tears in her eyes. The "weakness" view of mental symptoms has too strong a footing in our culture to allow one to let go of it in just one straightforward sentence.

I told her she might want to talk about this with a psychotherapist, explaining that people who have suffered a lot of depression end up distorting their lives in order to survive what they believe to be shameful pain. If she would take her medication she would be free of the pain and in a good state to work with a therapist to help her straighten out what she'd done to her life. She seemed skeptical, until I added that therapy was likely to help her understand and achieve her career goals. She brightened and asked me for the names of some therapists.

Once you determine that a "head problem" is, in fact, a body problem, the stigma evaporates. Until only a few years ago, an alcoholic in the family was the skeleton in the closet. Now we're calling alcoholism a disease, and it has become much easier to admit to needing help for it.

EMIL WHO?

Within the last century, Western psychiatry has followed separate "head" and "body" routes.

The founders of these two traditions were Sigmund Freud and Emil Kraepelin, both of whom were German-speaking men born in 1856. Although most Americans consider Freud the father of modern psychiatry, medical people, especially those in Europe, are likely to name Emil Kraepelin as the actual founder of the medical science of psychiatry. Sigmund Freud originated psychoanalysis, from which derive today's therapies based on psychodynamic theories and techniques.

Both men were physicians, Kraepelin practicing in Munich and Freud in Vienna. Freud's theories attempted to demonstrate an order within the chaos of the human mind. Kraepelin's work created order of the chaotic thinking about mental disease among doctors of the late nineteenth and early twentieth centuries.

Kraepelin's method was empirical: He observed mentally ill patients, described their symptoms, and followed their courses for some years. By doing so, he was able to discover similarities among patients and to identify distinct syndromes (a syndrome in medicine is a collection of symptoms that frequently occur together) and predict their outcome. He identified what he termed manic-depressive psychosis (now called bipolar disorder) and dementia praecox (schizophrenia). He showed that manic-depressives tended to get better spontaneously and that schizophrenics tended to deteriorate over time.

Before Kraepelin, psychiatrists were dealing with each patient as an idiosyncratic set of confusing symptoms whose causes, future course, and treatments were unknown and unpredictable. So-called diagnoses were descriptive and often had little relationship to anyone else's use of the same terms. Once Kraepelin showed that psychiatrists were dealing with the same illnesses among their patients, they could at last begin to make diagnoses.

A diagnosis in medicine implies prognosis (prediction of the probable course of an illness) and treatment. In those days, once a physician knew, for example, that manic-depressives get better in time, he could prepare the patient and the patient's family for a short-term hospitalization. These

serious mental diseases had no effective treatment, but at least psychiatrists could begin to research systematic treatment approaches.

Its house in order, late-nineteenth- and early-twentieth-century psychiatry was now in a position to take advantage of the medical advances of
those days. It was the era of the microbe, the disease-causing agent.
Using the available technology of the times, such as the microscope, and
applying the advances of the new science of bacteriology, psychiatrists
immediately made some startling discoveries. A number of their
"schizophrenic" patients had bacterial illnesses. These were syphilitics
suffering from general paresis, the late stage of that disease, which
causes schizophrenialike symptoms. These patients required medical
treatment, not psychiatric incarceration. Penicillin eventually proved to
be the treatment of choice, and lo and behold, the mental hospitals
emptied out by some 10 percent.

Even more dramatically, in the South, nearly half the patients in some
mental hospitals walked out suddenly sane when niacin was added to
their diet. They were discovered to be suffering from pellagra, which
results from a chronic deficiency of that B vitamin.

It seemed that the future of psychiatry was set on this firm medical
footing. The first part of the twentieth century, however, was to provide
psychiatrists with few advances with which to find the pathogens or
biochemical and structural defects in the brain they were hoping to
discover as the causes of mental illnesses. And the questionable use or
overenthusiastic application of such physical treatments as shock therapy, psychosurgery, and even teeth-pulling, combined with gross insen-
sitivity to the experiences of their patients, led medically oriented
psychiatrists quickly down the path of ignominy.

THE TALKING CURE

Biological research into the brain and its functions and the origins of
mental illness continued, but it fell increasingly to neuroscientists in fields
other than psychiatry. In psychiatry, for some forty years following World
War I, the dominant intellectual influence was psychoanalysis.

Sigmund Freud was a physician and began his career as a neurologist.
He was a brilliant physiologist, and many of his speculations about the
structure of the brain and its biochemistry have turned out to be accurate.

Like Kraepelin, Freud believed that biological correlates would be
found to explain mental malfunctioning. "In view of the intimate connec-

tion between things physical and mental," he once said, "we may look forward to a day when paths of knowledge will be opened up leading from organic biology and chemistry to the field of neurotic phenomena."

In the absence of the technical laboratory skills necessary to prove this point, Freud set up the best construct that he could: that neurosis (a disorder of personality rather than a disease syndrome) derived from key experiences of the child as it passed from one predictable developmental stage to another. The remedy was to explore the unconscious mind through uncensored talking and through the patient's reactions to the analyst, thereby identifying and reconstructing these early life experiences and working through their influence on adult life.

In theory and practice, Freud's ideas were revolutionary. Psychotherapy in the many forms it has taken since Freud has become an essential tool—sometimes the only tool—for mental health professionals. But it was never meant for serious illnesses. "Psychoses, states of confusion and deeply rooted (I might say toxic) depressions . . . are not suitable for psychoanalysis," Freud stated. All too many therapists have ignored Freud's advice and kept their patients with active brain disease on the couch for, literally, decades. These therapists don't believe in brain disease, despite all the recent evidence for it.

There are several other drawbacks to using "the talking cure" as the one and only method of treatment. For one thing, patients have to be sufficiently intelligent and motivated to apply the results of this learning experience to their lives. And, of course, they have to be good talkers. Not long ago the best candidates for psychotherapy were described as "young, physically attractive, well-educated members of the upper middle class, intelligent, verbal, willing to talk about and have responsibility for their problems, and showing no signs of gross pathology."

Of course, they have to be able to afford it as well. Got a spare hundred grand?

Still, Freud and his followers offered a rich and innovative approach to understanding human experience. The early decades of psychoanalytic influence were rife with intellectual fervor. Analysts saw themselves as medical subspecialists, researchers into the human psyche. They kept notes, went to meetings, presented cases, published articles in journals. Unfortunately, they and the therapists to come were never able to provide acceptable documentation that psychoanalysis works. Limited to each practitioner's private experience in the consulting room, without the presence of another therapist or film or videotape to document the progress of the analysis, "the self-congratulatory clinical histories in the analytic literature cannot be accepted as evidence of anything beyond the writers' self-regard," wrote one commentator recently.

Under the psychoanalytic influence, the 1930s and 1940s were the heyday of psychiatry and psychosomatic medicine. Many psychiatrists took additional training in internal medicine and walked around hospitals in white coats like the other doctors, and tried to figure out why people get ulcers, or ulcerative colitis, or high blood pressure. Without today's technology they didn't get very far. But their concern with the relationship of mind and body was appropriate for a physician. Today we see that relationship in the link between type A personality and heart disease, and between cancer and emotional stress (research, I might add, that was accomplished largely by nonpsychiatric investigators). These early psychoanalytic physicians recognized that their patients also had bodies!

Overall it was a time of enormous prestige for psychiatry, and the profession attracted the cream of the crop of medical school graduates.

As the years passed, however, practitioners of psychoanalytic psychotherapy were to abandon medical science altogether and all categories of mental diseases within it. In 1963, Karl Menninger, founder of the Menninger Clinic in Topeka, Kansas, published *The Vital Balance,* an influential book in which he insisted that all mental afflictions were degrees of a single disease and therefore responsive to the same technique: psychotherapy. This view doomed depressed people to another decade of non-cures on the couch. Psychiatrist Thomas Szasz, in *The Myth of Mental Illness,* published in 1961, insisted there wasn't even one disease.

Psychiatrists had become doctors who treated no diseases. How Kraepelin's ghost must have shuddered. Moreover, this theoretical stance blurred all distinctions between psychiatrists and psychologists, who had multiplied greatly since World War II. Psychotherapy requires no medical background. It's rather like getting eyeglasses fitted: Why go to an expensive ophthalmologist, a doctor who specializes in the eye, just to have your glasses checked, when you can consult an optometrist, who has gone to optometry school to learn this one technical skill? Ophthalmologists do, of course, fit eyeglasses, but as physicians they primarily diagnose and treat eye disease. If there were no more diseases for psychiatrists to treat, who would need them?

Psychologists and other nonmedical mental health workers (many of whom were trained by psychiatrists during the community mental health movement of the 1970s) further demedicalized prevailing views of the etiology of mental suffering and the corresponding treatment. Psycho-therapy is good for "whatever ails ya," from severe depression or mania to problems with your spouse. And if it has taken psychiatrists forever to begin to recognize the possibility that psychological symptoms may actually be symptoms of physical disease that must be treated, nonmedical therapists have yet to take this reality seriously.

THE PSYCHIATRIST AS CLOWN

Ironically, psychotherapy prospered in an illness-free environment: You didn't have to be "sick" to get your head on straight or to learn to open up or to sweeten your relationships or to handle money better or to overcome your sexual inhibitions. Whatever you wanted to accomplish, by the late 1960s there was sure to be a therapy somewhere to serve you. Psychotherapy was a growth industry. Shrinks with M.D.s or Ph.D.s or no degrees at all created liberating therapies founded on little legitimate theory and much popular hype. These might have been fun, even enlightening, for the participant who was basically okay, but the seriously depressed or otherwise ill person was likely to be lost in the melee.

Still, psychotherapists could see into your mind, predict your future, and cure you of anything that held you back. Such was the message of psychology and psychiatry, and the public wanted to hear it. Psychiatrists were elevated to the role of high priests of the courtroom and seers of the future. Supposedly the psychiatrists had the knowledge to determine whether a criminal or mentally ill individual would be dangerous to self or others, and therefore to determine his or her future. The courts listened; they continue to listen even as evidence piles up against psychiatric fortune-telling. A study published in 1984 suggested that nobody even knows what "dangerous" means. Psychiatrists and nonpsychiatrists were asked to rate sixteen criminals for dangerousness. Hardly any of the 193 raters agreed with each other; on only four of the cases was there as much as 60 percent agreement. Psychiatrists reached no higher level of agreement than anyone else.

Psychiatric performance in the courtroom has led to such absurdities as the "Twinkie defense" of Dan White, who killed San Francisco Supervisor Harvey Milk. Psychiatrists testified that White had become deranged by eating too much junk food. No research evidence was submitted.

The trial of John Hinckley for his attempted assassination of President

Ronald Reagan in 1981 was the last straw. So many psychiatrists were called to testify whether Hinckley was or was not insane that the public became convinced, once and for all, that psychiatrists could be paid by lawyers to say anything. In all, they were a bunch of silly people who didn't know much of anything. Why, Hinckley's own psychiatrist had thought he was essentially a normal kid who needed more discipline!

Psychiatrists came tumbling off the pedestal that society had helped put them on. Ironically, despite psychiatry's poor performance as an expert witness, the courts won't let it step down. The American Psychiatric Association in 1984 declared that psychiatry did not belong in the courtroom. Despite attacks on the legitimacy of psychiatric testimony in several recent court decisions, the Supreme Court has determined that psychiatrists can and should testify, even if their opinions are hypothetical and they never meet the person they are testifying about.

PILL TIME

The development of an arsenal of psychiatric medication by the 1970s both helped and hurt the profession's public image.

The age of the wonder drug in psychiatry had begun in the 1950s, when a French surgeon who was experimenting with a medication to reduce surgical shock discovered what would become the first antipsychotic drug: chlorpromazine (Thorazine). Many others soon were synthesized.

Prior to that time, most psychiatrists had dumped their psychotic patients in mental institutions and more or less forgotten about them, since there was no treatment to help them and few believed that psychotherapy made any sense for someone not grounded in reality. Medication liberated many of these patients both from lifetime sentences of bizarre behavior and thinking, and from the disregard of their psychiatrists.

The first of a class of drugs called tricyclic antidepressants, imipramine, entered the world as a possible new antipsychotic. It didn't relieve psychosis, but it did work to lift the spirits of depressed patients. Development of tricyclics and other classes of antidepressants immediately followed. Tranquilizers first appeared on the market in the late 1950s; lithium, finally, in 1970.

Pharmaceutical companies have poured billions of dollars into the development and marketing of psychiatric drugs. Despite this phenomenal amount of money and the proliferation of medications, few essentially new drugs had appeared until recently. Almost all were variations of earlier formulas or concepts. Each variation did, however, entitle the drug companies to a new patent, and it gave physicians who had little knowledge of psychopharmacology (but a lot of trust in the drug-company salesmen) hope that this new drug might work. Today, however, that is changing, and pharmaceutical companies have become an important partner on the cutting edge of the good news about anti-depressants.

Under attack for their inability to prove the effectiveness of psycho-therapy, frustrated by their lack of progress with severely depressed or anxious patients, and feeling the economic strain of competition from all the nonmedical therapists, psychiatrists were relieved to have chemical agents at their disposal. At last they had differentiated themselves from psychologists. And the prescriptions often worked.

Many psychiatrists and physicians in other specialties began to pre-scribe psychiatric medication with an excess of enthusiasm—a common phenomenon in medicine when a new cure makes its appearance. But the huge doses of antipsychotics they were dispensing turned out to have a ghastly and often irreversible side effect called tardive dyskinesia, which causes involuntary movements of the face and tongue. Tranquilizers were prescribed for every little twinge of anxiety, but they turned out to be addicting. Antidepressants caused such unpleasant, and occasionally dan-gerous, side effects that many patients quit taking them.

These excesses received wide public attention and further eroded the image of psychiatry. Psychiatrists came to be seen as pill-pushers, no better than the "druggies" who had emerged from the 1960s. Many psychi-atrists panicked. As a result, a serious problem in medicine today is the underprescription of medication for pain and for some psychiatric condi-tions, especially depression. Patients dying of cancer receive too little pain medication for fear they'll become addicted to it. And patients suffering the pain of depression are often given doses of medication so tiny that the brain doesn't even notice. We get so many cases of allegedly hopeless or intractable depression that we can cure in a blink simply by adjusting the medication level.

Still, despite their initial inexperience with the new psychiatric drugs, psychiatrists became convinced that at last they could actually do some-thing for their more seriously ill patients. For patients who had to be hospitalized, medication was usually the treatment of choice. Beyond a doubt, most depressed patients who were given a course of medication improved and went home. Books were written about the wondrous new cures. Psychiatry as a whole began to feel a lot better.

CRASH!

If all those books had been correct, you wouldn't be reading this one now. After nearly thirty years of these "miracle drugs," the verdict is in: They don't work miracles.

Study after study reveals that patients who are vigorously treated with drugs or even shock therapy by the most well-intentioned practitioners have a response rate that is about the same as those who receive cognitive psychotherapy (see Chapter 24). Even when the initial response is dramatic and the patient is soon discharged from the hospital, the risk of relapse is extraordinary. The ongoing National Institute of Mental Health (NIMH) Collaborative Study of the Psychobiology of Depression, conducted at America's premier academic hospitals, reports that only 60 percent of depressed patients have recovered six months after treatment, and only 34 percent are completely free of symptoms. Of those who fully recover during treatment, 19 percent relapse within six months and 24 percent develop new symptoms.

The fact is, depressed patients wonder whether they would be better off if psychiatrists left them alone. That same 60 percent will get better no matter what we do. The rate of spontaneous recovery is that high.

Findings such as these pulled the rug out from under traditional psychiatry. Down it went in a final crisis of confidence and credibility.

BIOPSYCHIATRY TO THE RESCUE

The apparent ineffectiveness of the most modern treatments for depression hardly surprised me. Having hung my hat with the new psychiatry, until then forced to remain behind the scenes, I knew why traditional methods had failed. It wasn't the fault of the treatments available; it was the failure of the practitioner to apply these treatments in rigorously scientific ways.

Antidepressant medication can work extraordinarily well if the patient needs it. Much of the work of biopsychiatry has gone into defining what biological depression is, developing a technology to aid in accurately diagnosing who has it, and determining through laboratory methods what is the most appropriate treatment.

Of course, success rates will turn out low if you're prescribing antidepressant medication for everybody who seems depressed, including the patients whose depressive symptoms are the result of other, undiagnosed diseases.

But let's say you are a psychiatrist and your patient really is biologically depressed. Which of all the medications available are you going to prescribe? For how long? How do you really know it's working? You'll have to use the laboratory to be sure. Many a patient starts to seem okay, but tests reveal that the biological condition remains active. Stopping medication at the patient's first sunny smile and or when the symptoms begin to remit virtually ensures relapse.

Biopsychiatry is rigorous medical science. That's the major reason why, using many of the same treatments at which others fail, we can make them work.

WHERE BIOPSYCHIATRY CAME FROM

The discovery of the psychiatric wonder drugs back in the 1950s led to some essential questions about the nature of psychiatric illness, questions only biological research scientists were equipped to resolve. Why did these drugs work? How? Which brain structures and processes were affected? If chemicals could alter the behavior of someone termed psychotic, but leave a depressed person essentially unchanged, was there some organic difference between these two individuals? Which conditions would be most responsive to which drugs, and why? If drugs altered brain chemistry, was brain chemistry the cause of mental illness? Suddenly a group of psychiatrists began to reconsider the discarded notion of separate psychiatric illnesses. Antidepressants worked on some people with symptoms of depression and not others. Were the differences in their brains or in their minds?

At the same time, neuroscientists in fields such as neurochemistry, neuroendocrinology (the study of the brain's hormonal system), and neurobehavior were asking a number of related questions about normal and abnormal brain function and its relation to feelings and behavior. The new organic psychiatrists remained alone and unloved in psychiatry, but they had lots of friends in these other sciences. All began to learn from one another. Suddenly there was an explosion in technological development, and the tools they all needed to answer their questions began to become available. They were peering into the very cells of the brain and beginning to discover how they worked, and how psychiatric drugs worked on the cells. The next step was to investigate the physiology of mental illness and perhaps even discover its causes. Then they could correct the problems.

THE GOOD NEWS: I AM A PSYCHIATRIST

I entered psychiatry at the very beginning of its recruitment crisis—no better time to get involved in the new psychiatry. The technology was in place, the greatest minds in the field were allying themselves with the new work, and the unraveling of the mysteries of the mind was imminent. Any serious psychiatrist who joined in could make a practical contribution to basic science and to patient care. Results were formidable. Traditional psychiatrists were in the doldrums, but we were a bunch of cheerful optimists.

We continue to provide evidence that patients with brain disease are different from those with problems of living. This couldn't be more important for depressed people, whose conditions can be anything from a perfectly appropriate reaction to a life situation to a serious biological illness. We are in the process of delineating subtypes of depression that respond to different treatments. We are discovering the relationship of genetics to the development of psychiatric illness and learning about the environmental, psychological, and biological factors that trigger it. We have amassed a gold mine of data on the relationship of illnesses such as depression to the endocrine system. We're discovering the biochemistry behind the relationship of depression to the immune system.

Overall, we've learned how to piece together the biochemistry, neuro-pharmacology, and neuroendocrinology of mental illness. Lab reports from high-performance liquid chromatographs, receptor-binding assays, and immunochemistry augment and rival more traditional psychiatric tools such as the notepad and the straitjacket. Educators now demand that psychiatrists must be skilled physicians who can diagnose illness using an interview, patient history, laboratory tests, and a complete physical exam, and that trainees have a broad knowledge of other specialties.

What does all this mean to the depressed person? It means that we are finally beginning to learn what depression is: a disease that is very treatable. Psychiatrists who treat depression traditionally with medication may not have to continue to use the trial-and-error method. They say that you have a 50 to 60 percent chance of getting better on the first antidepressant tried. If that doesn't work, you'll be switched to another one, which increases the chances to 65 to 80 percent. This will cost you twelve to thirty weeks in treatment.

We say that we'll test you to make sure you really are a candidate for medication. If you are, we'll test you again to make sure we hit on the first try. Biopsychiatry will get you better faster, more efficiently, and with less suffering. If you are not getting better in your current psychotherapeutic treatment, chances are close to 100 percent that biopsychiatric evaluation will yield either medical illness or active brain disease.

It means that you can begin to trust psychiatrists again. "That'll be the day," muttered a down-in-the-dumps patient who'd gone the shrink route and gave us a try only because she couldn't live with her condition and didn't know what else to do. She went home with a prescription for thyroid medication. No one had performed the right kind of thyroid test on her, so the thyroid disease that lay at the root of her mental symptoms had never been treated. "Maybe you guys aren't so bad after all," she said with a laugh in parting.

Yeah, maybe.

"Medicine is pragmatic," writes Canadian psychiatrist Myre Sim, M.D. "One must constantly seek better remedies and discard the old. Authority must have its credentials repeatedly examined and tested."

Addressing the American Psychiatric Association upon his election as president a few years ago, John Talbott, M.D., spoke of psychiatry's new agenda:

> While most physicians and, indeed, most laymen still perceive of psychiatry only as a couch-bound psychotherapeutic discipline, this is no longer the case, and we have to struggle not only with our sense of integrity in the face of such rapid changes but attempt to inform the rest of medicine and society about our changing world. This is not to say that psychotherapy no longer is valued or has value, but rather with our increasing ability to diagnose accurately and thereby treat effectively . . . we become more broad-based and better therapeutically armed.

So maybe it's time to have that depression of yours (or your spouse's or your child's or your grandfather's) looked at. By a biopsychiatrist.

PART II

DIAGNOSIS AND MISDIAGNOSIS

CHAPTER 3

All That Wheezes
Isn't Asthma

In medicine, treatment follows from diagnosis. If lab results show that you have a strep throat, you'll get a prescription for an antibiotic that will go to war with the streptococcus bacterium. Should your sore throat prove to be caused by a virus, against which antibiotics are ineffective, your doctor still may recommend antibiotics, feeling (improperly, of course) that he or she has to prescribe *something* to appear doctorlike and knowing that this kind of sore throat will go away anyway. As long as the doctor can figure out what's wrong with you, he or she can choose the treatment that is most likely to work. But should you really have a strep infection and your doctor jumps to the conclusion "It's just a virus; stay in bed, keep warm, it'll go away," you're in trouble. Wrong diagnosis leads to wrong treatment. Unless, of course, your doctor gets lucky and prescribes the right treatment from the wrong diagnosis.

Few doctors, psychiatrists included, can keep blind luck going for long. More likely, a high rate of misdiagnosis will yield a low rate of treatment response. This is what has happened in psychiatry.

The problem stems from (1) the medically outmoded diagnostic system psychiatry uses; (2) the nonmedical habits of some practitioners; (3) often-hostile competition among the many psychiatric approaches; and (4) reluctance, or downright refusal, to incorporate the new knowledge about brain function gained in the laboratory using the new technology.

"Psychiatry . . . tends to run about two hundred years behind the rest of medicine," comments Donald W. Goodwin, M.D., one of the new psychiatry's leading lights. The system of diagnosis, which classifies psychiatric illness largely through description of symptoms, was appropriate when doctors knew nothing about underlying causes or treatment. Today, psychiatric knowledge about both causes and treatments is exploding.

Nonetheless, when it comes to step one, diagnosis, psychiatry relies on a system that can at best yield incomplete information. At worst it encourages misdiagnosis. Adding insult to injury, when treatment fails, instead of questioning the diagnosis that encouraged them to choose an ineffective approach, psychiatrists accuse the patient of being a "nonresponder."

THE CASE OF MS. A.

Ms. A., the twenty-five-year-old patient of a Providence, Rhode Island, psychiatrist, had been misdiagnosed as schizophrenic by at least three different psychiatrists during the seven years before she consulted him. He correctly identified her illness as bipolar disorder (manic-depression). In this form of depression, periods of deep lows alternate with episodes of extreme highs (mania). Mania is marked by periods of high energy and nonstop activity. People go without sleep for days; they talk rapidly and have grandiose ideas. Often they spend huge sums of money and undertake ill-advised business ventures or massive, impossible projects. During a manic phase, bipolar and schizophrenic patients may behave in a similarly bizarre fashion. The bipolar patient, however, will exhibit powerful mood fluctuations, which are a dead giveaway if the psychiatrist is diagnosing only by the appearance of the patient. Confusing the two illnesses is common, although they are in fact very different, from diagnosis to treatment to prognosis. Bipolar illness responds almost immediately to lithium, which not only restores normality but controls the disease's seesaw course. Schizophrenics can be helped back into this world with neuroleptic (antipsychotic) medication, but their illness remains chronic, and medication only manages it.

Ms. A. did not believe that she was schizophrenic and refused to take her medication. Even so, her condition returned to normal between episodes—another bipolar diagnostic giveaway.

"The lack of early correct diagnosis led to a series of mutually reinforcing complications for Ms. A. that were all potentially avoidable," her psychiatrist wrote in a letter to the editor of the *American Journal of Psychiatry.*

Maintenance treatment was attempted with neuroleptics (with significant side effects) rather than with lithium, which might have minimized the chances of recurrences. Her dislike of the neuroleptics and her disagreement with her diagnosis led to confrontations with and distrust of her physicians. Her conflict with authority widened to her family, particularly her father, who blamed her for the episodes because she did not comply with the recommended treatment. She increasingly came to feel misunderstood and isolated. She did not know where to turn for guidance and support. This sense of isolation and confusion occurred during adolescence, a critical developmental stage, and was aggravated by the continued cycling of her illness. Once the initial diagnosis of schizophrenia was made, there seemed to be a strong reluctance to reexamine it, even with growing evidence against it.

Get it right from the beginning and you're more than halfway there, say the biopsychiatrists. Our treatment results are demonstrably better than those of psychiatry as a whole, because we begin by applying the more rigorous, medically current diagnostic system that is used in all other areas of medicine today.

MAKING A DIAGNOSIS, MEDICAL-STYLE

Arriving at a diagnosis can be the longest, most challenging, and most difficult step for a doctor. No two patients are identical in health or illness. Virtually no one will exhibit the "classic" patterns of symptoms and test results described in textbooks. Often, too, a physician will be searching for a disease that is in a stage of development in which it does not exhibit its characteristic appearance.

The time it may take a physician to diagnose your problem may be long and frustrating, but it's worth the wait. The doctor who can pinpoint your problem is best equipped to target the treatment precisely.

The process begins with a clinical interview in which the doctor takes a history of the specific complaint and of your overall health as well as your family's health patterns. The doctor next performs an examination in which he or she hopes to see, feel, or demonstrate the presence of a particular illness or condition. Usually the physician will order lab tests. The laboratory is central to modern medicine because it can provide highly specific, objective information of a kind that in previous years might have been available only at autopsy. (If you want the most accurate diagnosis, wait!) Together with the physician's clinical impression, the laboratory will help to confirm a diagnosis as well as to verify the progress of treatment.

Diagnoses made solely on the basis of a patient's symptoms are the least accurate or useful to a nonpsychiatric physician. Symptoms are usually vague and often difficult to describe and to remember. Emotional symptoms tend to be the most unreliable because the patient's description of them is colored by the emotion itself. For example, if you are depressed and a doctor asks you how long you have felt that way, unintentionally you will probably exaggerate because depression distorts your sense of time. In addition, when you're depressed, it's difficult to remember events or experiences that occurred when you were not depressed. Similarly, if you're not depressed now, you won't remember many of the details of your last depression.

The single greatest reason why symptoms are only part of the picture in medical diagnoses, however, is that symptoms are not specific. In other words, any one symptom can indicate a host of conditions. If you have a pain in your big toe, maybe you broke it. Or maybe you have gout. Or an ingrown toenail.

If you are depressed, maybe you have infectious mononucleosis. Or maybe you have a bad marriage. Or a genetic deficiency of enzymes that synthesize the brain chemical norepinephrine. Or a shortage of brain-endogenous morphine. Or an extreme sensitivity to cold, dark climates. Or insufficient exercise.

Before the development of objective measures to verify or clarify particular diagnoses, medicine had little choice but to depend on symptoms or clusters of symptoms (syndromes) to try to identify a disease. In medicine this era has ended.

MAKING A DIAGNOSIS, PSYCHIATRIC-STYLE

Despite their long years of medical training, and despite the increasing sophistication of the psychiatric laboratory, many, many psychiatrists still continue to diagnose their patients solely on the basis of their symptoms.

All too frequently a psychiatric diagnosis goes like this:

"Oh, Doctor, I'm so depressed."

"Tell me about it."

You talk about your feelings of worthlessness and hopelessness, your difficulties concentrating and making decisions, your insomnia, your loss of interest in just about everything, including food and sex. The psychiatrist asks how long this has been going on, whether you have experienced these feelings before, whether anything might have happened to bring on this episode.

At the end of the interview, the psychiatrist agrees that you are indeed depressed because the symptoms you describe fit the descriptive diagnostic criteria (see box on page 38).

It's as if you went to your internist with a sore throat only to discover that—sure enough—you have a sore throat.

The "diagnosis" thus quickly established, the psychiatrist will begin treatment equally peremptorily—no tests, no verification of the diagnosis, no uncertainty about what these symptoms may mean.

This, in a nutshell, is where most psychiatrists (and nonmedical therapists) still go astray: Instead of ruling out various potential problems, they rule in their diagnoses. In other words, they take the subjective details of symptoms and history described by their patients and fit them to the condition that appears the most obvious explanation for them.

It's Obvious

In medicine there's a saying: All that wheezes isn't asthma. This serves to remind physicians to look beyond the obvious before they jump to conclusions about their patients' conditions. And in fact, in the differential diagnosis of asthma, the treating physician must rule out thirty-four other possible causes for wheezing before he or she can safely rule in a diagnosis of asthma.

A friend of mine suddenly experienced a terrible pain and tightening in his chest. The pain radiated down his left arm. Dizzy and faint, nearly overwhelmed with nausea and barely able to breathe, he somehow managed to get himself to the nearest emergency room. "I'm having a heart attack!" he gasped, clutching his chest, and collapsed. In a split second he was on a hospital gurney surrounded by the ER staff. A doctor was listening to his heart while one nurse was hooking up the electrocardiogram, another taking his blood pressure, and another drawing blood to rush it to the lab for serum enzyme analysis. My friend lay there in terror of dying.

Thank goodness, he pulled through. His tests all turned out negative. He hadn't had a heart attack after all. He had had an anxiety attack.

Any doctor would have suspected a coronary, because my friend's symptoms so closely fit those we all learned about in medical school. But a decent medical workup always consists of a ruling out/ruling in—what we call a differential diagnostic procedure. This is absolutely essential to good medical practice, because what if it isn't the obvious condition? Jumping to conclusions can have tragic, irreversible consequences.

The Psychological Explanation

It is human nature to try to make sense of experience. Psychologically, there is almost always an explanation for why we feel the way we do. Sometimes that explanation is irresistible. Let's say you meet a middle-aged man who is in terrible pain from depression. After talking to him for a while, you find out he recently lost his wife in an automobile accident. Of course he's depressed! Need you explore further?

The answer is an unqualified yes, because it is precisely when the allure of the obvious is so powerful that serious mistakes are most likely to be made. Just because this explanation for the man's distress makes sense, who's to say it is the only one to make sense? Where is it written that the explanation for his distress must have a single facet? Indeed, with evidence mounting for a causal relationship between severe stress and physical, often fatal, illness, a physician is compelled to go further.

This man became our patient, and just in time. He had seen three doctors before he was referred to us for psychiatric evaluation. By the time he arrived he was only hours from death. He was deeply depressed and fit the necessary criteria for a major depressive episode. Within moments of his admission, our alert evaluation team noticed that his lips were vaguely blue. We took his blood pressure and discovered it was very low. Immediately, we ran emergency tests and found that his potassium level was high enough for his heart to stop beating. An electrocardiogram revealed a heart rhythm so disturbed he could indeed die at any moment. Quickly we provided intravenous fluids to bring down his potassium level and bring up his sodium level. This is standard procedure, but it didn't work. Within twenty-four hours we had discovered why. His cortisol test confirmed that he had Addison's disease, in which the adrenal glands shut down. Without treatment Addison's is fatal. Twenty minutes after we gave him intravenous cortisone, an adrenal hormone, he started feeling better.

Every physician knows that Addison's, an extremely rare disease, causes severe depression. Psychiatrists say: "Sure, Addison's causes depression, but I've never seen a case in all the years I've practiced." To this I respond, "When was the last time you looked for it, or any other not-so-obvious diagnosis? How can you find it when you hang your diagnostic hat on your patients' outward symptoms?"

THE DSM-IV

The Diagnostic and Statistical Manual of Mental Disorders, first published in 1952, is the bible of psychiatric diagnosis. Its influence is enormous even outside the field of psychiatry. For one thing, its diagnostic codes are used by all mental health providers whose services are reimbursable by insurance companies. For another, the book is available in bookstores, and many lay people read it to understand more about the problems they or their loved ones are struggling with. The book has been revised periodically to reflect developments in our understanding of psychiatric disorders. The fourth edition, known as the DSM-IV, was published in 1994.

Part of the new good news about depression is that, to some degree, the changes reflected in the DSM-IV indicate that the biopsychiatric approach is gaining greater acceptance within the psychiatric establishment. I still find the book's method of assessing disorders to contain problems and shortcomings, as I'll explain, but things are at least moving in the right direction.

One of the drawbacks of the DSM is that all psychiatric conditions are described using what, to my thinking, is a peculiar Chinese-menu approach: one symptom from column A, two from column B. . . . To see what I mean, take a look at the criteria for a major depressive episode (box, page 38). The diagnostician is supposed to size up patients and see how many criteria they meet. If they get the right score, bingo! They win the diagnosis. But I can't emphasize the point too strongly: Diagnosing by symptoms is often inaccurate, if not downright useless. In the field of medicine, a close-but-no-cigar style just doesn't cut it.

Here are some of the problems I see with the DSM-IV method:

1. *Diagnosing by symptoms makes it difficult to distinguish among disorders with similar symptom patterns.*

A patient shows up in my office talking a mile a minute about how God instructed him to take the Concorde to Paris and back. I recognize this symptom as grandiosity. According to the DSM-IV, though, grandiosity can be a feature of a manic episode, or cocaine intoxication, or schizophrenia. That's a pretty wide range. A doctor who gets the diagnosis wrong can effectively destroy a patient's life.

2. *Different patients experience and report symptoms differently.*

"How's your appetite?" I might ask a depressed patient who is obese. "Fine," she answers—and for her it *is* fine, because she is grateful that for once, due to her illness, she has no appetite.

"Are you in pain?" I ask another patient. "Not particularly," he answers—and he means it, because he has lived with pain for so long that for him it no longer seems unusual. Another patient, asked the same question, responds, "Oh, terrible!"—because her physical makeup and personality make her exquisitely sensitive to the slightest twinges of pain.

Criteria for Major Depressive Episode

A. Five (or more) of the following symptoms have been present during the same two-week period and represent a change from previous functioning; at least one of the symptoms is either (1) depressed mood or (2) loss of interest or pleasure.

Note: Do not include symptoms that are clearly due to a general medical condition, or mood-incongruent delusions or hallucinations.

  (1) depressed mood most of the day, nearly every day, as indicated by either subjective report (e.g., feels sad or empty) or observation made by others (e.g., appears tearful). **Note:** In children and adolescents, can be irritable mood.

  (2) markedly diminished interest or pleasure in all, or almost all, activities most of the day, nearly every day (as indicated by either subjective account or observation made by others)

  (3) significant weight loss when not dieting or weight gain (e.g., a change of more than 5 percent of body weight in a month), or decrease or increase in appetite nearly every day. **Note:** In children, consider failure to make expected weight gains.

  (4) insomnia or hypersomnia nearly every day

  (5) psychomotor agitation or retardation nearly every day (observable by others, not merely subjective feelings of restlessness or being slowed down)

  (6) fatigue or loss of energy nearly every day

  (7) feelings of worthlessness or excessive or inappropriate guilt (which may be delusional) nearly every day (not merely self-reproach or guilt about being sick)

  (8) diminished ability to think or concentrate, or indecisiveness, nearly every day (either by subjective account or as observed by others)

  (9) recurrent thought of death (not just fear of dying), recurrent suicidal ideation without a specific plan, or a suicide attempt or a specific plan for committing suicide

B. The symptoms do not meet criteria for a Mixed Episode.

C. The symptoms cause clinically significant distress or impairment in social, occupational, or other important areas of functioning.

D. The symptoms are not due to the direct physiological effects of a substance (e.g., a drug of abuse, a medication) or a general medical condition (e.g., hypothyroidism).

E. The symptoms are not better accounted for by Bereavement, i.e., after the loss of a loved one, the symptoms persist for longer than two months or are characterized by marked functional impairment, morbid preoccupation with worthlessness, suicidal ideation, psychotic symptoms, or psychomotor retardation.

3. *The impact of symptoms can vary depending on such factors as sex, age, and even culture.*

Women tend to display more of the emotional symptoms of depression — crying, sadness, irritability. In contrast, men are more likely to transform the emotional pain into physical complaints. Because many men are prone to doing rather than feeling, they may hide their depression, even from themselves, by engaging in activities. A colleague had a patient whose career had collapsed and whose wife had thrown him out of the house. Each time the man got depressed he would build a new piece of audio equipment. When he ran out of room in his studio apartment, he finally experienced the depression he'd been fending off and decided to go for help.

The previous edition of the DSM made no mention of how depression manifests itself among members of different cultures. This despite the fact that, in the last century, Kraepelin noted the existence of such clear differences. He observed, for instance, that his Japanese patients were neither guilt-ridden nor suicidal, whereas for Western patients guilt and suicidal thinking or behavior are common symptoms. More recent cross-cultural studies confirm that wide variation exists. For example, a study of Hawaii's ethnic groups showed that Japanese individuals with depression showed more suspiciousness, while Caucasians showed more helplessness. My point is that symptoms alone do not a diagnosis make.

After over forty years in existence, the DSM is at last waking up to this fact. A new section in the fourth edition notes:

Culture can influence the experience and communication of symptoms of depression. Underdiagnosis or misdiagnosis can be reduced by being alert to ethnic and cultural specificity in the presenting complaints of a Major Depressive Episode. For example, in some cultures, depression may be experienced largely in somatic terms, rather than with sadness or guilt. Complaints of "nerves" and headaches (in Latino and Mediterranean cultures), of weakness, tiredness, or "imbalance" (in Chinese and Asian cultures), of problems of the "heart" (in Middle Eastern cultures), or of being "heartbroken" (among Hopi), may express the depressive experience. . . . Cultures may also differ in judgments about the seriousness of experiencing or expressing dysphoria (e.g., irritability may provoke greater concern than sadness or withdrawal). Culturally distinctive experiences (e.g., fear of being hexed or bewitched, feelings of "heat in the head" or crawling sensations of worms or ants, or vivid feelings of being visited by those who have died) must be distinguished from actual hallucinations or delusions that may be part of a Major Depressive Episode, With Psychotic Features. It is also imperative that the clinician not routinely dismiss a symptom merely because it is viewed as the "norm" for a culture.

The last point is important. In this country, blacks and Latinos with bipolar illness are more likely than whites to be diagnosed as schizophrenic because they tend to have what admitting psychiatrists call delusions and hallucinations, which may actually be culturally based religious beliefs.

4. *Relying on symptoms often leads to inappropriate evaluation of the patient's progress.*

Biopsychiatrists have shown that patients may continue to show biological evidence of depressive illness even though many of their symptoms have disappeared. To stop treatment measures when symptoms abate puts these patients at high risk of relapse.

Shrewd patients can manipulate symptoms to get their shrinks off their backs. Others are in denial. Nobody likes to be hospitalized, and depressed patients need only appear to have all the right symptoms in order to get out. "How are you feeling today, Joanne?" "Just fine, Doctor. I'm sleeping and eating well and I'm full of energy. Why, I've been really excited about the great future ahead of me." So the psychiatrist releases Joanne prematurely. She goes home and kills herself.

5. *The absence of expected symptoms does not necessarily rule out the disease.*

Certain psychiatric patients diagnosed as suffering from schizophreniform disorder, for example, show none of the DSM-IV symptoms of mood disorders. Nonetheless, researchers have recently demonstrated that when these patients are diagnosed using all the tools of biopsychiatry, including the laboratory, they can be shown to be suffering from mood disorders. Most important, they respond favorably to treatment for depression or bipolar disorder.

Would you call a serial murderer normal? If you go only by symptoms you'd have to, because studies of murderers who kill many people show that, according to descriptive criteria, they appear utterly normal.

Despite its improvements, DSM-IV is still a trap for psychiatrists. It encourages them to believe that behavioral symptoms necessarily mean that a psychiatric problem exists. This comes from a notion, long discarded in the history of medicine, that the body consists of discrete systems having nothing to do with one another. Emotional symptoms come from the head and physical symptoms come from the body, and never the twain shall meet. If you're acting funny, you need a psychiatrist to straighten out your mind.

You *do* need a psychiatrist, but not necessarily for that reason. You need a psychiatrist to perform a sophisticated medical diagnosis so that you know exactly what you are suffering from that is affecting your behavior and emotions.

When a person tells me he or she is depressed, I say to myself, "So what? That doesn't tell me anything." If I know that someone is not sleeping, I'm no better off than I was before the patient walked in. Just because a patient meets DSM-IV criteria does not mean I know what caused the problem or what to do about it.

There is no mental symptom that is specific to psychiatric illness alone. You could be standing on a street corner having bizarre Technicolor hallucinations and still not be "crazy"; your visions may indicate you're in the midst of the aura that precedes some migraine headaches. Visual hallucinations could also be symptomatic of a brain tumor, of cocaine or hallucinogenic intoxication, or of alcohol or sleeping pill withdrawal. Or they could be a side effect of over-the-counter or other commonly prescribed medications. Catatonia—a condition in which the patient stays as still as a statue, utterly unmoving, despite an often bizarre and uncomfortable posture—is the quintessential psychotic symptom, right? Wrong. Catatonia is now known to be more indicative of neurological problems. The differential diagnosis of catatonia includes at least thirty-nine disorders, varying from lesions, tumors, and malformations of the brain to epilepsy, syphilis, encephalitis, and diabetic ketoacidosis, to chronic amphetamine intoxication and aspirin overdose.

Among the many flaws in previous editions of the DSM, perhaps the most shocking was that they did not even mention the organic conditions known to mimic psychiatric illnesses. The DSM-IV takes a significant step toward clearing up this confusion. For example, one of the criteria for Major Depressive Disorder is that "the symptoms are not due to the direct physiologic effects of a substance . . . or a general medical condition (e.g., hypothyroidism)." In another part of the book, the DSM-IV expands on the definition of an organic mood disorder—that is, one caused by some other medical problem:

A variety of general medical conditions may cause mood symptoms. These conditions include degenerative neurological conditions (e.g., Parkinson's disease, Huntington's disease), endocrine conditions (e.g., hyper- and hypothyroidism, hyper- and hypoparathyroidism, hyper- and hypoadrenocorticism), autoimmune conditions (e.g., systemic lupus erythematosus), viral or other infections (e.g., hepatitis, mononucleosis, human immunodeficiency virus [HIV]), and certain cancers (e.g., carcinoma of the pancreas). The associated physical examination findings, laboratory findings, and patterns of prevalence or onset reflect the etiological general medical condition.

A small step for the American Psychiatric Association; a giant leap for psychiatry! At last, as we approach the twenty-first century, the official book of psychiatric diagnosis generally acknowledges some of the more than seventy-five organic conditions that can mimic depression. Such improvements are due in no small measure to pressure from biopsychiatrists and the clear-cut results of the scientific studies they conduct. However, the manual still offers no guidance to physicians concerning how to rule these conditions in or out, nor does it suggest the further steps needed to identify the appropriate treatment. Chapters 5 through 9 of this book discuss these mimickers; read them and you may be better informed about the link between medical illness and depression than many doctors and the majority of nonmedical therapists.

To my way of thinking, this discussion of medical causes of mood disorders should be the first criterion for the differential diagnosis of depression. Out of ignorance a psychiatrist may misdiagnose depression when in fact the patient is suffering from a deficiency of zinc or folic acid or vitamin B_{12}—a fact easily demonstrable through careful laboratory testing. Such a physician is vulnerable to charges of malpractice.

As a medically oriented psychiatrist, I require far more than a list of symptoms to treat unhappy people who come to me in good faith, expecting me to help them. Fortunately, I know what to do. My physician's black bag is close at hand, and my lab is just down the hall.

Chapter 4

The Baby and the Bathwater

"**W**hat's wrong, Katharine?"

She sits across from me, hugging herself. She doesn't answer, and I'm worried.

"Katharine?" I repeat.

Finally, in a voice that is barely audible, she says, "I'm back just where I started, Dr. Gold. I thought there was a way out of this. That's why I came here. I don't know what I'm going to do now. . . ."

I've just told this bright, attractive, talented woman that all her tests are normal; no organic illness is causing her symptoms. She treats the news as if I have just proclaimed her death sentence. Katharine, a thirty-four-year-old artist, has been depressed for approximately seven years. She has had all the usual treatments and she has not improved. She came to me after seeing an article in a local newspaper about our success at diagnosing mimickers. As she sees it, unless she has a curable organic illness causing her depression, she has no hope.

Many psychiatrists would regard Katharine's reaction to my good news as typical of a depressed person's negative attitude. I find her despair understandable, considering what she has been through.

A Woman Robbed of Tears

Neither Katharine nor her husband, Steve, can remember exactly when she became depressed. She was fine—just the usual ups and downs—when they married, and she stayed fine for the first few years after their kids were born. Then "the uglies," as they called her dark moods, seemed to creep up on her. First they robbed her of the bright smile that Steve remembers most about her from "the old days." Ultimately, the uglies took everything away: her energy, her desire to paint, her pleasure in her family, her desire to live.

Ironically, Katharine is one of those people who seem to have everything. She has a solid, twelve-year marriage, a husband who loves her and understands the demands of her art, and two healthy, smart, well-behaved preteen kids. Her paintings have been well received by local critics, and she even has financial security now that Steve has been made a partner in his law firm.

Katharine makes a striking first impression. She's five feet seven, with long blond hair carefully combed in a quiet, conservative style. Her makeup is subtle, her clothes sophisticated and well chosen. She walks slowly and with apparent determination—determination not to reveal the struggle with depression that she says is always going on underneath that careful exterior. She is ashamed of her suffering.

Katharine's depression has robbed her of the chance to experience what otherwise would be a good, accomplished life. She hasn't painted in almost three years, since her first hospitalization. Her kids don't understand what's happening to her, and her youngest has suddenly begun to fail in school.

Steve seems devoted now, but reluctantly admits her illness is hard on him. Once he nearly left her, so convinced was he that her changed attitude toward the family and him meant that she had found someone else. Steve is a stoic, unused to sharing his feelings. He just couldn't talk to Katharine about his suspicions. Finally, at an elegant French restaurant, as he watched his wife pick at her meal, under the influence of one too many glasses of expensive wine, he burst out, "I can't stand this anymore, Katharine. The kids bore you, I bore you. Last night in bed you just lay there as if I were doing something detestable to you. I won't ask you who the guy is. I don't want to know. I just want you to go."

Steve gulped down the rest of his wine and asked for the check. Katharine hadn't said a word. She looked down at her hands, twisting the pink napkin.

Steve's outburst turned out to be what they both needed. Steve had to let go of some of his smoldering anger. Katharine had to talk about what was happening to her, and she had to understand that her depression was affecting the rest of the family. Both Katharine and Steve had to face that they were in trouble. For the first time since Katharine had become depressed, they talked honestly. She knew she'd been, as she put it, a "miserable blob." She hadn't had any energy, any motivation—hardly a state in which she could have an affair, she reassured Steve. "I'm dead inside, Steve," she said without emotion or expression.

With Steve's encouragement, Katharine made an appointment with their longtime family doctor. He did not examine her. Instead they talked, and he recommended a psychotherapist.

Katharine quit after four sessions. She told me, "He'd say things like, 'I can't understand why you are so unhappy when you're so pretty, Kathy.' I said, 'Oh, you mean that if I would realize I'm attractive, I wouldn't be depressed?'

" 'Well . . . ?' he responded with a big, wide smile.

"My heart just sank," Katharine said. "I felt I'd been trapped in another century, where no one could help me. Before that moment I'd never felt like killing myself. Fortunately I had enough self-esteem left to get up and leave."

She liked her second therapist very much. This woman treated Katharine and her problem seriously. Katharine went to her twice a week but, except for the first few sessions, when she was alive with hope that this would help her, her misery was ever-present. Without results, she couldn't see continuing beyond a year.

Several months later Katharine was referred to a psychiatrist, who prescribed a series of antidepressant medications. Katharine had trouble with the side effects, though. One antidepressant caused cramps; another made her eyes so blurry she couldn't watch TV (her one remaining "activity"); a third frequently made her dizzy and faint. The doctor urged her to hang in there, but she began to lose all hope. She thought seriously of suicide but naturally worried about the impact her death would have on her kids. Then again, she pondered, what kind of mother was she when all she could do on her worst days was stay in her room and watch television?

When her dismal mood plummeted to acute despair, she agreed to be hospitalized. She stayed there for a month while her doctor and the staff psychiatrists dosed her with medications that made her feel even more miserable and confused. After her discharge things stayed about the same.

A year and a half later she was rehospitalized by a different psychiatrist for a similar sudden "crash." The hospital he chose for her had a more active therapeutic program. Katharine had individual therapy, group therapy, and even family therapy. Although her pain lessened, it did not go away. A few months after she came home, when she seemed to be stabilizing, she left treatment.

"Now," Katharine confides to me in a flat voice, "a lot of nights, as I drift into sleep, I see my life as a short pencil line. There's a tiny dot on it that inches farther and farther toward the end of the line. I feel that I am that dot on that bleak line. Backward or forward, it all looks the same."

I wonder whether Katharine is thinking about taking an eraser and shortening the pencil line. I ask her. She merely shrugs.

I think, if only she could cry. Katharine has not cried in over three years.

Frankly, I am surprised that we have not turned up a physical condition that would explain Katharine's symptoms. A person such as Katharine, who has a history of nonresponse to treatment, is in the highest-risk group for a mimicker. I make a note to retest her periodically.

"Katharine," I say, "I understand you were hoping for a physical explanation of your depression. I understand too that you've had a lot of treatment for depression that didn't work. But we haven't even diagnosed your depression yet, so let's hang in there."

"Pardon me, Dr. Gold, but after all these years I don't need you to tell me what kind of depression I have." I have let her down and she is angry. "Good old incurable major depression," she says. Her cynicism is scary.

Quietly I say, "I don't consider 'major depression' a diagnosis."

Katharine stops hugging herself and for the first time today looks me in the eyes. I ask her, "Do you know about the steps we take today to diagnose and treat depression?"

She shakes her head.

"Chin up, kid," I say. "You ain't seen nothin' yet."

DSM-IV DOES IT AGAIN

The DSM-IV is an exercise in the classification of diseases, or nosology. In medicine we must classify diseases so that we can differentiate one from another for treatment, management, and research purposes. In the last chapter we saw that a nosology based on symptoms does not differentiate psychiatric depressive conditions from organic illnesses; instead it often leads to misdiagnosis and mistreatment. However, misdiagnosis and mistreatment can result even when, as in Katharine's case, the psychiatrist dutifully rules out organic symptom mimickers.

Katharine is depressed. Clinicians who have worked with depressed patients have long known that all depressions are not alike, and all stages of depression are not alike. Is it simply a matter of psychology versus physiology?

Do not look to the DSM-IV for answers. The DSM-IV criteria are so broad and overinclusive that they end up saying nothing much about anybody. To say that ten depressed people meet the DSM-IV criteria for major depression is not to say that they look, act, or talk alike; nor does it mean that they will respond to the same treatment—or even that they will respond at all. Furthermore, it does not indicate who is in spontaneous remission or who is at risk of suicide without hospitalization or who needs medication for life.

Doctors create categories to identify similar groups of patients. But two people with depression can have symptoms that are completely opposite and still meet the criteria: no appetite or overwhelming appetite; no sleep or too much sleep. No wonder psychiatrists dread going into court to explain how the same diagnosis can be applied to people who are so different!

Of the DSM-IV subtypes of depression, only melancholia lists objective and specific criteria: regularly worse in the morning upon awakening, loss of appetite and weight loss, early morning awakening, and so forth. But even these criteria don't tell the doctor what's wrong or what to do about it.

Neither do the DSM-IV categories reflect the biological subtypes of depression now being revealed through laboratory research. We are learning that there are important biological differences among depressed people. From this perspective, two people with a diagnosis of major depression can be as different as night and day; by the same token, their treatment will also be different. In contrast, a person with dysthymic disorder and another whose illness is diagnosed as atypical (a wastebasket category for anybody who doesn't fit existing categories) can reveal significant biological similarities and respond well to the same treatments. Only bipolar disorder (manic-depression) serves as a useful category biologically because it usually helps us predict which patients will respond to lithium (with anticonvulsants as back-up therapy).

Despite the rigor with which the DSM-IV writers have differentiated symptomatic categories of depression, none—with the exception of bipolar disorder—is clinically useful. Conclusion: The DSM-IV nosology of mood disorders is invalid.

But I have to begin somewhere. In order to relieve Katharine's suffering, first I have to understand her illness in terms of categories that mean something useful to me as a physician.

A DIAGNOSIS FOR KATHARINE: STEP ONE

Many of my biopsychiatric colleagues and I are guided by a nosology of *mood* disorders that is far more pragmatic than the DSM-IV. Following this scheme step by step, knowledgeable practitioners will recognize the

Nosology of Depression
Affective Disorders (Depression and Mania)

Primary affective disorder		Secondary affective disorder	
Unipolar affective disorder	Bipolar affective disorder	Other psychiatric disorder	Systemic medical diseases
|	|	|	|
Single or recurrent episode	Mania or manic-depressive disorder	Schizophrenia, alcoholism, dementia	CNS disorders, endocrine disorder, drug-induced disorder, infections

category of disease they are dealing with. From there they can take steps to identify the specific disorder. Treatment decisions easily follow. Faithful adherence to this scheme will steer the practitioner clear of misdiagnosis.

Let's say Katharine just walked in my door. I will show you how I organize my approach to her.

First I need to establish whether her symptoms represent a *primary* or a *secondary* mood disorder. A secondary illness is the result of another condition, such as an organic mimicker that could cause or worsen her symptoms. Or it may be a psychiatric condition other than depression that happens to produce depressive symptoms. If I find one of these to be true, I then identify precisely the causal condition from the list of mimickers.

In Katharine's case, through an extensive history (including a family history and a discussion with Steve), physical and psychological exam, and laboratory work, I have determined her illness is not secondary to some other cause. I must now work my way through the primary category. First I must establish whether Katharine's depression is bipolar or unipolar—in other words, does her mood also soar, or does it only plummet? Both Katharine and Steve have told me that hers is the plummet-only variety. Now all I need to know is whether this is her first episode or one among many; further conversations with Katharine reveal it is her fourteenth.

The result: Katharine's depression is of the primary unipolar recurrent type. In arriving at this finding I have been able to distinguish Katharine's depression from other disorders. Once I identify the precise subtype of her depression, I will know which specific treatment to try.

HOW PSYCHIATRISTS DECIDE ABOUT TREATMENT

Psychiatry offers three major approaches to the treatment of depression: psychotherapy, medication, and electroconvulsive therapy (ECT, also known as shock therapy). All of them work on some patients. Parts IV and V of this book cover the subject of treatment extensively. The point I want to make here, though, is that since the rise of biopsychiatry, the first choice in treatment has shifted from listen-and-talk therapy to medication.

What, then, is the best way to treat Katharine's major depression? In the old guidelines of psychiatry, the answer is: whatever works.

Following received wisdom, psychiatrists recommend ECT for patients who are having psychotic delusions, who cannot tolerate the pills, or who require emergency treatment to survive (such as those who are starving to death); patients with numerous physical symptoms get pills; all who have ups along with downs (bipolars) get lithium; and those with few physical symptoms and a chronic history get psychotherapy—or some combination of these four.

Usually, if one approach doesn't work, the psychiatrist tries another, or combines them, until something works, if only temporarily.

In other words, traditional psychiatric treatment is little more than trial and error, broadly aimed.

As Katharine's experience shows, psychiatry's poor record of treatment response results from this nonspecific approach combined with misdiagnosis of organic conditions. Unless they take a systematic approach, psychiatrists can never know why a treatment works or why it doesn't. Thus, they will rarely be able to replicate their success; they must start from scratch with each patient. With luck the patient will continue treatment and not quit out of frustration or become uncooperative—or even commit suicide—before the doctor happens upon the right formula.

Sometimes the right approach means giving the medication more time to work, adjusting the dosage, or switching to another type of drug that produces more tolerable side effects.

I recently saw a patient who illustrates this last point. I treated an obese woman who was referred to me as a nonresponder. She had been treated with many types of antidepressants, the last of which was a monoamine oxidase inhibitor (MAOI), but to no avail. It turned out that the woman had not been taking her MAOI as prescribed because she felt it made her gain weight. Her psychiatrist reassured her that it had no such effect, implying she was being neurotic. The last thing she needed was to gain more weight. So she stopped taking the pills, but she didn't tell her psychiatrist.

She was right about the weight gain; MAOIs do occasionally have that side effect. Her psychiatrist was not familiar with all the literature. MAOIs were a good choice of drug class for this patient. I switched her to a slightly different version, one that did not contribute to her weight problem. She took them as directed; within a month she experienced her first real relief in many years.

Each psychiatrist has a rationale for choosing a particular treatment for a particular patient, and each applies a set of criteria for evaluating the results. When subjected to scientific scrutiny, however, these choices and results may not hold up. Question: How would you, as the treating psychiatrist, know whether your depressed patient was better? When the symptoms went away—in other words, when the patient felt better? That seems to make sense and is, indeed, how most psychiatrists evaluate their patients' progress. However, upon close biopsychiatric investigation, it turns out that relief of symptoms is not a very reliable measure of progress. People who have biological depressions tend to relapse if treatment does not continue until their biological abnormalities disappear, regardless of how much better they feel and look and function.

How Patients Decide About Treatment

Few psychiatrists are generalists who use every treatment modality; most specialize in one or perhaps two approaches. Some provide medication, while others offer talk-only cures, and some (mostly those who work in hospitals) will even shock all comers. Each of these treatments is appropriate for different types of depression, or for the same type of depression at different times. Over time, for instance, psychotherapy and medication may prove equally effective, but using medication may stabilize a severely ill patient far more quickly. After the acute phase, medication maintenance plus psychotherapy may be the treatment of choice. Some patients require no somatic (bodily) treatment but would be more likely to respond to psychotherapy. But this therapy has several types. Should this patient undergo a long course of psychoanalysis or a short course of cognitive therapy?

Who decides? Often *you* decide, without even realizing it. You feel rotten, you ask a friend or a doctor for the name of a good shrink, you make an appointment, you go, and you take the cure that is offered. You may not know whether the therapist is an analyst, a medication specialist, a behaviorist, a cognitive specialist, or an orthomolecular practitioner. You may not even know whether this person is a doctor or a psychologist or a social worker. You take the cure that is offered, but if you went to the therapist down the hall, or the one down the street, you might get an entirely different treatment.

Ultimately, the burden of trial and error falls squarely on the depressed patient. Like many of my patients, Katharine has gone from therapist to therapist and cure to cure. Her depression only got worse.

ANOTHER MISSING LINK

We have seen that the DSM-IV employs broad, descriptive criteria that can apply to more than one disorder, and resulting diagnoses are not treatment-specific. There is another problem: The DSM-IV does not talk about what causes the illness or how it affects the body (its pathology). Without that knowledge, there's not much doctors can do except relieve symptoms. Probably the symptoms will come back. In medicine, diagnostic procedures are supposed to lead all physicians to a uniform understanding of the cause and the pathology underlying the patient's complaints. This information in turn yields uniform treatment options. For example, if a man has a persistent urethral discharge, his physician takes a gonorrheal culture; if the test is positive, the physician prescribes penicillin.

Psychiatry has no history of such uniform procedures. There are many schools of psychiatric theory. Some therapists even ignore these approaches and march to the idiosyncratic beat of their own drum.

One therapist decided Katharine's depression had to do with her early relationship with her mother. Accordingly, he applied a psychotherapeutic approach to lead her into the past and back again. Another therapist saw it as more a here-and-now problem; in her talk therapy sessions, this doctor discouraged Katharine from exploring her past relationships. She also prescribed medication to alleviate Katharine's symptoms quickly and make her feel better about psychotherapy. The first time Katharine was hospitalized, no testing was done to find out what was causing her condition. Instead, the resident doctors presumed her depression was caused by biological factors, and they gave her the medication they were most familiar with.

Why would the authors of the DSM-IV ignore the questions of causality and pathology? Perhaps they didn't want to rock the boat by appearing to endorse one psychiatric approach over another. From a political standpoint, this may have been prudent, but medically, it is disastrous. Existing in a conceptual vacuum, the DSM-IV is practically useless. It throws away the valuable lessons of biopsychiatric research. Down the drain goes the baby, and my patient, with the bathwater.

Dr. Donald Langsley, a past president of the APA, said: "We need conceptual frameworks within which to place our data of observation. It matters not if there are many; it matters much if there are none. With concepts, new data will distinguish those that are useful from those that are not. This has been the history of all medicine." Indeed, it is the history of *all* applied science.

In contrast, American psychiatry has a peculiar fondness for the *one* answer, the *one* concept with which all will be explained. This single-mindedness has contributed to the failure of psychiatrists to consider other vital questions, such as whether organic illness is present. The consequence is that psychiatry has been slow to integrate medical advances, or change of any kind, into the diagnosis and treatment of so many suffering human beings.

A DIAGNOSIS FOR KATHARINE: STEP TWO

Biopsychiatry is an integrative science of the mind, and those of us who practice it are equally a product of psychiatry and of the neurosciences. Conceptually we understand mental illness as a dysfunction with many aspects: brain, body, mind, environment. One of these aspects may outweigh others, and we may choose to intervene on that level using medical or psychological techniques. Still, our responsibility is to the entire patient—as a biological, psychological, and social being—from diagnosis through recovery.

To Katharine, I owe a diagnosis worthy of a medical doctor. Such a diagnosis must be practical: It must reflect causation and pathology and point toward a specific treatment. As you remember, I have decided that Katharine's illness falls within the primary unipolar recurrent category. Good medical practice dictates that I verify this largely subjective finding using objective measures. The fact is, any psychiatrist's clinical impression is likely to be inaccurate 25 percent of the time. Therefore I turn to biopsychiatry's essential resource, the right hand of modern medicine: the laboratory.

For example, I may give Katharine a battery of neuroendocrine tests. These tests reveal abnormalities in the brain-body systems that control both mood and endocrine-gland function; these abnormalities are thought to be biological markers of primary depression. Together the dexamethasone suppression test (DST) and the TRH (thyroid-releasing hormone) stimulation test would verify the presence of a neuroendocrine type of depression. If they do, I can be sure we are on a biological track. I will also have identified an important abnormality I can follow during treatment. I will also look for further markers that provide other clues to her particular subtype, such as a previous, or family history of, depression or response to a particular antidepressant.

Almost every day, biopsychiatric research reveals more extraordinary information about brain dysfunction in depression. We know, for example, that tiny amounts of chemicals called neurotransmitters carry signals across the synapses (spaces) between nerve cells in the brain. These chemicals regulate mood. If their levels are abnormal, depression can result. The task with every patient is to identify which of the many neurotransmitter systems seems to be at fault. The resulting diagnosis identifies a subtype of depression that we can match to a medication that acts on that specific system. We can't get a good and direct measurement of these neurotransmitters without poking around in a patient's brain. So we've developed clever ways to figure out indirectly what's going on by measuring the substances that are left over after the neurotransmitter has been used by the body. These substances, called metabolites, are found in blood, urine, or other fluids. As many as three depressive subtypes can be identified from the results of one urine test.

Katharine may suffer from a serotonin type of depression, a possible risk factor linked to other mood disorders and suicide. The discovery of serotonin's role in depression is one of the most important breakthroughs of the past decade, and is certainly the basis of most of the new good news. An important fact is that she has a positive family history of suicide. Her maternal grandfather—the skeleton in the family closet— shot himself to death "accidentally," according to the official family version. The unofficial version is that his death was self-inflicted. A few years ago Katharine's mother died in a car accident that may have been intentional, as many fatal crashes actually are. She supposedly fell asleep at the wheel and drove into a steep ravine. Katharine denied that her mother was depressed, but Steve thought that in some ways her persistent aloofness and coldness reminded him of Katharine during "the uglies."

Five out of every hundred people with depression kill themselves. The possibility of predicting true suicidal risk—and preventing tragedy—is almost too exciting for words, a psychiatrist's dream come true.

THE FINAL MISSING LINK

One of the biggest improvements in the DSM-IV over its predecessors is the acknowledgment that laboratory tests have a critical role in helping us recognize and understand psychiatric disorders, including depression. With this long-overdue step forward, the DSM at last is starting to catch up with the reality of psychiatry as practiced by biopsychiatrists over the past decade. For example, the DSM-IV notes that a number of laboratory findings are abnormal in people with major depressive disorder or bipolar disorder. Sleep changes, measured by the electroencephalograph (EEG), occur in 40 to 60 percent of outpatients and up to 90 percent of inpatients with major depression. And the DSM-IV also notes that tests of blood, cerebrospinal fluid, or urine can reveal abnormalities in the neurotransmitter systems thought to be involved in mood disorders (see Chapter 16). Other lab tests that provide vital clues to the nature of the person's illness include brain imaging, waking EEG, neuro- and psychological testing, and the dexamethasone suppression test (see page 221). Lab studies on people experiencing a manic episode also indicate increased secretion of a hormone called cortisol. The fact that some tests finally merit mention in the DSM-IV is very good news for patients, because it indicates that more psychiatrists are using an essential weapon—the lab—in their battle against mental disorders.

Most medical diagnoses derive from the physician's clinical suspicion combined with external, objective, verified laboratory tests. When clinical impression and test results differ, the physician will often give an abnormal test the greater weight. Certainly no doctor would ignore abnormal electrocardiogram results just because the patient feels fine and the stethoscope doesn't detect any problems.

Psychiatrists would never accept treatment for their own medical problems, or those of family members, without first being convinced that laboratory findings back up the diagnosis. Yet, until recently, many were willing to dispense powerful and possibly dangerous medications solely on the basis of a patient's history and behavior. Today, though, in psychiatry—as in all branches of medicine—the defining criteria for disease must ultimately be evidence of pathology, which can be demonstrated only with scans or in the laboratory.

The psychiatric laboratory is valuable in virtually all areas of clinical practice, from differential diagnosis to choice of medication and appropriate dosage to measurement of recovery and prediction of relapse. Yet many psychiatrists are still reluctant to test patients. Their stated reasons are these:

(1) The tests do not reliably confirm DSM-IV diagnostic categories;
(2) The tests do not provide a diagnosis;
(3) The causes of depression have not been proved, so testing is pointless.

Each of these objections is valid. Nonetheless, those who ignore tests for these reasons reveal their fundamental ignorance of the principles of laboratory medicine.

In the first place, the tests cannot confirm DSM-IV diagnoses because, as we have seen, the diagnoses are not true medical illnesses or categories. Just as Prozac can cure people who have varying degrees of depression or who do not even meet the criteria for depression, there is no one-to-one correspondence between a symptom and a specific pathology. It's impossible to come up with a test for feeling rotten and eating too much or too little and sleeping too much or too little. To insist that the only acceptable test would be one that "proves" the presence of major depression is like saying the only valid test for a sore throat is one that proves all sufferers have a strep throat.

The dexamethasone suppression test is continually being criticized because the results do not appear to be specific to depression. In other words, abnormal results can occur in patients with various diagnoses, such as borderline personality disorder. "See!" critics say. "The test doesn't work." Biopsychiatry's response is that we ought to rethink diagnostic criteria and reorganize them on the basis of neurophysiological measures, because persons with the same laboratory findings may respond to the same treatment or require long-term maintenance, regardless of descriptive diagnosis. Starting from these findings, we could then work backward to determine whether common behavioral criteria also exist.

Next, tests rarely in themselves provide a diagnosis. Laboratory results are pieces of the puzzle we combine with other clinical information to create a total picture. No test is the perfect final version; it is the best available at any point in time. The more clinicians use tests, the more the tests are improved and refined. But first, psychiatrists must reeducate themselves in laboratory medicine, which means they must overcome their reluctance to act and think like the doctors they are.

Finally, psychiatry is not the only medical field in which causes often elude us. The causes of most medical illnesses, ranging from heart and circulatory disease to diabetes and kidney disease to allergy and migraine headache to gastrointestinal disease to the common cold, remain to be proved. Nonetheless, the laboratory gives us important clues that we can use to refine our understanding and treatment. The lack of ultimate proof of a cause must never prevent us from applying what we have thus far learned to relieve our patients' suffering. Knowledge develops incrementally. What we learn today may show that we were wrong yesterday; more likely it will show that there's more to it than we thought yesterday.

THE GIFT OF HOPE

So I continue to diagnose Katharine's illness. I tell her about each step I will take. Should her neuroendocrine tests prove positive and further testing suggest a targeted treatment, I will not stop there. I'll test to see that the medication has reached the proper level in her blood to be effective. And I'll continue my diagnostic tests throughout her treatment to determine her progress; I won't stop treatment simply because she experiences relief of symptoms. I will also refer her for short-term psychotherapy designed particularly for people with depression.

If her neuroendocrine tests are negative, psychotherapy will be my sole treatment choice for the time being. I'll watch her progress carefully. If she still does not improve, I will retest her both for biological depression and for organic illness. Katharine might have an illness that is still developing and so does not yet show up in lab results.

"As soon as I have a final diagnosis for you, Katharine, I expect you to improve rapidly," I tell her, "because unlike any treatment you have received before, mine will be targeted to exactly what's wrong with you. Our research at this hospital shows that nine out of every ten women and men with your problem get better."

Katharine smiles shyly. I get a glimmer of the life that was once in her, and the hope that remains despite her pain.

Four months pass. Katharine comes in to have the level of medication in her blood checked. She is all smiles. She tells me she hopes to start painting again soon.

As it turns out, Katharine does not have a serotonin type of depression. (And, as you'll see in Part III of this book, I could have discovered this very easily by simply giving her Prozac or any of the other drugs in the SSRI class.) However, I did discover abnormalities on two other biological tests that help explain the chronic, relapsing course of her illness. I now begin to treat her with a type of antidepressant targeted to her diagnosed pathology. Katharine is far from pleased when she hears which drug I have chosen; one of her previous doctors had prescribed the same type of medication. Not only had it not worked, but Katharine had also suffered badly from its side effects. I tell her that I believe the dosage she had been given was far too low to be effective, and that there are strategies to help prevent side effects.

Through blood tests we discover that Katharine's body metabolizes most of the drug almost before it reaches her brain. As a result, she needs more than twice the amount of medication than she had been given before. The doctor who had prescribed it for her had not performed the laboratory work necessary to determine the required dosage. Frequently checking the amount of medication in her blood, I slowly build Katharine up to the effective dosage. She does not have as much difficulty with side effects as she expected. The greatest problem is drowsiness, so I change the timing instructions. Instead of taking the pills twice a day, she takes the full dose at bedtime; by the time she awakens, this side effect has worn off.

A month passes before we are able to get enough antidepressant medication into Katharine's system. Results are dramatic. She becomes able to laugh, able to cry.

Katharine feels a million times better, but is not cured yet. Her tests reveal that the fundamental biological abnormalities remain. I will continue her on the medication until they at least normalize. Only then can I be sure she will not suffer a relapse.

Six weeks ago Katharine entered short-term psychotherapy. I feel she needs to work on some of her depression-related attitudes. Katharine's depression has been central to her existence for so many years that she does not know how to live without it. For example, she has a great deal of time on her hands and does not know how to fill it. Before her illness she would have been grateful to have that time for her artwork. Now she feels that her depression has destroyed her talent.

When she tells me today she's off to buy art supplies, I know her faith in herself is returning. Four months after we established a diagnosis based on specific pathology, Katharine is on her way to a complete recovery.

CHAPTER 5

When Depression Isn't

Despite our understanding of biopsychiatry today, recent studies and reports by the U.S. Department of Health and Human Services show that between 12 and 36 percent of the average psychiatrist's patients are being treated for mental disorders they do not have. Their psychiatric symptoms are directly caused by a physical illness of which the psychiatrist is unaware. For hospitalized patients, the situation is just as grim, if not worse. Almost a third have undiagnosed physical diseases rather than the psychiatric illnesses for which they have been confined. Half have illnesses that substantially worsen their psychiatric symptoms.

In my own practice, I find previously undetected physical illness in approximately one out of four of my patients. This higher-than-average rate results from the nature of my practice, which includes a number of men and women who have been considered psychiatric treatment failures. Risk of a physical disease masquerading as an emotional problem is highest among this group. If you are treated by someone who does not look beyond your symptoms, you are less likely to recover than if you are treated by a biopsychiatrist.

At least seventy-five illnesses or conditions (some experts say ninety-one) can cause symptoms of apparent mental disorder. I call these diseases the great mimickers of psychiatry, because they imitate the disorders that psychiatrists are trained to treat. Without diagnostic examination and precise testing, rarely can any physician, or any patient, tell the difference between a true psychiatric illness and a mimicker.

Routine physical examination and testing are often insufficient. To uncover many mimickers, the examining physician must first stop to consider that an organic condition may be causing a patient's emotional symptoms. Then he or she must know which diseases to look for, and how.

The Most Unforgiving Organ

Confusion between physical and mental disorders occurs frequently because psychiatric symptoms are often the first and only signs of a developing illness. Mental symptoms may precede the appearance of overt physical symptoms by weeks, months, years, even decades. The Famous Actor's depression (Chapter 1) was his only symptom of testicular cancer for three and a half years. A sixty-six-year-old man was depressed for ten years before he developed jaundice and itching, the first physical symptoms of his pancreatic tumor. His depression finally abated after the removal of most of his pancreas.

Few if any diseases just "happen." You don't come down with an infectious illness the moment the offending virus or bacteria invades your body. Your immune system will struggle with the attackers, which continue to reproduce until finally you have that miserable feeling that you're coming down with something. Neither do you become diabetic the day your doctor announces you have diabetes; even if you "passed" your glucose tolerance test last year, the disease was there but undetectable by that particular measure. You may have felt depressed, but you would hardly have associated such a feeling with diabetes.

In all illness, the body undergoes subtle changes that may develop into the pathological states that doctors recognize as disease. One of the greatest challenges in medicine today is to detect these early stages *before* damage is done. This is a high priority in diseases such as heart disease and cancer, which often cannot be diagnosed until they are in their final stages. Early detection may be able to prevent the disease from developing further.

Early detection requires early suspicion. Standard screening exams reveal relatively little of what could possibly go wrong with your body. Generally the doctor starts a determined search only when you come in for treatment of specific complaints.

Ironically, considering psychiatry's longtime medical backwardness, our recognition that mental symptoms are frequently the earliest clues has finally moved biopsychiatry to the forefront of medical diagnostics. Psychiatric symptoms occur first, we have learned, because as many diseases develop they slowly, imperceptibly, alter the chemistry of the body. The brain will not forgive this; even the subtlest changes will affect it long before they appear to influence the normal functioning of other organ systems.

For example, the smallest reduction in the output of thyroid hormone can change the sensitivity of nerve-cell receptors in the brain. This chemical state can produce depression long before the classic physical symptoms of hypothyroidism emerge (see Chapter 9). Standard tests will show a normal amount of thyroid hormone in the blood. Only a supersensitive thyroid-hormone radioimmunoassay or the TRH test (see Chapter 9), rarely administered by doctors other than biopsychiatrists, can reveal this physical state. The difference between the two tests is often striking.

THE PSYCHIATRIST AS MEDICAL SUPERSPECIALIST

In an important study, Dr. Richard Hall found that most misdiagnosed psychiatric patients had no idea they were physically ill before they developed mental symptoms. Hall, a professor of psychiatry and internal medicine who is a seminal researcher in the mimickers, writes: "When a psychiatrist evaluates an adult who has recently developed a major psychiatric symptom or a severe personality change, a thorough, detailed physical examination should be conducted."

While all physicians would do well to take emotional symptoms as indications of early illness, differential diagnosis of the great mimickers is one area of medicine in which all psychiatrists must become better clinicians than internists, pediatricians, neurologists, and other medical and surgical specialists. The reason is practical: Because of the nature of the presenting symptoms, psychiatrists (indeed, all mental health practitioners) encounter more patients suffering from mimickers than do any other physicians. As you will see in upcoming chapters, some of these diseases have a fatal outcome if not detected very early in their course. Psychiatrists can—they must—save lives.

Referral to a psychiatrist is appropriate in any case, since a psychiatrist is—or is supposed to be—a medical specialist in all illnesses that affect a person's mental and emotional existence.

Admittedly, this is a lot to ask of most psychiatrists, who were relieved to abandon disease detection at the medical-school door. But there is no excuse for lack of awareness. All mental health practitioners must become aware of the mimickers, their prevalence within their practices, and the need for professional medical diagnosis of all patients before deciding on a treatment plan.

In the past only a biopsychiatrist would be likely to consider the presence of a mimicker in a patient complaining of depression, anxiety, confusion, and the myriad other symptoms these diseases may cause. Fortunately, that is finally changing. After all, diagnostic acumen should not become the rarefied province of only a few psychiatric subspecialists. Psychiatrists are physicians, not psychologists or social workers. All are obligated morally, ethically, and legally to provide state-of-the-art medical care to every patient.

How to Detect a Mimicker

An active evaluation program, at a hospital or in your own doctor's office, should first try to eliminate misdiagnosis. My biopsychiatric colleagues and I do not prejudge our patients' symptoms. We take a detailed personal and family history, then conduct a mental-status exam, and perform or order a complete physical, including neurological and endocrinological examinations. Now, working with clinical findings and the frequency with which each mimicker tends to occur in each of our settings, we develop an "index of suspicion."

The index of suspicion will determine which of the possible tests to run to rule out a diagnosis for which suspicion is high. The laboratory is always part of the process. Neither psychiatrist nor internist has sufficient clinical skills to pick up the majority of the mimickers without diagnostic testing. As I've noted, clinical impression alone is wrong one out of four times.

The expense of such an examination, which can take up to two weeks, is substantially higher, of course, than the one psychiatric session in which a person with depressive symptoms usually earns a diagnosis of major depression. Detection of a mimicker, however, will substantially shorten the hospital stay of many a patient previously considered to be a hopeless case—saving untold amounts of money for whoever foots the bill. Similarly, it can lop years off costly long-term psychotherapy.

One cannot, of course, put a price on the relief of suffering. At one hospital, at least eight out of every one hundred severely depressed patients we evaluate are found to be suffering from hypothyroidism, the most common mimicker and one that is easily treatable. These eight lives are utterly changed by the failure of the nonbiopsychiatric evaluation procedure. When their diagnosis and treatment are changed, their depression finally lifts and their lives go on.

Categories of Mimickers

The great mimickers of psychiatry fall into a few broad categories. The most common are (1) drug (illicit, prescribed, and over-the-counter) and alcohol reactions and (2) endocrine disorders (e.g., hypothyroidism, diabetes). Other categories include diseases of the central nervous system (including Alzheimer's disease and multiple sclerosis), infectious diseases, cancers, AIDS, metabolic conditions, and nutritional and toxic disorders, plus a large miscellaneous category.

In the remainder of this chapter and in the four that follow, we'll explore these categories, describing a number of the individual illnesses or conditions that fall within them. As you read, try to resist the natural temptation to believe that you or someone you know who is depressed has a certain mimicker, especially one that is fatal or most difficult to treat. When it comes to diagnosing their medical problems, most patients are as bad as most psychiatrists.

Cancer

Many types of tumors, found in various sites throughout the body, can cause mental symptoms, which may be the only symptoms to appear for weeks, months, or years. In fact, major depression occurs in 25 to 50 percent of patients with cancer, so it is vital to any patient's long-term survival that a proper diagnosis be made.

Cancers, however, are not the most common mimickers. Only 2 percent of all mimickers prove to be cancers. (Among depressed patients who do not respond to psychiatric medications and who have lost at least thirty pounds, however, the diagnosis of cancer is very common.) Cancer kills over 500,000 Americans a year. For that reason, among others, recognition of early psychiatric clues is urgent.

How many times have you heard the following story? "My mother has bone cancer. They found it in her hip. For years she's been depressed and feeling vaguely ill. Until the diagnosis was made, doctors told my mother it was all in her head. Now they give her six months to live."

Or this: "Aunt Lu was fifty-five when Uncle John told her he wanted a divorce so that he could marry another woman. Aunt Lu had been very dependent on Uncle John. Now here she was on her own. As you can imagine, she had a rough time starting a new life. Oddly, she didn't get really depressed for about a year after the divorce. Then she began to get backaches. They became more and more intense, until she could barely walk. My mother, Lu's sister, finally convinced her to go to a doctor. He talked about the back being a common focus for psychological stress and he prescribed pills for the pain. They didn't seem to work. And Aunt Lu started acting crazy—talking a mile a minute, often to herself, then suddenly bursting into tears. She ended up in a mental hospital. Everybody, including the doctors, blamed it on the divorce. My mother arranged to have Aunt Lu transferred to a private psychiatric hospital in our city. The doctor who admitted her said he thought her symptoms were medical. Everybody was shocked. Sure enough, she had a lymphoma. She was dead within a month."

Often, mental symptoms are the first signs of tumors of the central nervous system (brain and spine) and those that secrete hormones. Hormones are chemicals secreted by the brain and endocrine system that regulate many body functions, including metabolism, growth, and development. Hormones are related—sometimes identical—to neurotransmitters, the brain's chemical messengers. Hormones, as we shall see, are directly involved in the genesis of depression, whether mimicker-induced or biological.

Cancer and depression can produce similar symptoms, such as loss of interest in life, loss of appetite and weight, and insomnia. Careful testing for biological signposts, especially changes in neurochemical, endocrine, and sleep systems, must be performed. If the doctor finds abnormalities in the hypothalamic and pituitary systems, or changes in sleep patterns and certain neurotransmitters, then depression may be present and must be treated appropriately. Several studies have demonstrated that antidepressants can have a significant effect on improving quality of life and may enhance the longevity of cancer patients with depression. A high percentage of cancer patients treated with antidepressant medication report a better adjustment to their situation. While it hasn't been scientifically proven, I suspect that when their depression is treated, patients become more compliant with their cancer treatment, and thus may have a better course in their illness.

LUNG CANCER

Karen B. remembers that her sixty-six-year-old father became inexplicably depressed for three months before his lung cancer was detected. Claiming fatigue, he lost interest in playing golf, meeting friends, watching TV. "It just wasn't like him," says Karen. Her dad began to lose weight, but since loss of appetite is common with depression, no one recognized it as a bad sign. The family searched for a psychological explanation. Says Karen, "It didn't occur to us that there might be any other reason for a really awful mood like that." It was about time for her father to have a checkup, so he made an appointment and during the examination mentioned the mood change. The doctor answered that depression was common in older age, and if he wanted, he would prescribe some pills. Karen's father said he'd think about it.

By the very nature of the disease and its treatment, cancer patients are at high risk of developing a mood disorder. Among the risk factors they may encounter are:

- Social isolation
- Recent loss
- A tendency to pessimism
- Socioeconomic pressures
- A history of mood disorder
- Alcohol or substance abuse
- Previous suicide attempt(s)
- Poorly controlled pain
- Side effects of cancer medications

Cancer patients are also at high risk for suicide. Suicidal risk factors include:

- A prior psychiatric diagnosis (especially depression)
- Increasing age
- Family history of suicide
- Poor social support
- Delirium
- Advanced disease
- Disfiguring disease or surgery
- Substance abuse
- Poorly controlled pain

They never pursued the conversation, for his chest x-rays revealed an ominous spot on his right lung. It turned out to be cancer of the oat-cell type. Oat cells secrete ACTH, a pituitary hormone that stimulates the adrenal glands and is thought to cause or promote depression. Surgery and chemotherapy did not halt the course of the disease, which had already spread to his liver. Karen's father died almost a year after his cancer was diagnosed. Had the diagnosis come three months earlier, at the onset of the depressive symptoms, he might have had a chance.

PANCREATIC CANCER

Pituitary, thyroid, parathyroid, renal, ovarian, stomach, and particularly pancreatic cancers also secrete hormones. Pancreatic cancer, a swift and painful killer, is notorious for presenting first as depression in half to three-quarters of people with this form of the disease. The pancreas lies behind the stomach and normally secretes juices that are essential to digestion. The severe depression of pancreatic cancer is often accompanied by crying spells, insomnia unresponsive to medication, and anxiety associated with the fear of having a serious illness.

While a small percentage of patients with pancreatic cancer are candidates for surgery, which extends life for only 10 percent of them, half of all patients die within three months of the diagnosis, most within a year. The mortality may be so rapid because the disease is often clinically silent. When physical pain (constant and radiating toward the back), weight loss, and jaundice occur, the disease is quite advanced. Here is a real opportunity for a psychiatrist to save or prolong a life, because the depression of pancreatic cancer can precede the physical symptoms by as much as ten years.

Pancreatic cancer is somewhat more common among men than women and rarely occurs before age 40. Other symptoms include indigestion and constipation. The psychiatrist should be on the lookout for it when presented with a patient over age 50 who has severe depression and weight loss, or who has diabetes, or who may also be a heavy drinker (alcohol is a common cause of pancreatic disease).

CARCINOID SYNDROME

Carcinoid tumors, sometimes called functioning endocrine tumors, can occur throughout the body, but usually grow from endocrine cells in the small intestine, appendix, or stomach. Patients can live ten to fifteen years following diagnosis, even though the tumors usually spread to other organs. These tumors are accompanied by a bizarre set of symptoms called the carcinoid syndrome. Food, excitement, exertion, or alcohol may bring on an attack of flushing of the head and neck, color changes from bloodless to blue, and diarrhea and abdominal cramps. Forty percent of patients exhibit mental symptoms, especially depression.

Carcinoid tumors secrete substances, such as serotonin, that are implicated in depression.

CENTRAL NERVOUS SYSTEM TUMORS

Tumors of the left temporal (near the temple) and frontal (above the forehead) lobes of the brain and of the limbic system (deep inside the brain) are those most likely to produce early symptoms of depression and irritability. The most common psychiatric symptom of brain tumor, however, is personality change. Psychiatrists Linda Gay Peterson and Mark Perl report a case of a thirty-eight-year-old woman with multiple sclerosis (itself a frequent mimicker) who was hospitalized because of physical symptoms. Psychiatrists were called in because her husband mentioned that she had been acting strangely. A year earlier, he said, after ten years of marriage, she began having unexplained emotional outbursts. She started having an affair, which she flaunted, and moved back and forth several times between her mother's house and their own.

The consulting psychiatrists ordered a CAT scan and found brain tumors in the frontal, temporal, and parietal lobes (the parietal lobe is behind the frontal lobe, at the back of the head). Earlier diagnosis might have improved the woman's chances for survival. Undoubtedly, however, early recognition of the tumor could have reduced the marital strife and family disruption that occurred because of her symptoms.

Heart Disease

Every year, heart attacks and heart disease kill more people than cancer. More than 40 percent of all deaths each year are due to heart attack and vascular illness. Some 720,000 Americans are killed by heart attacks and another 69 million have high blood pressure, coronary artery disease, or related illnesses. The costs of heart disease are astronomical—over $108 billion in medical costs alone each year.

But there is some good news. Because we've begun to change our behavior through exercise, diet, and stress reduction, the death rate from heart attacks has declined by almost 25 percent in recent years. New medications that prevent the spread of heart disease or reduce the risk of death after a heart attack have saved countless lives. On the down side, these medications can provoke symptoms that appear to be depression.

Depressive symptoms can also result from the interactions among heart and high blood pressure medications and antidepressants. The combination of these drugs can cause such depressionlike symptoms as lethargy, fatigue, and sleeplessness.

Depression may also be an early clue to impending heart attack. A five-year study conducted by British researchers showed that men forty to sixty-five years old often had depressed moods, lost their sex drive, were exhausted, and worried excessively in the months before they suffered heart attacks. Examination prior to their attacks detected no physical symptoms of heart damage.

But actual episodes of serious depression can arise in patients with a history of myocardial infarction. Often these episodes increase in frequency in the years following heart attacks. Some studies estimate that depression is present in 40 to 65 percent of patients who have coronary artery disease, myocardial infarction, or a related disorder.

Infectious Diseases

Many infectious diseases can cause psychiatric symptoms (see table below). Viral pneumonia is often accompanied by depression. In the early stages of tuberculosis, many people become irritable and apathetic; excitement and hypomania (mild mania) characterize later stages. Commonly misdiagnosed infectious mimickers include mononucleosis and infectious hepatitis.

INFECTIOUS MONONUCLEOSIS

Doctors in student health services know that mono commonly shows up as depression—especially around exam time, when college students are generally run-down and susceptible. It occurs most commonly among adolescents and young adults, and has been called "the kissing disease," because it is spread by close oral contact. It is not very contagious, however.

Mono is caused by the Epstein-Barr virus (named for its discoverers), one of the many herpes viruses. The virus attacks the white blood cells that fight disease. For four to seven weeks no physical symptoms will be apparent. When symptoms do occur, they may be so mild, like a barely noticeable cold, that some people don't know they are ill. But others become extremely ill. Symptoms may include a persistent sore throat and fever, swollen glands in the neck, throat, armpit, and groin, plus headache, weakness, swollen eyelids, and a rash.

Infectious-Disease Mimickers

Disease	Major Depression	Manic-depression
Syphilis	+	+
Infectious mononucleosis	+	
Pneumonia (viral)	+	
Brucellosis	+	
Tuberculosis	+	
HIV	+	

Diseases Most Likely to Produce Psychiatric Symptoms

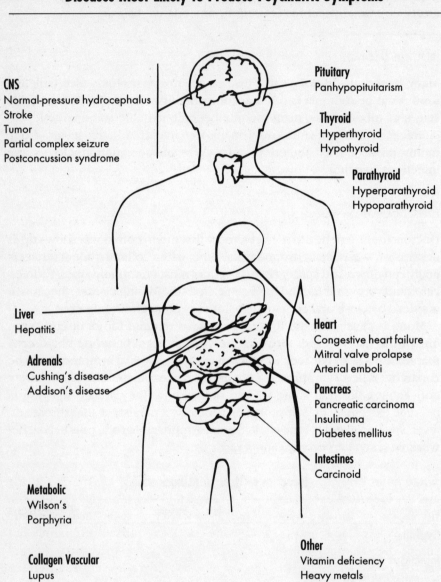

CNS
Normal-pressure hydrocephalus
Stroke
Tumor
Partial complex seizure
Postconcussion syndrome

Pituitary
Panhypopituitarism

Thyroid
Hyperthyroid
Hypothyroid

Parathyroid
Hyperparathyroid
Hypoparathyroid

Liver
Hepatitis

Adrenals
Cushing's disease
Addison's disease

Heart
Congestive heart failure
Mitral valve prolapse
Arterial emboli

Pancreas
Pancreatic carcinoma
Insulinoma
Diabetes mellitus

Intestines
Carcinoid

Metabolic
Wilson's
Porphyria

Collagen Vascular
Lupus

Other
Vitamin deficiency
Heavy metals
Toxins
Drug abuse or withdrawal
AIDS

The virus can infect many organs, making it difficult to diagnose and increasing the risk of complications. The liver is involved in almost all patients, and in about 50 percent the spleen is enlarged and may easily rupture.

Diagnosis is by blood tests, which are frequently negative. It may take two or three tests over several weeks to make an accurate diagnosis. Thus, when a student is so depressed he or she thinks she's going insane and tests negative the first time around, the doctor should resist delivering his standard speech about the stresses of exam time.

When depression and tiredness are the only symptoms, many young people will not seek medical help. A young man I know was so run-down and depressed that he actually left his Ivy League medical school. This was proof, he said to his therapist, that he didn't really want to be a doctor. When he told his father, a physician, about his decision to quit, the father convinced him to take a leave of absence and think it over. So he did his dad a favor and applied for and received a leave. He was certain that his symptoms would disappear with this decision. They didn't, so he gave it another week—after all, leaving medical school is itself a major stress. Another week went by and his eyes puffed up, his liver became swollen—and his next test for mono was positive.

Mono lasts from a couple of weeks to a few months to a few years. Treatment includes bed rest and relief of symptoms as necessary. A depressive syndrome may follow the disease and it may be the last symptom to depart.

CHRONIC FATIGUE SYNDROME

Chronic fatigue syndrome (CFS), a disease that gained widespread publicity in the mid-1980s, has been closely linked to depression. However, while its primary symptom—total fatigue that seems to strike suddenly and last for months to years—seems to indicate that it may be depression, no one knows for sure. Many victims have low-grade fever, headaches, and cognitive problems, and they often are unable to work or even carry out simple daily functions. In addition, the disease has appeared among clusters of people and in isolated communities, leading some experts to think that it may be caused by a virus. One suspect has been the Epstein-Barr virus; sometimes CFS has been called "EBV disease" and is considered another form of mono.

CFS also creates wide mood changes that mimic depression. In fact, results of a certain lab test conducted on people with depression are sometimes similar in people with CFS. Studies exploring the use of antidepressant medications to treat CFS have been inconclusive. In some isolated cases, drugs such as Prozac have been tried, but without significant results. In others, tricyclic antidepressants such as Wellbutrin have reduced symptoms.

Some studies find a resemblance between CFS and neurasthenia, a diagnosis common in the nineteenth century. These studies suggest that, like neurasthenia, the term *CFS* will disappear and the disorder itself will end up categorized as a psychiatric illness.

INFECTIOUS HEPATITIS

This liver infection can be caused by three or possibly four different viruses as well as by drugs and alcohol. Type A and type B hepatitis are more common. Type A is transmitted by contaminated water or food such as raw shellfish, or by contact with infected feces through sewage contamination and so on. Hepatitis B, also called serum hepatitis, usually enters the bloodstream directly through transfusion or infected needles, although it can be passed between sexual partners. A person may be a carrier of the virus, passing it on to others without actually becoming ill.

Following infection, symptoms of hepatitis may take from two to twenty-five weeks to appear. The resulting illness may be unnoticeably mild, fatal, or anything in between. While symptoms vary, they commonly begin with loss of appetite, malaise, nausea, vomiting, and fever. Itching and joint aches may occur. Next comes a darkening of the urine and then jaundice, a yellowing of the skin and the whites of the eyes. Following the jaundice, the disease usually begins to disappear, although type B may become chronic.

Strict bed rest is the treatment of choice for hepatitis, which the body will fight off eventually. Extremely ill patients may require hospitalization and transfusions.

Before, during, or after hepatitis of any type, mental symptoms ranging from mild lethargy to outright psychosis are possible. Anxiety or depression or both are very common. Suicides and acute delusional mania following hepatitis have been reported. Despite the regular occurrence of these symptoms, their existence is rarely mentioned in medical texts or in publications for the layperson. This is unfortunate, since hepatitis is a common disease throughout the world.

Immune and Autoimmune Disorders

The immune system protects the body from outside invaders. Sometimes, however, these invaders attack the cells of the immune system itself, weakening its effectiveness. In other cases the system may malfunction, mistaking some of our own cells for invaders and attacking them. These problems are called autoimmune disorders.

A relatively new topic of medical study, autoimmune factors appear to be at work in many diseases, including diabetes and endocrine gland failure (covered in Chapter 9), rheumatoid arthritis, and possibly some psychiatric afflictions.

Systemic Lupus Erythematosus

Usually called lupus or SLE, this serious, uncommon illness affects women in nine out of ten cases. Most victims are young, although the disease can strike at any age. It is a chronic and relapsing inflammatory disease of the connective tissue, and it can involve many organ systems in an unpredictable course. The disease may develop over years with frequent, unexplained fevers; in its early stages it is very difficult to diagnose. Painful joints, which may become misshapen, are common. Many sufferers have an itchy, scaly skin rash in the shape of a butterfly on body surfaces exposed to light. The lungs, spleen, kidneys, and heart often become diseased. Baldness, seizures, and anemia may occur. Lupus patients are weak and prone to infection.

Lupus has no cure. Treatment usually includes anti-inflammatory medication, but other strategies depend on how the disease affects the individual. Certain drugs may exacerbate lupus. Patients are urged to avoid emotional stress, physical fatigue, and overexposure to the sun.

Lupus can mimic many kinds of psychiatric disorders, ranging from mild anxiety to severe psychosis. Such symptoms occur early in the course of the illness and may be the only symptoms for quite some time. Among 140 lupus patients studied, 3 percent presented with solely psychiatric phenomena, and close to 24 percent had mental symptoms along with other symptoms prior to, or just after, diagnosis. Even though the psychiatric manifestations of lupus are well known, the diagnosis is routinely ignored or overlooked in young women who have psychiatric symptoms. The presence of joint pain, however, ought to be a clear giveaway.

Acquired Immune Deficiency Syndrome (AIDS)

Few diseases have been as controversial or confusing as AIDS. AIDS affects far fewer people than high blood pressure, cancer, or heart disease, but it has captured our attention because of its sudden, apocalyptic appearance and its almost certainly fatal outcome.

As its name indicates, AIDS is not a simple viral infection but a syndrome involving a number of symptoms and complications. There are no anti-viral drugs that can prevent the growth or spread of the virus. While Americans began to learn about AIDS in the early 1980s, the disease has been known worldwide for years, with many cases reported in Africa, South America, Asia, and parts of Europe.

In this country, according to the latest figures available at this writing, AIDS cases more than doubled between 1992 and 1993, from over 49,000 to 103,500. Some of the increase was due to further spread of the infection, although some was also due to a new, broader definition of the disease. When the AIDS epidemic struck, it first spread throughout the homosexual community, whose sexual practices put them in a high-risk group. Much of the increase in AIDS cases occurred among women, blacks, heterosexual intravenous drug users, and hemophiliacs. Among women, the incidence of AIDS rose by over 150 percent. Teens and young adults accounted for the greatest increase. AIDS cases resulting from heterosexual contact jumped 130 percent in 1993 compared to the year before, from 4,045 to 9,288; half of these were among blacks, and people age 13 to 29 accounted for 27 percent. Cases involving homosexual or bisexual contact increased 87 percent, to 48,266. Worldwide, the estimated number of AIDS cases increased by 60 percent—from 2.5 million to 4 million—between July 1993 and July 1994, according to the World Health Organization. Much of the increase has occurred within sub-Saharan Africa, but there was an eightfold increase in cases reported in Asia during this period. Even more frightening is the fact that an average of ten years elapses between the time people become infected with HIV and the time they begin to demonstrate signs of AIDS. Thus health experts assume that currently there are more than seventeen million people infected with HIV. By the end of the century somewhere between thirty and forty million people will be infected.

An estimated 1 to 1.5 million people are infected with the AIDS virus in the United States. While each year only 10 to 20 percent of these will develop the AIDS group of symptoms, all of them are capable of transmitting and spreading the virus.

AIDS is now the seventh leading cause of death in the United States and is the leading cause of death among intravenous (IV) drug users and hemophiliacs and among young adults in urban settings.

Thus far, apparently, no one has recovered from AIDS, but we have learned more as more cases have appeared. AIDS develops from a group of viruses referred to collectively as the human immunodeficiency virus (HIV). These viruses cause the body's immune system to weaken and eventually shut down, leaving the person vulnerable to severe infections, cancers, and brain lesions. One major difference between AIDS and other forms of immunological diseases (such as certain cancers) is that most AIDS victims have no history or risk factors for immune-system diseases. Who its victims are, and how they transmit the disease, are other controversial aspects of AIDS that have received enormous publicity and scientific study. No virus since polio has garnered such scientific attention, yet we still know very little about treatment and almost nothing about a cure.

Once the immune system has been invaded by HIV, the body's natural defenses become crippled. The victim is now susceptible to opportunistic infections, killers such as Kaposi's sarcoma, a once-rare skin cancer causing bruiselike lesions.

Many HIV-infected people have AIDS-related complex (ARC), considered to be an early sign of the disease. Symptoms include swollen glands, fever, fatigue, diarrhea, weight loss, and night sweats. An estimated 30 percent of AIDS patients reveal brain involvement, marked by depression, dementia, paralysis, seizures, and loss of control of body functions. Scientists now fear that the virus may infect the brain directly, independent of the immune system.

Over the past few years, it has become clear that psychiatric symptoms are common among AIDS victims. Many of the symptoms appear as dementias, but also may appear as depressionlike symptoms. It's thought that these can be early signs of AIDS or of the opportunistic infections common to AIDS. Because depression is so common among AIDS victims, antidepressant drugs such as lithium and desipramine have been tried with limited but promising results. One plus is that these drugs, which can affect the central nervous system, do not interfere with drugs used to treat AIDS itself.

CHAPTER 6

It's in Your Head

Diseases or injuries to the central nervous system (CNS) can be some of the trickiest mimickers for psychiatrists. The brain can produce both psychiatric and neurological symptoms. Some CNS diseases or injuries may mimic psychiatric syndromes so closely that the psychiatrist who does not always consider organic alternatives will easily be fooled. Delaying treatment for CNS diseases can lead to permanent brain damage.

THE DEMENTIAS

Dementia is a condition in which the brain and its ability to function deteriorate, often irreversibly. Between 17 and 50 percent of elderly patients may experience both depression and dementia. Over the years the outer layer of the brain (the cortex, site of most of our intellectual and social functioning) shrinks a little. This is a natural, if disagreeable, part of aging. But dementia is a different problem. Any degree of dementia means that some kind of pathological deterioration is taking place.

Eventually, as behavior and the ability to take care of oneself deteriorate, a person with a dementing disease will require total nursing care.

Dementia in younger persons is usually caused by alcoholism, chronic stimulant-drug abuse, infection, brain trauma, diabetes, or kidney failure.

Dementia may also occur in several central nervous system disorders, such as Huntington's chorea and Parkinson's disease (discussed on page 84), or in AIDS. Correct diagnosis is critical, because in certain illnesses the dementia may be reversible. The dementias discussed here, however, are primary—that is, they are diseases in themselves: pitilessly progressive and irreversible. Some recent studies suggest that patients who have signs of both depression and dementia should be treated for both disorders. Even if dementia is present, the depressive disorder should be treated first. Only in this way will it be clear whether or not the patient is suffering from dementia or depression. An experienced geriatric psychiatrist can make an accurate diagnosis and determine the best treatment.

Pseudodementia vs. Dementia: The Case of Mr. R.

As dementia progresses, a person's mood usually becomes flat. At first, however, the emotional responses can be highly exaggerated and produce quite peculiar behavior. Other early symptoms include changes in appetite and sleep habits and wild mood fluctuations. One of my patients, Jack K., had always been quiet and polite. With the onset of as-yet undiagnosed dementia, however, he demanded to be the center of attention at every opportunity. As soon as all eyes were on him, he'd start to tell jokes that only he could appreciate. His moods went from pussycat to tiger to cowardly lion. At this stage, all roads lead to the psychiatrist's office. Since depression in older age is very common, many doctors are tempted to (mis)diagnose a major affective disorder and thus overlook the presence of dementia.

In many cases depressed older persons develop a psychological dementia (sometimes called pseudodementia). This form is reversible when their depression is treated. The irony in this misdiagnosis is that depressed older persons have too often been tossed into nursing homes with an incorrect diagnosis of dementia.

"I am much gladdened by this recognition of the fact that many elderly people appear demented when they really have a treatable depression," comments Canadian psychiatrist Robert O. Jones. "I now have some feelings, however, that perhaps this concept of pseudodementia has gone too far and leads to diagnostic errors in the opposite direction, i.e., we call people with an organic dementia depressed, and miss the true diagnosis of the underlying dementia. As a result . . . we sometimes . . . make the dementia worse by our treatment."

Dr. Jones relates the case of Mr. R., who at age 62 was referred to him because he wasn't responding to treatment. A decade earlier the local government had taken over land on which Mr. R. had run a store. Three months after that, Mr. R. showed the classic symptoms of depression: He couldn't sleep, lost interest in his usual activities, and declared that life wasn't worth living. Dr. Jones diagnosed unipolar depression and hospitalized Mr. R. so he could give him high doses of antidepressant drugs. An EEG (electroencephalogram) and a mental-status examination revealed some abnormalities. Dr. Jones and the other doctors dismissed these findings as pseudodementia.

But the staff psychologist disagreed. She noted many areas in which Mr. R. seemed impaired. In her report she wrote, "While depression tends to interfere with one's efficiency in this area, the discrepancy revealed [in Mr. R.'s case] is marked and points to the likelihood of organic impairment."

Admits Jones, "With the weight of my medical authority (not to mention my medical arrogance), it was not hard to beat her into submission and have her agree to a diagnosis of pseudodementia."

The punch line is that the psychologist was right, and Mr. R.'s illness had to progress for eighteen more months before his doctor saw the light. "I was in the process of writing a prescription for more antidepressant medication at a higher dosage," relates Dr. Jones, "when he casually said, 'You know, there have been two or three times recently that I wet myself.' My pen stopped in midair. . . ." Detailed questioning of Mr. R. and his wife revealed that Mr. R.'s physical and intellectual functioning was deteriorating. Mrs. R. told Dr. Jones of an incident in which her husband looked a number up in the phone book quite correctly but then seemed completely unable to use the information to dial the phone.

Immediately Dr. Jones rehospitalized his patient. His EEG showed the same mild impairments as it had a year and a half before. But this time Dr. Jones investigated further. He ordered a CAT scan and called in a consulting neurologist, who immediately recognized that the CAT scan was abnormal. Mr. R. was ultimately diagnosed as having Binswanger's disease, a complication of chronic low-grade high blood pressure. "Unfortunately," concludes Dr. Jones, "these findings increase our medical satisfaction but not our ability to intervene in a useful way for Mr. R." There is no cure for the progressive dementia of Binswanger's.

Alzheimer's Disease

Approximately two million Americans, most over sixty-five, suffer from dementia of the Alzheimer's type, or Alzheimer's disease. The National Institute on Aging calls Alzheimer's "the most common cause of severe intellectual impairment in older individuals." The most serious form of the disease, however, strikes in middle age.

Studies show that up to 87 percent of Alzheimer's patients have symptoms of depression. As a result, the early symptoms of Alzheimer's disease are frequently mistaken for depression, partly resulting from differences, such as age of onset and overall health picture among Alzheimer's patients. For example, vascular disease and other concurrent diseases that appear among the aged can also cause depressive symptoms. However, some newer studies have shown that certain changes in the brain that occur in depressed patients also occur in Alzheimer's patients. Further links to depression and Alzheimer's disease are reported in recent studies that show the two conditions have overlapping clinical symptoms and biological markers.

Alzheimer's usually becomes apparent with the onset of mild confusion and forgetfulness, especially for recent events. Family members have a tough time dealing with Alzheimer's victims, who often deny that anything is out of the ordinary. People with Alzheimer's will drive others crazy repeating questions that have already been answered, and they'll show bad judgment that could get them into serious trouble. One undiagnosed Alzheimer's sufferer, for example, nearly lost his job as a road maintenance worker when he tickled a fellow crew member who was operating a chainsaw. Alzheimer's patients can be alternately loud and embarrassing, then sad and depressed. Frustrated families often force the person to see a psychiatrist. During the evaluation the patient will typically joke around and chatter, then possibly break into tears. The family's irritation and anxiety, combined with the patient's behavior and symptoms, may tempt the practitioner into a misdiagnosis of depression.

The disease progresses horribly. Memory gaps begin to include names, even identities of friends and family members. Comprehension of numbers and words starts to go. Victims lose their ability to organize their days or to complete tasks. They become painfully frustrated and irritable. Judgment, orientation, and concentration disappear. Victims often suffer from an extreme restlessness and need to move around constantly. Frequently they wander off. Eventually they lose control over bowels and bladder. In time, the Alzheimer's patient will require total care.

When Alzheimer's strikes in middle age, the course of the disease can be as long as twenty years. The patient will lose awareness of the agony, but the family will suffer the burden.

Alzheimer's disease has no cure. The disease is being studied extensively, however, in hopes of finding the causes of characteristic brain-cell changes. Scientists are studying the neurotransmitter acetylcholine, which is implicated in the disease, and are also looking at an enzyme necessary for the synthesis of acetylcholine. An accumulation of aluminum in the brain may contribute to the disease. Other possible causes include a slow-acting virus, damage to certain brain cells, or a newly identified infectious particle called a *prion*. Alzheimer's may be genetic, since it seems to cluster in families.

If Alzheimer's is correctly diagnosed in the early stages, experts can intervene to make life a little easier for the victim and for the family. Memory aids can help, and medication to reduce agitation, improve sleep, and treat depression can be effective.

INFECTIOUS BRAIN DISEASES

Virtually any brain infection can bring on a confusing array of psychiatric symptoms in lieu of physical symptoms. We will survey a few of them.

Syphilis (General Paresis)

One of the most devastating sexually transmitted diseases, syphilis can immediately invade the central nervous system. In addition, 10 to 15 percent of all untreated individuals will eventually develop a brain infection called general paresis or paretic neurosyphilis.

Early in the century, before antibiotics were discovered, general paresis was the greatest of all mimickers, accounting for 10 to 20 percent of all admissions to state hospitals for the insane. Today most psychiatrists have never seen it, and probably would not recognize it. In a study of one hundred state hospital patients in whom physical disorders had supposedly been eliminated, researchers found two cases of syphilis, one diagnosed as schizophrenia, the other as manic-depressive illness. General paresis can mimic virtually any psychiatric disorder.

Syphilis is caused by a spirochete, which is transmitted by sexual contact. Typically the chronic disease has active phases interspersed with long symptom-free periods. Symptoms, which progress to dementia, seizures, and paralysis, may be completely reversed if diagnosed and treated when they appear. Penicillin is the usual treatment at all stages.

Viral Encephalitis

This inflammation of the brain often occurs following other infections, such as measles or mumps. Also, in warm weather, it may be caused by bites from infected mosquitoes. The herpes simplex virus causes most cases of nonepidemic encephalitis, which usually will follow a skin infection by the same virus. It affects mostly children and young people, 50 to 70 percent of whom die of the disease. With immediate treatment, the mortality rate can be reduced to less than 30 percent. The physician who does not suspect a mimicker is not likely to diagnose encephalitis at this stage; behavioral changes, including psychosis and manic-depressive illness, may be the only initial signs.

Add those symptoms to a previous history of mental illness, and misdiagnosis is assured. Dr. Milton Erman relates just such a case. At 21, Miss V. had already been the victim of apparent psychiatric misdiagnosis. She had spent all but six months of the past two years hospitalized for schizophrenia, but she did not respond to antipsychotic medication. Once she was given lithium, however, her recovery was quick and impressive. Six months after she went home, she came to the emergency room with some physical symptoms, including headache, nausea, and blurred vision, and plenty of mental ones, including visual hallucinations and impaired thinking. The doctors tested the level of lithium in her blood to rule out lithium poisoning. A neurologist took a look at her and concluded—without performing a lumbar puncture, which would have revealed infection—that she had a hysterical psychosis. Back to the psychiatric floor she went. Her behavioral symptoms worsened in the following week. When organic involvement became painfully obvious—she was becoming less and less alert and beginning to wet herself—her doctors finally suspected an organic condition and performed the appropriate diagnostic tests. Miss V. had viral encephalitis. She survived, but it was five weeks before she was well enough to leave the hospital. A year later she felt she had not recovered her previous alertness.

NORMAL-PRESSURE HYDROCEPHALUS

When normal absorption of cerebrospinal fluid becomes blocked, it builds up in brain cavities. The accumulation produces a swelling, which compresses brain tissue. Dementia, loss of coordination or ability to walk, and incontinence mark this syndrome. Psychiatric symptoms may be the most apparent, however, ranging from behavior problems to persecutory delusions and psychotic depression. Since this condition is most common in older individuals, it should always be considered when an apparent psychiatric illness strikes seemingly out of nowhere. Timely diagnosis is critical: The only treatment is the insertion of a shunt (tube) in the brain to drain the fluid, and the earlier in the illness the shunt is inserted, the more likely it will help.

Causes of this syndrome are unclear. Prior brain infection or inflammation may predispose an individual to it.

POSTCONCUSSION SYNDROME

It doesn't happen only in the movies: A blow on the head can cause a personality change. We treated a man who had been a bystander at a barroom brawl and accidentally got hit with a nightstick when the police came to break it up. He had been a nice, placid guy, a cook at the restaurant across the street from the bar. The injury was bad, damaging the frontal lobe of his brain. He went from being a sweetheart to a living terror, prone to attacks of rage and severe depression. He also lost his sense of smell, so he was fired from his job as a cook. The psychiatrist who was treating him figured that his moods were related to the job loss. It was an obvious conclusion — except that when he was referred to us and we gave him an EEG, we discovered his attacks were actually seizures. The medication he takes now has restored his more pleasant nature, although he still cannot smell things.

Postconcussion syndrome occurs as the aftereffect of brain damage from severe head injury. Depending on which part of the brain is affected, it can mimic anxiety, depression, rage, loss of control over emotions or behavior, mood swings from euphoria to depression, and psychotic symptoms. Even mild injury may bring on fatigue, nervousness, anxiety, depression, restlessness, irritability, and prolonged elation for as long as several months after head trauma.

No tests exist for postconcussion syndrome. A history of severe head injury, particularly one that resulted in a coma lasting more than two days, is highly suggestive of this diagnosis. Treatment is aimed at relieving symptoms, but the damage may be permanent.

NARCOLEPSY

Narcoleptics suffer from a sleep disorder that makes their lives literally a nightmare. They continually fall asleep, often experiencing terribly vivid illusions or even hallucinations as they drift off. The desire to sleep, which may occur from a few to many times a day, is impossible to resist. Attacks may last from minutes to hours. Rousing a narcoleptic is no more difficult than waking a normal person. Nighttime sleep is poor and filled with bad dreams.

Sleep has two cycles, NREM and REM. REM stands for *rapid eye movement,* which is characteristic of dream states. NREM means non-REM. Normally in the first hour or so of sleep, a person sinks deeper and deeper into NREM before going into REM and starting to dream. In narcoleptics,

REM usually occurs immediately, and their dreams are usually vivid because they are barely asleep.

Other symptoms considered typical of narcolepsy include cataplexy (a brief paralysis usually brought on by strong emotion) and sleep paralysis (an occasional inability to move when falling asleep or waking up).

Firm diagnosis is often made by taking an EEG during sleep and finding the REM-sleep brain patterns at the beginning of sleep. Repeated testing may be necessary, however, because narcoleptics do not necessarily show the abnormal pattern every time they fall asleep. Few narcoleptics, in fact, evidence all the symptoms of this rare syndrome. In the absence of the complete symptom picture, or when a single test does not reveal the only measurable finding, narcoleptics are often condemned to misdiagnoses of major depression, schizophrenia, thyroid disease, or just plain malingering.

No one knows what causes narcolepsy, which is far more common among men than among women. The syndrome usually begins in adolescence or early adulthood and persists for a lifetime. Stimulant drugs are usually prescribed. Although narcolepsy is not a depressive disorder, recent evidence suggests certain antidepressants may be effective in treating it.

EPILEPSY

"The number of patients with schizophrenia diagnosed and treated as epilepsy by neurologists is equaled only by the number of patients with psychomotor epilepsy diagnosed and treated as schizophrenia by psychiatrists," noted Dr. D. A. Treffert in the *American Journal of Psychiatry* two decades ago. Not much has changed since then.

Epilepsy refers to any recurrent pattern of seizures. Along with syphilis, epilepsy is one of the all-time great mimickers of depression. Although seizure disorders are treatable, persons with epilepsy still must struggle against its stigma. Thus it is particularly tragic when psychiatric symptoms associated with certain types of epilepsy lead to a psychiatric rather than neurological diagnosis.

The brain is usually a smoothly functioning electrochemical system. In epilepsy, sudden surges of electricity disorganize brain activity and bring on a seizure. Just before the seizure, most people have premonitions, ranging from déjà vu and mystical experiences to headaches, visual hallucinations, or an overall undefinable feeling of oddness.

Stress, especially the everyday kind, is a potent seizure trigger. Not all persons suffering from epilepsy experience the classic convulsions, falling to the floor in a complete loss of control; this type of seizure, however, is the most common. Some will either stop all movement or begin to repeat actions inappropriately. Still others will briefly tune out, staring off into space as if daydreaming. Even if they remain conscious during the seizure, sufferers will have no memory of it. Undiagnosed epileptics often do not even know they are having subtle seizures.

Persons with partial complex seizures (temporal lobe epilepsy and psychomotor epilepsy) are most likely to suffer the symptoms that tempt psychiatrists into misdiagnosis. Between seizures, some become super-good—excessively religious and ethical, with a corresponding reduction of sexual interest and activity. In others this super-goodness may alternate with a super-badness, à la Jekyll and Hyde. These behaviors and hallucinations of any type may be associated with depression, anxiety, hysteria, hypochondriasis, apparent schizophrenia, confusion, and anti-social personality. Whether this form of epilepsy is related to violence and aggression is currently a hot topic among neurologists and psychiatrists.

Epilepsy can occur as a result of an unidentified inborn metabolic error, or possibly a birth injury or developmental defect. Other causes include brain injury, tumor, brain infections, drug overdose or withdrawal, poisoning, endocrine diseases such as hypoglycemia, drug allergy—virtually anything, in other words, that affects the brain. (Indeed, the term *seizure* or *epilepsy*, like *depression*, is more a statement of symptoms than a diagnosis.) Usually the seizures will disappear as the disease moderates or the drug or poison clears the system. But when misdiagnosis leads to incorrect or delayed treatment, seizures may continue, and permanent brain damage may occur.

Diagnosis of epilepsy consists of a careful history and examination to discover causative illnesses or conditions. The EEG can detect abnormal brain electrical activity, but it is not foolproof. A normal EEG does not rule out the disease, and, in the absence of clinical symptoms, an abnormal test does not always guarantee its presence.

Anticonvulsant medications, singly or in combination, are highly effective in helping to prevent or control epileptic seizures. In severe cases, brain surgery is usually effective. Once the disease is controlled, epileptics can lead virtually normal lives.

By the way, not all types of seizures are bad. ECT, or shock therapy, relieves symptoms of depression by inducing convulsions in an anesthetized patient.

MULTIPLE SCLEROSIS

Multiple sclerosis (MS) is a chronic degenerative disease of the central nervous system. Nerves lose the sheaths that protect and insulate them, and virtually all body systems slowly begin to deteriorate. It usually strikes between the ages of twenty and forty. Women are affected somewhat more often than men.

A puzzling array of psychiatric and neurological symptoms often appears years ahead of the diagnosis. Early neurological symptoms can include fleeting visual problems, transient weakness and tingling of an arm or leg, and vague bladder problems. Usually the psychiatric symptoms, including emotional upsets that can't be explained, depression, and euphoria, are more convincing. All the symptoms will come and go, which is another way that MS can mimic a primary emotional problem.

When MS ultimately reveals itself, limbs begin to go weak, an eye may lose its sight or its movement, or double vision may occur. Dizziness is frequent, loss of sensation is common, urinating becomes difficult, gait is unsteady, impotency and vaginal numbness strike, speech becomes slurred, seizures may occur, euphoria and/or depression continue, and bladder and rectal control are lost. Other symptoms may arise depending on how the disease progresses and which nerves are affected.

Usually MS does not continue on a steady downhill course. It is marked by unexplained remissions, which may last for years. Recurrence usually brings a worsening of symptoms. Most people with MS end up in wheelchairs.

Like many diseases of the central nervous system, the causes of MS are unknown. Possibilities include a virus to which the victim was once exposed and which eventually is activated either by reexposure or because of stress. Another culprit may be a defect in the immune system.

No cure for MS has been found, although there are now promising new medications that seem to delay its progression. Steroid medication may help shorten attacks. Care and treatment of symptoms is essential in order to strengthen muscles and to improve morale. An early diagnosis gives the MS sufferer the best possible chance to postpone or even avoid total invalidism. Needless to say, no progress can be made when a psychiatrist sets out to convince the unfortunate patient that the problem is in his or her head. I recall diagnosing MS in three psychiatric patients, each of them referred for depression. As serious as this diagnosis is, all three were relieved to have a doctor confirm what they'd been trying to get across: There was something wrong.

HUNTINGTON'S CHOREA

"The tendency to insanity and sometimes that form of insanity which leads to suicide is marked," noted George Sumner Huntington in 1872, when he described the hereditary degenerative disease that bears his name. Nonetheless, psychiatrists and other physicians continue to be deluded by obstinacy, moodiness, apathy, violence, paranoia, euphoria, psychosis, and a host of other psychiatric symptoms that mark Huntington's in its earliest presentation. While the giveaway should be the typical spasmodic, uncontrolled movements ("involuntary twisting and movements of the whole body, including the face and tongue," as Dr. Stephanie J. Bird describes it) and dementia, some psychiatrists will conclude that the movement problems are caused by the antipsychotic medication they have been prescribing. A family history of Huntington's should lock in the correct diagnosis of this disease.

Huntington's leads invariably to total mental deterioration. While medication can help control the movements, nothing can help the mind. Still, sufferers can live ten to twenty years.

Huntington's develops between ages 30 and 50. Genetically, half of all a sufferer's offspring will be affected. A genetic marker for the disease has very recently been identified, and development of a presymptomatic test is in the works. But there is no cure. The only preventive measure is for offspring carrying the defective gene not to be born.

The most commonly inherited neurological disease, Huntington's afflicts 10,000 to 25,000 persons in the United States; an additional 20,000 to 50,000 are at risk of passing it on.

PARKINSON'S DISEASE

Parkinson's has been called *shaking palsy,* which describes the most familiar aspect of this motor (movement) disorder. Except in sleep, the involuntary tremor in the hands is persistent. In resting as well as anxious states the shaking gets even worse over time, and yet under stress, when purposeful action must be taken, the tremor may briefly disappear.

Parkinson's, which primarily affects people after age 60, is chronic and progressive. It goes from a tremor to a slowing of movement and muscular rigidity. The facial expression becomes fixed, with unblinking, staring eyes and slightly open, drooling mouth. Posture is stooped, gait shuffling; worst of all, voluntary movement, such as walking, is difficult to get started, and once begun, is hard to stop. The speech of a Parkinson's patient becomes so soft and slow that it is unintelligible.

Between 38 and 46 percent of those with Parkinson's disease suffer with symptoms of mild to severe dementia during the course of their illness. It is not uncommon for these symptoms to go untreated. These changes may be directly related to the alterations of the brain's chemistry, specifically neurotransmitters—such as serotonin—that are connected to depression. Frequently, antidepressants are used in treating Parkinson's disease.

If all patients exhibited the textbook symptoms of every disease, and if nothing was happening during the presymptomatic phase, all doctors could go home early. A sixty-two-year-old woman we'll call Mrs. X. was referred to biopsychiatrist Harvey Sternbach because a few months earlier she had become increasingly depressed. She cried, couldn't sleep, had no hope, was agitated, and just couldn't complete a day's work. She had good reason to be depressed: Her alcoholic husband, who had recently had a heart attack, had just been demoted at work. Her internist gave her a clean bill of health, so she went to a psychiatrist, who prescribed antidepressant medication. But her depression and agitation worsened, and now Mrs. X. was becoming confused. A CAT scan revealed nothing significant, but neurological examination did show muscular changes in her legs.

What seemed more serious were the results of Mrs. X.'s electrocardiogram, which indicated that her heart could not tolerate the antidepressants. Dr. Sternbach took her off the medication and instead ordered a course of ECT. It worked, but the results did not last. Within four months, however, Mrs. X.'s depression was of less immediate interest than her increasingly apparent dementia. Neurological examination revealed some findings consistent with Parkinson's, and the CAT scan now revealed subtle changes in the basal ganglia, the area of the brain that controls starting and stopping movement. Dr. Sternbach prescribed an anti-Parkinson's drug, and Mrs. X.'s depression and movement difficulties began to subside. Her dementia improved also, but less dramatically. Mrs. X. does require help in the tasks of daily living, but at least her downward spiral has been halted.

The treatment of Parkinson's is one of the success stories of modern neuroscience—a good place to end this otherwise gloomy chapter.

The whys of Parkinson's are unknown—no hints of genetic factors, viruses, or autoimmune factors. The whats and hows, however, began to fall into place in 1955, when a German scientist discovered that Parkinson's sufferers had lost many brain cells in a certain area of the brain. These cells normally contain significant amounts of the neurotransmitter dopamine. It seemed a reasonable conclusion that because of the death of these cells, certain messages controlling muscle movement were not being effectively transmitted.

The logical treatment would be to replace the dopamine, but that proved easier said than done. Dopamine does not cross the blood-brain barrier (that is, the brain will not absorb it from the blood). The brain does absorb levodopa (L-dopa), however, which is a chemical from which the brain makes its own supply of dopamine. L-dopa prods the remaining cells to manufacture dopamine.

Years of experience with L-dopa have revealed it to be, like all drugs, less than perfect. It can have side effects varying from the annoying to the serious, depending on dosage and length of treatment. Unfortunately, large amounts must be taken because much of the chemical is metabolized by other organs before it reaches the brain. Over the years, however, other drugs have been developed that modulate, enhance, or mimic L-dopa's actions.

Speaking of mimicking: Mrs. X.'s first symptom of Parkinson's was a physiological depression brought on by the developing illness. The medication lifted her mood. Anti-Parkinson's drugs are not antidepressants, so why would they work in this way? We do not know precisely, but the interrelationship of physical illness and psychiatric symptomatology puts us in that most important, most exciting area where mind and body link. Mrs. X. consulted a psychiatrist because she was depressed. Later she developed a confusion similar to that suffered by many schizophrenic patients. But her problem was a disease of the central nervous system. Mr. Y. might go to a doctor with difficulties in initiating movement, even shaking, only to discover that his diagnosis is biological depression. Add profound confusion and the diagnosis might be schizophrenia.

We call Parkinson's an organic condition and depression or schizophrenia psychiatric conditions—in other words, not of the body. Nonetheless, neuroscientific study of diseases such as Parkinson's reveal important similarities between physical and mental processes.

Parkinson's, schizophrenia, and depression, for example, may all be related biochemically. Dopamine-cell circuitry is found in several areas of the brain. One pathway reaches from the midbrain to an area of the cortex believed to be involved in schizophrenia. In schizophrenia, one may be oversensitive to a normal amount of dopamine; we know that the drugs that help control schizophrenia block the body's use of that neurotransmitter. Unlike the action of L-dopa, antipsychotics reduce the body's supply of dopamine, as does Parkinson's; indeed, taken over a long period, antipsychotic drugs cause an irreversible movement disorder similar to Parkinson's (tardive dyskinesia).

The dopamine pathway extends from the hypothalamus to the pituitary in the limbic system. These brain structures regulate stress response, sleeping and waking, appetite, body temperature, hormones, sex, and emotion, all or many of which are involved in biological depression. Persons with depression often exhibit a slowness and difficulty in moving as in Parkinson's; many also suffer delusions while ill, as in schizophrenia.

Of course Parkinson's is different from schizophrenia, which is different from depression. The point of this chapter, after all, is that psychiatrists and physicians must learn to recognize the differences between them, so that their patients receive prompt, correct, and effective care. The differences are not to be found, as we have seen, by separating diseases into categories that simply list their mental or physical symptoms.

Overall, the study of diseases such as Parkinson's, schizophrenia, and depression is blurring the traditional conceptual distinctions between mental and physical diseases. Mental disease, too, is of the body. Elucidating its physical mechanisms has led to laboratory diagnostic tests for depression and to treatment that is much more scientifically based.

CHAPTER 7

Drugs: Rx or Otherwise

Courtesy of their doctors, bartenders, pharmacists, or dealers, virtually everybody in America takes drugs. All drugs are chemicals that enter the body and influence its physiology, causing desired effects as well as other, unwanted reactions.

In some segments of society illicit drug use is dropping, but the battle against illicit drugs and prescription drug abuse is far from over. Drug use still ruins lives, families, and communities in shocking numbers. For example:

- A federal Drug Abuse Warning Network report indicated that a record number of drug users—433,500—were treated in hospital emergency rooms in 1992.
- An estimated 17.8 million Americans are dependent on alcohol, 10.5 million of them meeting diagnostic criteria for alcoholism.
- National surveys show that 41 percent of teenagers indulge in binge drinking and that 5 percent drink daily.
- 9.7 million people admit that they smoke marijuana; 1.9 million people use cocaine.
- Over 500,000 people are addicted to heroin.
- If all workers were given a drug test on a given day, 14 to 25 percent would test positive, according to a study cited in *The Wall Street Journal*.
- A 1991 study estimated the cost of treating infants exposed to cocaine (i.e., crack babies) to be an astounding $500 million a year.
- The 1991 Household Survey on Drug Abuse found that 33 percent of the population age 12 or older had used marijuana.
- In 1989, 5.1 percent of college students used a hallucinogen during the past year; by 1992 the number had risen to 6.8 percent.
- Data from the 1992 National High School Senior Survey indicates that drug use among eighth graders, specifically use of LSD, marijuana, and inhalants, may be increasing.

From prescriptions to over-the-counter preparations to alcohol and illicit drugs, no drug is free of side or adverse effects. Some unwanted effects depend on the dose or the length of time the drug is used. Others vary with a person's age and state of health, while still others depend on the individual's genetic makeup and predispositions. When a drug directly or indirectly influences brain chemistry even slightly, psychiatric symptoms can result. Because of ignorance of the psychiatric effects of many drugs, or a quickness to jump to conclusions about mental symptoms, doctors often do not consider the adverse influence of drugs in the differential diagnoses of their patients. For all these reasons, drug effects are mimicker number one, causing more diagnostic confusion than any other substance, disease, or condition. Drugs must be considered in all psychiatric diagnoses because, as I said, everybody takes them.

RECREATIONAL DRUGS AND ALCOHOL

The Case of Alison R.

It was easy to see why her therapist believed that Alison's problem was her relationship with her parents. The daughter of prominent physicians, Alison was a junior at Harvard, and she was about to drop out of school. For a year Alison had been wrestling with an intractable depression, complete with lethargy and an inability to concentrate. Her parents paid for therapy, but when the therapist suggested, a year later, that Alison take

Drug Mimickers

Drug	Major Depression	Manic-depression
PCP	+	+
Toluene	+	
Marijuana	+	+
Amphetamines	+	+
Cocaine	+	+
Sedative-Hypnotic	+	
Heroin	+	
Methadone	+	

a leave of absence, get a menial job, and enter four-day-a-week psycho-analysis, her parents had had it and they called me in for a second opinion.

This physician couple was trouble from the very beginning. "You seem too smart to be a psychiatrist," her father said snidely. Her mother objected to my fee. I began, "If you have a financial hardship—" but the mother interrupted me: "We make more money in a month than you make in a year."

Finally I met with Alison. I was tempted to make the diagnosis on the basis of her downcast expression alone. She described a depressive-melancholic episode that had lasted for at least a year—decreased sex drive, loss of energy, memory problems, loss of interest in her friends and in her number-one love, skiing. When I asked how her physical health had been during the year, she said she had had a number of upper respiratory infections and an occasional cough. Also twice she had thought she was pregnant, but it turned out she had just skipped a period. She said she didn't use drugs, except for an occasional drink at a party; a couple of times she had taken some speed to stay up and study. "It really gave me energy, a real boost," she said, "but I was afraid to take it again."

I did a complete physical, including neurological and endocrinological examinations. I called her gynecologist about her last exam, which was normal. I interviewed her less-than-cooperative family. My examinations and interviews revealed nothing of interest. So far everything appeared to be within the depression spectrum. Depressed women frequently skip a period or even stop menstruating, and depressed people in general appear to be at greater risk for infections. Still, I told her, I wanted to do some tests.

"Do anything you want," answered Alison, "but I don't think anything is wrong with me except me." Score ten for depressed self-image.

But Alison's mother didn't want to spend the money on the tests. I'd had enough time with her, she said—did Alison seem depressed or not? If she did, did I think she needed to drop out or "just take a few antidepressants"?

I explained to the mother in no uncertain terms that lab tests were the tools of my trade, just as much as they were of hers. The mother backed off. I ordered a complete blood count (CBC) and a folate level. Folate, or folic acid, acts like a vitamin; a folic acid deficiency can eventually lead to anemia. A woman can have no obvious anemia on a CBC and still be deficient in folate. Birth control pills can reduce the available supply of folate, and Alison had been taking them until recently. I ordered a complete review of medical systems (liver, kidney, cholesterol, etc.), a comprehensive drug screen, and a pregnancy test. I would test for mono-nucleosis if all else was negative.

In addition I scheduled a test of thyroid function for the coming week. Early thyroid failure was possible, especially since one of Alison's maternal aunts had thyroid problems. I also scheduled a dexamethasone suppression test (DST) to confirm the diagnosis of biological, treatment-reversible depression. I ordered a blood-alcohol test for the first blood draw of the DST.

All the tests were normal, but her urine showed THC, the active ingredient in marijuana. Her blood workup was negative for alcohol, but the THC showed she had smoked marijuana recently.

When Alison and I met again I had a thick file of interviews and examinations and tests. I said, "My guess, Alison, is that something is going on with you at school and that you want to drop out." This she vigorously denied. I said that I'd try to help her stay in school, but she would have to stop smoking marijuana, see a psychiatrist who specialized in substance-induced syndromes, and be reevaluated in six weeks.

Alison blushed. She had not mentioned a word about marijuana. Now it all came out. She had been smoking three to four joints a day since she'd arrived at college. She'd gotten involved with a boy, a heavy marijuana user, who now wanted her to move in with him. Alison was feeling overwhelmed.

She agreed to sign a contract to refrain from using any mood-altering drugs or alcohol, go to ninety Alcoholics Anonymous meetings in the next ninety days (helpful for anyone who has a substance-abuse problem), go to the psychiatrist as often as that doctor suggested, and to have comprehensive urine testing for drugs at random.

It took six weeks for Alison's urine to stop showing evidence of THC. Her depression disappeared, and she asked her psychiatrist if she could return to her former therapist to continue to work out her feelings toward her parents. She became a prelaw student and eventually was accepted at an Ivy League law school. The last time I saw Alison she seemed very happy.

I'm Not a Cop . . .

. . . I'm a doctor. People like Alison come to me for help, and I can't provide it if I don't know the facts. You bet I test all my patients for drugs, because drug use is commonplace—and drugs cause more depressive symptoms than all diseases or substances. Most patients do not tell their doctors about their drug or alcohol use, or admit to its full extent, even if they come for help with a drug problem. They can't tell us, but they are relieved when we find out. I don't blame the patient—that's the reality of the behavior. I do blame the psychiatrist who rules out drug or alcohol reactions just because the patient has denied any significant use.

People like Alison often confess to occasional use of a particular drug but don't mention the drug that they use regularly. A priest came to me with depression and told me about his drinking problem, but did not confess to using cocaine. An airline pilot told me he occasionally smoked a little marijuana. What he *didn't* say was that he had a huge cocaine habit and snorted constantly, including before and during flights. And I treated a senior flight attendant who complained of a classical medical depression and who said that she smoked a few joints of marijuana a week. Tests confirmed her use of marijuana—as well as cocaine and opium. She told me, "I was sure you'd throw me out of the office if you knew I smoke opium as often as I can get it, and I use coke to stay awake enough to go to work."

"Recreational" Drugs and Depression

The most recent data available suggests that alcohol use, like most other drugs, has decreased since 1985. However, with at least 103 million current users and over 50 percent of senior high school students and 30 percent of junior high school students admitting to alcohol use, alcoholism and alcohol-related depression must always be considered. Because of their memory problems, social isolation, and urinary incontinence, elderly patients may seem to be suffering from dementia or Alzheimer's disease. In fact, however, these problems can all be caused by alcohol use. We have found that alcoholics who are referred to a residential rehab program are often depressed and seem to meet the standard laundry-list criteria for depression. They are frequently placed on antidepressant drugs immediately. We find in these cases, however, that when the alcoholism is treated first and the toxic effects of the drug are gone, and the patient is involved in a twelve-step or group-therapy program, the depressive symptoms disappear. In other words, we treat the alcohol symptoms before we treat the mood disorder. In most cases, the symptoms of depression are produced by the drug. Interestingly, this is a different approach from the one we take when depressive symptoms appear in other disorders, such as cancer. In these cases, while the cancer is being treated vigorously, we find that using an antidepressant at the same time can significantly improve the person's outlook and quality of life.

We used to think that people used drugs and drank because they were depressed to begin with. While certain people say they get high to escape a rotten mood, evidence now suggests that most often it's the drugs themselves that *create* the depression. One study found, for example, that 95 percent of people addicted to opiates (heroin, methadone) who also have a diagnosis of major depression experienced their first depression only after they started using the drugs.

We studied seventy consecutive patients admitted to our alcohol rehabilitation program. While a large number were seriously depressed on
admission, only 7 percent remained in the dumps two to three weeks
following detoxification.

Another study showed quite dramatically that alcohol increases depression. Alcoholics in a hospital detox center were briefly allowed to drink as
much as they wanted. Twelve percent were depressed before, 41 percent
after. Once they were abstinent, their rate of depression was no greater
than that of the general population.

Cocaine abusers have a terrible time with depression. Most callers to a
national cocaine helpline—83 percent—reported how down they were.
Chronic fatigue and sleep problems are the rule. The depression will remit
spontaneously in the majority of those who quit in a supportive, struc-
tured setting or after prolonged abstinence.

Another common drug syndrome commonly confused with depression
is "burnout." Chronic apathy, low energy, inability to function in a meaningful way in society, plus some intellectual deterioration are the consequences of long-term, chronic drug use.

We are beginning to understand more and more how drugs of abuse can
be models in helping us understand a number of naturally occurring
psychiatric diseases. In the late 1970s I became interested in both opiates
and cocaine. With Professor Bob Byck I proposed that the effects of
cocaine might serve as a model for bipolar disorder, commonly known as
manic-depression. Cocaine produces euphoria and can induce changes in
appetite, sleep, sex drive, and other behaviors; these changes look identical to mania. However, continued cocaine use produces the opposite
effect: depression. We thought that the brains of people with bipolar
disorder might produce a cocainelike molecule and that the continued
production of this substance would trigger dramatic mood switches. Our
research showed we were right: Cocaine exerts many of its effects by
binding to the same cell receptors as the neurotransmitter dopamine (see
page 95). With new evidence that the dopamine receptor might be the
source of cocaine's effects, a whole new generation of treatments for
psychosis and mood disorders might be developed that target the dopamine system and thus also block cocaine cravings.

Low-Level Drug Use

"But I only smoke maybe half a joint every couple of days. Don't tell me I
have a drug problem."

"I don't really drink—a couple of cocktails after work."

"Listen, Dr. Gold. You're not going to convince me I'm hooked on coke because I do a few lines on weekends."

I hear these kinds of comments frequently from persons who use drugs regularly but in small quantities. Their lives continue as productively as always; they are not experiencing the well-publicized horrors of drug use. Many of them, however, are feeling kind of anxious or down, tired, perhaps less able to sustain their concentration—nothing "serious." They don't mention their symptoms to me because they don't associate them with their drug use. Instead, they see their mood as something rooted in their emotional makeup, or as a reaction to life events. Worse, so do their psychiatrists, who commonly do not realize that low-level drug use may prove to be the genesis of a depressive syndrome. No drug use is without consequence.

Drugs and the Brain

Drugs and alcohol are powerful mood-altering substances—that's why most people take them. They achieve their effects by interacting with the brain's own mood-regulating systems. The high from drugs may be short-lived, but the effect on the brain's chemical physiology can be long-lasting. With regular use, drugs replace certain natural chemicals in the brain. Either the brain stops making these chemicals, or they lose their potency because they can't compete with the more powerful drugs. But when drug use stops, the brain's chemical-manufacturing systems do not necessarily return to working order immediately; during this phase withdrawal occurs.

The big question is, Will the mood-regulating systems resume functioning *at all*? Sometimes the answer is no, and just as if you'd contracted an irreversible neurological illness, this means brain damage.

Sleep, appetite, sexual function, and energy are often profoundly affected by the psychological and physiological effects of drugs and withdrawal from them. Related nutritional deficiencies and infections, such as viral hepatitis, common in intravenous drug users, or hepatitis or cirrhosis in alcoholics, can all contribute to a very convincing "major depression."

Depression is but one of the psychiatric symptoms of drug use, overuse, and abuse. Adverse reactions to any abusable drug can resemble any known psychiatric symptom—from psychosis to mild anxiety states.

The Biological Pathway of Addiction

Many factors, beginning with genetic vulnerability from the moment of conception, contribute to the biological process of addiction. The drugs consumed by the mother during pregnancy and biological imbalances in important brain chemicals can combine with psychological factors, such as low self-esteem, stress, and dysfunctional family life, to pave the road for future addiction.

Recently, researchers have discovered that an addict's body responds differently to various chemicals and environmental factors and that this different response may increase the chance of addiction. Many of these varying responses occur in the area of the brain called the limbic system. The limbic system contains nerve cells that help to regulate our moods. Other areas of the limbic system are involved in the perception of *reward,* which means the pleasure we feel after doing something good. (Eating, for example, is essential for our survival. The limbic system rewards eating by making it a pleasurable activity.)

All drugs that are addictive in humans are now considered to be rewarding, in that drug use stimulates further use. This reinforcing property is one of the key elements of their addictive nature. While this may seem obvious, until recently many people still believed that drugs were not addictive unless they caused a person to experience withdrawal effects. As a result, some drugs with overt withdrawal symptoms, such as heroin, were considered addictive, while drugs such as cocaine, with less obvious withdrawal symptoms, were considered to be nonaddicting.

Drugs such as cocaine trick the limbic system by triggering the reward response through the release of neurotransmitters. Cocaine, for example, leads to the release of dopamine, which causes nerve cells to fire. The result is euphoria, a feeling so strong that the brain views dopamine as a substance necessary for survival. The brain then "asks" for more cocaine; further use of cocaine means excessive amounts of dopamine are released. Normally any surplus dopamine released by the nerve cells is eventually reabsorbed by them; cocaine, however, interferes with this reabsorption. Molecules of dopamine are left floating in the bloodstream, where they are broken down by enzymes and flushed out of the body in the urine. Eventually the brain's store of dopamine is depleted. Cocaine users then experience intense cravings for more cocaine. The limbic system remembers its pleasurable response to cocaine, a memory that can even be triggered by visual stimuli such as talcum powder!

Given enough repetitions, drug and alcohol use become as entrenched in our limbic reward system as our desire for food, water, or sex. In fact, in animal studies cocaine even overpowered the animal's desire to eat or have sex, to the point where the animal would rather use cocaine and die than eat and live. Furthermore, drugs affect the frontal lobe of the brain—the area responsible for judgment and insight. Not only do drugs cause the addict's brain to demand more drugs; the addict's ability to handle this demand rationally in the context of other everyday demands (such as work, family responsibilities, and health and safety concerns) is also distorted. The end result is the out-of-control addict.

Given the complexity of the body and the brain, it is likely that no simple cause of addiction will ever be found. However, researchers are using sophisticated diagnostic exams to uncover more information. The information gleaned from these exams may result in more effective treatment and prevention strategies.

Psychiatric Diagnosis of Drug Effects

There is some more good news. In the past, except for practitioners who specialized in substance abuse, most psychiatrists remained inexcusably naive about diagnosing drug problems. In the DSM-IV, the criteria for cocaine intoxication (see box, page 97) are a prime example of how psychiatry's diagnostic practices in this all-important area are changing. To my mind, there is still room for improvement.

The Medical Version

The American Medical Association (AMA) has always been wiser than psychiatry when it comes to diagnosing substance abuse. If you want to know whether your patient's maladaptive behavioral effects result from cocaine intoxication, the AMA manual will tell you to find cocaine levels in blood and/or urine that reflect intoxication.

This is what the DSM-IV should recommend first. But instead of listing lab tests as a criterion for diagnosis, the DSM-IV tucks this vital fact into a paragraph a few pages later, under the heading "Additional Information." Additional? It's essential! There are simple laboratory procedures that provide important data fast. Treatment for the patient's actual problem can begin almost immediately.

Not using the lab to rule out drug use also can affect future psychiatric patients profoundly. Many persons with drug-related mimickers make their way into studies of depressed subjects, polluting the results. In my own research, I test for drug-related problems before embarking on a study. And as I said, I test all patients who come for diagnosis and treatment of an apparent psychiatric condition.

Diagnostic Criteria for Cocaine Intoxication

A. Recent use of cocaine ("Oh, I've done a little coke at parties, but nothing regular, Doctor." "When was the last time?" "Gee, let me think. Yeah, must have been three weeks ago . . .")

B. Maladaptive behavior changes, e.g., euphoria, fighting, grandiosity, hypervigilance, psychomotor agitation, impaired judgment, impaired social or occupational functioning (effects that are hardly specific to cocaine)

C. At least two of the following signs within one hour of using cocaine

  1. Rapid, slowed, or irregular heartbeat
  2. Widening of the pupils
  3. Elevated or lowered blood pressure
  4. Perspiration or chills
  5. Nausea or vomiting
  6. Visual or tactile hallucinations
  7. Weight loss
  8. Agitation or slowed movements
  9. Muscle weakness, breathing irregularities, or chest pain
  10. Confusion, seizures, or coma

  (All these are dose- and duration-related effects that can also result from fever, caffeine, atropine, and hundreds of other causes.)

D. Not due to any physical or mental disorder

SOURCE: Adapted from DSM-IV

Washing Out Depression

But the testing is only the first step in determining the contribution of drugs to the patient's misery. Next comes a two-week drug-free "washout." All drugs, including prescribed medications whenever possible, are stopped so that we can see what impact their absence has on the patient. All patients are supervised closely and supported during this period.

It is gratifying to observe a severe depression lift during this period. Drug-induced depressions will usually clear up in users of alcohol and other sedatives, marijuana, and cocaine; detoxification from heroin and especially methadone often causes a long-term depression. Unfortunately, too many psychiatrists immediately prescribe antidepressants and/or tranquilizers for the depressed recovering drug user. At best, medication at this time muddles our ability to determine what the patient's depression comes from; at worst, it creates yet another drug problem, especially when addictive drugs such as tranquilizers are prescribed.

Prescribed Drugs

The drug washout can be equally dramatic for persons who were doing no more than following doctor's orders. Laurie K. suffered ferocious depressions two weeks out of every month, during which she would berate her husband and then herself. She was convinced she was both evil and crazy. Her psychiatrist suggested she stop taking birth control pills. She pooh-poohed his advice, convinced her moods were far too complicated for something as simple as that. When she heard about our diagnostic work, she was certain we would correctly diagnose her severe mental illness. We took her off birth control pills, and to her husband's relief, and her own, her "severe mental illness" disappeared.

In 1971, investigators found that approximately 3 percent of all people taking any prescribed drug experienced psychiatric symptoms. Hallucinations, delusions, psychosis, agitation, anxiety, weird feelings, depression, fatigue, nervousness, and nightmares were all reported.

Today the incidence is probably much higher, because, for one thing, so many medications have been introduced since 1971. Second, advances in disease control have led to concurrent use of numerous drugs, which separately might be safe but in some persons interact dangerously. Older people, who do not metabolize drugs as efficiently as younger people or clear them from their systems in the same way, are at risk for this category of mimicker. Yet when psychiatric symptoms develop, they often are whisked into nursing homes without being properly evaluated.

Know What You're Taking

The list of prescribed drugs that have provoked mimickers is encyclopedic. The drug or drug types we'll be discussing are those that have caused the greatest number of psychiatric reactions. Be aware as you read these pages that most drugs have more than one use, often unrelated to their primary application. Dilantin, for example, is classified as an anticonvulsive drug, but it is also sometimes given for ventricular arrhythmias. Tranquilizers, listed as psychiatric medication, are commonly prescribed for high blood pressure and muscle relaxation. Even antipsychotics such as Thorazine have other medical applications.

If you are medically ill, getting on in age, or have a predisposition to or history of depression or other psychiatric illness, you are especially vulnerable to the psychiatric side effects of the following drugs. When a doctor prescribes a medication, be sure to find out what it is and what is in it. Your pharmacist may also be a good source of information. You can also consult one of the many reference books available for the layperson; there are inclusive drug guides as well as separate reference guides for particular kinds of drugs or conditions. Whether or not you are among the more vulnerable population, it is always a good idea to know what you're taking and to volunteer the information to the doctors whom you consult.

Psychiatric Medications

Antidepressants can make you more depressed, tranquilizers more anxious, antipsychotics more psychotic. These reactions are most likely to occur when the medications are removed suddenly. The tricyclic type of antidepressants may cause a severe mania or even a psychotic episode in a

---

Selected Medications Reportedly Associated With Depression

Cardiovascular Drugs
Alpha-methyldopa
Reserpine
Propranolol
Guanethidine
Clonidine
Thiazide diuretics
Digitalis

Hormones
Oral contraceptives
ACTH (corticotropin) and
  glucocorticoids
Anabolic steroids

Psychotropics
Benzodiazepines
Neuroleptics

Anticancer Agents
Cycloserine

Anti-inflammatory/Anti-infective Agents
Nonsteroidal anti-inflammatory
  agents
Ethambutol
Disulfiram
Sulfonamides
Baclofen
Metoclopramide

Others
Cocaine (withdrawal)
Amphetamines (withdrawal)
L-dopa
Cimetidine
Ranitidine

person who is in a depressed phase of bipolar illness. Tricyclics can also make a schizophrenic person more psychotic. Monoamine oxidase inhibitor antidepressants (MAOIs) can cause anxiety, nervousness, agitation, insomnia, depression and/or euphoria, or full-blown mania.

Antipsychotics can create a host of mimickers, including vocal silence (mutism), catatonia, parkinsonism (symptoms similar to those seen in Parkinson's disease), involuntary muscle movements, extreme restlessness, and delirium. Woe to the patient whose psychiatrist thinks that the medication isn't working and prescribes more of the same.

When blood levels of lithium (prescribed for bipolar disorder and often for depression) get too high, symptoms such as inability to concentrate, depression, and sometimes delirium may result. At greatest risk are patients of doctors who do not carefully monitor blood levels.

Benzodiazepine tranquilizers and sleeping pills, which include Valium, Librium, Xanax, and Restoril, have been known to cause severe depression involving suicidal thoughts, even psychosis. These medications will produce dependency over the long term; sudden withdrawal can bring on a host of psychiatric symptoms and invite misdiagnosis and inappropriate treatment.

Antabuse is prescribed for alcoholics to make them sick to their stomachs if they take a drink. Additional reactions have included anxiety, severe depression, successful suicide, manic psychosis, schizophrenia, and delirium. The doctor who is unaware either that the patient has taken this medication or that it can have these side effects risks exacerbating the symptoms by prescribing antipsychotics.

For more information about drugs prescribed by psychiatrists, see the sections that follow on anticonvulsants and barbiturates.

Antihypertensive Agents

Many of the ingredients in medications prescribed for high blood pressure are notorious for precipitating depression. Some studies have found a 5 to 20 percent risk of depression in patients treated with reserpine. People with a history of depression are most vulnerable to a reserpine-induced depression. Hank, a sixty-two-year-old shoe salesman, had the misfortune to fall into a deep depression a few months after his internist switched him to a blood pressure medication that contained reserpine. Hank wasn't the kind of person to talk about his emotions, so he didn't tell his internist how rotten he was feeling. His wife finally convinced him to return to the psychiatrist he had seen when he'd become depressed several years before. He felt ashamed to return—he felt as if he'd failed.

"How's your health, Hank?" inquired the doctor. "Fine," Hank replied. Hank didn't think to mention the blood pressure pills, and the psychiatrist did not inquire specifically about medications he was taking. He wrote a prescription for the same antidepressant that had worked for Hank the last time. It didn't work this time. Now Hank was positive he'd failed. The psychiatrist wanted to try a different medication, but Hank quit. He couldn't see the point of going to a psychiatrist if the treatment didn't work. His depression continued. It was Hank's wife who came to see us. She said her husband was depressed but she couldn't get him to go to another psychiatrist. We asked if his depression had been medically evaluated, and she said no. It took her months to get Hank to make an appointment with us, but when he called he said he wanted a "physical doctor." He got one: me.

I identified the culprit: the reserpine in his blood pressure pills. I called his internist and discussed changing to a different medication. For me this was a simple case. Not so for Hank, because of a series of errors and omissions by doctors and because of his own reticence to share his feelings. The internist did not ask about Hank's history of depression or inquire specifically about side effects while Hank was on the medication. His previous psychiatrist committed a serious, potentially life-threatening error in prescribing a drug without asking which other medications Hank was taking. He also made a false assumption that Hank's present depression was a recurrence of his last depression.

Alpha-methyldopa, another antihypertensive agent, causes depression at high dosages. Other psychiatric side effects include sleep problems complete with bad dreams and nightmares and, in rare cases, psychosis. Clonidine occasionally will induce depression, nervousness, irritability, paranoia, and hypomania (a low-level mania). And propranolol (Inderal), besides occasional depression and sleep problems, has been known to cause sleep-related hallucinations.

Cardiovascular Drugs

Mental symptoms may be the first and only signs of digitalis overdose. Digitalis toxicity is often confused with "intensive care unit psychosis," a syndrome resulting from the sensory deprivation of the intensive care unit environment, and usually treated psychiatrically. Death from heart failure, heart block, or cardiovascular collapse can be the result of this misdiagnosis and mistreatment. Monitoring of digitalis blood levels prevents overdose.

Psychosis is also a possibility with antiarrhythmics such as lidocaine and procainamide, which are generally administered in the emergency room.

Drugs for Arthritis and Joint/Muscle Pain

Nonsteroidal anti-inflammatory drugs (NSAIDs) are prescribed for joint diseases such as arthritis and bursitis and for sports injuries. The pills act much like aspirin to relieve pain, reduce swelling, and lower fever. Two drugs in this category, Indocin and Clinoril, have been reported to cause psychiatric symptoms with only one dose. Indocin has caused anxiety, agitation, hostility, paranoia, depersonalization (feelings of unreality about oneself or the environment), hallucinations, and psychosis. For Clinoril the list includes bizarre behavior, obsessive talking, delusions, paranoia, combative behavior, irritability, depression, and homicidal threats.

Gastrointestinal Medication

Cimetidine (Tagamet) is widely prescribed for ulcers and other conditions marked by excessive gastrointestinal secretions. A wide spectrum of mental changes has been reported from cimetidine therapy, especially among alcoholics with liver damage, the elderly, and persons who are seriously ill. Symptoms range from mild to severe confusion, depression, agitation, hallucinations, peculiar speech, fluctuating levels of consciousness, and extreme paranoia.

Anticonvulsants

Traditionally these medications are used to treat seizure disorders. Lately, however, some of the drugs in this category are proving helpful for persons with bipolar disorder who do not respond to lithium.

Phenytoin (Dilantin) has long been the drug of choice for seizure control. High blood levels will bring on symptoms that are easily confused with psychosis: delirium, hallucinations of all kinds, delusions. Carbamazepine (Tegretol), lately a psychiatric as well as a neurological drug, has fewer mimicking effects but is not free of them. One study showed that 40 percent of patients on anticonvulsant drugs suffer from a major depression. Phenobarbital seems to produce more depression than carbamazepine, and recent government guidelines recommend close monitoring of all patients on phenobarbital for signs of depression, especially those with a personal or family history of depression.

Barbiturates

Barbiturates have a wide range of uses. They are sedative-hypnotic drugs, inducing sedation or sleep. They are often ingredients in pain medication, such as Fiorinal, which is prescribed for headaches. Some types of barbiturates, notably phenobarbital, are also used as anticonvulsants. Still others are used as antispasmodic medications. All types of barbiturates are potentially addictive drugs of abuse.

Barbiturates are among the more challenging mimickers, since they tend to cause opposite psychiatric effects in adults and children. Adults suffer confusion, drowsiness, oversedation, and depression, while kids are more prone to excitement, irritability, tearfulness, aggression, and hyperactivity. Many of these effects will besiege those who are in withdrawal from a barbiturate, which can be addictive whether it is used to get high or to get better. Toxic or withdrawal reactions frequently are not recognized for what they are.

Anti-Parkinson's Drugs

Parkinson's disease is a top mimicker among older patients; so too are the drugs used to treat it. L-dopa has a 20 percent rate of psychiatric side effects, including confusion, delirium, depression, agitation or activation, psychosis, delusion or paranoia, hypomania, and hypersexuality. Bromocriptine, related to LSD, tends to encourage hallucinations, vivid dreams, mania, and paranoid delusions, symptoms that can be quite prolonged. (I have recently begun to use bromocriptine very successfully in the treatment of cocaine addiction. Side effects are rare in such cases because the drug is taken at low dosage over a short period of time.) Recent APA guidelines report that "bupropion exerts a beneficial effect on symptoms of Parkinson's disease in some patients, but may also induce psychotic symptoms."

Cancer Chemotherapy

If your Aunt Sylvia is depressed and she has cancer, everybody around her whispers, "Well, of course Aunt Sylvia's depressed. She's got cancer." Her doctors also think her frame of mind is natural and understandable. They may be right, but they may not realize that the drugs they are giving her may be making matters much worse. Even if Aunt Sylvia starts acting "crazy," the family may believe it is her way of dealing with her illness. Or they begin to pull away from her, believing her survival to be hopeless.

Side effects of cancer chemotherapy are not limited to nausea, vomiting, or hair loss. Psychiatric side effects are numerous. Chemical treatments for cancer can cause Aunt Sylvia to suffer depression along with confusion, hallucinations, anxiety, agitation, delirium, and so on. Vinblastine, for example, produces depression and anxiety in 80 percent of patients within two to three days of treatment. Twenty percent of patients treated with hexamethylamine have had severe psychiatric side effects, including attempts at suicide.

State of mind is all-important in the struggle against cancer (indeed, against all disease). Aunt Sylvia can put up a fight if she realizes that the depression and confusion, the bizarre behavior, are neither her nor the deadly effects of the disease. The family too will be helped, relieved, and better able to remain close to her.

Corticosteroids

Corticosteroids can replace the natural hormones produced by the adrenal glands when the glands no longer function adequately on their own. Because they are very powerful anti-inflammatory agents, corticosteroids are also useful in a wide variety of diseases and conditions. Lupus, asthma, hay fever, drug and transfusion reactions, skin rashes, psoriasis, eye inflammations, cancer . . . the list is endless. Patients are usually warned about the many physical side effects of these drugs. That they also have mental manifestations comes as a terrible surprise—everything from depression to mania to schizophrenialike psychosis. These reactions occur in approximately 5 percent of people taking the drugs.

A major corporation referred an employee to a colleague of mine, Dr. Irl Extein, for hospitalization. The man was fifty years old and had already been in three general-hospital psychiatric units for depression.

No contributing medical problems, concluded his internist.

Dependent personality, concluded his psychiatrist.

Hypoadrenal state, concluded Dr. Extein.

The man gave every appearance of major depression: He felt worthless and hopeless, he had no interest in anything anymore, and he cried a lot. Dr. Extein, a biopsychiatrist, did a depression workup, which included a standard measurement of the adrenal hormone cortisol at various times throughout the day. "The levels were extremely low," says Dr. Extein. "On careful review of this man's medical history, it was revealed for the first time that he had been treated with corticosteroid hormones for a gastrointestinal condition. This medication had been stopped just prior to the onset of his depression. In retrospect, the diagnosis was clear—his own adrenal glands had 'turned off' when he was prescribed corticosteroids and, as is sometimes the case, had not 'turned on' again. His depression was a result of his hypoadrenal state.

"The treatment was then clear also. He was prescribed corticosteroid replacement medication and within a few weeks his depression and apathy vanished. He did not require antidepressant medications. He returned happily to his family and to his job. Once more he was a productive employee."

Other Rx's

Half of all women taking oral contraceptives experience varying degrees of depression, irritability, tiredness, reduced sex drive, and even reduced capacity for orgasm. . . . Certain general anesthesias can produce a month's worth of depression and other symptoms that are indistinguishable from the real thing. . . . Many of the drugs for tuberculosis have a long list of psychiatric side effects. . . . Temporary psychosis could be the result of therapy with chloroquine for malaria or skin problems, or quinacrine for intestinal parasites. . . .

Over-the-counter Medications

"The availability of approximately 100,000 over-the-counter (OTC) drugs complicates the picture," write Dr. Richard Hall and colleagues. "Adverse drug reactions to OTC preparations occur more frequently than most people imagine. The elderly, children, patients with medical and psychiatric illness, and those using other prescribed or OTC medications are the populations most at risk. Psychiatric complications may include nervousness, anxiety, depression, psychosis, or delirium."

The medical community now frowns upon doctors who prescribe diet pills (amphetamines, also known as "speed"), which produce too many physical and mental side effects—including dependency and addiction, depression, and psychosis—to be worth the loss of a few pounds. Reducing pills are easily obtained at the drugstore, however, complete with their share of problems. These pills contain stimulants that mimic both the effects and the side effects of amphetamines.

In a personal communication Dr. Hall tells me about a twenty-year-old college student who came to him because she was so anxious and depressed that she couldn't concentrate and would suddenly break into tears without any reason. She couldn't sleep, either, which always makes everything worse. She'd been in this state for about a month and a half. A couple of weeks before her symptoms had started, she had decided she needed to do something about those extra fifteen pounds, so she bought some diet pills at her local drugstore. "Sometimes she took more than the manufacturer recommended on the label," Dr. Hall says. "The symptoms abated when the diet pills were discontinued."

Cold and cough preparations contain similar stimulant ingredients, plus antihistamines and nonnarcotic anticough chemicals. From these last two ingredients some people suffer tiredness, slowed or impaired judgment, central nervous system depression, possibly convulsions. According to Hall and colleagues, cough and cold remedies are the most frequently used OTC drugs.

And watch out for laxatives. Overuse of types that contain mercurous chloride (usually foreign brands) can lead to the tremor and dementia of mercury poisoning. Anorexics and the elderly most frequently overdo laxatives.

OTC medications must list all ingredients on the label. Phenyl-propanolamine, ephedrine, pseudoephedrine, and aminophylline are among the greatest offenders.

CHAPTER 8

You Are What You Eat . . . and Breathe

Your body requires a basic environmental survival kit of food, water, air. It's fussy about this threesome, though. To thrive, it insists on a particular balance of ingredients in each category. All bodies will react to a major deficiency of an essential ingredient or an overabundance of a potentially toxic material. The fine tuning, however, is individual. The amount of nutrients you need to be at your best is unique to you. Similarly individual is the point at which a substance in air, food, or water will be toxic to you.

The brain is greedy and supersensitive. Over all other organs, its cells have first call on oxygen and energy-producing sugars. Deprive the brain of even small amounts of these and other nutrients, and it will often turn "psychiatric" on you. Introduce a toxin and it will often be the first organ to react.

Nutritional and toxic disorders are making a comeback in biopsychiatric circles. Diet, air, and water are changing, yielding new deficiencies, new pollutants. Of course these changes will affect us. Sometimes it seems as if the only thing that is not changing is our way of thinking about mental disturbance and nutrition.

Nutritional and toxic disorders will not be discovered without laboratory testing. Even so, deficiencies or excesses that are marginal or subclinical may not be considered significant, and your doctor may tell you your vague complaints are all in your mind. "Among doctors, the idea of a marginal nutrient deficiency has been about as prevalent as belief in a marginal broken leg," quipped one pundit. Thus, unless the index of suspicion is extremely high—as it might be if you work in a garage, breathing exhaust fumes laden with carbon monoxide—nutritional and toxic mimickers may not be detected.

Certain populations are more vulnerable to mild nutritional and toxic mimickers. The elderly are the most susceptible and, as always, end up the victims of antiquated thinking. "I think it likely that in older people subclinical deficiencies can indeed lead to less-than-optimal mental performance," says Dr. James S. Goodwin.

VITAMINS

"I asked my shrink whether he thought my depression might have something to do with a vitamin deficiency and he was dead silent," reports thirty-six-year-old Linda F. " 'Well, I guess you don't think so,' I said, feeling more depressed than when I'd walked in for my session. Then I couldn't think of anything else to say. Finally my shrink suggested that my asking about vitamins and my subsequent silence meant I was trying to avoid the 'real' work of the therapy."

Linda, in fact, turned out to have a deficiency of vitamin B_6. With treatment, her longtime depression lifted substantially.

Some psychiatrists think that a patient's interest in a vitamin "cure" is yet another neurotic symptom. Others go the opposite route and believe that all mental problems result from nutritional deficiencies.

"The psychiatrist should . . . realize that there is tremendous lay interest in the role that vitamins play in mental disorders," says Dr. Frederick C. Goggans, addressing his psychiatric colleagues. "While there is no evidence that the use of vitamins in the therapy of patients without true deficiencies is of value, absolute or relative deficiencies will never be discovered if patients are not tested."

Some vitamin deficiencies, particularly of the B vitamins, do indeed present psychiatrically. This should come as no surprise to a physician, since the B vitamins play an important role in brain metabolism. The deficiency is extremely common. Over half of 127 consecutive admissions to a British general-hospital psychiatric unit, for example, were deficient in at least one B vitamin, a 1982 study found.

Treatment of vitamin deficiencies should result in the reversal of psychiatric and neurological symptoms. Failure to detect and treat them, however, may result in permanent psychiatric or neurological damage.

Niacin

Pellagra, which earlier this century affected as many as 200,000 people, a third of whom died of the disease, is one of the great historical mimickers. In the South, as many as half the state mental hospital beds were occupied by demented pellagra victims. Pellagra is caused by a dietary deficiency of niacin, which was especially common in the South, where many people existed on a diet of corn, fatback, and molasses. After 1937, when the niacin factor was discovered, the vitamin was added to most commercial cereal products and pellagra disappeared. Besides dermatitis and gastrointestinal problems, pellagra victims suffered depression, intellectual impairment, psychosis, or dementia sufficient to send them to mental institutions. Niacin deficiencies and their attendant mental symptoms are now found principally among drug addicts, alcoholics, elderly persons, and some persons with liver disease. Anti-parkinsonian drugs also can reduce necessary niacin levels.

Agitation and anxiety as well as mental and physical slowing, depression included, are among the symptoms of developing deficiency. Niacin usually cures the condition rapidly, except in cases of longtime niacin dementia.

Vitamin B_{12}

Ms. A. was forty-seven when she began to see UFOs. Then Jesus commanded her to board one of them. Her family thought she would be better off in a car heading for a hospital. The doctors who saw her thought she looked older than she was. She was tired, sad, and reclusive. "Jesus has hold of my soul," she declared. "He'll come down in a cloud to take me to be his bride." She would burst out laughing and then just as suddenly dissolve into tears.

Out of her mind or out of B_{12}? Ms. A., who had had no previous psychiatric history, was definitely out of B_{12}. Monthly B_{12} injections sent the spaceship back to its home planet and returned Ms. A. from organic psychosis to mental health.

B_{12} shortage ultimately leads to pernicious anemia. *Anemia* refers to a deficiency of red blood cells or of hemoglobin, which transports oxygen to body tissues. B_{12} is necessary for the production of red blood cells in bone marrow. Intrinsic factor, an enzyme secreted in the stomach, allows the vitamin to be absorbed in the intestine. Pernicious anemia occurs most often because of a deficiency of intrinsic factor. Stomach illnesses, thyroid disease, and certain drugs are among other causes. B_{12} is found most commonly in meat and animal protein foods; thus, vegans (vegetarians who eat neither eggs nor dairy products) are at risk for a dietary deficiency. So too are older persons.

The body stores B_{12} in the liver, generally building up a three- to five-year reserve. Symptoms develop as the stores are slowly used up; psychiatric and neurological manifestations often appear long before the anemia becomes diagnosable. Early diagnosis is crucial, however, because mental changes can become permanent. These include dementia, mood changes, paranoia, irritability, hallucinations, confusion, and mania. Physical symptoms of pernicious anemia include weakness, shortness of breath, heart palpitations, appetite loss, diarrhea, dizziness, burning of the tongue, and tingling sensations in the limbs. In addition, gait is often disturbed.

Folic Acid

Folic acid, or folate, is essential to hemoglobin production; deficiency leads to anemia. But here too, psychiatric symptoms commonly appear before a diagnosable anemia does. A number of recent studies have shown that psychiatric patients have lower folic acid levels than normal subjects and that at least 20 percent of depressed inpatients with no anemia have abnormally low levels. Deficiency of this B vitamin was present in 67 percent of people in one geriatric psychiatric unit. Still another study showed that folic acid treatment shortened the hospital stays of patients with depression, schizophrenia, and organic psychosis.

Green leafy vegetables are the main source of folic acid, but cooking destroys more than half the available vitamin, making deficiency of this vitamin the most common overall. "In general, folate levels reflect the overall nutritional status of an individual," says Dr. Goggans.

A nutritionally inadequate diet, as often occurs with alcoholism (alcohol also interferes with metabolism of the vitamin), illness, poverty, poor eating habits, and many reducing diets, contributes to folic acid deficiency. In addition, barbiturates, aspirin, anticonvulsants, oral contraceptives, and other drugs interfere with its absorption into the body.

Fatigue and lassitude are early signs of folic acid deficiency. As the condition worsens, depression, burning feet, restless-leg syndrome, and dementia are common. Deficiency during pregnancy increases the likelihood of premature delivery and birth defects.

Vitamin B$_6$ (Pyridoxine)

In research among hospitalized patients or those taking part in depression treatment studies, B$_6$ deficiency has been strongly correlated with depression. As many as 20 percent of study subjects revealed a B$_6$ deficiency without any physical symptoms, or with neurological symptoms such as tingling sensations in the limbs, numbness, and sensations reminiscent of electric shocks. B_6 is important for blood, the nervous system, and skin. Deficiency in it is yet another path to anemia. In children convulsions are a major consequence.

Vitamin B_6 is present in most foods. Deficiency results from malabsorption diseases, certain drugs (including antihypertensive medication containing hydralazine, oral contraceptives containing estrogen, L-dopa, and MAO inhibitor antidepressant medications), and increased metabolism.

Caution: Vitamin B_6 is damaging to sensory nerves at high doses.

Vitamin B_2 (Riboflavin)

Like vitamin B_6, B_2 is associated with depression in the absence of signs of malnutrition or other evidence of disease. A British study of 127 consecutive admissions to a psychiatric unit in a general hospital found B_2 deficiency in 29 percent of patients, most of whom exhibited symptoms of depression.

Vitamin B_2 is essential for growth and tissue function. In deficiency states, the lips and mouth can become cracked and scaly, vulnerable to fungus infection. The skin around the nose, ears, eyelids, and genitals becomes red, scaly, and greasy, producing a condition called "shark skin." The eyes too can become ulcerated, and vision may be impaired.

Deficiency is common in the second trimester of pregnancy. Oral contraceptives reduce available vitamin levels.

Vitamin B_1 (Thiamine)

Fatigue, irritation, memory problems, difficulty sleeping, chest pain, loss of appetite, abdominal miseries, and constipation—all symptoms of depression—may mark the onset of vitamin B_1 deficiency. Severe deficiency leads to beriberi, a now-uncommon nutritional illness. Cerebral beriberi, or Wernike-Korsakoff syndrome, can be mistaken for severe depression. This syndrome, common among chronic alcoholics, is characterized psychiatrically by anything from personality change to apathy to confusion. Korsakoff's psychosis resembles alcoholic delirium tremens (DTs). Also at risk are pregnant and nursing mothers, who have an increased need for the vitamin, and persons who suffer frequent bouts of diarrhea.

Milder forms of B_1 deficiency are more common, especially among alcoholics, drug addicts, schizophrenics, the elderly, the chronically ill, and people existing on polished rice. Junk-food consumers are also at risk.

In one study, adolescents who ate a lot of junk food, carbonated sugary drinks, and candy showed early symptoms of beriberi.

Vitamin B_1 is necessary for brain carbohydrate metabolism. Untreated, deficiency can lead to death. Treatment must begin early to reverse the condition completely.

Vitamin C (Ascorbic Acid)

Marginal deficiencies of vitamin C have been reported to influence mood and behavior. Severe deficiency leads to scurvy, in which depression, hypochondria, and hysteria are quite common.

Vitamin C is a busy vitamin. It participates in the formation of connective tissue, collagen, and teeth, and it is necessary for wound healing and recovery from burns. In addition, it facilitates iron absorption and is involved in the actions of folic acid and the amino acids phenylalanine and tyrosine (see page 113).

Oral contraceptives, tetracycline, aspirin, stress, pregnancy, lactation, aging, inflammatory diseases, surgery, and burns all increase the body's need for vitamin C. If the increased requirement is not met, deficiency will occur, as it will in a nutritionally poor diet.

In true mimicker fashion, tiredness, weakness, apathy, weight loss, vague pains, and depression appear three to twelve months before scurvy shows up. Finally, sores will begin to appear, often containing coiled hairs, on the buttocks, thighs, and calves especially. The gums swell and bleed, teeth loosen, and wounds fail to heal.

AMINO ACIDS

All body substances, neurotransmitters included, consist of proteins, which are made of complex molecules called amino acids. The body can produce some of its own amino acid building blocks, but others must come from food. Technically, then, dietary amino acids are vitamins, which *Dorland's Illustrated Medical Dictionary* defines as "a general term for a number of unrelated organic substances that occur in many foods in small amounts and that are necessary in trace amounts for the normal metabolic functioning of the body."

Does a deficiency of dietary amino acids mimic depression? As Dr. Goggans puts it, "Although it is inherently obvious that availability of the substances in the diet and their presence in blood and brain would be important in the evaluation of mood states, appreciation of their roles and the clinical investigation of such issues as prevalence of amino acid deficiencies in major affective disorder patients and their role as therapeutic agents have only just begun."

In the brain, neurotransmitters are manufactured (synthesized) by enzyme action on substances called *precursors*. The amino acid tryptophan is a precursor of the neurotransmitter serotonin; serotonin levels are low in some depressed people. Tyrosine, another amino acid, is a precursor of both norepinephrine and dopamine, both of which are known to be involved in mood; dopamine may play a major role in schizophrenia. Phenylalanine is yet another critical amino acid. All three of these must be obtained through diet.

Amino-acid replacement therapy for apparent deficiency states is not as easy as it may sound. Ingesting a high-protein meal or the pure amino acid itself does not insure that it will arrive in the brain in the required amount. Some researchers believe that the ratio of desired precursor to other amino acids is all-important. Following a high-protein meal, amino acids will compete with one another to penetrate the blood-brain barrier. A high-carbohydrate, low-protein meal apparently increases brain tryptophan levels by causing insulin secretion, which in turn lowers levels of serotonin's amino acid competitors. But ingesting large amounts of tryptophan is likely to inhibit tyrosine uptake. Phenylalanine may not be metabolized without the addition of vitamin B_6. But B_6 can be toxic at high levels, and phenylalanine can trigger hypomania.

Right now we know all too little about amino-acid replacement therapy. The good news, however, is that psychiatry is beginning to take seriously the complex interrelationships of food, mood, and behavior. "In the past," notes psychiatrist John W. Crayton, a therapist might have attributed a patient's craving for sweets to a "symbolic feeding of the self by a defeated and depleted psyche." Today the practitioner might also consider the effects of carbohydrate loading on brain neurotransmitter metabolism. "Increasing the proportion of carbohydrate in the diet tends to increase the amount of tryptophan entering the brain and consequently raises the amount of serotonin available for neurotransmission," Crayton notes. Since some depressed people reveal a low level of serotonin, the carbohydrate craver could be attempting to raise serotonin levels via this mechanism. "Evidence that central serotonin levels can influence the proportions of carbohydrate and protein selected in the diet support this notion," he reports.

Amino acids hold the most promise as supplements to standard depression treatments.

METALS

Although your mother never said, "Eat your metals, dear," she probably did have a few words to say about finishing your spinach. Spinach is a source of iron, one of many metals essential to health. Essential metals, usually called minerals, include sodium, magnesium, potassium, calcium, vanadium, chromium, manganese, iron, cobalt, copper, zinc, molybdenum, nickel, strontium, and selenium. Most of the essential metals are necessary to the functioning of enzymes, which in turn are essential to metabolic processes throughout the body. When you don't get enough of the essential metals, either because of diet or inability to metabolize them properly, deficiency diseases result. But you can also get too much of a good thing, and that spells toxicity—in a word, poisoning.

"Metals are ubiquitous in our environment," notes Neil Edwards, M.D. "Of the naturally occurring elements, sixty-nine are metals." Our bodies require fifteen of these metals, but we come in contact with many more.

Toxic Mimickers

Toxin	Major Depression	Manic-depression
Magnesium	+	
Hypocalcemia	+	
Hypercalcemia	+	
Zinc	+	
Manganese	+	
Lead	+	
Mercury	+	+
Thalium	+	
Bismuth	+	
Aluminum		
Lithium		
Arsenic	+	
Bromides	+	
Organophosphates	+	

Since 5000 B.C. we have learned to use them with increasing sophistication in tools, shelter, medicines, fuels, jewelry, structural materials, makeup, hair spray, herbicides, kitchen cleansers, insecticides . . . Overdoing our contact with many nonessential metals turns out not to be so good for us, especially when we eat or breathe them. Lead, mercury, and radioactive metals—not to mention the favorite poison of a good old whodunit, arsenic—can wreak havoc.

The psychiatric complications of essential or nonessential metal deficiency or toxicity, even at low levels, are many. The brain is quicker to react than the rest of the body; thus mental and behavioral symptoms may be more apparent than organic signs. The result is the usual mimicker story: inappropriate psychiatric treatment or incarceration. We'll look at the most common of these metal mimickers.

Essential Metals

SODIUM

Hyponatremia is the term used to indicate a decrease in sodium (salt) concentration in body water. Usually it represents an increase in body water rather than a decrease in sodium. "Hyponatremia has been associated with numerous psychiatric conditions," says Dr. Goggans. "To some extent symptoms depend on the speed with which hyponatremia develops." When it comes on suddenly, agitated delirium or psychosis often results. In chronic, slowly developing states, however, depression and/or dementia are more likely.

Overdoing diuretic medication, which causes the kidneys to excrete water by removing too much salt from the system, can induce hyponatremia. If you are taking "water pills," be sure to follow your doctor's directions. Call your doctor if you start to feel weird or moody while taking the medication. Other causes of hyponatremia include vomiting, diarrhea, or porphyria, or kidney, adrenal, pituitary, thyroid, brain, lung, heart, or liver diseases. For more information on hyponatremia, see page 144.

POTASSIUM

Diuretics are also a common cause of potassium deficiency, or hypokalemia. Depression is the primary mental manifestation. Reduced potassium slows the whole body, to the point of paralysis and respiratory failure. When the potassium level falls far enough, the heart will lose its rhythm and stop. Hypokalemia is the most frequent cause of sudden death in anorexics and bulimics, usually because of cardiac complications. People with these eating disorders deplete themselves of potassium through vomiting and through abuse of laxatives and diuretics.

IRON

Iron deficiency is on the increase worldwide, possibly because of increased consumption of refined foods and decreased use of iron cookware. One study indicates that perhaps half of all premenopausal women and a third of all children do not receive enough iron. Athletes—runners in particular—apparently are prone to low-level iron deficiency.

American Health magazine published a story about world-class marathoner Alberto Salazar, who suddenly began to run poorly under even the best of conditions. After one race he poured out his frustrations about his physical state on national television, reported author Paul Perry. He hadn't slept well in more than a year. He was listless, irritable, and depressed. Canadian sports-medicine specialist Doug Clement, M.D., suggested a special diagnostic test to Salazar's coach, and sure enough, he was deficient in iron. He began to take a supplement, and within two months he ran his second-best time ever.

Doctors often wait for anemia to appear before they will diagnose iron deficiency. In iron-deficiency anemia, the body forms too few red blood cells and tissues become deprived of oxygen. Anemia may progress from weakness, tiredness, loss of stamina, dizziness, ringing in the ears, irritability, or strange behavior to cessation of menstrual periods, loss of sex drive, congestive heart failure, or shock. Some persons with iron-deficiency anemia crave dirt, paint, or ice. Blood loss is a major cause of anemia.

Symptoms of marginal deficiency include depression, fatigue, irritability, reduced attention span, poor work performance, and possibly sleep disturbance. It can be caused by an iron-poor diet, heavy exercise (World War II troops became deficient in iron after long marches), insufficient vitamin C, increased nutritional demands (as in pregnancy and adolescence), malabsorption diseases, and menstruation, in addition to the causes mentioned above.

Too much iron, however, can lead to toxicity. Iron poisoning occurs in conjunction with a genetic condition (hemachromatosis) in which iron is overabsorbed, or with various diseases such as alcoholic cirrhosis or diabetes. Taking iron supplements can quickly lead to vomiting, upper abdominal pain, diarrhea, drowsiness, and shock. Hemachromatosis generally develops slowly, however. Skin color turns bronze, cardiac symptoms develop, sex drive is lost, and behavioral changes occur. Hemachromatosis usually develops after the age of fifty.

Iron poisoning can happen to anyone, though, due to overuse of dietary supplements. In children, particularly, iron poisoning from multivitamins can often result in death.

CALCIUM

Depression is common in calcium toxicity—but that doesn't mean that doctors will automatically check a depressed patient's calcium level. Jerry G. was a cranky guy in his mid-seventies who had been depressed on and off for years. He had refused psychiatric help, saying it was nobody's business what went on in his mind. His wife, Frances, died from cancer shortly after they moved to a retirement community in the Southwest. Soon after, Jerry's condition worsened, mentally and physically. He was sure everybody was against him. His blood pressure zoomed, he had digestive problems, and finally he even had triple-bypass surgery. Although his recovery was complete, he was frightened of an imminent heart attack or stroke. He would go from doctor to doctor, all of whom quickly tired of his anxieties.

When Jerry's depression worsened suddenly and severely, nobody thought too much about it. Even his children, who tended to be kind and sensitive to him, shrugged it off with, "What do you expect at his age, with Mom gone?" Jerry couldn't sleep, yet he barely had the energy to get up. When he went out of the house he became panicky. He worried continually. He was afraid of dying, but he talked of suicide. He began to lose weight because he couldn't eat; he couldn't keep food down. His regular doctor assured him he was okay; he should "get out more and make some friends." The doctor shooed him off to the nurse, who took his blood pressure and told him to come back in two months.

Finally he went to a new doctor. This time the doctor hospitalized Jerry for testing. Jerry's calcium level was "almost off the charts," as the gastroenterologist put it. Jerry was suffering from two diseases: parathyroid tumors and acute, severe pancreatitis. The parathyroid hormone helps control the body's calcium (see page 147). In Jerry's case the tumors caused oversecretion of the hormone, which in turn increased the concentration of calcium in his blood. The doctors believed that the long-undiagnosed hyperparathyroid condition had led to an accumulation of calcium in Jerry's pancreas, poisoning the digestive organ. Two months after a doctor finally paid attention to Jerry's symptoms, he was dead from complications of the pancreatic illness.

The body is acutely sensitive to changes in calcium. Brain cells will not function normally in the presence of too much of this essential metal. Psychiatric symptoms—typical depressive symptoms plus possible personality change, disorientation, delusions, hallucinations—parallel calcium levels. It is possible that Jerry's "usual" depression was related to calcium, since the parathyroid condition develops slowly over decades.

Depression also occurs in calcium deficiency. Other psychiatric symptoms include anxiety, tiredness, weakness, irritability, and psychosis. Calcium deficiency sometimes results from vitamin D deficiency, but more often is the product of disease, including kidney failure, hypoparathyroidism, intestinal malabsorption, magnesium deficiency, leukemia, or fluoride intoxication. Here too, the psychiatric symptoms may long predate the appearance of the organic condition.

Many women have begun to take calcium supplements to prevent osteoporosis, the bone weakening they are subject to with advancing age. The best way to increase calcium is to eat more dairy products and vegetables. Calcium supplements can provoke kidney stones in vulnerable individuals.

MAGNESIUM

Deficiency of magnesium can result from numerous causes, among them inadequate diet, kidney disease, chronic alcoholism, parathyroid disease, or impairment of the intestines, through which magnesium is absorbed into the body. Lactating mothers have an increased need for magnesium and can become deficient by not adding more to their diet. Premature infants tend to suffer from it, as do normal-term babies of mothers with diabetes mellitus.

Psychiatric symptoms of magnesium deficiency not only may be the first to appear, but may continue after the others disappear. These include depression, agitation, disorientation, confusion, anxiety, and hallucinations. Patients suffering from the deficiency are irritable and uncooperative; this behavior can lead internists to make a too-hasty referral to a psychiatrist.

Persons with poor kidney function are most prone to magnesium toxicity because healthy kidneys usually clear it out of the body fairly rapidly. Generally the poisoning is associated with medical use of magnesium sulfate, which may be given intravenously for high blood pressure or convulsions, or by mouth as a cathartic or antacid. The toxicity results in lassitude, depression, and changes in perception, attention, intellectual function, and personality.

Zinc

More than fifty enzymes need zinc in order to function properly. Thus, zinc deficiency can lead to a number of disorders and difficulties, including loss of appetite, taste, and smell, compromised immune-system functioning, mental slowing, irritability, emotional disorders, impaired healing, and rough skin. Zinc-deficiency depression is seen particularly among the elderly; their complaints about appetite and taste often suggest a (false) psychiatric diagnosis. Consequences for children include retarded growth, possibly even mental retardation and learning disabilities. Experiments with pregnant monkeys indicate that even slight zinc deficiencies can seriously affect the health of pregnant women.

Zinc deficiency can result from diets high in whole grains, intestinal malabsorption disorders, infectious conditions, anemias, diabetes, cirrhosis, dialysis, anorexia, and many other conditions—including, of course, a diet poor in zinc.

Manganese

Manic excitement, incoherent speech, depression, irritability, insomnia, refusal of food, spontaneous laughing and crying—these are the symptoms of "manganese madness," and they occur in people who work in manganese mines, steel foundries, and ore-crushing plants, and in anyone who inhales manganese dust regularly. Prolonged exposure leads eventually to symptoms similar to those of Wilson's disease (see page 125) or Parkinson's disease (see page 84), although once again mental manifestations come first.

Nonessential Metals

Lead

Lead poisoning causes a biochemical malfunction similar to porphyria (see page 124), complete with its wide range of psychiatric manifestations. In children, lead poisoning leads to mental retardation in 25 percent of all cases. Most common are hyperactivity and lower intellectual functioning. It behooves the careful clinician dealing with children who are hyperactive, learning disabled, retarded, or even autistic to obtain a careful history for possible lead exposure and to administer the appropriate tests.

Adults exposed to lead often exhibit depression and cognitive and behavioral changes, even at low levels of toxicity. Indications of high-dose lead poisoning can be abdominal cramps, nerve disorders (especially in the wrists and ankles), personality changes, metallic taste, headache, vomiting, and constipation.

The symptoms of lead poisoning in adults and children can develop slowly or suddenly, often recurring long after the toxicity has been treated, since lead is stored in bone tissue.

Lead is so much a part of our environment that sources of poisoning are numerous. A partial list includes paint chips from lead-based paints in old homes (a common source among young children, who put the chips in their mouths and swallow them), water that has been standing in lead pipes, solder and fumes from lead-emitting smelters, automobile exhaust from old cars using leaded gas, "moonshine" whiskey made in lead stills, the burning of lead-containing painted wood or battery casings, and ceramic ware (usually homemade) that has been improperly lead-glazed.

If you work in the manufacture of ammunition, pipes, brass, bronze, solder cables, lead shielding, pigments, chemicals, or processed metals, you are at risk for low-level lead poisoning.

MERCURY

Do you know anyone who is mad as a hatter? Then your friend must be suffering from mercury poisoning. The expression probably comes from the behavior of English felt-hat makers in the last century, who were exposed to mercury vapor in their work. They suffered severe depression with retarded (slowed) movement, severe irritability, a profound fear of strangers (xenophobia), and such embarrassment and self-consciousness that they could no longer function under direct supervision. Then as now, mercury poisoning progresses to a permanent dementia if the source of exposure is not discovered and avoided. Children with mercury poisoning may appear to have learning disabilities.

Besides mercury vapor, poisoning can occur from mercury-containing dental fillings, douches, skin creams, diuretics, and laxatives, and food and water contamination resulting from improper disposal of industrial wastes.

ARSENIC

Arsenic is an ingredient in insecticides, herbicides, rat poisons, antibiotic preparations for amebic infections, and detective novels. The poison causes death within hours if ingested in large quantities, or illness and a rather dramatic madness followed by death if exposure occurs over a longer term. Arsenic poisoning generally begins with a feeling of burning in the throat, followed by gastrointestinal symptoms. Psychiatric symptoms of arsenic poisoning can include depression, anorexia, lassitude, confusion, disorientation, crying, agitation, paranoia, and visual hallucinations.

If you are inexplicably losing your hair, if your skin is thickening and becoming darker, if you find a white line running across your fingernails, and if you are suffering from any or all of the above symptoms, this may be a case for Agatha Christie.

Bismuth

Most cases of bismuth poisoning go unrecognized in this country. Worldwide, bismuth is most often used in oral gastrointestinal preparations, including some laxatives, chronic ingestion of which can lead to toxicity. In the United States, skin-lightening creams, unbeknownst to most doctors, are the major culprit; bismuth, which can be absorbed into the body through the skin, is a major ingredient in these preparations.

Psychiatric symptoms predominate in the first phase of toxicity. Depression, anxiety, loss of interest, slowed thinking, antisocial behavior, delusions, and hallucinations mark this phase. Often they come and go, just like a psychiatric condition. Complete mental confusion, tremor, and involuntary behavior (walking, standing, speaking) typify later stages. Death can follow.

Correct diagnosis is simple—measure bismuth levels in blood and urine. Simple, that is, if it occurs to the treating psychiatrist to take some tests.

Aluminum

The principal risk for aluminum poisoning is among people undergoing kidney dialysis. In one study, 86 percent of the dialysis patients eventually developed psychiatric symptoms that were misdiagnosed as major depression and mistreated with antidepressants. Dialysis dementia is characterized by progressive mental deterioration. Behavioral changes range from severe depression to memory problems to hallucinations. Reducing aluminum levels in dialysis fluids will prevent the disorder. Continued exposure will lead to coma and death.

Bromides—a Literary Case History

Bromides used to be popular as sedative-hypnotics and anticonvulsants. They were a major mimicker of their day, accounting for 21 percent of all psychiatric admissions in 1927. Since supplanted by modern medications, bromide toxicity accounts for a tiny percentage of mimickers today.

The late British author Evelyn Waugh had used bromides for sleep for ten years prior to his breakdown in 1954. His psychotic collapse was actually a case of bromide poisoning. In his 1957 novel *The Ordeal of Gilbert Pinfold,* Waugh details this experience through the fictional character Pinfold.

Pinfold, like Waugh at this period, is an ill-humored, cranky writer who becomes depressed and can no longer write or sleep. Convinced that he requires a stronger dose of his medication, he talks his pharmacist into not diluting his bromides. Instead he dilutes them himself with alcohol. Soon Pinfold begins to suffer from bromide poisoning. Waugh describes the symptoms of Pinfold's bromide toxicity as skin blotches, memory lapses, an inability to spell, aches and pains, clumsiness, and irritability with his wife. A doctor misdiagnoses his condition as an allergy to an unidentified substance, and his advice is to escape the allergen. Pinfold books passage for Ceylon. On board ship he becomes at first delirious, then quickly psychotic, convinced he is involved in an international conspiracy. He hears voices, one of which falls in love with him. Pinfold prepares for an affair. When nothing happens, other voices accuse him of impotence.

In his confusion Pinfold has not packed enough bromide, and his supply runs out on the second day. Instead, he takes pills and alcohol. The psychosis continues, interspersed with periods of lucidity as he now goes into withdrawal from his long habit. He returns to London within a month and gradually recovers. The family doctor, who now knows of the bromide use, says, "It sounds like a perfectly simple case of poisoning to me." But the way Pinfold looks at it, "he had endured a great ordeal and, unaided, had emerged the victor." When Waugh himself returned from his own journey, a psychiatrist correctly diagnosed his breakdown for what it was.

TO SUPPLEMENT OR NOT TO SUPPLEMENT?

All the vitamins, amino acids, and metals we have discussed are available as supplements from drugstores, health food stores, and vitamin suppliers. Self-treating a depression with one or more of them makes little sense, however. Unless a biopsychiatrist diagnoses your depression as a nutritional mimicker, you cannot know whether your problem is lurking in your diet. Neither can you know which substance to take or how much; that is something only laboratory testing can reveal. The body depends on a balance of nutrients, which can be dangerously altered by adjusting intake of one. The megadoses often recommended by the "expert" behind the counter can be toxic. Taking large doses of amino acids, for example, can lead to lowered food intake, massive tissue damage, and death. Furthermore, dosing yourself with vitamins, minerals, and amino acids will only confound your diagnosis when you are finally ready to get one.

You're better off joining a health club. As you will see in Chapter 23, there are a number of ways for you to treat your own depression, but do-it-yourself dietary prescriptions are not one of them. The best way to be sure you're getting the nutrition you need for your head is to eat a balanced diet.

ENVIRONMENTAL POISONS

These are the poisons that modern "progress" has created. Does a day go by without a report of toxic-waste pollution or disaster from chemical fumes? Environmental poisoning need not come from an exotic source, however. The exhaust from any car will do.

Carbon Monoxide

Virtually all of us are exposed daily to this colorless, odorless gas. It is a component of automobile exhaust, tobacco smoke, and the gases from burning wood, coal, and charcoal, to name a few sources. Poisoning will occur after prolonged exposure. A faulty automobile exhaust system or fireplace chimney, or a job in a parking garage, will do it. Running a car engine in an enclosed space and breathing the fumes will do it unto death.

Carbon monoxide steals oxygen from the body. The symptoms of carbon monoxide poisoning are so unpredictable, however, that it has been misdiagnosed as hysterical psychosis, borderline personality, schizophrenia, psychotic depression, catatonia, or hysteria. Poisoning must be treated to avoid permanent brain and heart damage.

Organophosphate Insecticides

Organophosphate insecticides act in the same way as nerve gases used in chemical warfare: they inhibit acetylcholinesterase, an essential brain enzyme. Chronic exposure results in irritability, tension, anxiety, jitteriness, restlessness, giddiness, emotional withdrawal, depression, drowsiness, decreased concentration, confusion, and bizarre dreams. Atropine, administered intravenously, usually reverses the condition.

Volatile Substances

Painters, refinery workers, and persons who work with fuel for many years are at risk of personality change, depression, fatigue, lowered intellectual capacity, irritability, panic disorder symptoms—the works.

Children and adolescents who sniff glue, toluene (a solvent), gasoline, cleaning fluid, and nitrous oxide ("laughing gas") are also in for it, and not just from their parents. After the euphoria come hallucinations and what we psychiatrists call conduct-disordered behavior. These resulting behavior patterns are usually considered part of the "bad behavior" that led to the drug abuse, rather than the brain's organic response to poison. Most of the toxic effects disappear with removal of the substance.

METABOLIC DISEASES

All the chemical reactions that release energy from food and that convert food into more complex chemical compounds equal the process of metabolism, which takes place in every cell. Some individuals are born with chemical defects that affect this highly complex, essential functioning. In some cases these diseases produce symptoms similar to psychiatric conditions. Some of the more common of these are:

Acute Intermittent Porphyria

This is one of a rare group of diseases caused by an inherited defect in the enzymes that produce a constituent of blood. A speaker at the 1985 annual meeting of the American Association for the Advancement of Science suggested that early victims of these diseases could have inspired the myths of werewolves and vampires, because sufferers used to ingest blood to right this defect. Acute intermittent porphyria affects the nervous system and is more common among women. It can exist in a latent form with no physical symptoms. Attacks, however, can be precipitated by various drugs, alcohol, crash diets, or simply reduced intake of carbohydrates; by pregnancy, menstruation, or oral contraceptives; and by infection.

Since the disease can affect any part of the nervous system, symptoms can include nausea and vomiting or constipation, muscular weakness, loss of vision, paralysis, and psychiatric problems. These problems run the gamut of virtually everything a psychiatrist has ever seen or studied, including neurosis, hysteria, organic brain syndrome, psychosis, conversion disorder, and depression, which is most common between attacks.

A screening of 2,500 psychiatric patients discovered the presence of the disease in thirty-five patients, a 1.5 percent incidence.

Acute intermittent porphyria can often be controlled by a high-sugar diet or by injections of a blood product. Although porphyria is not a psychiatric disease, phenothiazine, ordinarily prescribed for psychosis, may be helpful in controlling the disease's pain and psychiatric symptoms.

Avoidance of stressors that provoke attacks is the best approach. Obviously, if menstruation is the trigger, this is not always possible. Neither is it possible when a psychiatrist misdiagnoses a patient with the disease and prescribes medication that will promptly precipitate an attack.

Wilson's Disease

Another rare, inherited disorder, Wilson's disease is caused by an error in copper metabolism that results in copper accumulation in body tissues. Symptoms begin to occur early in life, between the ages of six and twenty, when binding sites in the liver become saturated with copper. Some Wilson's patients suffer liver disease at this point, which can lead to liver failure. About half of patients develop a golden-brown or gray-green ring around the corneas of their eyes. Eventually the copper will begin to destroy nerve cells, causing tremors, peculiar movements and rigidity, personality changes, and dementia. None but psychiatric symptoms may be present, however, and more Wilson's sufferers are initially sent to psychiatrists than to pediatricians or other physicians. Wilson's symptoms can mimic mania, depression, schizophrenia, schizoaffective disorder, hysteria, conversion disorder, anxiety, confusional state, neurosis, hyperactivity, and school phobia.

Wilson's disease is reversible if it is properly diagnosed when symptoms first begin. Certain death follows on the heels of misdiagnosis.

An Apple a Day

Biopsychiatrist A. James Giannini, not one to fall for a mimicker, recently solved a one-of-a-kind metabolic deficiency case.

His patient, a supermarket owner in his early thirties, had emigrated from Greece four years earlier. Every September since his arrival he would suffer disabling depression with anxiety. Every December it would lift.

"During this time he had the changes in mood, appetite, sex drive, energy levels, and confidence characteristic of a biological depression," Dr. Giannini tells us. Psychiatrists had dosed him with antidepressants, but to no effect. Dr. Giannini gave him a battery of biopsychiatric and psychological tests. Negative. "Finally," says Dr. Giannini, "in the manner of a fishing expedition, we gave him virtually every test available. His only abnormality was a deficiency of the enzyme G-6-P-D.

"Levels of the enzyme G-6-P-D are frequently lower in Southern Europeans," he explains. "Usually this causes no problem, unless the reduced level of enzyme is overloaded with salicylates. Salicylates are found in aspirin, wintergreen, and most importantly in this case . . . apples.

"This patient rarely ate apples on his Greek isle of birth. Here in Ohio, however, apples are abundant. During the autumn season the excess apple crop is pressed into cider. This patient, who acquired a passion for apple cider, drank several quarts daily throughout the entire cider season— which lasts from September until mid-December.

"When the apples and apple cider were discontinued, the depression lifted." Dr. Giannini is happy to report that his patient has been without cider, and without symptoms, for two years.

Case closed.

CHAPTER 9

Hormones

One of the most rewarding parts of scientific research and its subsequent application to clinical activity is that its basic concepts often lead to widespread understanding of disease. A decade ago we had a basic understanding of the important relationship between hormonal activity and depression. But not everyone was convinced, as the following story illustrates. Some years ago the hospital where I practice wanted to expand its outpatient evaluation program. We knew it would not be easy to find a psychiatrist with the right qualifications: excellence in psychiatry combined with a strong medical background. The man we ultimately decided on had terrific medical and psychiatric training. But he was young and brash, convinced that already he had seen everything.

"All this testing is bogus," he declared. "None of these patients are going to be physically sick."

I smiled—how many times had I heard that before? "Do me a favor," I said. "Just work up fifty patients in a row my way. Then write a paper on your results, whatever they are. If the patients turn out to be physically healthy, fine. Then you can go ahead and expose me."

It was his turn to smile. "A deal!" he said.

His paper appeared in the *Journal of the American Medical Association.* It was about how thyroid disease was commonly misdiagnosed as psychiatric illness.

"If you don't take a temperature, you won't find the fever," the saying goes. Had this young doctor not performed the necessary workups, he never would have been convinced that early thyroid failure is the most common medical condition to mimic depression. Today, most young physicians and psychiatrists are fully aware of the relationship between the neuroendocrine system and depression. We know that the endocrine system as a whole, of which the thyroid is one small part, is the organ system most commonly associated with psychiatric symptoms. Studies

Endocrine Mimickers

Toxin	Major Depression	Manic-depression
Hypothyroid	+	+
Hyperthyroid	+	+
Hypoglycemia	+	
Cushing's disease	+	+
Addison's disease	+	
Hyperparathyroidism	+	
Hypoparathyroidism	+	
Pheochromocytoma	+	
Carcinoid	+	+
Ovarian failure	+	
Testicular failure	+	
Panhypopituitarism	+	+

report that depression occurs almost three times more frequently in patients with clinical hypothyroidism than those without that disorder. As many as one-third of misdiagnosed patients will have one or another endocrine mimicker (including diabetes), with underactive thyroid being the most frequent.

A CRASH COURSE IN NEUROENDOCRINOLOGY

Endocrine glands are found throughout the body. The thyroid is located in the neck, where it is surrounded by the parathyroid glands. The thymus gland is below the neck. The islets of Langerhans are situated on the pancreas, which is the digestive organ found behind the stomach. The adrenals sit atop the kidneys. Our sex organs, the ovaries and testes, are also endocrine glands. The brain too has its endocrine glands—the pituitary, the hypothalamus, and the pineal. These are the "traditional" endocrine glands. We are discovering, however, pockets of cells throughout the body that act like endocrine glands.

Hormones

All endocrine glands secrete hormones into the blood. Hormones are the body's chemical regulators. Growth and development, reproduction, response to stress, sexual activity, energy, heart rate, blood pressure, body temperature, appetite—all are mediated by hormones. Hormones work to keep the body in a state of balance, or homeostasis. If your electrolyte balance is off, for example, the adrenal cortex will secrete aldosterone to increase sodium and decrease potassium and make sure that the body's electrical transmission system can continue to function uninterruptedly.

The endocrine system functions remarkably like an extension of the nervous system, communicating with organs and tissues throughout the body to control their functioning. The differences between the two are that the endocrine system is slower to respond than are nerves, and its effects are longer-lasting. Also, it relies on the nerves in the sense organs to tell it what is happening outside the body. The electrochemical nerve impulses triggered by the sight of a bull charging at you are immediate but brief. Nerves communicate the news to the endocrine system, which takes over to direct the response. The pituitary gland will begin to secrete one of its hormones (ACTH) into the blood. When the circulating blood reaches the adrenals, the ACTH tells the cortex to secrete cortisol, which helps to stimulate the adrenal medulla to secrete epinephrine (adrenaline) and norepinephrine, its stress hormones. Only now will the "fight or flight" reaction begin; your heart will start pounding, your legs will take you to the nearest tree, and your arms will help pull you up, even though you may never have climbed a tree in your life.

Glands in the Brain

Like the nervous system, the endocrine system has a control center, or centers, in the brain, which direct its activity. The pituitary gland has long been called the "master gland," because its hormones initiate the secretions of other glands. However, it is the hypothalamus that directs the pituitary.

The pea-sized hypothalamus has been called the "brain of the brain." It has connections to nearly all parts of the brain. Its responsibilities are awesome indeed: to regulate sleep, waking, heart rate, body temperature, hormones, hunger, thirst, sex, and emotions. Keeping them all in balance—particularly that last item—is some chore. No wonder the hypothalamus (and the limbic system of the brain, of which it and the pituitary are a part) is of major interest to psychiatry today. Limbic-system structures are also involved in learning, long-term memory, creative thinking, decision making, and behavioral control. Some psychiatrists believe that mental illness originates right here. Depression, whether primary or secondary, appears to be a hypothalamic/limbic phenomenon.

Mind-Brain-Body Bond

The more we can see into the brain, the more we are discovering just how interconnected are the nervous system and the endocrine system. Here are just a few of the many extraordinary ways in which they interlock and interact:

• The brain's all-important neurotransmitters, those chemicals that carry nerve messages across the gaps (synapses) between neurons (nerve cells), are identical to some hormones. For instance, epinephrine and norepinephrine are adrenal hormones. They are also brain neurotransmitters, playing an important role in the genesis of depression.

• The neurotransmitters that regulate the hypothalamus are the same as those that regulate moods.

• Thyroid hormone as well as the neurotransmitters norepinephrine and dopamine are all made from the same amino acid, tyrosine.

• The brain is itself a target organ for endocrine hormones. Thyroid hormones, for example, set the tone of receptors for mood-message neurotransmitters. After a drop in thyroid hormone, receptors become "deaf" to messages of good cheer.

• In earlier chapters we referred to the new diagnostic tests for the existence of biological depression. All of them test particular functions of what we have come to call the neuroendocrine system. The great majority of people with biological depressions demonstrate a variety of brain-endocrine abnormalities.

The endocrine system, then, is powerfully involved in what depression is as well as what it is not. We will investigate more of this intriguing organ system in depth as we move, in the next chapter, from the mimickers to true depression.

THE DIAGNOSIS DILEMMA

"Since the endocrine system and the nervous system are intimately linked, it is often difficult to distinguish cause from effect," says Dr. Arthur J. Prange, Jr. "In depression, for example, one usually assumes that mental changes cause endocrine changes; in certain endocrinopathies [disorders of endocrine glands], depressive changes or other mental aberrations are usually seen as results."

Little wonder that the psychiatrist or internist who does not test depressed patients confuses these relationships utterly.

But testing itself is not enough. The physician must know which tests to perform, and how to interpret their results.

When an endocrine gland malfunctions, it secretes too little or too much hormone, or it stops secreting altogether or stops responding to "command" hormones. Because of the interrelationship of the brain and the endocrine system with its hormones, mental symptoms of gland disease will occur far earlier than bodily symptoms. Even the smallest alterations in hormonal secretions can upset the chemical balance the brain requires. Traditional endocrinology, however, still relies on a concept of disease that waits for physical pathology to appear. Also, many of the diagnostic tests that endocrinologists use, particularly thyroid function measures, cannot detect developing gland failure. Following these tests, the patient will be told he or she is "normal," despite mood and behavioral changes.

The psychiatrist who bases his or her own judgment on the standard indices will have to conclude that the patient's mood misery is primary. Out comes the prescription pad. But the antidepressants don't work, and the psychiatrist decides that the patient is a nonresponder. The patient feels guilty and probably quits treatment. If she or he is "lucky," in ten or fifteen years the dysfunction will have developed into full-blown disease, which a doctor at last will diagnose and treat.

Biopsychiatrists are frequently subspecialists in the branch of medicine that combines endocrinology and neurology. Most other psychiatrists today are also learning more about the field of neuroendocrinology. We look at the failing systems on a continuum that is unique to each person. Each stage of organ failure, from subclinical beginning to traditional disease state, is marked by deviations from the hormone level at which the individual functions best. The hormone level may technically fall within a normal range, but if it causes symptoms, it is not normal for *you*.

THE THYROID

Sometimes at conferences I'll be talking about all the tests that can be run on patients with mood problems. Often somebody will ask, "After a drug screen, if you could do only one test, which one would it be?"

I always answer, "The TRH stimulation test. With this test you will find that ten to fifteen percent of the patients you think are depressed have one form or another of thyroid disease that you wouldn't have found otherwise. Thyroid dysfunction is the single most important area of misdiagnosis."

The thyroid lies in the neck, just below the larynx and straddling the windpipe. Every cell in the body, brain cells included, depends on thyroid hormones T3 and T4 to function effectively, because the hormones control their rate of metabolism. Thus, this one gland determines the speed of all chemical reactions involved in consuming oxygen and burning energy in each and every cell. Normal growth and development are possible only if the gland is functioning properly. Mental and physical retardation are the tragic results of thyroid illness in a fetus or young child.

As noted earlier, the thyroid is part of a neuroendocrine minisystem called the hypothalamic-pituitary-thyroid (HPT) axis. The hypothalamus secretes a hormone called thyrotropin-releasing hormone (TRH), which travels to the pituitary and stimulates that gland to release thyroid-stimulating hormone (TSH). TSH in turn acts on the thyroid to promote release of thyroid hormones into general circulation. Levels of thyroid hormone in the blood modulate the pituitary's continued release of TSH. This feedback mechanism ultimately switches off the pituitary.

Things start going wrong when the thyroid goes "off-system," secreting its hormones against pituitary orders. Thyroid dysfunction will result too, if disease strikes elsewhere in the HPT axis.

Inherited defects in the immune system are probably responsible for most thyroid malfunction. Other known causes include iodine deficiency or excess, lithium (a common cause of hypothyroidism), and diseases of other endocrine glands.

Thyroid disease is extremely common, especially among women. Perhaps as many as one woman in fifteen is prone to thyroid problems. Overall, an estimated ten million people in the United States have some form of thyroid dysfunction, whether they know it or not. The only signs may be depression or fatigue.

Thyroid diseases fall into two categories: hypothyroidism, in which the gland slows down and secretes less and less thyroid hormone; and hyperthyroidism, the reverse condition, in which the gland secretes more hormone than is normal for the person. In either case, and at any level of illness, psychiatric symptoms are the rule.

Hypothyroidism: A Tale of Three Patients

It was Ms. A.'s second overdose in six months. She'd swallowed a bottleful of the antidepressants that were supposed to make her feel better. "I tried to commit suicide twice. I guess that means I'm depressed," she told the emergency room staff sardonically. She was angry that they had pumped her out and ruined her attempt. She said to the admitting psychiatrist at the psychiatric hospital to which she was subsequently referred, "I'll probably try again."

No sense trying to convince Ms. A. that she had a good life ahead of her. She was only twenty-seven and held down a responsible executive position with a major corporation. For a year she had been trying to work out her depression in therapy with a psychologist. During the previous nine months she had also been seeing a psychiatrist for medication.

Ms. A.'s depression had appeared out of nowhere. She'd never been this depressed before, and there was no history of mood problems in her family. She had zero energy, she said; she needed far more sleep than she ever had needed before, and nothing gave her pleasure anymore. Although she had always liked to go out and have fun, she had withdrawn from her friends and preferred to stay home nights and weekends. She couldn't pay attention, her memory was awful—what was the use of going on?

Meanwhile, in another city, Mrs. T. was talking suicide, if not yet acting on it. She was in the midst of an awful crisis: Her husband had just announced he was leaving her. When she started talking suicide, her psychiatrist had her admitted to the hospital. Hers seemed as sure a case of depression as anyone ever did see: no energy, daily variation in her mood, problems with concentration and paying attention, no appetite, insomnia, bouts of tearfulness. For six months her depression had regularly been getting worse. And for the last two months her marriage had been on the rocks. Now her husband was leaving her. At only twenty-six years old, Mrs. T. was in bad shape. As she saw it, she was utterly without a future.

At the same time in still another city, a police cruiser received instructions to go to the local Catholic church and take away the "crazy." There they found Ms. U., a well-dressed forty-four-year-old woman, declaring in no uncertain terms that she had the same rights to the church as the priests who ran it. No indeed, she would not leave. The police had to arrest her, but they let her go as soon as she seemed calm. Right back to the church she went and up the winding stone steps to the bell tower. There she rang the church bells, singing out her right to run this church as she wished, denouncing the priests and the religious hierarchy for all to hear.

A trip to the local hospital was next on Ms. U.'s itinerary. The emergency-room personnel noticed her lethargy and puffy face, but they did not have time to finish their physical examination before an orderly from the psychiatric service came to get her. They kept her in the psychiatric ward for twenty-four hours for observation but released her without a formal diagnosis. Ms. U. returned to her own city. Some days later she turned up at the local hospital emergency room, saying she was so tired, so depressed. When she told the staff what she had done when she was away, they quickly transferred her to the psychiatric service with a diagnosis of psychotic depression.

The admitting psychiatrist walked into her room. Ms. U. was sitting on the bed in a very warm room wrapped in a blanket and wearing a scarf and cap. She was cold, she said, and no wonder: Her body temperature was only 96.4 degrees. Her pulse was so slow that the psychiatrist could hardly believe it: 46! Her expression was dull; she was puffy and swollen, her eyelids drooping. She spoke with a raspy, hoarse voice. The psychiatrist could make a diagnosis virtually by looking at her.

Fortunately, all three women, in separate hospitals across the country, had ended up in the care of biopsychiatrists. The correct diagnosis of their "depression" could now be made. Ms. A., Ms. U., and Mrs. T. were all suffering from differing grades of hypothyroidism—symptomatically indistinguishable from major depression. Once the correct tests were administered and the diagnoses made, each woman's condition was treatable with hormone replacement medication.

Ms. U.'s Myxedema Madness

Biopsychiatry has identified three stages of thyroid illness. Ms. U. had stage 1, the full-blown thyroid illness called myxedema; her thyroid had virtually ceased functioning. The symptoms are obvious: puffiness, drooping eyelids, flat expression, sensitivity to cold, raspy voice. Ms. U. was constipated, another typical finding. Her skin was thick and dry, her hair sparse and coarse. Yet, despite all evidence of disease, because she was acting so "crazy," almost everyone jumped to the wrong conclusion. Had she been transferred to a psychiatric hospital for long-term treatment, the diagnosis might have been missed completely.

Ms. U. was suffering from "myxedema madness," which can occur with end-stage hypothyroidism. Her thyroid was swollen (a condition called goiter), her heart was enlarged, her reflexes slow, her menstrual flow heavy. The longer her condition continued, the more she was at risk of heart attack, coma, and death. At this level of illness, all the standard tests—once someone thinks to take them—reveal frank illness. Indeed, Ms. U.'s T4 level was 0.5 mcg/dl; normal is nine to twenty-five times that, ranging from 4.5 to 12.5 mcg/dl.

Signs and Symptoms of
Hypothyroidism and Depression

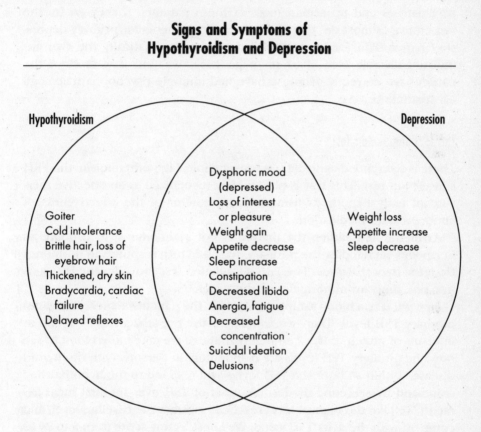

Hypothyroidism

Goiter
Cold intolerance
Brittle hair, loss of
  eyebrow hair
Thickened, dry skin
Bradycardia, cardiac
  failure
Delayed reflexes

Dysphoric mood
  (depressed)
Loss of interest
  or pleasure
Weight gain
Appetite decrease
Sleep increase
Constipation
Decreased libido
Anergia, fatigue
Decreased
  concentration
Suicidal ideation
Delusions

Depression

Weight loss
Appetite increase
Sleep decrease

Ms. A.'s Subclinical Hypothyroidism

Ms. A., although she was actively suicidal, was suffering from stage 3 hypothyroidism, the lowest level of dysfunction. Her thyroid was just beginning to go, and her ferocious depression was the only symptom. We call stage 3 illness chemical, or subclinical, hypothyroidism. Stage 2 is termed mild hypothyroidism and reveals a few other symptoms, such as fatigue, dry skin, constipation, and weight gain. Data suggest that both forms of illness will develop into myxedema if untreated.

Over 90 percent of the patients with hypothyroid depression have stages 3 and 2 illness—neither of which is generally detectable on standard tests. Even the use of the ultrasensitive radioimmunoassays may not detect the earliest and most subtle functional thyroid deficits. Thus, psychiatrists end up seeing most of these patients. If they go by the symptoms, as most do, they will institute treatments for primary depression rather than for hypothyroidism, for symptomatically the two are indistinguishable (see chart on page 135). We find that most of the patients we correctly diagnose have had multiple psychopharmacological treatments.

The TRH Stimulation Test

There is a surefire diagnostic test for subclinical hypothyroidism: the TRH stimulation test. This test is now widely recognized as an effective measure of early hypothyroidism and as predictor of the effectiveness of antidepressant medications.

As mentioned earlier, the thyroid is not autonomous; it responds to hormones secreted by the pituitary, which in turn responds to hormones from the hypothalamus. The TRH stimulation test provokes the HPT axis into revealing any abnormality in the system.

First we take a blood sample to measure the patient's regular (baseline) pituitary TSH level. Then we administer the hypothalamic TRH, and at intervals of fifteen, thirty, and ninety minutes we take more blood to see how the pituitary TSH levels are responding. In persons with no thyroid disease, within an hour the TSH levels will respond to the hypothalamic command by secreting modest amounts of TSH over the first measurement. We take the highest level reached, subtract the baseline level, and come up with the delta TSH value. We consider any score from 5 to 20 as normal.

In subclinical hypothyroid patients, the delta TSH is markedly increased, even though the thyroid hormone is utterly normal. Apparently, in early thyroid failure, the pituitary has become supersensitive to TRH and secretes lots more hormone trying to stimulate the sluggish thyroid to "put out." For the time being it works. But although the thyroid hormone level remains normal via this mechanism, all is not right in the brain.

Ms. A.'s Symptomless Autoimmune Thyroiditis

Ms. A.'s delta TSH score was 27.1. Mrs. T.'s delta score was similar, at 27.3. But that wasn't the end of Mrs. T.'s story. She became a patient of Dr. Ronald Bloodworth, who found antithyroid antibodies in her blood. Diagnosis: subclinical hypothyroidism secondary to symptomless autoimmune thyroiditis (SAT). Her thyroid had begun to fail because her immune system was attacking the gland. The more research we do on this condition, the more common SAT turns out to be. As many as 60 percent of the patients we test have these antibodies.

The whys of SAT are not known. It affects 5 to 15 percent of the general population and is four to eight times more common among women than men. SAT runs in families. It appears most commonly between the ages of thirty and fifty, and may be associated with other diseases, such as anemia, diabetes, allergies, and arthritis.

The treatment for SAT is the same as for other thyroid conditions: thyroid hormone replacement.

When Mrs. T. began to take this medication, she showed gradual and sustained improvement despite the stress of her failed marriage. She continued in psychotherapy and at last was able to become actively involved in it. An endocrinologist took over her treatment for SAT.

Hyperthyroidism

In hypothyroidism the metabolic rate gets slower and slower as the gland fails. In hyperthyroidism, as the gland secretes excess hormone, the metabolic rate is correspondingly speeded up.

Consequently, hyperthyroid individuals are often restless and have to keep moving around. They can't pay attention for long. Neither can they sleep. They are hungrier than usual, but they may lose weight. Physically, too much thyroid hormone can cause abundant sweating, heat sensitivity, tremor, fatigue, skin that is soft and moist, heart palpitations, frequent bowel movements, muscular weakness, and protruding eyeballs. Women have scant periods. In men, swelling of tissue of one or both breasts (gynecomastia) may occur.

A hyperthyroid person will feel anxious, jittery, and irritable, and may have frequent mood swings and emotional explosions. At its emotional worst, the condition is often misdiagnosed as mania or psychosis.

Depression occurs in hyperthyroidism too, and can substantially worsen a life-events depression.

Dr. John J. Schwab had a patient consult him for depression. He turned out to have Graves' disease, a form of hyperthyroidism. The man was thirty-six, a successful and well-to-do accountant. During the first visit he told Dr. Schwab that he no longer felt pleasure or gratification in any area of his life. He was afraid that his gloom and despondency might increase to the point where he would harm himself. He worried about his marriage and his work. He had been married ten years and had three young children. Although he cared for his family, he had become increasingly irritable with them and they just weren't getting along. At work he had begun to pass on the more challenging work to his partner.

"During the last six months," reported Dr. Schwab, "he had had difficulties with sleeping, especially with frequent awakening, a loss of energy, diminished interest in sexual activity, and some increase in appetite. Prominent mental symptoms were difficulty with concentration, distractibility, and pessimism."

During the second visit, he continued to talk about how depressed he was and when it all had started. The alert psychiatrist noticed that his patient had a fine tremor of the hands and fingers. He denied any history of alcoholism and of tremor in the family. Also, he admitted to perspiring excessively for six to nine months, to some heat intolerance, and to a feeling of muscular weakness.

Subsequent physical examination and testing revealed the existence of hyperthyroidism. The most common treatment, radiation with radioactive iodine, worked. "Many of the symptoms of depression have lessened considerably," reports Dr. Schwab, "and he has begun to enter actively into therapy in order to resolve the conflicts that have imperiled his marriage. He has not needed antidepressant medication."

Because hyperthyroidism is far less common a mimicker than hypothyroidism, we have not yet studied it as deeply. We have reason to believe, however, that it too can be understood on a continuum of malfunction, from subclinical to mild to overt illness. Recently a form of disease called silent thyroiditis has been identified. It consists of a mild hyperthyroid condition lasting weeks to months, often followed by a brief bout of hypothyroidism. Then the thyroid function returns to normal.

Untreated, severe hyperthyroidism can lead to thyroid storm, which can be fatal. It comes on abruptly, often preceded by a physical stress such as surgery, diabetic shock, or toxemia of pregnancy. However, severe fright can bring it on as well, as can sudden discontinuance of hyperthyroid medication. Thyroid storm is marked by fever, severe weakness, muscle wasting, extreme emotionality and restlessness, confusion, psychosis, swollen liver, cardiovascular collapse, and shock. Even with treat-

---

A Paradox

Administer the TRH stimulation test to a hyperthyroid individual, and the resulting delta scores will be below average. In other words, stimulate the pituitary to produce thyroid-stimulating hormone, and it will secrete very little, because the thyroid is independently putting out so much on its own.

Now give the same test to a biologically depressed person who has no thyroid disease and what will you find? Twenty-five percent of depressed people will show a *low* delta TSH score, as if the person were *hyper*thyroid! This result occurs so consistently that it has become a biological marker for the existence of depression as well as a predictor of response to treatment.

This finding seems to make no sense. It's the *hypo*thyroid people who characteristically are depressed. Why does it happen? You'll find the answer (or at least the theory) in upcoming chapters.

---

ment, one-fourth of patients die. Like hypothyroidism, hyperthyroidism appears to be a genetic autoimmune disorder. It too is most common among women, especially those between the ages of 20 and 40.

CELL SELF-HATRED?

We've been talking about thyroid illness as autoimmune—the body mobilizing to fight off its own tissue, as if it were a foreign invader. An important area of medicine explores the question, Why does the system fail? For the body to attack its own cells is the ultimate in self-hatred. Could depression have anything to do with it? Research is providing some surprising answers. Stay tuned.

THE ADRENAL GLANDS

In talking about the adrenals we introduce a second neuroendocrine axis that is central to mood regulation: the hypothalamic-pituitary-adrenal (HPA) axis. While diseases of the adrenals are less common mimickers than thyroid malfunction, they too develop along a continuum. Emotional and behavioral symptoms occur earliest, and only the psychiatrist with a nose for medical causation is likely to differentiate adrenal dysfunction from primary psychiatric states.

Diseases of the adrenals can be extremely serious, and waiting to diagnose them until they develop fully can be dangerous—as witness the near-death of the man with Addison's disease we discussed back in Chapter 3; until he came to me, all the doctors he consulted were convinced his depression was caused by the recent accidental death of his wife.

What They Do and How They Do It

Each of the two adrenal glands, perched atop the kidneys, is two separate glands in one: the adrenal cortex and the adrenal medulla. The hormones secreted by the cortex are called *corticoids* or *corticosteroids*. Among them are aldosterone, which increases sodium and decreases potassium in the blood; androgens, male sex hormones (which are also present in women, although at lesser levels); and a number of hormones called glucocorticoids. Glucocorticoids help maintain blood sugar at appropriate levels; they play a role in blood pressure, reduce inflammation, and help fight infection, allergy, and stress. Cortisol, or hydrocortisone, is a major hormone in this category—and one in which psychiatry is extremely interested (see below). Some steroid medications such as prednisone and cortisone, are chemically related to adrenal hormones. That steroids are themselves potent mimickers is not surprising.

The hormones produced by the adrenal medulla are the catecholamines, epinephrine and norepinephrine. These are the "fight or flight" hormones released by the adrenal glands under stress. These hormones also exist in the brain, where they are among the most significant neurotransmitters in depression. They instruct the hypothalamus to secrete the releasing factors that control pituitary function and that control the cortex of the adrenal glands. (Specifically, hypothalamic corticoreleasing factor, or CRF, stimulates the pituitary to release ACTH, which triggers the hormones of the cortex.) The adrenal medulla is triggered directly by the nervous system as well as by some of the cortical hormones.

Several new studies have confirmed that patients whose adrenal glands are enlarged—a condition known as adrenocorticohypertrophy—are more likely to suffer from depression. More important, postmortem studies of suicide victims often reveal enlarged adrenal glands. This condition is also considered a marker for repeated bouts of depression and may be useful in predicting relapse. A variety of tests can identify those whose adrenal systems are out of whack. So not only are there CRF, ACTH, and cortisol changes seen in blood, but the glands themselves are abnormal in depression.

Addison's Disease

President John F. Kennedy suffered from this rare disease, in which the adrenal cortex progressively fails. Tuberculosis used to be the major cause of Addison's. Now, however, in the large majority of cases the gland atrophies for no known reason. Addison's may not be detected or diagnosed until severe stress causes an Addisonian crisis. However, symptoms of depression and emotional instability may have existed for a long time. Dr. Richard Hall mentions that "mental changes are common [in Addison's], occurring in 64 percent to 84 percent of the cases, and may vary from mild neurotic traits to gross psychosis. The most frequent mental changes are mild disturbances in the level of consciousness, manifested as apathy, somnolence, insomnia, and dulling of intellect. These disturbances are fluctuating and episodic. Most observers report apathetic or depressive moods, poverty of thought, and lack of initiative."

Weakness, fatigue, shortness of breath, and low blood pressure are other early signs. Skin usually becomes darker and black freckles may appear. Loss of appetite, nausea, vomiting, dizziness, sensitivity to cold, and hypoglycemia (low blood sugar) are possibilities. In later stages, resistance to infection and stress is lowered. Addisonian crisis is marked by severe pain in the legs, belly, or lower back, plus collapse of blood vessels and kidneys. Without treatment, death will follow. Treatment with steroid medications brings a return to normal functioning.

Cushing's Syndrome/Disease

Cushing's *syndrome,* the reverse of Addison's disease, is overactivity of the adrenal cortex, usually as a result of adrenal tumors or ACTH-secreting tumors elsewhere in the body (as in some lung cancers). Cushing's *disease* refers to overproduction of pituitary ACTH, to which the adrenals are overresponding. The disease represents two-thirds of all Cushing's cases; most victims are women of child-bearing age. In both types, the disease and the syndrome, behavior is affected in as high as 90 percent of cases. Depression is the most commonly mentioned symptom; euphoria, anxiety, and psychosis complete the list.

Physical signs of Cushing's include a moon-faced appearance, weight gain, purple stripes on the belly, and accumulations of fat in pads ("buffalo hump"). Wounds heal poorly, and bruising is common. High blood pressure, kidney stones, muscle wasting, bone weakness (osteoporosis), acne, and diabetes occur frequently, as do menstrual irregularities and excessive hairiness in women.

Frequently, however, none of these symptoms occur, and the only indications of malfunction are periodic behavioral symptoms plus increased cortisol secretions—which earn Cushing's sufferers beds in psychiatric wards, since these symptoms are typical of major depression. Clearly there are subclinical forms of this adrenal malfunction.

Treatment is surgery, radiation, or drugs, depending on the cause.

Cushing's Test for Depression?

The dexamethasone suppression test (DST), highly touted as the diagnostic test for biological depression, was first developed to discover the excess secretion of cortisol in Cushing's. Then one day not so long ago we discovered that many biologically depressed people also secrete excess cortisol. As a matter of fact, nearly all of the HPA abnormalities arising in Cushing's syndrome can occur in patients with a primary psychiatric disorder.

Pheochromocytoma

Pheochromocytomas are tiny tumors, generally benign, that form on the adrenal medulla (although occasionally they occur in other areas of the body) and that secrete catecholamines. They can occur at any age but are most common between five and twenty-five. High blood pressure is the most significant physical sign; it may be constant or it may occur only during attacks.

Emotional stress, abdominal massage, standing up or sitting down, anesthesia, laughing, sleeping, sexual intercourse, shaving, gargling, straining during a bowel movement, sneezing, hyperventilating, urinating, pregnancy in young women—all these have been known to provoke acute attacks in vulnerable individuals. Headache, perspiration, and palpitations often characterize attacks. Nausea, weakness, nervousness, chest pain, difficulty breathing, tingling and other strange feelings in the arms and legs, tightness in the throat, dizziness, and faintness have also been reported. From headache to faintness, the list of symptoms is consistent with a panic attack; during pheochromocytoma attacks, the anxiety may be so intense that it produces acute temporary psychosis. Add to this the fact that symptoms other than the possibly chronic hypertension show up only during attacks, and pheochromocytoma's place among the mimickers is assured. The tumors have also been noted to produce severe chronic depression and depressive psychoses.

The disease is frequently associated with a familial tendency to multiple benign endocrine tumors. Surgical removal cures pheochromocytomas 90 percent of the time.

THE PITUITARY

Deep inside the brain is this tiny blockbuster of a gland. It influences a number of metabolic processes essential to growth and development, and maintains the functioning of other endocrine glands.

Attached by a kind of stalk to the hypothalamus, the pituitary, like the adrenals, is two glands in one. The anterior pituitary alone secretes six major hormones and some minor ones, each triggered by hypothalamic hormones. Four of the most important anterior pituitary hormones stimulate other endocrine glands to perform their various functions. These include thyroid-secreting hormone (TSH); adrenocorticotropic hormone (ACTH), which stimulates the adrenal cortex; follicle-stimulating hormone (FSH); and luteinizing hormone (LH). In women, both FSH and LH are involved in ovulation. In men, LH is called interstitial cell-stimulating hormone (ICSH), and it stimulates the testicles to secrete testosterone. The other two hormones of the anterior pituitary include growth hormone (GH), a metabolic hormone that regulates growth in children, and possibly controls healing and tissue repair in adults; and prolactin (PRL), which in women stimulates the growth of breasts during pregnancy and lactation afterward.

The posterior pituitary releases two hormones that are not really pituitary hormones at all. They are manufactured in the hypothalamus and are simply stored in and released by the pituitary. They are oxytocin, which causes labor contractions, and vasopressin (also called antidiuretic hormone, or ADH), which stimulates the kidneys to reabsorb water.

What with all the hormones flowing to and through this gland, and its direct involvement with the hypothalamus and limbic system, anything that goes wrong with the pituitary is bound to affect mental life. Accordingly, since most of the body's hormones seem to be controlled by the same neurotransmitters that we believe are involved in mood disorders, the functioning of the pituitary and its client glands may well provide a window into the brains of depressed people. Many of our neuroendocrine tests for depression do indeed measure fluctuations in pituitary hormone output.

Recently, magnetic resonance imaging (MRI) has been used to show active disease in the brain of depressed patients. MRIs clearly show that enlargement of the pituitary gland due to hypersecretion can provoke depression and vice versa.

Panhypopituitarism

This condition is a general slowing of the anterior pituitary, often due to a tumor or some other space-occupying mass in the brain or to damage to the gland from a disease or a burst vessel. Symptoms encompass those of the endocrine glands, which are affected. Mental symptoms are present at least 70 percent of the time, usually beginning with depression and lack of sex drive. When the disease comes on suddenly, it is likely to be diagnosed properly. But when it develops slowly, misdiagnosis is common. Besides depression, panhypopituitarism commonly mimics anorexia nervosa.

As the illness progresses, infertility, decreased secondary sex characteristics, hypoglycemia, hypothyroidism, hypotension, low stress tolerance, and susceptibility to infection may arise if the disease is not caught in time.

Panhypopituitarism is treated by replacing the hormones of the target glands, which can no longer function in the absence of pituitary control. Often the gland must also be surgically removed.

Acromegaly

Acromegaly refers to pituitary oversecretion of growth hormone in adults. In children the excess hormone leads to pituitary gigantism and growth to a height of more than seven or eight feet.

In acromegaly the bones begin to enlarge. Face, hands, and feet particularly are affected, changing the person's appearance completely and unpleasantly. "Little attention has been paid to the psychiatric aspects of acromegaly," says Dr. Richard Hall. "Although it generally does not produce a psychosis, it is regularly accompanied by alterations of personality such as decreased initiative and spontaneity, and mood change."

Pituitary adenomas (benign tumors) are likely to produce this condition; excessive secretion of hypothalamic hormones may also be a factor. Such growth does not happen overnight. Once again, mental symptoms may be important clues. Surgery or radiation is the usual treatment.

Hyponatremia

If the posterior pituitary releases excessive vasopressin (ADH), then too much water is reabsorbed by the kidneys and delivered into the blood. The blood becomes too dilute, which decreases the salt concentration and leads to hyponatremia. This condition may not reveal itself clinically, but it may well trigger delusional depression. Psychiatric researchers have dis-

covered cases of people who had frequently been hospitalized with delusional depression but who in fact were hyponatremic. Fluid restriction
and a high-sodium diet substantially cleared up their symptoms.

DIABETES MELLITUS

You'll need a microscope to spot the groups of cells called the islets of
Langerhans on the pancreas. These cells, discovered by Paul Langerhans,
secrete the hormones glucagon and insulin. Glucagon helps liver cells
convert a substance called glycogen into glucose. Insulin helps transport
the glucose out of the blood and into cells, where it is used as fuel, or back
to the liver, where it is stored as glycogen.

When the islets of Langerhans underproduce insulin, or when the body
cannot use it, glucose continues to accumulate in the blood and the tissues
cannot get at it. Diabetes mellitus is the result. There are at least five forms
of the disease.

Type I diabetes, usually called insulin-dependent diabetes, most often
occurs in persons under thirty. The islet cells in these people do not
produce adequate insulin, and they must take replacement hormone for
the rest of their lives. Complications include kidney failure, stroke, blindness, or loss of the use of limbs. This is the most severe form of diabetes,
affecting about half a million persons in the United States and causing over
48,000 deaths each year.

Evidence is beginning to accumulate that type I diabetes is an autoimmune disease in which the body attacks its own insulin-secreting cells.
Research in this area also reveals that often the antibodies are present long
before the disease becomes manifest. Treatment with drugs that inhibit
the immune system has met with varying success. The key seems to be to
catch the disease before it becomes symptomatic. The best way to do that,
researchers have learned, is to screen children for the presence of the
damaging antibody. Type I diabetics have a genetic tendency to the disease, which may be triggered by a virus or some other unknown cause.

Type II diabetes, non-insulin-dependent, usually occurs in persons over
the age of thirty. Perhaps as many as nine to ten million people have this
form, although they have not necessarily been diagnosed. Many of them
are obese at the time of diagnosis or have a history of obesity. Type II
diabetics usually have a combination of insulin deficiency and inability to
use insulin. Weight loss, controlled diet, and, if necessary, antidiabetic
drugs can improve both aspects markedly. Type II becomes more common with increasing age.

Diabetes can also occur secondary to other conditions, such as pancreatic disease or Cushing's. A fourth type occurs during or after pregnancy and usually disappears spontaneously. Women who have gestational diabetes tend to develop type II diabetes.

The final variety is impaired glucose tolerance, or subclinical diabetes. Excessive thirst, urination, and hunger with weight loss are classic symptoms. Weakness, lethargy, itching, boils, fungus-type vaginal infections, blurred vision problems, slow healing, and easy bruising are among the symptoms of manifest disease. Complaints of tiredness, low energy, and altered appetite, even blurred vision, will signal depression in the absence of gross physical signs. And, in true endocrinological style, diabetes causes its share of serious emotional symptoms. Patients who have diabetes often meet all the criteria for major depression, schizophrenia, and personality disorders. One researcher has noted that undiagnosed diabetics may appear for psychiatric consultation because of impotence and marital problems.

If one day testing for the autoimmune type of diabetes enables us to prevent the disease, it will be interesting to see how many depressed people will "miraculously" be cured.

Recent studies show clearly that diabetics are several times more likely to suffer from depression compared to the rest of the population. It is not known, though, whether people with diabetes suffer from depression more frequently than those with other chronic illnesses. But it is clear from these reports that diabetes can be a mimicker of depression. Diabetics also suffer from the reduced neurotransmitter functions that are associated with depression, and this link may give us some further tools to make a proper diagnosis in diabetics with ambiguous symptoms.

HYPOGLYCEMIA

A fifty-five-year-old woman appeared in a hospital emergency room and started taking off her clothes in the waiting area. Clearly a psych case, concluded the nurses, who summoned a psychiatrist. In another emergency setting, a forty-five-year-old man was labeled drunk and crazy, and the staff ignored him. A thirty-nine-year-old man was lying on a New York street babbling and looking wild-eyed. Inured to drunks and street people, pedestrians walked around or over him on their way to work. It made no difference that he was well dressed, wearing a suit and tie.

These "drunks" or "crazies" were all insulin-dependent diabetics who had taken too much insulin and were suffering hypoglycemic reactions; now they had too little glucose in their blood.

Hypoglycemia can produce bizarre behavior that in appearance is indistinguishable from schizophrenia, depression, dementia, or anxiety attacks. In less severe states, the person may appear drunk, with slurred speech, an unsteady walk, and some confusion. In chronic, undiagnosed conditions, changes in personality, occasional attacks of paranoid psychosis, and progressive deterioration resulting in dementia may ultimately be irreversible.

Physically, depending on the cause, faintness, weakness, hunger, shakiness, nervousness, headache, and visual problems can progress to palsy, loss of consciousness, convulsions, and coma.

Many conditions can cause hypoglycemia, including insulin-secreting tumors of the pancreas or overdose of insulin in diabetics. Early mild diabetes may cause so-called reactive hypoglycemia, which strikes a few hours after a meal rich in carbohydrates. It can happen for no apparent reason, however, in which case it is termed *functional.* Fasting hypoglycemia, usually quite mild, is familiar to many people who have missed a meal. If severe, however, it may signify underlying illness and should be checked out. Eating carbohydrates will take away the immediate symptoms, but the control of the condition depends, of course, on the cause.

Just don't tell your psychiatrist that you think you have hypoglycemia—he'll think you really are crazy. A few years ago hypoglycemia was a fad diagnosis—everybody, especially women, had it. As a result, now nobody has it.

Nevertheless, the psychiatrist should not overlook mild or subacute forms of hypoglycemia in his or her patients. Standards for its diagnosis are far more strict than in the days of overdiagnosis, and the diagnosis can now be made with confidence.

THE PARATHYROIDS

Four tiny parathyroid glands lie behind the thyroid. They secrete parathyroid hormone, which increases blood concentration of calcium. The body is extremely sensitive to changes in calcium concentration: too little (hypocalcemia) causes muscles to go into spasm and the mind into depression, dementia, or psychosis; too much (hypercalcemia) leads to severe emotional disturbance and heart malfunction. These conditions result primarily from the undersecretion or oversecretion, respectively, of parathyroid hormone. The alert physician can predict a person's mood on the basis of his or her calcium level. Details of the effects of hypercalcemia, the far more common condition, are discussed on page 117.

Hyperparathyroidism is usually caused by benign tumors, sometimes by cancer. Surgery is the usual treatment; but the surgeon often removes the parathyroids too, sometimes inadvertently. The result can be hypo-parathyroidism.

THE SEX GLANDS

Last—but no one would say least—are the male and female sex glands and their hormones. The female sex glands are the two ovaries, each of which contains two endocrine structures. The ovarian follicles secrete estrogens, and the corpus luteum secretes progesterone as well as estrogens. The hypothalamus and pituitary control the timing of these hormones in menstrual and reproductive behavior.

Also under hypothalamic-pituitary control are the endocrine interstitial cells within the testes of the male. The more ICSH from the pituitary, the more testosterone is secreted. When testosterone reaches a high blood concentration, it signals the pituitary to stop releasing ICSH.

Unfortunately, little systematic research has been conducted on the possible psychiatric presentations of sexual hormone abnormalities. To judge from how bizarrely we can behave under the influence of normal sex-hormone secretions, surely abnormalities of the sex glands are bound to be trouble!

Estrogens and progesterone have been given to women to influence mood states encountered during menopause and during premenstrual syndrome (PMS). Estrogen makes some women less depressed and other women more depressed. We'll talk more about this when we tackle PMS and postpartum depression in Chapter 25.

One of the cases I am most proud of concerned a woman in her mid-thirties whom I'll call Susan. Susan, a Ph.D. biochemist, was referred to me for severe depression. She felt completely overwhelmed and had isolated herself in her home. This was the second time she had had such a crisis. The first was in 1976, while she was in graduate school and could not tackle her dissertation. At the time a psychiatrist gave her a very small amount of antidepressant medication. It had no effect. Susan gave up and quit the therapy, and eventually she came out of her depression. She had been in and out of therapy for milder depressions several times since.

Susan's father was a psychologist and her brother was a gynecologist with an endocrinological subspecialty. What's more, Susan was referred to me by a very close friend of mine in another city. The pressure was really on to do something.

Susan's father and brother were very concerned about her. Her dad believed that her present episode had to do with Susan's recent promotion at the drug company for which she worked. Her brother was worried that she was going to blow a great career.

I began to take her history. While we were talking about her two major bouts of depression, Susan mentioned, "You know, making matters even worse, both times I got very hairy. My legs got hairy—so did my thighs, and particularly my face. Ugh!"

Unusual growth of hair—hirsutism—is an endocrine problem. Immediately I had Susan doing temperature charts to find out if she was ovulating. She wasn't. At first I thought she might be overproducing adrenal androgens, male hormones that females also have. But her level was normal. When I checked her pituitary-stimulating hormones, I confirmed this finding.

The other common cause for female hirsutism is polycystic ovaries, which would also be consistent with lack of ovulation. But here Susan threw me a curve ball. She said she'd had an abortion. That didn't fit with polycystic ovaries, because if she hadn't ovulated, she could hardly have become pregnant. Susan said she had been sexually inactive at the time and couldn't imagine how she could have become pregnant. But she had missed her period and had all the signs of apparent pregnancy; the hospital where she went for the abortion tested her hormones and her progesterone was high enough for pregnancy. Then she told us that they hadn't found a fetus.

We sent for the pathology report; sure enough, no fetus. The doctors believed that she had what is called an exuberant growth of the uterus, overstimulated by hormones. This too is consistent with polycystic ovaries.

A diagnostic procedure confirmed the existence of polycystic ovary disease in our "psychiatric" patient. But when Susan filed a claim for insurance reimbursement, her insurance company wanted to send me for peer review (a hearing before other doctors). Susan had been in therapy for twelve years with a depression that came and went but always came back again—a dozen years of psychotherapy at a cost to her insurance company of thousands and thousands of dollars. During all this time no one had asked for a peer review to analyze her doctors' treatment of her. I agreed to the review, but I insisted that these peers be psychiatrists who knew something about medicine, because this patient did not have a psychiatric diagnosis.

No peer review proved necessary. I had diagnosed in our patient a condition that had been missed probably her whole adult life. The insurance company saw the light. The best news is, Susan's all right.

PART III

DEPRESSION
IS . . .

CHAPTER 10

Of Depression and Elephants

In the previous sections of this book, we examined what medicine has learned about diagnosing depression over the last decade. We also discussed the conditions that resemble—but that are not—depression. And in the next section we'll look at the phenomenal advances in treatment, and how these advances may actually change the way we define depression. But in between what it is not and how it is treated are the most intriguing questions of all: What is depression? What causes it and how do we diagnose it properly?

For many years now, biopsychiatrists, neuroanatomists, and psychopharmacologists have been deeply involved in research, hoping to unlock the secrets of the origin of depression. Today depression is the most widely studied of all psychiatric illnesses. This past decade has seen a quantum leap forward in our knowledge of the brain and the complex inner workings of the mind and body.

But the answers still are not complete. For one thing, the more we learn about the brain's function, the more we find to study. As James Watson, the Nobel laureate who helped unlock the secrets of DNA, has said, "The brain is the most complex thing we have yet discovered in our universe." One good example of this complexity is the lack of success we've had trying to replicate human intelligence with computers. While there are some promising starts, many brain researchers doubt whether we'll ever be able to re-create the millions of neuronal pathways in the brain that carry chemical messages, adapt to changes in the environment, and keep us alive each day. Can we really hope to duplicate this system on a sliver of silicon?

Probably not. But if we can understand some of the brain's biochemical functions, we may be able to create treatments that target specific psychiatric illnesses, from panic attacks to drug addiction, freeing millions from unnecessary suffering. Unraveling the mysteries of how the brain works is perhaps the greatest frontier in science. As you will see in Part IV of this book, understanding the role of neurotransmitters—the brain's chemical messengers—is the leading edge of this research.

Genetics is the other great medical frontier. A few years ago, researchers claimed they had identified a specific gene for bipolar illness (manic-depression). Unfortunately, it did not turn out to be true. According to Dr. Miron Baron, of the New York State Psychiatric Institute at Columbia University, who studied the single-gene theory extensively, "We know that there is no single major gene for psychiatric illness. The model of three or four or five interacting genes operating in tandem to produce an illness is becoming more and more appealing."

Over the past decades, many studies of fraternal and identical twins lend support to the theory that a predisposition to various forms of depression exists in families. Such research will in turn lead to early detection and more treatments for major mental illness. So part of the good news is that biopsychiatrists and other researchers have not only embarked on a search for better medications, but, in fact, are deeply involved in a search for what causes depression—what depression *is*.

Here's a quick quiz. How would you answer?

Is depression:

a. a normal part of life?
b. a psychological problem?
c. a symptom of medical and/or psychiatric illness?
d. an illness in itself?
e. several possible illnesses?

The answer you get depends on who's talking. *Depression* is still a term with many seemingly contradictory meanings. To the individual who is aware of being depressed (and not everyone is), it signifies a miserable, subjective personal experience. When one friend says to another, "I'm so depressed," they both understand that "ugh" feeling upon which the statement is based.

But professionals who study depression and work with patients who suffer from it aren't yet able to agree on a definition so readily. Depression is a psychological reaction to early life experience, says one. Depression is the unavoidable reaction to oppressive social conditions, says another. You're all wrong, says a third: Depression is a learned behavioral style. No way, says a fourth: Depression is a biochemical disorder, entirely physiological. A fifth professional will insist that depression is an expression of a genetically determined behavioral trait.

It reminds me of the story of the blind men and the elephant. Four blind men encounter an elephant. They seek to understand this impressive phenomenon. The first man feels the tusk and thoughtfully concludes that an elephant is a kind of spear. The second man explores the elephant's legs and decides it is a tree, while the third man, at the tail, insists it's a rope. The fourth man tells his friends that this thing is a snake; moving back from the trunk, he cautions the three to take care.

Their answers obviously depend on which part of the elephant each man has experienced. The blind men have each discovered valid aspects of elephantness. Now they require not sight but insight into what all their data mean. They need to step back, gather all of the information they have, and create the big picture. Each aspect of the elephant, while significant, is but a part of a greater entity. Many animals have tails and legs, and some even have tusks. All of those individual features combine to make this specific animal what it is.

Similarly, my professional colleagues, past and present, are correct in what they have discovered about depression. The answer to the above quiz is: All the above—and then some.

Here's What We Are Sure of Today

Depression is a condition of the mind. It is a physical affliction. It is environmentally induced. It is a genetic tendency. It is learned. It is a "biological clock" disorder. It is many separate biochemical illnesses.

According to C. Robert Cloninger, M.D., a professor of both psychiatry and genetics at the Washington University School of Medicine in St. Louis, studies of twins who have depression indicate that life events, social supports, personality, and unspecified genetic factors show that various risk factors can interact to provoke depression. Dr. Cloninger points out that in the past a recent stressful life event was a predictor of high risk for depression. "However," he writes, "we really still do not know whether a report of stressful life events around the time of a depression is a *cause* or a *consequence* of depression" (emphasis added).

In science we are all blind. Therefore the best way to comprehend depression is first to approach it as if it were an elephant—to encounter all its many features and dimensions. Facts and facets will build upon one another as the chapters proceed; by the end of this section, we will perhaps have imagined the very nature of this most oppressive beast.

The good news today is that we know more about what the whole elephant looks like, and we can usually tell when the circus is in town.

DEPRESSION IS ALSO A FACT

Depression is the most common adult psychiatric disorder. Ten to 25 percent of us will experience an episode of depression at some time in our lives—5 to 6 percent of us are in the throes of one right now. It is estimated that 50 percent of people who have had one bout with depression will probably have others. Depression is believed to be on the rise worldwide, and is perhaps even epidemic. In the United States alone, mood disorders (depression and bipolar illness) currently affect nine to sixteen million people. The rate of suicide among bipolar and depressed people ranges from 15 to 20 percent!

No one, rich or poor, white or yellow or brown or black, famous or unknown, infant or ancient, is immune to the mental and physical ravages of depression.

Depressive illness disrupts the lives of sufferers and their families. Whether or not they go for help—and more than two out of three will not—their illness will exact a heavy toll. Overall, the illness of depression costs this country $7 to $10 billion every year. According to a 1985 special

---

U.S. President: "I Am Now the Most Miserable Man Living."

He continued, "If what I feel were equally distributed to the whole human family, there would not be one cheerful face on earth. Whether I shall ever be better, I cannot tell; I awfully forebode I shall not. To remain as I am is impossible. I must die or be better, it appears to me."

These words belong to Abraham Lincoln, who was plagued with severe bouts of depression, complete with headaches and profound fatigue.

"He was a sad-looking man; his melancholy dripped from him as he walked," wrote his former law partner, W. H. Herndon. So depressed was Lincoln the January day in 1841 on which he was supposed to marry Mary Todd that he did not appear at the ceremony. Alarmed, his friends went searching for him. They found him walking by himself, desperately depressed. Afraid he would kill himself, they instituted a suicide watch over him. Abe and Mary eventually married, presumably on a more cheerful day.

report from the Institute of Medicine, "The affective [mood] disorders . . . are probably the most destructive group of mental illnesses in the United States in terms of prevalence, mortality, economic cost, and impact on families." Affective illness is the third most commonly diagnosed condition in the United States, following cardiovascular disease and musculoskeletal disease.

Depressive illness is the most common cause of psychiatric hospitalization. It is the bread and butter of a psychiatrist's practice. Family and internal physicians see even more of it than do psychiatrists or psychologists, and they write most of the prescriptions for antidepressant medication.

Bipolar illness tends to show up first when people are in their twenties, although about a third of cases emerge during adolescence. The age of onset of unipolar depression is less easy to pinpoint, probably because the depressive syndrome represents many separate subtypes. Most cases appear from the late thirties to early forties, although depression can appear at any age from childhood to old age. In women the illness may occur somewhat earlier. The first episode of unipolar depression may in fact go undiagnosed, since it often appears as a masked condition or is dismissed as "just" a reaction to a life difficulty. Earlier-onset depressions are now believed to be bipolar II depressions (see next chapter).

Mood disorders are the most common psychological problems among college students. One out of three college students will have experienced a unipolar or bipolar episode by the time he or she has graduated. In the freshman year alone, one out of five experiences depression or manic-depression.

MORE STATISTICS

While depression is usually precipitated by a life event, its severity and course may be unrelated to the reality of that situation. In 80 to 85 percent of all cases, the episode will abate within six to nine months whether or not the illness is treated and no matter what triggered it.

It will also recur, treated or untreated. Seventy to 90 percent of people who endure one episode of severe depression can expect to go through it again at least once. Four recurrences is the lifetime median. Months, years, or decades with or without related symptoms can pass between episodes. The risk of recurrence is said to be greatest within four to six months after initial symptoms pass. (Unfortunately, most studies use remission of symptoms as a measure of recovery. But symptoms provide no indication that the internal biological condition has abated.)

Episodes of bipolar disorder recur far more frequently; the median number is ten. However, for the majority of people, lithium treatment will reduce the number of recurrences by half; for as many as 30 percent, it will put a halt to all future episodes.

Even though the symptoms of severe depression will most likely disappear in time, we treat it so that it will lift as quickly as possible. The longer an episode of depression continues, the greater the risk of the illness becoming chronic.

In a chronic course, symptoms do not go away; they fluctuate between more intense and less intense. Inadequate treatment will assure this result as certainly as no treatment at all. A panel convened by the National Institutes of Health (NIH) recently concluded that recurrent mood disorders are both underdiagnosed and undertreated. Other factors that appear to predict depression taking a chronic course are preexisting alcoholism, older age at onset, minor depression, other psychiatric disorders, and low income. ("The substantial association between lower family income and a more pernicious course seems all too familiar, and serves as a reminder that many powerful factors influencing the course of illness are not susceptible to the clinician's art and science," report the authors of one study.)

EPIDEMIOLOGY TO THE RESCUE

Doctors treat disease in individual patients. No disease strikes just one person, of course, and any disease will be expressed differently in each individual. Epidemiologists are public-health specialists who contribute to the understanding of disease by studying its expression within the population as a whole. Does a disease strike uniformly throughout the country, the world? Or are there geographical areas in which it is more prevalent? If so, what are the factors that contribute to the isolated outbreaks? Does the disease strike equally among men and women and adults and children? Does it have similar manifestations in each age group? How is the disease transmitted? Does it appear in families? What factors or characteristics seem to favor the appearance of this disease? Other than the disease itself, do persons with the disease have anything in common? For example, can they trace their ancestry to one area of the world? Or do they also have any other illness? Are identical twins affected similarly?

In other words, epidemiologists unearth the incidence, distribution, and variations within the population of illness and health problems. In doing so they detect the factors that most influence its expression within the population or group: social, economic, genetic, environmental, psychological, medical, and so forth. They also evaluate diagnostic criteria and treatment effectiveness. Ultimately epidemiologists trace patterns of disease and identify vulnerability factors and risks. Knowing how the disease behaves within the larger population, a physician can see the patient's reported symptoms and examination findings in a sufficiently broad context to make a diagnosis. This holds true as well in mental illness. Epidemiology supplies many of the missing pieces that allow the puzzle to begin to reveal a clear picture.

Elicited during the history, or in an interview with the family, an epidemiological finding can often clarify an otherwise iffy diagnosis. For instance, let's say that you, as a doctor, do not know whether a patient's depression is symptomatic of bipolar or unipolar illness. You find out that the first significant depression occurred in the patient's early twenties and that since then there have been at least three recurrences a year. Epidemiology has shown this to be a bipolar II pattern, so you begin to lean in this direction.

Biopsychiatrists and epidemiologists work hand in hand, often to correct flaws of an earlier era. Among these have been the notion that research among hospitalized populations can tell us all we need to know about the vastly larger number of people on the outside, most of whom have never even sought help for their depressions. Today, ambitious studies of larger community populations are shedding new light on old ideas. The chapters that follow discuss the new understanding of depression in greater detail.

COURSE OF ILLNESS

Some forms of depression are self-limiting. By that I mean they will go away by themselves, without treatment, after a period of time. According to the DSM-IV, an episode of major depression typically lasts six months or longer, regardless of the person's age when the episode begins. In most cases symptoms vanish entirely. But for perhaps three out of ten people, symptoms may persist for months or even years. If people in this group experience a subsequent bout of depression, this same pattern is likely to repeat itself: severe depression that continues causing misery for a very long time. In about two-thirds of cases, people with a major depressive disorder (recurring episodes of depression) may recover completely and enjoy months or years of normal mood before the next depression strikes. About one in three people with this diagnosis, however, never recover completely. They don't quite reach the plateau of normal feeling before they are plunged into darkness again.

Episodes of mania typically begin suddenly; if untreated, the symptoms escalate rapidly over a few days. The manic phase is usually shorter than the depressed phase, in most people lasting for a few weeks to several months. Mania ends more abruptly than depression, which often lifts only after six months or more pass.

Some people reading the above paragraphs may think, "Well, if depression goes away by itself after a few months, then maybe I can tough it out. I don't need to see a doctor and I don't need any kind of treatment, especially medication. I'll just be stoic and hang on until the storm blows over." I can't emphasize strongly enough how misguided such a conclusion is. For one thing, treatment can prevent the physical and emotional agony of depression from dominating your life, even if the episode lasts for "only" six months. Why should you weather a storm for that long when treatment will help you "move to a sunnier climate" within a short time? What's more, people with depression often think seriously about killing themselves; many try it, and a significant number succeed. The longer a depressed person goes without treatment, the greater the risk of self-harm.

There's another reason to get help: Depression can leave dangerous and lasting scars. The neurological storm of a mood disorder may pass, but the devastation it leaves behind can be enormous. A brain and a psyche damaged by depression are more vulnerable to future episodes. It might take less of an emotional shock (such as bereavement) or a physical trauma (such as disease or substance abuse) to trigger the next round of illness. There is evidence, too, that a severe major depressive disorder can "graduate" into some form of manic-depression. Getting treatment, therefore, is a valuable form of protection against future onslaughts of recurrences or different forms of mood disorder.

CHAPTER 11

Depression Is a Feeling

Depression is like love. It is a state of mind that overwhelms and distorts the senses; the whole world looks and feels different. Love seems to imbue all the molecules of the earth with a light, heavenly energy. Depression, in contrast, increases the weight of the world until finally it is too dense and dark to stand up in. Worse, the self loses its value in such an atmosphere. The depressed person is but one more grain of sand washed up on an endless, meaningless beach.

"AY, THERE'S THE RUB"

Like the man or woman in love, if you're depressed, you think about or feel little beyond that experience—it is all-encompassing. It is a feeling that colors life and living; in other words, it is a mood. A mood can exist for as little as a moment, called forth perhaps by a memory, but for that speck in time, the mood represents your perception of past, present, and future. The experience seems final—you can't imagine ever feeling differently; you believe that the joy and meaning that depression takes from you will never return. Never.

Some people feel angry when they get depressed. Others feel an inner apathy or a host of physical discomforts. Some harbor a secret burden of guilt for the duration. Others loudly blame the very heavens for this agony. A few people are not aware of anything being wrong, or anything being right.

Although most people who are depressed feel a lack of energy and a blunting of all appetites, the actual experience of depression is utterly individual.

My son Steven once said, "Depression is when you really like to go fishing and then all of a sudden you don't really care about going fishing anymore."

The Storm Within: Signs and Symptoms of Depression

Nearly everyone suffering from depression has pervasive *feelings of sadness.* In addition, depressed people may feel *helpless, hopeless, and irritable.* You should seek professional help if you or someone you know has four or more of the following symptoms continually, for more than two weeks:

- Noticeable *change of appetite,* with either significant weight gain or weight loss not attributable to dieting.
- Noticeable *change in sleeping patterns,* such as fitful sleep, inability to sleep, early-morning awaking, or sleeping too much.
- *Loss of interest* and pleasure in activities formerly enjoyed.
- Loss of energy, *fatigue.*
- Feelings of *worthlessness.*
- Persistent feelings of *hopelessness and/or helplessness.*
- Feelings of inappropriate *guilt.*
- *Inability to concentrate* or think; indecisiveness.
- Recurring *thoughts of death* or suicide; wishing to die or attempting suicide.
- *Melancholia* (overwhelming feelings of sadness and grief) accompanied by waking at least two hours earlier than normal in the morning, feeling more depressed in the morning, and moving significantly more slowly.
- *Disturbed thinking,* a symptom developed by some severely depressed persons. For example, severely depressed people sometimes have beliefs not based in reality about physical disease, sinfulness, or poverty.
- *Physical symptoms* such as headaches or stomachaches.

A fifty-five-year-old clergyman I treated reported: "It was like getting run over by a steamroller. You lie there flat on the ground with your brain telling your arms to move—but it's all going on in slow motion."

And a sixteen-year-old cheerleader told me, "All I could do was sleep and eat. It seemed like I was sleeping eighteen hours a day. I would eat and sleep and then eat and sleep some more until my boyfriend gave me some cocaine. It made me so depressed that all I could do was sleep, eat, and cry for a whole day."

A sixty-four-year-old clothing executive: "I worked my way up. I assure you, no one ever accused me of being a soft or sentimental woman. But last year I suddenly became tearful. I felt like crying after doing just about anything—going to a movie, reading the newspaper. One day I burst into tears when a young woman at the office said hello to me. After that I stopped going out to lunch—I felt like staying in my office with the door closed instead of having to eat with people."

A forty-two-year-old investment banker: "I didn't feel especially depressed—I just didn't feel the optimism that had always been with me."

A thirty-nine-year-old real-estate agent: "I felt like Dr. Jekyll and Mr. Hyde. I'd go along, even-tempered and easy to be with. Then suddenly, right before I'd get my period, I'd get extraordinarily hostile to everybody—my husband, my kids, myself, my clients. But a few days later I'd wake up and feel my old self again."

A twenty-year-old bass guitarist: "Usually I'm a very up guy. I'm on top of the world when I'm performing—high as a kite on nothing but my music. But after Shari and I broke up I was empty inside. The emptiness was totally heavy—like a black hole. All my sense of pleasure vanished into blackness. I couldn't taste, feel, love. There was no music. I didn't want to go back to her, and I couldn't perceive a future that was any different from how I was feeling."

A prince of Denmark:

To be, or not to be: that is the question:
Whether 'tis nobler in the mind to suffer
The slings and arrows of outrageous fortune,
Or to take arms against a sea of troubles,
And by opposing end them? To die: to sleep;
No more; and, by a sleep to say we end
The heartache and the thousand natural shocks
That flesh is heir to, 'tis a consummation
Devoutly to be wish'd. To die, to sleep;
To sleep: perchance to dream: ay, there's the rub;
For in that sleep of death, what dreams may come. . . .

This last speaker, of course, is Hamlet, desperately depressed. He cannot accept his heartache and, typical of depressed people, cannot foresee a time when this pain will end. He feels helpless to alter his fate, ever. He is angry and wishes to strike out. But how? Where? Against life itself?

Does depression strike certain types—melancholy Danes, for example? In fact, there is some evidence that depression, and especially manic-depression, seems to affect the more creative among us. In *Touched With Fire,* a classic study of manic-depressive illness and the artistic temperament, Dr. Kay Redfield Jamison discusses the effects of depression. She describes it as "a morbidity and flatness of mood along with a slowing down of virtually all aspects of human thought, feeling and behavior that are most personally meaningful. . . . Mood is bleak, pessimistic and despairing. A deep sense of futility is frequently accompanied, if not preceded, by the belief that the ability to experience pleasure is permanently gone."

Dr. Jamison's remarkable book explores the "fine madness" of the mood swings of manic-depression. She includes many references to depression among artists throughout the past decades. One description in particular is similar to what I hear often from my own patients. Dr. Jamison reports that the famous French composer Hector Berlioz referred to his depression as "the most terrible of all the evils of existence," saying, "It is difficult to put into words what I suffered—the longing that seemed to be tearing my heart out by the roots, the dreadful sense of being alone in an empty universe, the agonies that thrilled through me as if the blood were running ice-cold in my veins."

A GLASS HISTORICALLY HALF EMPTY

Shakespeare must have been no stranger to the feeling of depression to have put the extraordinary soliloquy in Hamlet's mouth. He had a lot to say about depression throughout his plays. The people of Shakespeare's time were as familiar with depression as we are. Melancholy, or melancholia (meaning unwarranted sadness and the loss of the ability to achieve pleasure), was known as "the Elizabethan malady" in sixteenth-century England. "If there be a hell upon earth, it is to be found in a melancholy man's heart," commented Robert Burton some 360 years ago in a book called *The Anatomy of Melancholy.* It became a bestseller of its day.

Miseries were foremost in everyone's mind in those days: "One [melancholic person] complains of want, a second of servitude, another of a secret or incurable disease; of some deformity of body, of some loss, danger, death of friends, shipwreck, persecution, imprisonment, disgrace, repulse, contumely, calumny, abuse, injury, contempt, ingratitude, unkindness . . . unfortunate marriages, single life, too many children, no children . . . etc.," wrote Burton.

Sound familiar? While everyone's experience of depression may differ, feelings of despair, of loss, of frustration pervade all sufferers' thoughts. In the absence of depression, we may see the glass as half full; when depressed, it is half empty, and it will never be filled.

Depression feels like a kind of death-in-life, the (usually) temporary disappearance of faith and hope. It shares many of the features of grief and

Complaints of People With and Without Depression

With Depression		Without Depression
90%	Impaired Concentration	30%
85%	Weakness	10%
60%	Rapid Breathing	4%
50%	Constipation	15%
50%	Ringing in Ears	10%
40%	Speech Problems	5%
35%	Loss of Sex Drive	4%

mourning. Frequently it follows on the heels of loss—loss of love, of a loved one, of employment, of opportunity, of possessions, of youth, of everything, of anything.

THE FEELING IS A NORMAL ADAPTATION

Three and a half centuries ago, Robert Burton recognized that depression "is either a disposition or habit. In disposition, it is that transitory melancholy which goes and comes upon every small occasion of sorrow, need, sickness, trouble, fear, grief, passion or perturbation of the mind. . . . And from these melancholy dispositions, no man is free."

When depression corresponds to a recent or present experience, and the degree of reaction is appropriate to the cause, it can be a completely normal adaptation. The bank forecloses on you and you lose the farm that has been in your family for generations. You would be abnormal if you didn't get depressed. You "close down," lick your wounds, and eventually begin to cope with the reality of your new situation, however unpleasant. You begin to hope for a better future; the urge to survive has returned. You may not be cheerful, but you are no longer depressed. You never did lose your capacity to obtain pleasure; a visit from your grandchildren was a joy, no matter how dark a time you were going through. And throughout the experience, no matter how bad you felt, you did not hate yourself.

Depression as a normal reaction is equivalent to unhappiness or sadness and can affect great numbers of people at any one time. There seem to be times in history—as in Robert Burton's day—when the incidence of this rotten mood is extraordinary. Apparently we are enduring such a time now. One writer estimated that 80 percent of the entire population is suffering from some type of depression at this very moment!

Life in sixteenth- and seventeenth-century Europe was marked by fundamental changes in all aspects of life—social, religious, economic—as people adjusted to Renaissance upheavals in long-standing traditions. Our times, too, are marked by extreme, and exceedingly rapid, changes. Throughout the world, we are in an era of social, political, and technological revolution. The science we learn in school is invalid by the time we reach adulthood. The computer is second nature to our children, but to many parents and grandparents this fundamental new tool remains a mystery. Children have a power and independence unheard of just a short time ago. Teenagers murder. Teenagers commit suicide.

Life expectancy is longer, but money runs out. Conquer heart disease and what do you get? Cancer. Horrible diseases such as AIDS appear out of nowhere. One plane crashes and five hundred people die. Acid rain. Toxic waste. Drug addiction. Child abuse. Park your car in a city and the cassette deck is gone when you come back. Terrorists blow up airplanes, shoot cripples. Nuclear war threatens doom.

The operative word of our times: *stress.* Constant stress. You can't win. Your hopes for the future cannot be fulfilled. Today the turbulence is too much for you. Depression.

Tomorrow maybe you'll see it another way.

Survival of the Depressed

Depression is perfectly human—or shall we say *mammalian?* Mammals get depressed, too, in reaction to stresses of loss and frustration (as well as from alcohol and other drugs, experimentally speaking). Remove an infant monkey from its mother, for example, and it will demonstrate characteristically depressed behavior. After displaying obvious, loud distress, like a human infant whose mother does not come, a young monkey will "despair," withdrawing, slouching, and curling up, ceasing to play. Its face will have that same downcast expression and gaze and furrowed brow that gives our human moods away, no matter how much we might insist to others that we're feeling okay. Charles Darwin noted that all mammals will display this expression.

This animal response suggests one evolutionary advantage conferred by depressed behavior. There must be something useful about depression for the trait to hang on through the evolutionary millennia from mammals to humans. Isolated in the wild, the baby monkey becomes easy prey. The withdrawn, silent nature of depression insures that the monkey will not reveal

continued

itself to potential enemies and that it will not wander off before its mother returns or until other monkeys appear to whom it can attach itself. In addition, with all its functions slowed, it cannot deplete its energy reserves. Thus, the natural depressed response to separation enables the monkey to survive.

Animal response to loss or abandonment demonstrates how mood serves to motivate. A depressed mood motivates us to inaction when the appropriate response to stress is, in effect, to play dead. Loss of a loved one, through death or severing of the relationship, is a terrible blow for most people, an extremely common depression trigger. A normal, adaptive "downing" allows us to temporarily remove ourselves from the fray and bandage our psychological wounds. This healing step is important, for a major loss often precedes the onset of serious illness. (Depression of the maladaptive type, however, can prove even more stressful than the loss that triggered it. Then the depression becomes the illness risk factor.)

Psychiatrists Paul Wender and Donald Klein reason that moods have survived because they help us to cope with a changing environment and with danger. If we are continually defeated by a hostile environment, it makes no sense to continue to take risks. The safest course is to throw in the towel. A pessimistic attitude that accompanies a depressed mood— "There's no point in trying; I lose no matter what I do"—evolved from an animal's avoidance of a losing battle.

By the same token, mania has its evolutionary advantages. An optimistic attitude, no matter how apparently unrealistic, maximizes use of available or scarce resources. Manics can be amazingly productive. They race around getting things done, not sleeping, hatching creative, seemingly crazy schemes and plans. They proceed whether others agree with them or not. They can be very likable, even charismatic. They'll attract a mate and reproduce their genes for sure. Their energy is bottomless—unless they crash. At their most intense, moods are nearly always short-lived. In an evolutionary sense, they guide our survival temporarily.

Yet another theory of the survival of depression suggests that the genetic trait may confer an evolutionary advantage that has nothing to do with depression. This follows the model of diseases such as sickle-cell anemia, a fatal anemia common among blacks. Inheriting the affected gene from only one parent appears to confer a resistance to malaria, a killer in ancestral Africa; anemia does not develop. Persons who had acquired this protective trait would have tended to survive; thus the gene would have proliferated. Unfortunately, possession of two of these genes, one from each parent, leads to the development of sickle-cell anemia.

This last theory may explain why pathological, long-lasting forms of depression afflict our species to the extent that they do. The nature of the possible genetic advantage associated with this miserable trait has yet to be suggested, however, let alone imagined.

DEPRESSION IS A BAD FEELING THAT WON'T GO AWAY

Normal, nonclinical depression is a drain on energy and psychic resources. But it does not truly interfere with your ability to go about the necessary business of living, although it may well reduce your motivation. To repeat, it does not rob you of self-worth. You remain the person you always were. Gloomy though you may be, you can do your work and relate to other people. You feel lousy, period. Normal depression is ultimately, if unpleasantly, benign.

For some people, though, the mood creeps into every corner of life. Tomorrow's view of the world will be just about as negative as today's and yesterday's. These individuals see and feel the bad side of everything, especially themselves—the mirror reveals nothing but flaws. All experience, no matter how objectively gratifying, is ultimately disappointing. Although those close to them are always telling them to stop looking at the dark side, their behavior is based on a genuinely pained perception of the world and of themselves that they cannot easily relinquish. Nor do they feel there is anything they can do about it.

Overall, it is a chronic misery, even though there will be periods in which it lifts.

This persistent depression is a maladaptive state of mind, hindering a normal experience of life. Generally it affects thinking, feeling, and energy, and results in withdrawal from others. But the afflicted person can still participate in essential life activities.

Normal Grief

Trauma	Rumination	Resolution
Crying	Depression	Regaining of interest in people, appearance, and activities
Numbness	Insomnia	
Sense of unreality	Loss of appetite	
Denial	Fatigue	
Disbelief	Thoughts of death	
	Social isolation	
	Loss of pleasure	

Regardless of resolution, death of a parent before the child reaches the age of seventeen is associated with very high risk of eventual adult depression.

Psychiatrists and psychologists have many names for depression with these descriptive symptoms, including *depressive personality disorder, characterological depression, depressive neurosis,* and *minor depression.* DSM-IV calls it *dysthymic disorder* (chronic disturbance of mood). Some community studies have shown that 9 to 20 percent of the adult population have symptoms of depression. One recent study of patients who presented symptoms of dysthymia were found a year later either to be at higher risk for depression or to have full-blown depression.

Whatever its name, this persistent bad mood is usually considered to be either a largely psychological problem in and of itself or symptomatic of a psychiatric condition such as alcoholism or obsessive-compulsive neurosis. But watch out for a psychiatrist or other practitioner who jumps immediately to this conclusion.

"How long have you been depressed?" the doctor will ask. "All my life," you sigh. Immediately you are hustled off for psychotherapy, because to many therapists, *chronic* equals *neurotic.*

Any depressive difficulty that becomes maladaptive requires a complete differential diagnostic procedure. Even if it is not symptomatic of a mimicker or of another psychiatric illness, who is to say it isn't biological? The symptoms may not be typical of biological depression (which we discuss in the next chapter), but symptoms are not the best way to tell what is going on inside your brain; laboratory tests are needed to provide objective data.

Keep in mind, too, that your "minor" depression (which to you feels far from minor) may become chronic if nobody treats it correctly in the first place. This type of depression can begin following a bout with biological depression. Or vice versa: 15 percent of all biological (also called clinical, major, or endogenous) depressions erupt out of minor depression. We call this phenomenon double depression. The minor form tends to persist after the major form clears up.

Still, the most probable diagnoses are psychological for a clinical picture that consists mostly of a persistently depressed mood. Which doesn't mean the depression is not serious. Being depressed all the time is an awful way to live. Besides, anyone who is depressed runs the risk of suicide.

What does *psychological* or *neurotic* mean? In their broadest sense these terms refer to patterns of thinking and behaving caused by mental or emotional conflicts rather than by physiological factors. These conflicts may have been generated in early life in response to internal or external stresses or learned throughout life because of psychosocial factors, such as socioeconomic status.

Why a Rat Will Sing the Blues

Apparent depression can be experimentally induced in rats. Yoke two rats together in a cage with a wheel on one wall. Give control of the wheel only to the rat on the left. Now give them both an identical electric shock. The shock will stop when the rat on the left turns the wheel. Although the shock begins and ends at the same time for both rats, it's the rat on the right who gets depressed. This rat has no control over what has happened to it, and ends up just giving up on life—the *learned helplessness* effect. Now, if you put that rat in a situation where it can escape the shock, it will not be able to learn how. It will eat less, lose weight, develop stomach problems, and be less aggressive.

Learned helplessness has been proposed as one model for human depression as well. Disadvantaged or scapegoated segments of society are at risk. Family dynamics can produce this kind of depression in the child who learns through the horrors of experience that she or he is helpless and unable to control abuse; or, more subtly, in the family member, adult or child, who is consistently deprived of respect and power.

CHAPTER 12

Depression Is an Affliction of Mind and Body

When depression persistently interferes with pleasure, social functioning, thinking, eating, working, initiative, sex, memory, satisfaction, sleeping, self-esteem, self-care, peace of mind, assessment of reality, movement, health, and will to live, the bad mood is often the least of it. This depression is more than maladaptive—it's downright pathological. This collection of symptoms has an exhausting list of names, a few of which are: biological depression, major depression, clinical depression, vital depression, endogenous depression. Assuming I had already ruled out mimickers and other psychiatric illnesses, and that I had not yet discovered the subtype, I would simply refer to it as primary depression (see page 48 for my preferred nosology of depression).

Depression produces cognitive and emotional symptoms. (*Cognitive* refers to our ability to reason, comprehend, and concentrate.) Depression of this nature includes what we call atypical or vegetative symptoms. These refer to essential functions of the organism: sleeping, eating, procreating, remaining alert, and so forth. Vegetative symptoms (also called hypothalamic symptoms) may indicate brain malfunction, particularly of the hypothalamus, which regulates these body functions. Such symptoms tend to appear in younger patients, but it's not clear whether or not they are familial traits or associated with a specific genetic characteristic.

PATIENT PORTRAITS

Primary depression syndromes have any number of symptoms and symptom combinations.

Judy Y.'s symptoms presented perhaps the most common picture. She

171

came to us with a fierce bad mood and a load of guilt. "This is a terrible thing I'm doing to my family," cried the forty-two-year-old mother of three, as if she had asked for this affliction. Her self-esteem was down to about ground level. She'd lost, she said, twenty-five pounds. She was five feet seven and fairly large-boned, but weighed only 125 pounds. She just didn't care about eating. Or about how she looked, to judge from her appearance; her hair just hung, unstyled, unwashed. Normally sexually active ("Every night," she said with that guilty glance, as if something were wrong with that), Judy had "given up," as she put it. She was far less interested in sex now, but the major problem turned out to be that she could no longer have an orgasm.

Judy walked heavily and spoke very slowly, a sign of psychomotor retardation. She had difficulty concentrating. She wasn't interested in much of anything anymore, not even the afternoon TV soap operas, which for years she had tuned into with delicious anticipation. She was constipated (this, too, she "confessed" as if it were some kind of crime). Her worst time of day was morning, which is typical of most biologically depressed people, whose mood fluctuates throughout the day. Mornings, she said, were when she wished she were dead. She thought her husband probably wished the same for her, too.

Judy was having a horrible time, but some people have it even worse. They have delusions or hallucinations on top of everything else. These delusions have the same miserable, guilty, down tone as the depressed mood itself—they're mood-congruent, as we say. The nature of the delusions or hallucination distinguishes this psychotic depression from schizophrenia. I had a patient, Harvey L., for example, who was utterly convinced that he had murdered his wife and that his execution was imminent. In fact, his wife had recently died from cancer. Harvey's depressive syndrome was of the psychotic type.

John R., age fifty-four, came in so agitated he couldn't stay seated. He spoke quickly as he moved nervously around the room, pulling variously at his sleeve, his hair, his pants legs. He complained less of a depressed mood than of this awful anxiety and restlessness. The remainder of his symptoms fit the depressed picture.

Finally, Ellen P., a nineteen-year-old college student, was plagued by a weight gain of fifteen pounds and an appetite that wouldn't quit. When she wasn't eating, she said, she was sleeping—twelve, even fourteen hours a day. She felt okay once she got up, though. By nighttime she was ready to kill herself.

A BACKACHE, A STOMACHACHE, CONSTIPATION . . .

For some people, depression involves few of the mental or physical experiences we have discussed so far. Instead, their depression manifests itself as stomach pains, headaches, backaches, palpitations, weird tingly feelings in the extremities (paresthesia), dizziness, and a host of other entirely physical complaints. They claim to have no agonized, helpless, depressed feelings, although sometimes they'll admit to being upset about their health.

These individuals are depressed, but theirs is called *masked depression*. Their physical pains are real; instead of signifying an actual physical illness, however, these pains become a physical expression of a mental phenomenon that is too painful to experience directly. Other names for a physical condition that serves as a masked depression are *depressive equivalent* and, when the patient is all smiles, *smiling depression*.

People suffering from this depressive syndrome consult internists and family physicians, not psychiatrists. Why would a physician suspect that a patient's physical complaint is depression? To the alert and concerned physician, these patients offer a host of clues. For one, the symptoms often will result in difficulty concentrating, sleep and memory problems, lack of appetite, and other depression-associated vegetative symptoms. Their health problems may provide the explanation for the social withdrawal so frequently found in depression. Drug use is another possible clue. The patient may have started taking drugs or drinking excessively to distance himself or herself farther from the depression.

In addition, these individuals often look depressed—that nearly universal downcast expression and slow, heavy demeanor or jumpiness are important clues. For another, the pain or complaint frequently does not follow a disease pattern. Moreover, a family history of depression is common, and the appearance of symptoms often coincides with major losses or frustrations, which are common depression triggers. The final diagnostic factor is that a thorough physical examination reveals no physiological basis for the distress.

Clues notwithstanding, the diagnosis of masked depression requires considerable care on the part of the physician, and caution on the part of the patient. Misdiagnosis presents two serious risks: Is it really masked depression, or is it a mimicker? Although the patient may present a masked-depression appearance, the physical symptoms may indeed express a disease process. Watch out for the doctor who announces a masked-depression verdict without taking an extensive history and physical. On the other side of the coin is the doctor who would rather treat a patient for bodily complaints than deal with an emotional problem. The physician's avoidance can result in inordinate expense and permanent suffering for the patient with masked depression whose aches and pains are taken too seriously, perhaps even treated surgically.

PANIC DISORDERS AND EATING DISORDERS AS DEPRESSIVE EQUIVALENTS

Antidepressants can be effective in treating panic disorders and apparent anxiety. Recent attempts to treat eating disorders with these types of medications have produced hopeful results. The question arises: Are these illnesses also depressive equivalents, or are the antidepressants effective in treating a number of different conditions?

Panic disorders now appear to be present in 10 to 20 percent of patients with major depressive disorder. About 30 percent of all depressed people also have symptoms associated with general anxiety disorder. In about 50 percent of these cases, the anxiety disorder was a precursor to the depression. Phobias are also quite common. Studies report that over 90 percent of all people with agoraphobia also develop some sort of mood disorder; interestingly, more than 85 percent of those have a family history of depression.

The bad news is that those with concurrent anxiety or panic disorders are more likely to have more severe and frequent depressive episodes, and they are more likely to attempt suicide. Therefore, anyone with these symptoms can be assumed to be at risk for a more serious and life-threatening problem.

Several biopsychiatric studies confirm that some forms of bulimia (binge-purge syndrome) and anorexia nervosa (self-induced starvation) are related to depression in the way they cause changes—possibly permanent—in both brain chemistry and brain function. As many as one-third to one-half of all eating-disorder patients also suffer from depression. And 50 to 75 percent of eating-disorder patients suffer from some sort of major depression over their lifetime. This finding would explain why some antidepressants are effective in treating these disorders. In addition, genetic studies indicate a multigeneration family "pedigree" of depression in persons with eating disorders, the significance of which is discussed in Chapter 14. Finally, poor nutrition can often create depressionlike symptoms. Thus, women who suffer from anorexia nervosa may also be at high risk for depression or be misdiagnosed as depressed.

MISERABLE MOOD, MISERABLE BODY

Depressed people with classic symptoms are not exempt from bodily ills. Aches and pains of all kinds are common. Many depressed people feel a kind of pressure in the chest or in the head. "I feel like I've been socked in the stomach," said one patient. The discomforts of constipation are all too

Undiagnosed Depression

Common Single Complaints of 100 Patients Seeing Their Internists or Family Practitioners

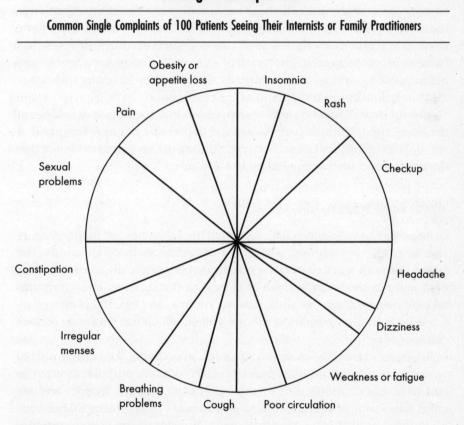

familiar to depressed people. In addition to these miscellaneous aches and pains, however, folks who are chronically or frequently depressed are prone to three particular medical conditions: irritable bowel syndrome, hypertension, and fibromyalgia.

Can depression cause disease? Over forty studies in the last decade show that there is some relationship between depression and the immune system's ability to function. The jury is still out on what exactly that relationship is. Does depression cause the immune system to become weaker, thus leaving people vulnerable to illness? Or does illness weaken the immune system (and perhaps the neurotransmitter systems in the brain), leaving people susceptible to depression? In a way, this is the biochemical version of the classic problem of which came first, the chicken or the egg. Some researchers are also exploring the question of whether antidepressant medications may affect the immune system, and if so, how.

This issue of the connection between depression and illness is by no means easy to study. After all, there are as many variables in the equation as there are people who suffer from depression. Some people smoke, some drink, some take prescription medications, some use illicit drugs. Often these substances need to be "washed out" of the body for a few weeks before a doctor will be able to identify whether they have any cause-and-effect relationship to the person's depressed mood.

Like the search for the roots of depression in the complex workings of the brain, the relationship of disease and depression is a new frontier that will be part of the good news to come. Still, we do have clear evidence that depression and disease are linked in a few areas.

Irritable Bowel Syndrome (IBS)

Irritable bowel syndrome (IBS), in which the intestines are highly responsive to stress, is a chronic functional disturbance. In other words, the bowel does not work correctly, even though it is not really diseased. IBS is not nearly as medically serious as it feels to the sufferer. The symptoms include constipation, diarrhea, nausea, cramps, and gas. IBS is often confused with another condition, spastic colitis, which can be a very serious disease indeed.

IBS is an extremely common disorder, accounting for a high rate of worker absenteeism. Studies evaluating IBS sufferers find that as many as half have mood disorders. It's surprising, then, as Paul Wender and Michael Kalm comment in the *American Journal of Psychiatry*, that there is no discussion of IBS as a psychosomatic disorder in the current premier psychiatric textbook.

Hypertension

Some researchers have found that the prevalence of depression is five times higher among people with hypertension than it is among the general population. One study on psychiatric outpatients found diagnoses of major depression three times as common among those with hypertensive disease as those without it.

This relationship makes it harder to treat high blood pressure because antihypertensive medications tend to cause or exacerbate depression.

Fibromyalgia (Fibrositis)

Chronic tenderness, pain, and stiffness of connective tissue in muscles, joints, tendons, and ligaments are the features of fibromyalgia, also known as fibrositis. The pain can be severe and disabling. This common rheumatic condition has a strong association with depression as well as with irritable bowel syndrome. Persons with the disorder, of which the cause is unknown, have a strong family history of depression. One study found that 71 percent of fibromyalgia sufferers had a history of significant mood disorder, compared to 14 percent of patients with rheumatic arthritis.

CHAPTER 13

When Depression Is Half the Story

If you have experienced a depressive episode, you are at risk for a manic episode as well. In fact, 95 percent of those with bipolar disorder also have recurring bouts of depression. In terms of symptoms, depression and mania are polar opposites—hence the name *bipolar illness,* currently the preferred name for manic-depression (in this book I use them both interchangeably). Mania is as up as depression is down. During a depression you can't get moving. During a manic phase you can't stop.

Manics talk a mile a minute, but often cannot complete a thought before they go on to another one. They are impulsive, to say the least, and this, coupled with an overwhelming and unrealistic self-confidence, spells trouble.

The rotten mood of depression is matched by the euphoria of mania. The high, however, commonly turns to or is accompanied by irritability and a ferocious temper when someone prevents a manic person from undertaking ill-considered projects.

Manic activity—the hypermania so closely associated with this disorder—causes sufferers to doggedly pursue a specific activity constantly, continuously, and unrelentingly, until they are literally driving everyone else crazy. The other important aspect of the "high end" of bipolar disorder is the overresponse to a specific situation—swinging from excessive joy to a switch to equally intense anger.

FLYING HIGH WITH DAVID, CRYSTAL, AND RANDY

David S., thirty-nine, a stockbroker, had a manic inspiration. He sank nearly a million dollars of his clients' funds into three worthless stocks, which he was sure would rise to extraordinary heights. To no one's surprise but his, the stocks lost further ground. He lost his job and reputation, and by sheer good fortune managed to avoid going to jail. If David had been depressed, he probably would have mistrusted his own good judgment of the market and therefore he would have had difficulty making an appropriate decision.

All the energy and appetite that is lacking in depression, mania has in spades. Manic individuals usually have little need for sleep. They often are overly social. They may believe, for example, that someone they just met feels a special closeness to them. Hypersexuality is frequently a symptom, as it was with Crystal. A few years ago her mother, in a panic, phoned a colleague of mine. She had gone to visit her twenty-five-year-old daughter. When she arrived, Crystal was standing naked by the elevator in her apartment house, issuing invitations for sex to any man who got off the elevator. Her mother could not convince her to stop and return to her apartment. When the police arrived, Crystal happily propositioned them too.

A patient I'll call Randy was a tall, thin, arrogant, aggressive CEO of a multinational corporation whose real name is familiar to anyone who reads the business pages. Rumors of his sexual prowess spread around the world. Was it true that this forty-year-old self-made billionaire could have sex nonstop for six hours running?

Yes—during his once-a-month, weeklong manic episodes. But then there was another week in which he could not even get an erection.

Neither his associates, acquaintances, or lovers recognized Randy for the manic-depressive he was, although his wife knew something was wrong with him. He was a rapid cycler, riding the high waves two weeks a month, going under for one week, and floating in a calm sea for another week. In his high phase, one week would be truly manic, filled with work and sex and generally frenzied behavior that was accepted as allowably idiosyncratic by someone of his stature. His depressions, regular as clockwork, were severe for only two or three days, when he could not drag himself out of bed to go to work. The remaining down days were characterized by a general lack of energy or interest. He had to travel frequently and would try to arrange to fly during a down time, so he could sleep through it.

Randy came to me because his wife insisted; otherwise, she would have left him. Despite his numerous adulterous relationships, he could not bear to lose her, and during one of his depressed swings he nearly succumbed to suicidal despair.

Randy did not respond to lithium, but he is doing very well now on anticonvulsant medication. He may appear less "brilliant" to columnists, but his wife, as well as his company's board of directors, are far more pleased.

THE BIPOLAR LIFE

As you can see, going through life on the roller coaster of bipolar disorder can be a nightmare for both the victim and the family. Like many other severe mental health problems, bipolar disorder had long gone unrecognized. However, in recent years, the National Depressive and Manic-Depressive Association was formed by patients to bring a message of hope and education to their fellow sufferers. Organized to provide support services and eliminate the stigma associated with depression and manic-depression, this volunteer self-help group has made major changes in the public perception of manic-depressives. Their publications and conferences have spurred research and treatment innovations.

But, as the organization points out, far too little has been accomplished. Recently the association in conjunction with the American Psychiatric Association conducted a comprehensive study. The results, released at the APA Annual Scientific Meeting in May, 1993, were startling:

- Fifty-nine percent of those studied said they had experienced and reported symptoms as adolescents, but over 50 percent of that group went untreated for at least another five years.
- Amazingly, 37 percent of the group studied had been misdiagnosed three times before a correct diagnosis was made. (Think about what the results would be in a specialty such as cardiology if one out of three heart attack victims was told, "Don't worry, it's only indigestion!")
- Those surveyed said that they had each seen three or four different doctors before a correct diagnosis was made.
- Fifty-nine percent of those who were untreated had failed marriages or other personal relationships. Surprisingly, 32 percent of those whose illness was "properly managed" also had similar failures in their relationships.
- More than half of those surveyed reported that their families were permanently damaged because of their illness, and in fact, they were having trouble maintaining any sort of friendships.
- One-third of the respondents reported that they had been fired when their illness was out of control, and another 40 percent said they were given fewer or diminished responsibilities when their illness was not

managed properly. More than half of the group studied had been forced to stop working or found themselves on a merry-go-round of frequent new jobs.

The voices of bipolar disorder victims are being heard, but it's not easy. Often their own symptoms conspire against them. Manics are commonly misdiagnosed as schizophrenic. This mistake is easy to make, because, like schizophrenics, they can become delusional, and they may experience racing thoughts and speak in peculiar ways. As in depression, the content of the delusions, or hallucination, is significant. The admitting psychiatrist must be alert to excessive self-esteem and grandiosity. Ron, twenty-nine, said he was directed by God to take a supersonic transport to London to be the bearer of holy tidings to Prince Charles and Princess Diana upon the birth of their first child. He was traveling without luggage because he expected to move in with the royal family, who would, of course, provide him with a new wardrobe. That very night he was outfitted with pajamas and a robe at the New York hospital where his before-takeoff ravings earned him a bed.

At first glance, the seemingly endless energy and reduced need for sleep experienced by people with mania may seem enviable, especially to those of us who have many projects to finish and little time. But there's a hidden danger. "Before modern treatments for mania were available, it was a life-threatening illness: Approximately 15 percent of manic patients died from physical exhaustion," psychiatrist Nancy Andreasen reminds us. "Even in the era of modern treatment, the excessive activity level continues to be a serious risk in patients with cardiac problems."

A fairly strait-laced Wall Street lawyer, Ron was later horrified at what he had attempted to do. It had been his first full-blown manic episode. He claimed to be a "pretty even guy." But after taking a history and speaking to Ron's parents and his wife, the psychiatrists were able to point out to Ron that he had had several milder ups since his early twenties. These were interspersed with mild, infrequent downs. Ron had moved from one form of bipolar disorder to another, as I'll explain.

ADDICTION TO MANIA

Manic-depressive illness bears an intriguing resemblance to cocaine addiction. (Many of Randy's friends and colleagues believed his peculiar behavior was due to cocaine, which Randy said he had never used.) In fact, the down stage has many biochemical similarities to changes that take place in the brain during addiction. For example, studies have found that during manic episodes, there is an overstimulation of the noradrenergic and dopamine systems, which can reduce the supply of dopamine. This is one reason why those addicted to drugs such as cocaine often have an initial up period, but eventually the system is so overrevved that it collapses on itself in a state of depression. Recently, studies using positron emission tomography (PET) scans have confirmed that the dopamine receptor sites, key to the operation of this system, are altered by bipolar disorder. This means that the normal neurotransmitter release, binding, and reuptake process for dopamine is changed, and ultimately the brain neurochemistry is altered. As you may recall from the previous chapter, this again raises the chicken-or-egg question: Which occurs first, the disease or changes in the biological systems?

Creative Highs and Woes

For many years, Dr. Kay Redfield Jamison has been studying the connection between creativity and depressive illness. More recently she has focused on the relationship between creativity and bipolar disorder. Her studies, recapped in her wonderful book *Touched With Fire,* recount the lives of English and American poets, musicians, and writers to demonstrate the "fine madness" that runs through these groups.

Byron, Shelley, Poe, Delmore Schwartz, Robert Lowell, Sylvia Plath, Anne Sexton, and Theodore Roethke are only a few of the bipolar poetic greats. Byron, she reports, described his manic depression this way: "We of the craft are all crazy. Some are affected by gaiety, others by melancholy, but all are more or less touched with fire."

Studies involving thousands of writers and artists show that the rates of mood disorders in this group range from 30 to 50 percent, more than six times the rate found within the general population. Many of them had been hospitalized for the disorder, and more than half had received medication for mania or depression. In fact, writers are at far higher risk for any sort of mental illness than the rest of the population.

Well or ill, however, close to 90 percent of the writers and artists experienced powerful, productive, creative highs for two weeks at a time—periods corresponding to the length of the usual manic high.

Jamison concludes that creativity and mood disturbance go hand in hand: no mood swings, no poetry. But one does not need such ups and downs to be a successful poet or creative artist, she says. To which I might add that just because you're moody, you are not necessarily guaranteed a place in the pantheon of great ones.

The effect is simple: sufferers become addicted to their own neurochemical manic explosions and prefer this sick state to any other. Like cocaine addicts, they do not come for help until their lives are in shambles, with job, finances, family, and health heading down the drain.

One of the greatest challenges in treating manic patients is keeping them on their medication. Once their lives are back in order, many manics prefer a recurrence of their illness to a normal experience of life. They stop taking the lithium and succumb to mania. Because this behavior is so common, bipolar-treatment programs such as ours offer support groups, just as we do in our drug treatment programs. And, of course, we check blood levels of drugs—lithium for the manic-depressives, illicit drugs for the abusers.

The similarities between mania and a drugged state are widely recognized in research circles. Can drugs that work to reduce addiction also combat mania? Experiments are ongoing.

Not surprisingly, there is also a higher rate of substance abuse within populations of bipolar patients, as there is in psychiatric patients as a whole. According to studies by the NIMH, alcoholism and substance abuse, particularly cocaine dependence, are far more common in bipolar patients. There is also evidence that these patients have a more serious course of illness. This has led researchers to suspect that there may, in fact, be a genetic link between drug abuse and depression. But, again, the evidence is not clear and we have yet to unlock these secrets.

I must point out that cocaine is not an antidote for depression. Cocaine makes severe depression worse, often triggering hallucinations. Manic-depressives often try cocaine or amphetamines to switch themselves from depression into mania. Some end up feeling a slight improvement, but they crash to the depths within a couple of days.

THE BIPOLARS

Bipolar illness is broken down into several categories by the DSM-IV. Some of the categories seem at times to be overlapping or ambiguous. Recently experts have called for either a new system of categorization or a scale system. However, there is no single best method of describing illness because, as one writer put it, "mental illness may not be a jointed creature, easily divisible into its component parts." Here, then, is a brief rundown of the current definitions.

Bipolar I

Bipolar I illness is classic manic-depression: one or more episodes of major mania alternating with major depression. It is rarely a one-for-one cycle, though. One pole or the other usually predominates. Men tend to experience more manic episodes and fewer depressions, while women have more depression, less mania. Depressed phases generally last longer than manic periods.

Long periods can separate episodes of either kind, and during these times the person is fine, much better off, in fact, than people who suffer from depression alone. Bipolars tend to experience more recurrences of the illness than do unipolars, however. The median lifetime episode frequency is ten. Those unfortunate persons who suffer four or more episodes per year are known as rapid cyclers and are problematic to treat.

Bipolar victims are often young, with recent studies reporting that 50 percent of those studied had symptoms in high school but only 3 percent were diagnosed. This, of course, has often had a devastating effect, with 67 percent reporting difficulty socializing and an inability to concentrate on schoolwork. Still, many forge ahead and complete their education. A national study of manic-depressive patients reported that the vast majority of respondents had symptoms in college and were not well controlled. Still, most had graduated from college and more than a quarter went on to complete postgraduate studies.

Bipolar I illness has the distinction of being probably the truest descriptive category among all the lists of mood disorders in terms of consistency of symptom pictures, prognosis, and treatment indication. In other words, while some psychiatrists (including myself) question the DSM-IV depression categories, we all agree that bipolar illness is a discrete illness in everything from symptoms to biochemistry. Generally, bipolar I disorder is effectively controlled with lithium, a naturally occurring salt (see page 275 for a complete discussion of this drug). Bipolar illness can also be effectively treated with anticonvulsants.

While the depression occurring in bipolar disorder is symptomatically indistinguishable from unipolar depression, it's essential that the doctor diagnose the problem accurately, even if a manic episode has not yet occurred. The goals of treatment in bipolar illness are to stabilize the cycling and treat the particular mood. Treating the depression only with tricyclic antidepressants, one of the most often used medications for depression, could send a bipolar patient flying into mania, or it could increase the frequency of the cycles (from perhaps one up and one down episode per year to three of each). Such a reaction to medication will help identify an undiagnosed bipolar disorder, but it is not the best way to go about helping a patient. Indeed, some people suffer depression and mania at the same time—a truly miserable condition.

Bipolar II

Until recently we believed the risk of bipolar disorder among depressed patients to be a relatively low 10 percent. That was before we discovered the existence of another, milder form of the disorder, known as bipolar II. Now we believe that 25 to 35 percent of depressions are in fact the down side of all forms of bipolar disorder. About half the time the disease is bipolar I; the other half it is a bipolar II disorder that has not yet been diagnosed.

The manic phase of bipolar II disorder is what we call hypomania, meaning "low high." If you're hypomanic, your behavior does not appear bizarre, the way manic behavior often does. In fact, you may not seem at all ill. You're in an extremely good mood, have a lot of energy, you feel sexy, you don't need a whole lot of sleep, your self-esteem is great, you're full of ideas and plans and enthusiasms. You're the ideal person of the 1990s.

Is such a great state of mind really abnormal—or are psychiatrists a bunch of grouches?

The difference between normal and abnormal in all aspects of mood is often extremely subtle and may depend on the accumulation of consequences. Everyone has mood shifts. In bipolar II disorder, your judgment may be affected. Is your decision to change jobs based on a realistic appraisal of your abilities and opportunities, or on a sudden spurt of self-esteem? Do you really need all those new clothes or audio equipment or computer add-ons that you are about to buy? Even more to the point, can you really afford them?

Despite the consequences, however—and there may be few—who would seek psychiatric help because they feel good? Since it is the depression that brings a person with bipolar II to the psychiatrist's office, the illness is sometimes called pseudo-unipolar depression or atypical bipolar disorder. It looks like a DSM-IV form of depression and it acts like it, only it isn't. Even if the patient has never experienced hypomania, here too the psychiatrist has to be able to predict it in order to best treat the disorder. The pain that brought the patient in requires mood-stabilizing treatment in addition to antidepressants.

Obtaining an accurate history from depressed patients is tricky, however, because as psychiatrist Frederick Goodwin points out, they are looking at the world through "blue-colored glasses." Very commonly, however, one can pick this up from family members. In a study at the NIMH, physicians took a history of the patient alone first, then interviewed family members. A large portion of the patients who had been diagnosed as unipolar were rediagnosed as bipolar II after doctors obtained more complete histories.

Less is known about bipolar II disorder than about bipolar I. We know that patients with bipolar II tend to have a history of bipolar I in their families, and that their own illnesses began in the age range in which we generally begin to see manic-depressive illness.

Some of my colleagues have suggested that bipolar II is the category in which to place those depressed patients who have reverse symptom patterns: those who oversleep as opposed to those who can't sleep, and those who eat and eat instead of losing their appetites.

Is There a Mania in Your Future?

Assessing the Risks

For almost six and a half years, psychiatrist Hagop Akiskal and his colleagues followed 206 outpatients with a history of depression only. Mania eventually appeared in 20 percent of them.

These people differed from the 80 percent who continued their depressed-only course in six ways:

1.   They had had their first clinically significant depression before age twenty-five.
2. and 3. Not only did they have a history of bipolar illness in their families, they also had "loaded pedigrees," meaning at least three family members had the illness.
4.   The women suffered from depression following childbirth (postpartum depression).
5.   When depressed, they tended to oversleep rather than sleep too little, as is common in unipolar depression.
6.   Antidepressant medication caused a hypomanic episode.

You could already be subject to mania but not know it, until you move to a particular geographic area. That's because in some areas (west Texas, European spas, and mineral springs, for example) high levels of lithium occur naturally in the drinking water. This can prevent the appearance of bipolar symptoms.

Cyclothymia

There is a separate category of bipolar disorders that is reserved for those whose ups and downs are believed to be caused by neurosis or by difficulties with character or personality. This pattern is called cyclothymia, and it involves chronic low mood (dysthmia) mixed with phases of hypomania.

Recent evidence suggests that cyclothymia is a low-level bipolar illness and that cyclothymics come from bipolar families. They may not be any more or less neurotic than anyone else with a mood-cycling disorder.

I'll say it again: The actual categories of mental illness can never be described by symptoms alone. We must employ every diagnostic means available if we're ever going to provide treatment that makes sense.

Bipolar Disorder = Seizure Disorder?

Lithium is not the only medication used to control manic-depression. Anticonvulsant medications used in the treatment of epilepsy, such as carbamazapine (Tegretol) and sodium valproate, hold promise for treatment of bipolar disorder. Similarly, lithium acts also to control epileptic seizures. Antiseizure medications could be effective in both illnesses either because the two types of disorders are related, or because the drugs have several different actions in the body (like Valium, which relaxes muscles and relieves anxiety).

Two research psychiatrists from the NIMH recently found that some bipolar patients (plus a relatively few unipolar depressives) and epileptics with complex partial seizures share a number of symptoms. These include illusions of significance, jumbled thoughts, altered perceptions of sound and odor intensity, hallucinations of hearing and smell, periods of amnesia, visual distortions of shape and distance, feelings of detachment from the environment, and others.

The scientists concluded that perhaps the electrical physiology of certain parts of the brain is similarly and subtly altered in both conditions, accounting for the common symptoms.

One small study does not prove the point, but there is no doubt that for many manic-depressives, anticonvulsants work. This is good news, as is the possible relationship to seizure disorders, for it is a line of research that can provide an understanding and eventual answers for those who suffer either disorder.

CHAPTER 14

Depression Is in Your Genes

Depression runs in families, often for generations. Within the past decade scientists have determined, with reasonable certainty, that the neuro-chemical deficiencies seen in depression are transmitted genetically from parents to offspring. Children who receive the affected gene or genes are vulnerable to affective disorders.

There is a 1 to 2 percent risk of bipolar disorder in the general popula-tion. But the risk that a first-degree relative of someone with a bipolar illness will also have some form of manic-depression is as high as 15 to 25 percent. Sixty-eight percent of identical twins with bipolar depression share certain genetic traits, and 23 percent of fraternal twins have similar traits linked to bipolar illness. A child with one depressed parent has a 26 percent higher risk than the rest of the population for depression. With two depressed parents, the rate increases to 46 percent. It is clear that depression can be inherited.

But genetics are only part of the picture. The environment and other external stressors can interact with certain biological triggers to set off depression in people who are genetically susceptible. So many questions still remain unanswered—which genes, which people, which genera-tions, and, of course, why some in a family and not others? When these and other questions are answered, there will be even more good news for patients like Leslie, a young woman I recently treated.

DOWN THROUGH THE GENERATIONS

The family of Leslie Y. presents a typical pedigree of depression. Leslie is the oldest of four daughters; the second two are twins. Leslie has some-how managed to survive five suicide attempts. Her father had become severely depressed when he was in his forties. Leslie remembers that he developed a painfully sour outlook on life. Although he had been a successful lawyer, he began to believe that he was not good enough. He became convinced that he was about to have a heart attack and went from doctor to doctor seeking this diagnosis. Some assured him he was fine; others suggested psychiatric help, which he angrily refused. Often he stayed home in bed rather than face the prospect of running his business, and he withdrew from friends and formerly enjoyable activities as well as from his family.

Leslie at first insisted that her mother was "more than okay mood-wise." Leslie's description, however, revealed a woman who arose daily at 5 A.M. because she couldn't sleep and whom the children would not dare disturb before her morning coffee because her frame of mind was so awful. Once the morning mood passed, her mother sometimes became "speedy and superefficient," Leslie reported enviously. Her mother was also prone to apparently excessive socializing and occasional spending sprees. Hearing this story, I strongly suspected a bipolar II pattern.

Although both sets of grandparents had died in Leslie's early childhood, she knew about them, and their moods, from her parents. Both grandmothers had also been depressed. Leslie's paternal grandmother, an Eastern European immigrant, could see no future for herself or her family, although her husband within a decade progressed from pushing a cart to owning buildings; her only son, Leslie's father, was far more educated and successful than his father had ever been. The woman was excessively fearful, a trait that Leslie's father exhibited as he grew older. Like his mother, too, Leslie's dad grew to believe that "everyone was out to get him."

Leslie's maternal grandmother suffered extreme mood swings, from fits of laughter to torrents of tears. Leslie's mother was the fourth of seven children; the older children cared for the younger, since their mother was often emotionally incapacitated.

In Leslie's generation, both she and her youngest sister had a history of depression. Her sister's depressions, less severe, began in her mid-thirties, shortly after her second child was born. Leslie's twin sisters were spared the family illness.

Leslie's own difficulties dated from high school; she attempted suicide for the first time at age seventeen. Four attempts followed when her three-year marriage broke up in her late twenties. She was shocked to hear that I believed her to be bipolar, since her many previous psychiatrists had treated her only for depression. I had asked Leslie to describe the last time she remembered being happy—not an easy question for a depressed person whose dark state of mind dominates and distorts every thought and memory. With pained nostalgia, Leslie described a period of euphoria, reduced need for sleep and food, and unusual productivity—in a word, hypomania.

POPULATION GENETICS

Family trees such as Leslie's first alerted scientists to the possible inheritability of depression. Most of the evidence is statistical; biological data are highly suggestive but still not conclusive. Direct proof awaits further research, which itself depends on identification of the biochemical, neuroendocrinological, and neurophysiological components of depression. As you will soon see, this research is proceeding at a furious pace. Genetic epidemiologists have been in the field for decades, gathering data. While early studies may be in doubt because of methodological problems, data from recent family, twin, and adoption studies are increasingly convincing.

Family studies consist of interviews with as many members of the family of a depressed person as possible to determine diagnoses and ultimate family patterns of illness. Often family members will be asked to supply information about members of past generations.

BIOLOGICAL GENETICS

Some geneticists believe that all affective disorders, from manic-depression to dysthymia, are controlled by one gene. Others claim that many genes must be involved. In either case, biological geneticists hunt for trait markers to reveal how the disorder is transmitted and who is vulnerable.

A genetic trait marker, explain Dr. Robert Hirschfeld, the former chief of the NIMH Center for Studies of Affective Disorders, and Brana Lobel, is a biological characteristic that is clearly associated with a tendency toward clinical depression. "If scientists had an ideal," they say, "it would be a trait marker that could be traced to a specific location on a particular chromosome; it would be inheritable; it would be observable in well but susceptible people and recovered ill people, not merely in those who were currently ill; and its presence would be associated with the illness—ill people would always have the marker, while their healthy relatives might or might not."

Linkage markers are one type of trait marker. These are characteristics unrelated to mood—color blindness, for example—that afflicted individuals and their relatives tend to inherit along with the mood-related trait and whose genetic location is known.

We each inherit a pair of genes for every characteristic, one from our mothers and one from our fathers. Each pair is located on one of our forty-six chromosomes. Geneticists have discovered that genes that are close together on a chromosome tend to be inherited together—a group from Mom, a group from Dad. The linkage marker is one that presumably is inherited along with the gene or genes that carry affective disorders.

The possible linkage markers that have been suggested apply primarily to bipolar illness. This is the form of affective illness geneticists like to work with, because it is the most clearly defined of the affective disorders and, as population studies reveal, it has the strongest genetic pattern. Some of the inheritance mechanisms may prove to be the same as those for unipolar depression.

The X (female) chromosome is home to many of the bipolar linkage markers, including red-green color blindness and a certain blood antigen. In other words, some geneticists have found that within certain families, the manic-depressives are also color-blind and have the blood factor. Not all families with bipolar pedigrees possess these traits, which suggests that bipolar disorder can be transmitted in more than one way. And, to repeat, not all people who are color-blind have manic-depression. There is no functional tie between these factors; color blindness and the blood antigen are merely a convenient way of trying to locate the mood problem.

Some geneticists are searching for biological trait markers specific to the physiology of the mood disorder itself. Genes control the activity of many enzymes, certain cell membrane processes, and immunological mechanisms, all of which are believed to be involved in the vulnerability to depressive disorders. The closer we come to identifying the biochemistry of depression, the easier their job will become. That day is dawning.

THE AMISH STUDIES

Homogeneous populations, or inbred groups, such as the Old Order Amish of Pennsylvania, are ideal for genetic studies because complicating environmental and cultural influences are minimal. The Amish have maintained their own customs in rural communities separated from the non-Amish for two centuries. Their excellent record-keeping includes detailed family trees dating back to European times. Since they do not drink or take drugs, are all employed, and have strong family ties from birth to death, we can rule out many nongenetic influences in the development of mood disorders. Studies consistently show that mood disorders cluster along family trees within this population too, thus giving strong evidence that genetic factors are involved.

Several studies of the Amish have helped us reach our conclusions about genetic links. The biggest and best-known of these is one conducted by Kelsoe, Ginns, and England, and published in the prestigious journal *Nature.* That study, which looked into the family histories of Amish who suffered from major depression, revealed a disruption on a marker called chromosome 11. Although more recent studies have indicated that chromosome 11 is not the only culprit, this was a discovery of significant magnitude.

Other studies reveal a genetic link even in suicidal behavior. Suicide is uncommon among the Amish because their religion forbids it. Nevertheless, the research team was able to find evidence of twenty-six suicides over the past century. Seventy-three percent of them occurred within only four families. One family had seven suicides in one hundred years. "The role of inheritance was suggested by the way in which suicides followed the distribution of affective disorders in these kinship lines," reported researchers in the *Journal of the American Medical Association.* Lending further support for the inheritability of suicidal behavior is the team's finding that, although the suicides occurred within families with a high rate of mood disorders, other families in which depression was common claimed no suicides. Although the majority of suicides occur among depressed people, depression itself, then, may not be the sole deciding factor.

Other, more recent work by Yale University researchers showed that persons who suffered their first major depression before they reached age 20 had the most relatives with the same condition. On the other hand, those who first developed depression at 40 or older had a family rate of depression barely greater than normal.

Interestingly, inheritance patterns appear to differ among bipolar and

Depression à Deux

One in five married depressed patients has a depressed spouse. Geneticists want to know why. Is this an example of assortive mating—our human tendency to pair off with someone who shares the same problems? Or is it that life with a severely depressed spouse can get you down? Obviously, the validity of many genetic epidemiological studies depends on a correct answer in each instance.

unipolar groups. Bipolar individuals tend to have an equal number of first-degree relatives with bipolar as well as unipolar problems. Unipolar individuals, however, tend to have mostly unipolar relatives. This tantalizing finding suggests that there is a genetic relationship between the two manifestations of affective illness, with bipolar illness possibly the more severe form.

TWIN AND ADOPTION STUDIES

Identical twins are the darlings of epidemiological geneticists because they share an identical genetic makeup. If one twin inherits depression, odds are the other will develop the disorder too. Studies reveal a significant difference in concordance between identical twins and nonidentical (fraternal) twins. Depending on the criteria used to define depression, both members of a set of identical twins become depressed in 40 to 70 percent of the cases; rates of concordance for bipolar illness are even higher. Among nonidentical twins the corresponding rate is the same as it is for nontwin siblings: 0 to 13 percent.

To test whether one twin's depression would depress the other, epidemiological geneticists also study twins who have been raised apart from each other. The results are the same.

Studies of adopted (nontwin) children yield similarly valuable information. Scientists look at adopted children whose natural parents have mood disorders and compare them with adopted children whose natural parents are not depressed. The goal is to determine whether the adoptive parents or the natural parents have the most influence over the future moods of the children. It turns out that adopted children whose natural parents suffer from affective illnesses are most likely to develop similar difficulties, a finding that adds more weight to the theory that mood disorders are passed on by parents.

THE (SE)X FACTOR

If depression, at least in some families, is passed on via the X chromosome, it could explain why more females than males are depressed. The X and Y chromosomes determine sex; females have two X chromosomes, males one X and one Y.

Genes are either dominant or recessive. Of the pair of genes inherited, any dominant gene will determine the characteristic in the presence of a recessive gene. Some geneticists think that the depression trait is dominant. The odds go against a female, who could be stuck with the vulnerability from either of her X chromosomes. The odds are better for a male, who has only one X of a chance to inherit the trait. If there is no depression lurking on the chromosome, presumably he's home free.

X-linkage is not reported in all studies, however. If it were valid, a depressed father could pass his vulnerability on only to a daughter. But various investigators have found father-son lines of inheritance. Thus, either X-linkage is erroneous, or, more likely, it is true only in certain families.

Do women, as is popularly believed, suffer from depression more frequently? The answer is yes and no. Several studies seem to indicate that bipolar disorder is an equal-opportunity disease, as is mild to moderate depression. The prevalence for men and women is about the same. However, women, it seems, are far more likely to develop major depression. In fact, the rate is about two to three times higher among women than men. Among married and divorced persons, women number among the more depressed. Men take the depressed cake among those who have never married or whose spouses have died. Men experience more of the manic form of bipolar I. Bipolar II claims more women on both sides.

We are not sure why this should be the case, but there are some clues in recent studies. A report in the *American Journal of Psychiatry* suggests that a combination of stressful life events, genetic factors, previous history of major depression, and neuroticism may be more prevalent in women. Other studies of depression in women show that heredity and genetics play a strong role in depression in women. Environmental factors play a significant role, but in the long run the effects of environment probably don't increase vulnerability to depression.

NATURE OR NURTURE?

Let us return to the family of Leslie Y. For at least three generations the family had suffered from depression. Statistical implications notwithstanding, their pattern does not prove that depression is genetically inherited. Might Leslie's illness have arisen because her parents were unable to establish a healthy family experience due to their own mood problems and those of the previous generation? It is depressing to grow up with depressed parents. Did Leslie's dad learn his mother's attitudes? Was her mother mimicking her own mother? Did her mother's child-rearing practices contribute to Leslie's own problems?

Obviously, these are difficult questions to answer. Assessing the impact of genetic and environmental factors is a complex problem. As the authors of a report issued by the NIMH state, "There may be more than one genetic predisposition capable of producing a clinical syndrome. Nongenetic factors that may be significant in the etiology of depression, such as poverty and child-rearing practices, tend to run in families from generation to generation just as genetic traits do."

Nature or nurture? The answer: both. Nurture (environment) triggers nature (heredity). That is, experience makes us vulnerable to our inherited predispositions. And experience makes it possible to correct many of them.

A tendency toward depression is but one of many predispositions we inherit. Perhaps you have a family history of type II, or adult-onset, diabetes. Will you get it? Even if you inherit the vulnerability, the answer at best is maybe. Predisposed does not mean predestined. Grow fat and you are more likely to trigger the tendency to become diabetic. But mend your nutritional ways after you receive the diagnosis, and in time you may not even know you have the disease.

In depression as in diabetes, geneticists calculate that many more people possess the gene(s) than actually develop the disorder. Some combination of environmental, biological, and social factors must act on the predisposition: even then, other factors may work to offset it. In the words of another NIMH report: "Protective factors, genetic or environmental, interact with genetic predisposition or vulnerability and can prevent the expression of a disorder."

Leslie's twin sisters were at high risk to develop the family mood disorders, and yet they remain free of any sign of it. Perhaps their strong, positive attachment to each other acted as a kind of buffer against family and environmental stresses. In some families with a history of multigenerational depression, only one identical twin develops the illness. Genetically they are as close as any two people can be; clearly other factors intervene. Personality factors can influence a predisposition; for example, people who are worriers and perfectionists are known to be vulnerable to depression. Extraordinarily dependent individuals as well as introverts are also at risk.

VULNERABILITY TRIGGERS

Other than personality factors, among the known or suspected genetic vulnerability triggers are early life experience, overall stress, illness, socioeconomic status (in itself or change in it), geographic mobility, nutrition, physical or mental illness, individual biochemistry, and so on.

The contribution of these factors to the expression of an underlying predisposition probably depends on the relative weight of both inheritance and experience at any given time. During any severe economic recession, the environment will likely awaken a depressive tendency in great numbers of people. Similarly, among disadvantaged groups, rates of depression and mental illness in general are higher than among the remainder of the population. (Bipolar illness is a curious exception—it tends to be a disorder of those who are well-off.)

For strongly predisposed individuals, biochemistry alone may be sufficient to trigger the illness. And in families with many ill members, such as Leslie's, triggers may be almost impossible to avoid. Leslie was very close to her dad when she was young. For him to suddenly drop out when she was a teenager must have been a terrible blow.

The Best News Yet

Our genes are not our destiny; this is perhaps the great lesson of genetic research. Inborn errors can be corrected. Vulnerabilities can be avoided. We can change. Better than that, the research that is going on will also help us unlock a whole host of mental health problems from alcoholism to stress to phobias.

Biopsychiatric treatments for depression work because they counter or correct many of the genetic as well as experiential factors that trigger depression. The psychiatric lab is beginning to differentiate among several different biochemical subtypes of depression; we can then proceed to correct these genetically controlled processes. Similarly, specific psychotherapies have been developed to counter interpersonal, cognitive, and behavioral depression triggers. Psychotherapy in general often helps to provide strength to cope with life-event and psychological stressors that can touch off a depression in a vulnerable individual.

As you will see in Chapter 24, you can do much yourself to strengthen your resistance to depression and at least soften the blow. Self-help measures in mild cases or self-help in conjunction with biopsychiatric treatment in more severe illness may even prevent the next depressive episode.

Prevention will be the greatest gift of genetic research. Once biological markers are found, children in high-risk families can be tested and treated before illness becomes a life pattern. This scenario is not necessarily far off, considering the progress we have made in the laboratory in detecting the biological underpinnings of depression. The future of genetic research, the development of accurate diagnostic procedures, specific treatments, and ultimately cures for this horrifyingly common source of human suffering depend on what we are doing in the psychiatric laboratory right now.

Let us not forget, as we depart this chapter, that inheritance is also a good thing. In Chapter 13 we mentioned Kay Redfield Jamison's study of writers and artists, which showed that they had much higher rates of mood disorders than one would expect within the general population. But even the healthy individuals in this group tended to experience creative, maniclike highs during which they were extremely productive. To geneticists these data suggest that a carrier of the manic-depressive gene or genes might receive a great gift instead of a disease. Genes confer the best as well as the worst possibilities.

CHAPTER 15

Depression Is Mortal

"To tell you the truth," Dr. L., one of my close colleagues, told me, "one of the reasons I chose psychiatry was because I couldn't deal with patients dying. The deaths that result most directly from psychiatric illness are suicides. Naive as I was, I believed I would be able to prevent or avoid them.

"Little did I realize the nightmare of sitting there with patients in therapy session after therapy session worrying about who was going to do it and who wasn't. The quiet ones—were they the risk? The ones who threatened time and time again? What if my attention wandered and I missed something that would be the giveaway? When my practice grew to the point where I could afford to turn away patients, I began to accept only those who I felt were not or would not become suicidal.

"Then it happened—one of my patients committed suicide. She was a forty-five-year-old woman whom I had seen three times. She had come to me because she felt stuck in life, she'd said. Her job was going nowhere, her marriage was boring. She seemed depressed, but not seriously. I asked her, as I asked all patients in the initial interview, whether she ever felt like killing herself. 'No,' she'd said matter-of-factly.

"She did not show up for her fourth session. I phoned her home and no one answered. I called her at work and they told me she had died. 'How?' I asked, shocked. Her secretary would not tell me. Finally I reached her husband, who told me she had shot herself in the head. His tone was icy cold—I felt he was aiming that gun at me. I wanted to throw the phone down and run. I don't remember what I said. The next thing I knew, the phone was back on the hook and I was crying. For her, for me. I had had no idea she was suicidal. What kind of psychiatrist was I?

"She shot herself!" repeated Dr. L., reliving the event as if it had happened last week, not twelve years before. Six months after his patient's death, he abandoned the consulting room for the laboratory.

Many physicians fear death; some can translate this mortal fear into a powerful desire to save or extend their patients' lives. For the others, there are few corners in clinical medicine in which to hide. Psychiatry is not one of them.

"Psychiatric patients are known to have high death rates relative to the general population," comment Drs. Donald Black, Giles Warrack, and George Winokur, authors of a study of psychiatric mortality. "During the last fifty years, in different samples, in different parts of the world, researchers have consistently shown this to be true. The excess of deaths has been found in all types of clinical settings and in patients with varied psychiatric diagnoses." Their own work, conducted from 1972 through 1981 among former hospital inpatients, revealed a high rate of unnatural deaths—i.e., suicide and accidents. Among depressed patients, these excessive deaths occurred particularly among women during the two years following their hospitalization. Drugs and alcohol are often contributing factors in the high death rate among all psychiatric patients.

THE AWFUL FACTS OF SUICIDE

Suicide is a terrible epidemic in this country. For every seven people who attempt it, one succeeds. The rate may be even higher, because some suicides don't make it into the statistical charts. For example, "accidental" deaths, such as single-car automobile fatalities, are often a form of suicide. Suicide claims the lives of at least 15 percent of depressed patients. Many more try but fail. It is well established that the highest rates of suicide are among psychiatric patients. In fact, at least 70 percent of those who succeed in killing themselves have at least one concurrent medical disorder in addition to the psychiatric problems they are experiencing. If you are white, male, and elderly, your potential risk for suicide is even higher than the rest of the population. Twenty-five percent of all suicides occur among older people, who represent less than 10 percent of the U.S. population. Alcoholism, always linked to a variety of disorders, is also a high-risk factor for suicide.

Among depressed nonpatients, no one really knows how many people take their own lives; suicides are grossly underreported to spare the family the stigma, and among those that are reported, we do not know who was or was not depressed. Some experts believe that there may be ten thousand suicides for every million untreated episodes of depression. The reported number of suicide deaths is thirty thousand per year. The NIMH estimates that the actual number is closer to seventy-five thousand.

The reported number alone makes suicide the tenth leading cause of death in this country. According to Dr. M. Harvey Brenner, a member of the National Commission on Mental Health and Unemployment, every time the U.S. unemployment rate goes up one point, suicides as well as homicides increase by 4 to 6 percent within the next six years.

MALE SUPERIORITY

Men have the tragic distinction of being "better" at suicide. While four times as many women as men attempt suicide, men tend to succeed; in other words, men outnumber women as successful suicides four to one. Explanations abound for this phenomenon. "For women, attempts often are a way to express their distress, something men may be less able to do until the pain has gotten too great," says NIMH psychiatrist Susan Blumenthal. It also may be that women take pills and men use more violent means, such as guns, which are more likely to succeed.

THE LINK WITH HOMICIDE

Men also commit more homicides, which we mention because of the deadly close relationship between suicide and homicide. Fact: Some 10 percent of homicides are associated with suicides, as when a mother kills herself and her children. Fact: Violent, murderous rage is one of many possible motives for suicide. (Among others: escape from pain and unconscious rebirth fantasies.) Fact: Depression may fuel homicidal as well as suicidal tendencies.

Here's another fact: Women are catching up in both homicides and violent suicides.

WHO'S AT RISK

By far the group at highest risk for suicide is the elderly. In people over sixty-five, the rate of suicide is fifteen times higher than among the population generally. Even so, the rate for persons over forty-four is lower than it was in 1950. Not so for the people under forty-four—especially those twenty-four or younger, among whom the rate of suicide has been on the rise.

For adolescents and young adults age fifteen to twenty-four, the rate has more than doubled since 1950. Nobody seemed to notice this until the early 1980s. Now this alarming trend is taken seriously indeed. In a flurry of professional and public activity, we have developed a deeper understanding of adolescent depression and suicide and its warning signs. Turn to Chapter 25 for a discussion of depression's special populations, including children and older people.

PREDICTING SUICIDE

Speaking of warning signs, my colleague Dr. L. was not alone in his inability to foresee his patient's suicide. Prime risk factors include depression (a factor in 80 percent of all suicides), alcoholism, drug addiction, and schizophrenia, but none of these factors applied in this case. Dr. L.'s patient was depressed, but to his knowledge she had made no previous suicide attempts; she did not indicate her intention; she did not tell him she was writing a will or otherwise finalizing her affairs; she was not delusional; and she had not recently suffered a severe stress—all of which would have put him on a suicide alert.

If Dr. L. knew that his patient was contemplating suicide, her degree of hopelessness could have proved an important predictor of eventual success. Chances are that her husband or a friend knew, though. A pity no one told her psychiatrist. Probably her husband did not want to face it either, or perhaps he was one of the many who expect a psychiatrist to be a mind-reader.

Dr. L. would have been overjoyed if someone had handed him a foolproof suicide-prevention checklist. Wouldn't we all! Many dedicated people have attempted to develop one. Unfortunately, while they are able to identify high-risk groups and characteristics of people who have already committed suicide (such as a family history of affective disorders or suicide), they cannot predict whether any individual will or will not do it. The greatest risk of suicide is when the patient is beginning to come out of a profound depression and has recovered sufficient energy to act on the deadly impulse. Apparent recovery brings the energy with which to act. Clinicians must use their subjective judgment of the patient's behavior, attitude, and shared thoughts to decide whether and when the patient is in danger. Possibly Dr. L.'s anxiety obscured his clinical skills; clearly he was not cut out to be a psychotherapist. Yet even the most competent, intuitive clinicians lose patients to suicide.

Suicide Risk Factors

1. A history of previous attempts.
2. A lethal suicide plan.
3. A family history of suicide, which is more common in suicidal patients than in the general population.
4. Marital status: Patients who have never married are at greatest risk, followed by those widowed, separated, and divorced, married with no children, and married with children.
5. Failure at, or loss of, occupation.
6. Having certain occupations (e.g., psychiatrists, police officers, musicians, and lawyers seem more prone to suicide).
7. Gender: Men are more likely to be successful at suicide, while women make more attempts.
8. Age: Risk generally increases with age, although teenage suicides are increasing.
9. Health status: Certain patient populations are at high risk, including those recently having undergone major surgery, patients in great physical pain, and patients with a chronic or terminal illness.
10. Location: Rates are higher in urban areas than in rural ones.
11. Drug or alcohol use.
12. Paranoia: withdrawal from healthy human contact.
13. Hopelessness: sense of inevitable doom.
14. Surviving the death of a spouse.

THE BIOLOGY OF SUICIDE

The biopsychiatric laboratory has produced some extraordinary findings about the biology of suicide. Many new studies have shown that a problem in the body's hypothalamus-pituitary system (the HPA axis) is a possible sign of suicidal tendencies. Changes in some of the receptor sites in the brain that respond to tranquilizers may also play some role in triggering suicidal feelings. Other studies indicate that reduced transmission of the neurotransmitter dopamine may play a part in the suicidal behavior associated with depression. Some studies even suggest that abnormalities in the human growth hormone system may be a marker or risk factor that can help predict suicidal behavior.

Finally, as you'll see in Part IV of this book, treatment breakthroughs resulting from our greater understanding of the role of serotonin will also reduce the rate of suicide linked to depression.

Suicidal individuals have abnormally low levels of the brain chemical serotonin. Serotonin is one of the neurotransmitters strongly implicated in certain types of depression; it is also involved in the regulation of impulsive behavior and aggression, whether or not depression is present. This finding, as well as others under study, promise the clinician objective, case-by-case diagnostic data. For the patient, the same finding offers the hope of eliminating the violent urge to die.

We determine serotonin brain levels indirectly, by measuring levels of its principal metabolic breakdown product, 5-HIAA (5-hydroxyindoleacetic acid), in the cerebrospinal fluid (CSF). Almost two decades ago in Sweden, Dr. Marie Asberg began to notice the correlation between low CSF 5-HIAA levels and both suicide attempts and high levels of aggression. Her finding has been replicated again and again. In one study of suicide attempters who had their CSF 5-HIAA measured, Asberg discovered that 20 percent of those with low levels succeeded in killing themselves during the subsequent year; of those with normal levels, only 2 percent killed themselves.

Asberg and numerous additional researchers have since found that persons prone to violent suicides (shooting, jumping, hanging) have especially low levels, as do violent criminals. In still another study, both unipolar and bipolar depressed patients with low CSF 5-HIAA levels scored particularly high on the anger-related items on a psychological questionnaire.

The serotonin discovery fits in nicely with genetic findings about suicide and depression. Identical twins tend to have similar levels of CSF 5-HIAA; nonidentical twins do not. Healthy persons with low values have significantly more affective illness in their families than do healthy persons with normal values. The serotonin factor thus marks an inherited trait rather than a temporary state; it is a trait marker rather than a state marker. This is just the sort of information biopsychiatrists are searching for: biochemical markers linked to suicidal behavior. The markers are used to develop both reliable tests to identify persons at risk and medication to reverse the illness. Combine these objective tools with our additional clinical skills, and we will be better able, as Dr. L. was not, to save our patients' lives.

The desire to self-destruct is in itself a nightmare. Paula D., now fifty-one, made four serious attempts on her life in a two-year period, after she discovered her husband's infidelities with two of her close friends. "At the time, I thought that the humiliation and betrayal I felt were the worst pain I had ever experienced. Looking back on it now, though," she muses, "the need to destroy myself was by far the most excruciating part of the whole horrible time."

That Paula survived seems proof that somebody up there wanted her to live. She survived two gunshot wounds, one overdose of pills, and one attempt at gassing herself in a closed garage. She had been depressed much of her life, before and after the attempts. She was and is in treatment with a psychiatrist well known as a psychotherapist, but who did not at the time believe in the use of medication. Paula herself urged him to prescribe antidepressants for her, which he did but at too low a dose to be effective, an all-too-common error. When Paula finally came to me for evaluation, tests revealed she was a good candidate for medication. Within one month her most recent depression had substantially lifted. At the end of the year, when we slowly tapered her off the pills, it was gone. She has not had a recurrence, or an urge to die, in four years.

"Now I know what most people mean when they say they're depressed," she says. "I get depressed. It's a down frame of mind, usually in response to something that's just happened or to something that has come up in my therapy—not a blackening of my entire existence. I deal with it and it goes away. Or I don't deal with it—and it still goes away!"

Paula's therapy is no longer a perpetual battle with her moods. "I've been able to understand and avoid the self-destructive relationships I was always getting myself into. I'm finally getting some work done there!" she says with a laugh and a grimace. Paula has been in therapy for almost twenty years.

CHAPTER 16

Depression Is a Brain Disease

Thus far we have encountered numerous aspects of depression. Subsequent chapters will reveal still others, deeper and deeper inside the brain and body. Let us take a few steps back now, however, and see what we have so far.

WHAT IS DEPRESSION?

Depression is a psychobiological mood disorder—in other words, an interaction of psychological and biological variables. The extent to which these factors contribute to depression depends on the relative strength of environmental and genetic influences. Long-standing economic stress, chronic medical or psychiatric illness, destructive family patterns, or an overload of stressful situations can cause depression even if genetic factors are absent. Similarly, inherited body chemistry can assure the onset of depression even if other triggers are few or mild or—in rare cases—absent altogether. Factors and variables differ for everyone. Depression is utterly individual, utterly personal. The treatment of depression depends on this understanding.

In medicine we often find the cure before we understand the illness. When we attempt to understand why the treatment works, we often end up understanding the illness. This knowledge leads us to more effective treatments, to better diagnostic tests, to new cures, and ultimately to preventive measures. Such is the story with depression.

Depression is a brain disease. We know that because of two decades of extraordinary exploration of the brain as we have attempted to figure out why and how antidepressants achieve their results.

A HEADY TIME

Our success in treating depression is actually the result of our success in the treatment of schizophrenia. A French surgeon was searching for a drug to prevent the fall of blood pressure that leads to surgical shock. He tried an antihistamine on his patients; it did not achieve the desired results, but it had interesting calming properties that left the person's awareness intact. He added the drug to his presurgical repertoire. Other surgeons became interested; chemists set out to produce more effective compounds. Chlorpromazine (Thorazine) proved to be just such a drug. In the early 1950s this drug was elevated to wonder-drug status when French psychiatrists discovered that it could do what no other treatment had ever accomplished: bring schizophrenic patients back into this world.

Then came a mad dash by pharmaceutical companies to come up with a drug that was even better and that had fewer side effects. A common strategy in doing this is to alter or add to the chemical formulation of the existing drug. By fiddling with chlorpromazine, Swiss chemists created imipramine (Tofranil). It failed as an antipsychotic, but it did seem to reduce depressive symptoms.

Thus was born the tricyclic class of antidepressant drugs. (*Tricyclic* refers to the drug's three-ring chemical structure.) Meanwhile, physicians in tuberculosis hospitals happened upon another major class of antidepressants, monoamine oxidase inhibitors (MAOIs). The MAOI iproniazid, an antibiotic developed specially for TB, seemed to lift the cloud from many of the depressed patients.

It was a truly heady time in the history of psychiatry. Freud himself had postulated a chemical imbalance in severe mental illness, but he lacked the technology to find it. In our time, advanced technology was opening the portals to a golden age of neuroscience.

A major breakthrough came when research scientists were able to demonstrate that the nature of communication in the brain was both electrical (which we knew) and chemical (which had been hypothesized but never confirmed). It became immediately clear that chemicals were the fundamental units of communication between nerve cells. This finding gave biological psychiatrists and neuroscientists the go-ahead to search for the biochemical malfunctioning that they believed generated mental illness. Even so, physiological explorations of severe mental suffering enjoyed little support among the psychiatric establishment, which followed a largely psychoanalytic approach that preferred psychological explanations for the entire spectrum of mental illness.

There was little doubt, however, that antipsychotics and antidepressants worked by affecting the chemistry of the brain directly. Ready or not, it was time for psychiatry to widen its perspective. It was time for the brain to resume its proper place inside our heads, from which it had long been banished in favor of the mind. The question remained: How do medications for the mind affect the chemistry of the brain?

THE COMMUNICATION NETWORK OF THE BRAIN

Strangely, throughout much of the history of medicine, the brain has been considered off-limits. A brain at autopsy could reveal structural information, but it took to the grave most of its working secrets. That's because, until recently, tinkering with a living brain would destroy it; the brain is the only organ in our bodies that does not generate new cells after birth. (It does, however, generate new connections between cells as we learn and experience.)

The Whats

The brain is essentially a mushy mass of nerve cells—between ten billion and a trillion of them. These cells come in two types: glial cells and neurons. Glial cells outnumber neurons nine to one; these cells keep the brain supported, protected, and fed, but their additional functions are poorly understood. As far as we know now, the neurons do all the actual brain work.

Nerve cells are organized into structures and specialized functional areas that often look identical but control quite different activities and systems.

The anatomical structures of the brain evolved over millions of years. The brainstem, rising from the spinal cord, is often called the "reptilian brain," because it is remarkably like a reptile's brain. Basic body functions necessary to survival—heart rate, breathing—are regulated here. All communication to and from the body passes through the brainstem. The cerebellum, one of the brain structures concerned with movement, is behind the brainstem.

The diencephalon is deep within the brain. It consists of groups of neurons sometimes called the "mammalian brain" because these structures are most highly evolved in mammals. Within this part of the brain is the limbic system, the "emotional brain," containing, among other structures, the hypothalamus and the pituitary gland. Body temperature, blood pressure, eating, sleeping, hormones, behavior, and emotions, including pleasure and displeasure—our mammalian selves—are kept in balance here. Or not, as the case may be. Those of us who study depression are most concerned with this area of the brain, particularly the hypothalamus. It is a limbic system regulator, integrating messages through this complex area. The hypothalamus appears also to be a major motivation center, highly influenced by rewarding stimuli.

Lying atop it all is the largest part of the brain, the cerebrum, site of our most evolved, cerebral selves. The cerebrum is covered with an eighth of an inch of gray matter, the cortex, that contains our uniquely human capabilities: reason, planning, understanding, behavior control, speech, decision making, imagination, writing, nuclear bomb-making . . .

The two hemispheres of the cerebrum are somewhat specialized. In most people, the left side is more logical, mathematical, and verbal. The right side is more concerned with patterns and spatial relationships. Each hemisphere controls opposite sides of the body—the left hemisphere directs the right side, and the right hemisphere directs the left side.

The cortex is divided into four lobes, each with highly specialized areas corresponding to different body functions and systems, such as recognizing and processing visual stimuli, control of delicate movements, interpreting sounds, and so on.

The neuron is the basic functional unit of these structures and areas. The neuron consists of a cell body, containing the nucleus. A web of tubular filaments called dendrites protrudes from the cell body. The dendrites receive information and deliver it to the cell body, which gets the message and communicates it to other neurons via the axon. The axon projects like a stem from the cell body. At the end of the axon are hundreds of branches, each with a terminal.

Each cell has a legion of dendrites and some as many as a thousand axon terminals. "In a single human brain the number of possible interconnections between these cells is greater than the number of atoms in the universe!" Robert Ornstein and Richard F. Thompson appropriately exclaim in their book *The Amazing Brain!* that calculation should relieve the anxieties of those who worry that scientific study of the anatomical structures and biological processes of the mind robs us of our individuality and free will.

The Hows

No two neurons are directly connected to each other. A space of a millionth of an inch—the synapse—separates each of them. An electrical impulse zips down the axon from the cell body. Q: How does it get to the next neuron? A: It never does. Each axon terminal contains little sacs (vesicles) that hold chemicals; when the impulse reaches the end of the axon, it triggers the vesicle to release its chemical contents.

The chemicals at the terminals are called neurotransmitters. They travel across the synapse to the adjacent neurons, where they attach to receptors. A receptor is a structure on the surface of the cell. Each receptor will accept a chemical only with a particular molecular shape. The traditional analogy is that of a lock and key. If the neurotransmitter fits precisely into the receptor molecule, changes will occur in the membrane of the next, or postsynaptic, neuron; sodium ions will rush in and excite that next neuron into generating a new impulse, called an action potential. Thus the message continues from neuron to neuron.

Neurotransmitters deliver basically two messages: excite (fire); inhibit (don't fire). Translation: Gimme some more of that delicious neurotransmitter; I'm feeling really terrific today. Or: Turn the stuff off, will you? I'm in a crummy mood. When a neurotransmitter is delivering an inhibitory message, negatively charged chloride ions permeate the membrane and prevent the target neuron from firing. (Actually, it takes neurotransmitters from hundreds of terminals to get a complete message across to the neuron.)

A neuron will use only one type of neurotransmitter at every connecting point, from dendrites to axon terminals. The brain probably manufactures several hundred neurotransmitters. We have identified some thirty of them so far. They are difficult to find because they are released in minute quantities. Another problem is that unused or excess quantities are immediately withdrawn from circulation. Either enzymes break them down, or they are sucked back into the presynaptic terminal (a process we call reuptake) to be broken down and recycled.

DEPRESSION, DRUGS, AND THE BRAIN

Once we had the technology to work at a cellular level in the brain, we began to understand how antidepressants worked.

In Parts IV and V of this book, we take a very close look at the treatment for depression. As you read it you will realize that we have truly crossed a new frontier in our understanding of the basic activity of the brain when it becomes depressed. It is the best news of all, and the final part of the picture you need in order to understand what depression is. Not surprisingly, this technology has been behind the breakthrough drugs described in Part IV that have helped us understand much of what we now know about depression and the brain.

The Catecholamine Hypothesis

A decade ago, a basic theory was devised to explain the biological process that leads to depression. That theory focused on decreased concentrations in the brain of the neurotransmitter norepinephrine. (Norepinephrine is a chemical of the catecholamine family. Like serotonin and some other neurotransmitters, norepinephrine molecules contain only one of a certain kind of protein, called an amine, and so it is classified a monoamine.) One of the functions of norepinephrine is to regulate mood.

Researchers found that the two main types of antidepressant medications each increase norepinephrine levels, but they do so in different ways. The tricyclic antidepressants (TCAs) prevent neurons from reabsorbing norepinephrine. In contrast, the other kind of medication works by inhibiting a brain enzyme called monoamine oxidase (MAO) from doing its job, which is to break down monoamine molecules. These antidepressants are thus called MAO inhibitors, or MAOIs.

Scientists realized that if symptoms of depression arise because of *low* norepinephrine levels, then symptoms of mania may be the result of *excess* norepinephrine. We began to test this theory, called the catecholamine hypothesis, through the use of lab tests. Of course, we couldn't take tissue samples from people's brains, the way we can take samples of other tissues for study. Instead we had to devise indirect ways of measuring neurotransmitter activity. We found that by analyzing a person's urine, we can detect the substances that remain after the MAO enzyme dissolves the norepinephrine molecule. These substances, called metabolites, give us clues about how much norepinephrine is present and how fast it is being broken down. Low levels of a metabolite called MHPG (short for 3-methoxy-4-hydroxyphenylglycol) indicate low levels of norepinephrine. Indeed, depressed people tend to have low MHPG levels, which suggests that they have low levels of norepinephrine. The reverse is true in people with mania. Today we can use advanced machines such as the PET scanner to create images of the living, functioning brain. But we still have to rely on these indirect measures of neurotransmitter activity to study how the brain is working on the molecular level.

Scientists also developed other tests to show biochemical activity, tests that provided other evidence to support the catecholamine hypothesis. For example, depressed people were found to have too much of a hormone called cortisol. In these people, the biological clock fails to regulate the normal secretion of cortisol, and thus the hormone is released in high quantities throughout the day. (Norepinephrine is partly responsible for

regulating cortisol, so it makes sense that a breakdown in the norepinephrine system might also lead to high cortisol levels.)

The use of TCAs proved reasonably effective in people whose depression involved a malfunctioning norepinephrine system. But not everyone
with depression got better using TCAs. Clearly some other faulty biological mechanism was at work. Another puzzling question concerned the
fact that sometimes weeks, even months, would pass before the patient
felt the antidepressant effects of TCAs. We knew that these drugs boosted
neurotransmitter levels immediately. But why, then, did they take so long
to reduce symptoms of depression?

As is so often the case in science, answers led to more questions.
Further digging revealed that the brain has many different receptor
subtypes that respond to the same neurotransmitter. For example, there
are at least five receptors for dopamine. It is possible that a defect
in one type of receptor, but not others, could be involved in mood
disorders. Researchers also discovered new classes of brain chemicals,
such as the natural opiates known as endorphins, that had their own
variety of receptors and that were also found to be involved in mood
regulation.

Things soon got even more complicated when it was discovered that
some receptors can even adapt to changes in the brain's chemical environment. For example, if antidepressants raise the level of a neurotransmitter,
the neurons might respond by producing less of the substance, or their
receptors might become less sensitive to the presence of neurotransmitter
molecules.

The era of naive simplicity was over. We could explain how a medication
worked at the molecular or cellular level. But we began to discover that
antidepressants also triggered many intermediary reactions involving other
neurological transmitters, hormones, and modulators—some of which
had yet to be discovered.

It seemed nearly an impossible task to state with absolute certainty
how a medication worked in depressed people who had lost their
appetite, sex drive, and normal sleep patterns. As an interim measure,
the catecholamine hypothesis was fine, but a more complete theory was
needed.

The Biogenic Amine Hypothesis

Laboratories throughout the world began identifying other biogenic amine neurotransmitter culprits. Depression seemed to be not one but several illnesses that shared a common symptom constellation. In other

words, depression has several subtypes. As a rule, each subtype responds to treatment with a certain kind of antidepressant. In contrast, the various depressions described in the DSM-IV bear little relationship to the biochemical disruptions that result in illness. In my fantasy, the next DSM will not list bipolar I or cyclothymia, but entirely new categories, such as MAOI-susceptible or TCA-susceptible depression!

A few years after the discovery of imipramine, scientists realized that a different neurotransmitter, serotonin (another monoamine), was also involved in depression. A new variety of TCA, amitriptyline, was found to influence serotonin rather than norepinephrine. Serotonin's metabolite, 5-HIAA, leaves the brain via the spinal fluid, where it can be measured. Some persons who respond to amitriptyline but not to imipramine do indeed have low levels of 5-HIAA. Very low levels of 5-HIAA often correspond to suicidal behavior or even homicidal behavior, as discussed in the previous chapter.

Further complicating the biogenic amine hypothesis were findings that some depressed people had high instead of low levels of norepinephrine and serotonin.

Although norepinephrine and serotonin remain the neurotransmitters most directly implicated in depression, other neurotransmitters have been added to the list, including dopamine, which previously was thought to be involved primarily in schizophrenia. Others undoubtedly play a role in mood alteration as well as in the production of antidepressant side effects. A common side effect, for example, is dry mouth—blame acetylcholine for that. And histamine is the apparent culprit when sedating side effects are noted.

Neuropeptides

Another of the most fascinating research areas over the past decade involves a whole new class of chemical substances, the neuropeptides (also called polypeptides or just peptides). These are chemicals that have properties of both hormones and neurotransmitters. They work in conjunction with neurotransmitters, making cells more or less receptive to the message.

The endorphins, a relatively new class of neuropeptides, have captured public and scientific imagination because their structure and function is similar to opiate drugs such as morphine. Besides killing pain, opiates can bring on depression and elation (the runner's high, for example). Our natural brain opioids (the word means "opiatelike")—the endorphins and related substances—are clearly important to the biochemistry of depression. For example, my colleagues and I have found that people with some types of minor depression, particularly those patients who mutilate or cut themselves, have low beta-endorphin levels. Endorphins may function to reinforce important behaviors and produce a sense of well-being, such as occurs in breast-feeding women.

Somatostatin is a peptide found in the gastrointestinal system and in the

---

The Biochemistry of the Placebo

Antidepressants, no matter which type, are guaranteed to work in at least one out of three patients. That's because of a phenomenon called the placebo effect. Aspirin would have the same effect if it were called an antidepressant, because it too has a high placebo response rate. Medicine typically looks down its nose at patients who respond to placebos, as if their response to a pill with no active ingredients proves that they are not really ill.

The placebo and the placebo responder deserve more respect.

Step 1. A research team appeared at a dental clinic in California. Dental pain is supposed to be the worst physical pain we feel, and they came bearing pain pills for the patients awaiting their dental work with the usual dread. Little did anyone in the waiting room know that half of them were about to receive placebos. Nonetheless, all subsequently reported a substantial reduction or elimination of pain.

Step 2. The team reappeared at the clinic. Again, half the unsuspecting patients received genuine medication and half received placebos. Only this time half of the placebo group also received a drug called naloxone. The naloxone group was the only segment to report substantial pain.

Naloxone is an endorphin antagonist; it is designed to fit into endorphin receptors and block them so that our natural painkillers cannot work.

The results of this experiment, and many others before and since, tell us that the lowly placebo acts on our endorphin system. All it requires is the belief that the medicine we're taking is the real thing.

We do not actually know whether endorphins are responsible for the placebo effect of antidepressants. We do know, though, that endorphin receptors are abundant in the limbic and hypothalamic areas linked to depression, and that endorphins regulate important catecholamine systems.

And now for the bad news: The placebo effect in depressive illness is usually short-lived. The good news: If it's an isolated bout, the placebo effect may be what cures you. Which is possibly why so many psychiatrists prescribe these extremely potent drugs with such abandon.

brain. During a depressive episode, some depressed persons show a low level of this substance.

No doubt other brain substances will prove to fluctuate along with moods—and a new generation of drugs will alter their levels in the brain. It may turn out that some still-to-be-discovered neurotransmitter is the answer to everything. At present we can study only those substances that are both known and measurable.

Amino Acids

Amino acids are the building blocks of proteins. They have neurotransmitter properties. A few years ago the amino acid GABA (gamma-aminobutyric acid) was identified as our natural antianxiety neurotransmitter. Anxiety and depression are frequent companions, which may explain why low GABA levels have been found in some depressed people.

Focusing on the Receptor

Evidence exists that the functional defect in depression is not so much in the transmitter itself but in the receptor that receives it. In other words, the key is all right; it's the lock that is broken.

Focusing on the receptor could help answer a question that has continued to plague researchers: Why do antidepressants typically take two to three weeks to work when they increase the amount of available neurotransmitter almost immediately? Perhaps antidepressants end up changing the sensitivity of receptors, an adjustment that would take time.

This point of view has become the new catecholamine hypothesis: that altered levels of neurotransmitters result from the brain's attempt to compensate for the reduced sensitivity of receptors. The synapses have feedback receptors that normally determine when the neurotransmitter levels are appropriate; they issue the order to cease firing. Depression has deafened this feedback system, however. The cell keeps pouring the stuff out and the synapse becomes flooded with neurotransmitter. The brain is always trying to keep itself in balance; thus receptors on the postsynaptic side refuse to respond. In time, the effect of the antidepressant would be to set those receptors straight once more.

Systems, Electrolytes, Enzymes

Another approach to the delayed effects of antidepressants is to study the relationships among adjacent neurotransmitter systems. Evidence suggests that when an antidepressant affects one neurotransmitter system, neighboring systems may adjust themselves accordingly to restore harmony.

Investigating electrolytes has also proved productive. Electrolytes such as sodium, calcium, potassium, and magnesium assist in electrical conductivity across cell membranes. Electrolyte imbalances appear in certain types of depression. Lithium, a salt that is similar to an electrolyte, appears to assist in transport of the sodium ion.

MAO: The "Personality Enzyme"

When is a platelet not a little plate? When it is a component of blood cells. We can monitor levels of the enzyme MAO in platelets, which resemble brain cells in the way their receptors and membranes function. Until recently, platelet MAO measurements have been used mostly to diagnose (MAO is low in bipolar depression), to determine how a person is responding to MAOI medication (the medication appears useful in persons with high MAO activity plus anxiety, agitation, and bodily complaints), and to improve MAOI response (reduction of platelet MAO by 50 to 80 percent).

Lately, platelet MAO levels are also providing a quick and easy assessment of certain personality traits—easier than the paper-and-pencil psychological test approach. In study after study, decreased MAO levels, associated with bipolar disorder, correlate with sensation- or thrill-seeking and impulsivity. Low MAO is a possible suicide marker, as is low serotonin.

Eventually, MAO levels may be able to predict future vulnerability to mood disorders. In one experiment, researchers measured MAO levels in college students, then contacted them again two years later. Compared with the high-MAO and normal group, the low-MAO group had more psychiatric and legal problems and had fallen an average of a half year behind in school; those who had graduated or simply left school reported greater job instability. Some had experienced no serious problems, but they reported significantly more depression, alcoholism, suicide, and contact with the mental health system in their families. Platelet MAO levels may qualify, therefore, as a genetic trait marker, identification of which could potentially help prevent serious mental suffering.

The ability of serotonin to bind to receptors, can also be measured in blood platelets. Low levels of serotonin correlate with such personality traits as violence, impulsivity, and suicidality. A high level of serotonin is associated with leadership. In one report, dominant monkeys had twice the amount of serotonin than the others—and in a college fraternity, the officers had higher serotonin values than the brothers.

Then there's COMT (catechol-O-methyltransferase), an enzyme that breaks down neurotransmitters within the synapse. Abnormal COMT levels have been reported in different types of depression.

MAPPING DEPRESSION IN THE BRAIN

To repeat: The neuron is the basic functional unit of the brain, and the neurotransmitter is the fundamental unit of communication. Our brain-power comes from the "wiring" of neurons—the pathways—among the specialized structures and areas of the brain. Emotional reactions do not come blasting helter-skelter out of the limbic system. The circuitry connects the system to the cortex and many other areas of the brain, including memory centers, all of which may encourage or inhibit a response and determine how it is to be expressed. The response is different in every person because the interconnections among nerves are as individual as fingerprints. Interconnections are continually being formed by learning and experience.

Neurotransmitters carry the messages throughout the brain, but they do not determine the content of the message. The meaning of the message can be inferred from where in the brain it goes.

If we follow the pathways of norepinephrine (called the noradrenergic system), serotonin (the serotonergic system), and other biogenic amines, we see the brain areas likely to be involved in depression. The neurons in these systems have very long axons and plentiful terminals, so that their interconnections number in the many thousands.

There are actually two noradrenergic brain pathways. One leads to the hypothalamus and limbic system, with terminals in the so-called pleasure centers. The other is concentrated in a small brainstem area known as the locus ceruleus. This tiny brain area is associated with fear, and is involved in drug withdrawal states. This noradrenergic pathway terminates in the cortex and hippocampus, which is involved in memory. The serotonergic system follows a pathway similar to that of norepinephrine, originating, however, in certain cells that may help regulate agitation and sleep. One part of the dopaminergic system connects to an area of the cortex that is associated with emotional behavior.

The point of tracing these neurochemical routes is to show why depression affects us on many experiential and physiological levels. The neurotransmitters are particularly involved in the limbic system, disruption of which can produce depression's emotional and physical symptoms. The nerve patterns within the cortex demonstrate that depression affects the highest brain functions and controls.

High-tech Mapping

Positron emission tomography (PET) offers an intriguing way to see where depression is located in the brain. It is a latter-day computer-assisted x-ray, which reveals body tissue in action. In research psychiatry, PET reveals rates of glucose metabolism in the brain. Glucose — sugar — provides the energy for the brain. Subjects receive radioactively tagged glucose; forty minutes later their brains are scanned. If certain areas of the depressed brain are more or less active during depression, they will show up using this procedure.

In a 1985 study, PET scans on depressed persons revealed significant sluggishness in the part of the brain called the caudate nucleus. Connected to the limbic system but not actually part of it, the caudate nucleus helps to regulate movement and muscle tone, but it may be involved as well with attention and arousal. The caudate nucleus is one of the most highly evolved dopamine-containing areas of the brain.

One more difference showed up on the scans, but only in certain patients: The left side of the frontal lobe of the cortex was substantially slowed. For years there have been numerous reports that the brain may segregate positive and negative emotions, with rotten moods being the right hemisphere's burden to bear. Stroke victims whose brains have been damaged in the left frontal areas show severe depression. So it seems that if your "cheerful side" is impaired, depression may await you.

Electrical "Behavioral" Maps

How the brain responds to a brief stimulus, such as a flash of light, provides an inner look at a possible explanation for outward behavioral style. The method is called evoked potential.

The subject is attached to an electroencephalograph (EEG), which measures the brain's electrical response to changes in a given stimulus (light, sound, etc.). The evoked potential of depressed persons typically differs from that of nondepressed individuals. As the stimulus becomes more intense, the brain waves of depressed individuals barely increase in amplitude; sometimes they may even show a reduction. In other words, brain activity in depression is inhibited, underaroused. Depressed persons cannot maintain appropriate sensory attention to the world around them—further indication that our responses to the environment depend on the electrical and chemical environment within the brain.

The hyperresponsiveness of mania is revealed in results of evoked potential tests by the way brain waves intensify beyond the normal.

Evoked potential response parallels neurotransmitter defects. Give a depressed person L-dopa, which will increase dopamine, and brain-wave response will return to normal levels.

CHAPTER 17

Depression Is Too Many Hormones and a Mistimed Bio-Clock

As you've seen, the route of depression is a direct path to your entire being. Something occurs outside your body that affects you internally; then depression literally flows out of the brain and into the body. The endocrine system provides the channel.

So common are biochemical derangements of the endocrine system that we have come to regard them as state markers for biological depression. Unlike a trait marker, which is present in health and illness and signifies a vulnerability to disease, a state marker comes and goes with the illness. In other words, a state marker is a diagnostic flag. In the biopsychiatric laboratory, your hormones are such a good indication of what is happening in your head that we call them a window into the brain.

A WINDOW INTO THE BRAIN

Some years ago, Dr. Edward J. Sachar began a study of the levels of the hormone cortisol among depressed persons undergoing psychotherapy. Cortisol is a stress hormone secreted by the cortex of the adrenal glands. Sachar wanted to see whether psychotherapy causes changes in stress levels. Instead he stumbled upon a major discovery about the biology of depression.

Sachar discovered that a large percentage of seriously depressed people have a level of cortisol in their bodies that is even higher than in persons suffering from severe anxiety, psychosis, or other equally stressful conditions. It did not make any sense. Cortisol is an activating hormone that helps to stimulate body systems to respond to stress. But depressed persons with high cortisol levels were anything but stimulated. In addition, while oversecretion of cortisol is a symptom of Cushing's disease, Sachar's depressed subjects had normal adrenal glands.

No Feedback

Investigators began looking for other abnormal hormonal patterns in depressed persons. The search soon yielded another paradoxical finding. Many depressed persons with healthy thyroid glands showed evidence of excessive secretions of thyroid hormone. Persons with too little thyroid hormone (hypothyroidism) are often misdiagnosed as depressed (see Chapter 9), but, as with cortisol, too much of the hormone generally produces opposite symptoms.

Indeed, evidence of too many hormones began to show up in many endocrine subsystems. But the glands themselves were normal.

The endocrine glands function to keep complex body systems in a well-balanced, well-regulated state, or homeostasis; they continuously and smoothly adapt to changes in our inner and outer environments. Clearly, depression disrupted this delicate balance. But neuroendocrinologists could find no evidence that the glands themselves were damaged.

The site of the malfunctioning had to be the brain. The endocrine system is a kind of extension of the nervous system into the remainder of the body. Indeed, the two are inseparable, since they are linked at the hypothalamus. We have seen that the hypothalamus and the limbic system of which it is a part are central to emotions in general, depression in particular. The hypothalamus also has charge of the endocrine system, via the same neurotransmitters implicated in depression. The imbalances in neurotransmitter-receptor systems that produce depression also influence the hypothalamus's ability to regulate the endocrine system.

Thus, via the hypothalamus, emotions influence the physiological functioning of the body, and the malfunctioning of body systems influences emotional experience.

We have seen as well that diseased endocrine glands are among the most common mimickers of depression. Disease causes a gland to oversecrete, undersecrete, or cease secreting hormones; the resulting hormonal imbalance produces emotional symptoms through neuroendocrine channels.

Depression, however, works from the brain downward. It affects the elaborate feedback mechanisms that establish and monitor the correct level of hormonal secretions throughout the endocrine networks. Some of these mechanisms function like thermostats, turning off secretions when hormone levels reach a certain set point. In biological depression, these sensors do not operate properly. The depressed person awakens at unusual hours and cannot return to sleep; he loses his appetite; she does not get her menstrual period even though she is not pregnant.

ENDOCRINE TESTS FOR DEPRESSION

Thanks to the work of neuroendocrinologists and biopsychiatrists since Sachar's original discovery, we now have concrete physiological evidence of disruption in this essential homeostatic balance in depression. Since not all patients reveal the same endocrine abnormalities, we have developed a number of neuroendocrine measures.

The dexamethasone suppression test (DST) and the TRH stimulation test are challenge, or provocative, tests. We administer a dose of hormone and challenge the system to behave or misbehave. The TRH stimulation test was described in Chapter 9. The DST works in a similar way. Dexamethasone is a synthetic version of the adrenal hormone cortisol. We administer a dose of dexamethasone that the hypothalamus should recognize as excessive cortisol. The normal, nondepressed hypothalamus responds by telling the pituitary gland to signal the adrenal cortex to stop its usual daily secretions of cortisol for a while, until levels return to normal. But in about half of depressed people, no such response takes place. In the absence of functioning feedback mechanisms, the adrenal cortex continues to pump out cortisol.

Together the DST and the TRH stimulation tests can identify biological malfunction in approximately 85 percent of unipolar depressives. The DST alone will identify about half of them; the TRH stimulation test alone is abnormal in nearly 64 percent. Thirty percent of patients show abnormalities on both tests.

We know that these endocrine disinhibitions are depression-related, because treating the depression makes them go away. Normal endocrine regulation resumes. Thus we use these tests not only to detect biological depression but also to determine when the episode truly has ended. Symptoms may disappear, but when the underlying imbalance remains, we now know that depression is bound to return. The tests are our feedback mechanisms. Once they are normal, we can cease aggressive treatment of the acute phases and move on to long-term prevention.

THE CLOCK THAT COULDN'T

Dr. Sachar's work led to another important discovery about hormonal functioning in depressed persons. Sometimes their overall levels of hormones are normal, but the timing of secretions is odd indeed. In normal individuals, for example, cortisol levels are lowest in the middle of the night and highest at about 8 A.M. and 4 P.M. Depressed people often reveal no day-night differences, or they may even show a reversed pattern, with the high occurring in the wee hours.

Emotionally, depressed persons are out of sync with the rest of the world. Biologically, too, they march to a different drummer.

A Sad Patient

I remember the first time I heard her voice. It was during the World Series. I was about to turn off the radio so I could watch the game on TV. But when I touched the radio dial she started to sing. The quality of that voice—you would know what I mean if I could reveal her name—transformed the next several hours of my life. Even when the song had ended, I remained mesmerized. The baseball game was exciting, but it takes second place in my memory of that long-ago day.

I bought a number of her recordings over the years, for hers were the kind of voice and personality that live forever. But then she stopped singing. I heard a vague rumor that she was ill. Cancer, somebody said. I shook my head in sadness.

Shock is too mild a word for my reaction when she was shown into my consulting room. My appointment book indicated a new patient, but the name was not hers. She had used her real name instead of the stage name the world knew her by.

She certainly did not look like she had cancer. Her shapeliness had disappeared under the thirty pounds she said she had gained in the last few months. "I get these cravings," she admitted. "Anything sugary or sweet. I could eat a box of donuts this minute—all of them, no joke."

Our tests ruled out cancer along with other mimickers. Nonetheless, she was severely ill—desperately depressed. At that moment she was spiraling downward, she said, but sooner or later she would "snap upward like a released rubber band." While she had been going back and forth like this for at least ten years, it hadn't been a significant problem until three years earlier, when her manic-depression was diagnosed. She had been through the gamut of psychological and pharmaceutical therapies without noticeable change. She had had a brief flirtation with alcohol, marijuana, and cocaine in order to keep up with her demanding career. She ended up on such a "bummer," she said, that she gave them up along with her career.

During depressed phases she drifted away from everybody she knew. She had no energy. Mostly she slept. At first she would return to the world when her spirits lightened. Her disappearances lasted so long, however— half the year—that she lost contact with most of her circle. She traveled for a while but found it too difficult, ultimately, to keep up the interest or the pace. Even in a good phase she felt a little lonely and lost. She spent most of the time sleeping in her hotel rooms in some of the most fascinating places in the world.

Only one trip seemed to bring her out of it, she said. She'd spent part of one winter in the Caribbean at the estate of an old friend. She had had a wonderful time. She didn't do anything special; she just felt great, like her old self again. She went back to New York to see about resuming her career, and within the week she had plummeted.

The proverbial lightbulb went off in my head. Close questioning revealed a pattern to her moods: down in fall and winter, up in spring and summer. "I've always been down in winter," she said, "since I was a kid. But it was nothing like what's happened to me during the last few years. I've spent a lot of time talking to shrinks about why I close up in winter." She added, "I'm really neurotic about it."

"Maybe, maybe not," I said. "Your mood swings may be physiological. We have recently discovered that some depressed people are highly responsive to light, or rather the absence of it. Their moods fluctuate seasonally in response to the length of day and the intensity of the light."

Her visit occurred years ago, when the discovery of seasonal affective disorder (SAD) was brand-new. Now we know a great deal more about it, including the hormone that seems to be responsible: melatonin. Melatonin is produced by the pineal gland, located in the brain. Not that the seasonal nature of moods had escaped notice. Even Hippocrates had known that mania and depression peak in spring and fall.

In our time we regard these seasonal moods as psychologically motivated events, as they often are. But sometimes they have to do with the biological rhythm of melatonin.

Why we secrete melatonin has long been a mystery. In animals it controls seasonal reproductive rhythms; offspring are born as the hormonal secretions diminish in spring and summer. Melatonin secretions occur in the dark of night; nights grow longer in winter, when few animals give birth and many hibernate. Darkness stimulates melatonin; light suppresses it.

Human reproductive behavior does not follow such a pattern. Light and dark have far less of an overall influence on our behavior, or so we have long believed.

Nonetheless, our pineal glands secrete melatonin at night. Natural or bright light will suppress it. Those afflicted with SAD are sensitive to this hormone. Other than depression, their symptoms, which grow stronger as the days grow shorter, suggest impending hibernation: lethargy, large appetite and overeating, weight gain, carbohydrate craving. And according to one report, women with SAD tend to conceive in late summer, giving birth at a low-melatonin point nine months later.

SHE SINGS IN THE SUNSHINE

New studies indicate that there are actually two forms of SAD—winter depression and summer depression. And in fact, they may have differing symptoms. Winter depressives were more likely to have increased appetite, carbohydrate craving, increased weight gain, and excessive sleep patterns. The summer depressives had almost opposite symptoms, with insomnia and loss of appetite. These studies, which are not conclusive, show that specific treatment for summer depression is unclear, although everything from ECT to medication has been tried.

The treatment for winter SAD is simple: more light. Spend the winter closer to the equator or sit under intense light, five to ten times brighter than usual indoor light, for three hours at the beginning and end of the day or for five hours at the end. My singer-patient chose the "Caribbean cure." Every year she winters with friends in the South. She'll come north for brief concert dates or recording sessions, since it takes about three days for the depressive syndrome to return.

Light put her back in sync with the rest of the world. She sings again. All depressed people wish to sing again in their own way. Resynchronization may just be the key.

There is some not-so-good news about light treatment for SAD. Some very preliminary studies show that there are side effects to light treatment, such as eye strain, headache, and insomnia. There are also some other reports of maniclike symptoms with treatment that lasts more than two weeks. Still, overall, light seems to be the answer for most winter SADs.

The Loss of Rhythm

We live in a world of cycles and rhythms, daily, monthly, yearly, lunar, seasonal. No matter how "civilized" we become, our existences are tied

---

The World through Rose-Colored Glasses or Blue-Green Ones

Put on a pair of specs with 50 percent rose gradient plastic lenses and you'll be cured. Unless you are one of those people who require blue-green lenses, says Dr. Peter Mueller. He refers to the novel treatment he has developed for the seasonal down-up phenomenon he calls light-sensitive Seasonal Energy Syndrome (SES).

Dr. Mueller studied a group of severely seasonally affected individuals for whom light therapy did not work. He discovered they had an unusual set of mental and physical symptoms for each of the fall/winter and spring/summer illness phases.

During the fall/winter period, for example, besides the symptoms ordinarily found in SAD, his patients commonly suffered from such vascular problems as chronic migraine, easy bruisability, and Raynaud's phenomenon (in which fingers and toes become extremely cold and painful). Women, he also found, were markedly more depressed as a group than were the men during this phase.

In the spring/summer phase, men suffered the more extreme emotional symptoms. All patients were up in this period, but the men as a group tended to lose control, become violent, and move into psychosis. Migraine was common at this time too, but it tended to be acute instead of chronic.

Dr. Mueller performed extensive tests on these patients, including EEGs and CAT scans. Most of them, he discovered, suffered from attention deficit disorder (which in children used to be called hyperactivity) and about half had a form of epilepsy.

Light exposure did not work—and the worst of the symptoms, the violent behavior, occurred during periods of ample light.

He traced most of the symptoms to melatonin and its chemical precursors. He prescribed medications where necessary—and glasses.

For the fall/winter group, rose-colored glasses did the trick; for the spring/summer set, blue-green polarized lenses. On the basis of this initially fortuitous discovery, he suggests that visible light in the red spectrum inhibits the melatonin, while the blue-green increases it.

---

inextricably to them. When the weather grows colder we must dress more warmly, to cite but one simple but essential example.

The basic unit of our lives is the twenty-four-hour day; we must adapt all our activities—sleeping, working, eating, playing, maintaining a family—to this environmentally imposed cycle. Our bodies have corresponding rhythms, some attuned to the outward environment, some working only according to internal, repetitive rhythms, and all working in complex harmony with one another.

From the cycles of sleeping/waking and rest/activity to body-temperature rhythms and hormonal secretions, smooth and ordered functioning of our biological clocks is essential to physical and mental well-being. Think of the havoc that jet lag can wreak on our lives. Adjusting our daily clocks a few hours ahead or back can throw off concentration, energy, digestion, behavior, sleep, hunger, immunity to illness, and mood.

Physiologically, jet lag is the result of our two daily oscillators, or pacemakers, losing their mutual synchronization. Researchers believe that our daily rhythms are driven by at least two such oscillators. One is strong and consistent; it controls body-temperature ups and downs, some hormonal secretions, and REM (dream) sleep. The other oscillator controls sleep/waking, activity/rest, and sleep-dependent hormones. It is said to be weaker and more capable of fluctuating in time. For instance, unless you have insomnia, you can go to bed at eleven tonight and two A.M. the next night and midnight the night after that without too much difficulty getting to sleep and sleeping through the night. But your temperature will doggedly stick to its pattern; it will peak at the same time every afternoon and dip to its lowest in early morning.

Both of these systems are usually keyed to the day-night, light-dark cycle imposed from the outside, which also keeps them in sync with each other. Head for Bora Bora, however, and these cycles will have to adapt to a different day-night cycle. According to one calculation, after a five-hour flight west, the sleep/wake pacemaker will catch on in two days, while the more stubborn temperature system will continue on home time for three more days. Misery. Only when this cycle eventually adapts to the change and operates in harmony with the weak oscillator will you feel yourself again.

Evidence is mounting that depression represents a periodic desynchronization with respect to internal and environmental stimuli, especially when hormonal secretions are out of sync. Experiments have been conducted in which normal volunteers spend time in environments with no clocks or windows or other time cues. Characteristically, their days lengthen to an average of twenty-five hours (called a circadian rhythm, meaning "about a day"), their two pacemakers separate, and they end up with biological rhythms much like those of depressed people. Some subjects also become seriously depressed.

Depression has its own pathological rhythms. Bipolars have two distinct mood cycles. All mood disorders are episodic: sometimes better, sometimes worse. Recurrences often occur with precise regularity. Besides a seasonal worsening, for most depressed people the bad mood intensifies in the morning, letting up a little toward the end of the day. Some persons exhibit the reverse pattern. Twenty-eight-day lunar rhythms in depressed moods occur in women with premenstrual syndrome (PMS).

The Sleep of Depression

Virtually all persons with mood problems experience irregularities in the sleep/wake cycle, which is the most fundamental rhythm in our lives. Some can't fall asleep, others can't stay asleep, most awaken too early in the morning. Still others require enormous amounts of sleep.

Sleep researchers have been peering into sleeping depressed brains for some time. Using EEGs they have discovered that the sleep cycles of depressed people run backward.

Sleep consists of four stages plus REM (rapid eye movement) sleep, in which dreaming occurs. All stages plus REM repeat themselves every ninety minutes throughout the night, although the different stages occupy more or less of the time relative to one another as the night progresses. The typical, normal pattern is for deepest sleep to take up most of the ninety minutes at the beginning of sleep and to grow shorter toward morning. REM sleep, however, which is close to a waking state, occupies perhaps as little as ten minutes per ninety-minute cycle early in sleep but can lengthen to as much as an hour as wake-up time approaches.

The pattern is reversed in depression. REM sleep occurs far more quickly after the onset of sleep (we call this shortened REM latency) and diminishes toward morning. The shortened REM latency is so characteristic that it has become the single most accurate diagnostic test for biological depression, with an 85 percent yield.

Depressed people also get less overall deep sleep, which is the most restorative and refreshing of all.

This peculiar pattern of depressed sleep is evidence of desynchronization, since REM sleep and sleep/wake are on separate timing "devices."

The REM finding also supports the view that the basic disturbance in depression is in the biological clock. Other distorted biorhythms involve cortisol (previously mentioned), body temperature, and secretions of hypothalamic TSH and prolactin. MHPG, the metabolite of norepinephrine, also reveals an "off" rhythm. Explanation: The temperature-REM pacemaker is running too fast in relation to the sleep/activity cycle. The good news is that antidepressants slow the cycle and return the biological clock to its proper, complex timing system.

The Master Timekeeper

Our biological rhythm pacemakers are a central nervous system phenome-non, requiring contact with both the outside and inside world. When changes occur, the brain works hard to correct them and to resume the balanced, functioning state (homeostasis) that enables us to survive. Intro-duce cocaine into your brain, for example, and your brain will feel as if it's received a rush of norepinephrine, which cocaine resembles. Keep on flooding those receptors, though, and soon the brain will fight to regain its "composure," the receptors becoming insensitive to the drug. Balance is achieved anew—unless the dose of cocaine is increased, which will start the process over again. Keep on increasing and eventually you'll die from the effects of the drug on the cardiovascular system.

Depression can be seen as a similar phenomenon. You go out of sync and the brain eventually resets the clock. It goes out of sync again, though, because the illness remains. Thus the struggle continues. If, however, the depression is not treated (and if suicide does not intervene), the brain will begin to see depression as normal. It will no longer work to resume its previous balance. The depressed state will become chronic.

The puzzle is: From where in the brain does this timing control ema-nate? We don't actually have little machines spinning around in there, or ticking, for that matter. Chronobiologists (*chrono* means "time") believe that they may have located such a center. Guess where they found it? Right, the hypothalamus. Which brings us back, like a well-functioning clock, to neurotransmitters and hormones.

The suprachiasmatic nuclei (SCN) are small cell clusters in the hypo-thalamus that are linked to the pineal gland and to the eyes. They are believed to be the brain area that integrates daily rhythms, if not all biological rhythms, according to the most prominent environmental stimulus, light. Via the nerve pathways excited by the neurotransmit-ter acetylcholine, light travels from the eyes to the SCN, then via a norepinephrine pathway to the pineal. Here norepinephrine acts as an inhibitor, to stop the manufacture of melatonin. In the absence of light, melatonin is synthesized directly from serotonin. The pineal, in fact, possesses the highest concentration of serotonin in the body.

THE FINAL COMMON PATHWAY

"The major neurotransmitters which we relate to depression are all in-volved in the control of melatonin synthesis," said pioneering researcher Daniel F. Kripke, M.D.

"So what you're saying," an interviewer responded, "is that light may affect the metabolism of these key neurotransmitters, and that this can lead to an effect on melatonin secretion (which regulates the body's circadian rhythms—one of which may involve mood)."

"Correct," said Dr. Kripke. "We don't know the full details of where and how melatonin acts, but it appears that melatonin acts on the hypothalamus in a way that alters the secretion of hypothalamic polypeptides. Thus, melatonin secretion appears to influence the secretion of certain hypothalamic-releasing hormones."

We have seen that many types of depressive syndromes (psychological, drug-induced, biological) produce similar symptoms. Is the SCN-to-pineal pathway the final common pathway that produces this constellation? "Genetic, biological, environmental, and psychological effects could all trigger disorders of this system," says Dr. Kripke.

THE GOOD NEWS

The biological clock can be reset. Antidepressants and lithium are one way, light another, eyeglasses another. Careful use of melatonin itself, or of other drugs that affect these mechanisms, may prove to alleviate depression. Shifting synchronizers has been attempted with some success—such as treating chronic depression by timing bedtime and waking five or six hours earlier, then gradually returning to the usual time. If this doesn't lift mood, it may nonetheless increase the effectiveness of antidepressants. Waking a depressed person during REM phases has sometimes also been successful in the treatment of acute depression.

Or skip a synchronizer altogether. Stay up all night. The next day you'll feel fine. It's one of the best ways we know to snap somebody out of depression. Unfortunately, it does not necessarily work for long. By day two you'll probably be feeling lousy again. You'll be ripe for more long-lasting, perhaps permanent treatments.

You might try the natural, organic approach. Lead a regular life. Every day, even on weekends, get up at the same time, go to sleep at the same time, eat at the same time, and so on. All these activities are synchronizers that may ease you back on track. Also, stay away from drugs and alcohol, which are desynchronizers. This path is commonly recommended to persons suffering from insomnia, chronic headaches, and stress-triggered problems of all kinds.

Depression, Hormones, Clocks, and the Immune System

Our nervous, endocrine, and circadian systems all share mind-body links. The immune system may be the last missing link. It too is modulated by hypothalamic hormones as well as by adrenal, thyroid, sex, and growth hormones. Depression alters the secretions of all these hormones.

The field of psychoneuroimmunology is busy turning out evidence of these and other extraordinary interrelationships. Among them:

1. Depression indeed influences susceptibility to disease. Lymphocytes are the primary disease-fighting units of the immune system. Several studies now show weakened lymphocyte response among severely depressed patients, which would make them more vulnerable to disease. Intense grieving resembles depression in many ways, and landmark studies have demonstrated similar changes in lymphocytes following bereavement, particularly among men.

    Depression increases vulnerability to certain infections, including those caused by the herpes simplex virus. Possibly it raises the risk of cancer.
2. Cortisol plays a powerful role in suppressing the immune response. At least half of all biologically depressed persons oversecrete this hormone.

    Normally, cortisol may turn off the system in response to hormonal signals that the "invaders" are done for. However, in depressed people, feedback mechanisms do not function normally, and cortisol continues to flow, damaging the body's ability to fend off illness.
3. States of learned helplessness (see page 170) in animals parallel some types of human depression. Laboratory animals in which learned helplessness is induced show impaired immune systems.

    When rats are subjected to stressful experiences early in life, including loss of a mother, their immune responses function poorly even in adulthood.

    Loss among human beings has been associated with the onset of many diseases, including hypertension, rheumatoid arthritis, skin conditions, and ulcers.
4. Loss of circadian hormonal rhythms can adversely affect the efficiency of the immune system.
5. Just as a depressed mind can suppress the immune system, positive emotions can enhance it. A study of depressed persons undergoing psychotherapy showed a strong relationship between increased hopefulness and improved lymphocyte function.
6. Antidepressants and lithium help to regulate immune-system reactivity and return it to normal.

PART IV

THE STATE OF THE ART
Treatment of Depression in Biopsychiatry's New Golden Age

Chapter 18

Treatment That Works: The State of the Art Today

Depressed people deserve and need help as quickly as possible. Thankfully, today we can meet that need more frequently, and with better results, than we could even a decade ago. In this section you'll see that there is plenty of good news about treatment for depression.

Biopsychiatric methods can usually achieve results that are faster and more lasting than traditional psychiatric treatments. We have no magic elixir or arcane cures. Like most psychiatrists, we use one or a combination of the same treatment modalities: medication, psychotherapy, sometimes ECT (shock therapy). The difference in effectiveness lies mostly in how we use them.

Using a medical approach to diagnois provides benefits by:

1. Drastically reducing the often long wait for treatment to become effective
2. Increasing the odds against first-time failure
3. Preventing relapse for a vast number of patients
4. Limiting distressing side effects
5. Contributing to the storehouse of knowledge that can be applied to all depressed patients

That's what I call *really good news*!

Today there is better than a 90 percent success rate in the treatment of depression. Eight out of ten patients experience complete relief promptly; most of the rest are likely to experience the same freedom with additional aggressive treatment.

In the previous decade many psychiatrists simply skipped the diagnostic phase and began to treat patients immediately. Many wrote prescriptions for medication during their patients' first visit, choosing the antidepressant with which they were most familiar. In general, within six weeks of dutiful pill-taking, at least half of their depressed patients began to feel much, much better.

But the other half weren't so fortunate. So, there was a next medicine, and then a next. Eventually, some responded to different medication. For those who did not, yet a fourth or fifth medication trial, or shock therapy, might be the turning point. Each change of medication or treatment modality extended the treatment time; often there was a six-week to six-month wait for results. This approach also required a degree of hopefulness that is rare in a depressed person. The risk of suicide increased as the "cure" dragged on.

Many factors influence the amount of time a patient must wait before feeling better. Antidepressant drugs never take effect immediately. While symptoms such as insomnia may disappear within a week or two, the heart of the depression hangs on for another week or two. Before antidepressants can do their job, you must be taking the full therapeutic dosage.

Therapeutic dosage signifies the amount of medication you require daily in order to receive the maximum antidepressant benefit. This amount varies greatly from individual to individual. An effective dosage for you may leave another person as depressed as ever, and it may prove literally poisonous for a third person. Everyone metabolizes antidepressant drugs differently. How much ends up in the blood for delivery to the brain depends on factors such as genetics, other drugs, age, and the overall health of your liver.

Response to an antidepressant drug, if any, will be seen within ten days to three weeks at full therapeutic dosage. Since you must build up to your maximum dosage slowly, the wait to know whether this drug is right for you may be closer to six weeks. Part of the good news, however, is that newer antidepressants may work much faster in some people, thus reducing the waiting period by up to several weeks.

Until biopsychiatric methods became widespread, about the only way psychiatrists could determine your therapeutic dosage was guesswork. If they estimated correctly and you responded quickly, well and good. But if you remained depressed, the guesswork became complicated: Is it because the dose was too small or because you were nonresponsive to this particular pill? Possibly you were not a candidate for medication to begin with.

Now we know better how to match the dosage to the patient. If you don't respond to the medication, we no longer watch and wait, wasting precious time. We know now that when a medicine doesn't work, it's not anyone's fault—contrary to what patients were once made to feel. The problem, instead, is that this particular pill is not the right one for your body and your particular form of depression.

The Influence of Side Effects

Antidepressants are powerful chemicals that can adversely affect many body systems. Any side effects you experience may keep you from taking the medication as prescribed, thus delaying your recovery. In this new era, however, new medications have a decreased rate of side effects. They're also simpler to use and, in many cases, are even more effective than their predecessors. Any side effects that emerge are often more tolerable and easier to manage. Thus more people are able to continue taking the pills for longer periods, and enjoy greater relief.

The Story of Steve and Trudy:
An Overview of Treatment in the 1990s

As we've seen, depression doesn't just appear one day. And, likewise, treatment for depression isn't as simple as a visit to your family practitioner or the emergency room. The symptoms begin to appear slowly, then increase in severity and frequency over a few weeks. Finally, one day, perhaps months later, they reach a crisis point.

Take the case of a "normal" guy like Steve N., who, one Saturday, wouldn't and couldn't get out of bed. Steve's wife, Trudy, was concerned, but she was too busy that weekend to really notice. By the time she did, Steve was in real trouble. The first signs were almost unnoticed until one day Trudy's cheerful "Let's go to the pool" was greeted with "Leave me alone—I feel like death." Trudy was surprised. The weekends were the only time they really had to spend with their children, and it was almost a house rule that they spend Sundays doing something as a family. This weekend, though, was different. The kids had a party to go to, and Trudy's sister Margot was in town, so she simply let it go. Margot's interpretation of Steve's remark was, "He's burned out from work or coming down with something. If he's been feeling lousy off and on for a few weeks, let him be. If he wants help, he'll ask for it."

Steve didn't make it to work on Monday—or Tuesday. This time, Trudy took a close look at him. He had no fever and yet he felt flushed and listless. Trudy had noticed over the past few weeks that he had lost some weight. He looked almost gaunt. He either wandered the house at night or slept all day. Now she remembered another thing. Every few nights they jogged around the park. Just before he'd gotten sick, he had complained during one of the jogs that he was having muscle spasms or cramps. Maybe he was really sick, she thought.

"Steve, I'm calling your doctor," Trudy said. "I think you'd better get some antibiotics." When he didn't respond, she said, "You're going to lose your job. This isn't funny any longer." If pleading wouldn't work, then, she thought, perhaps threats or guilt would. But they didn't. To her great shock, he simply pulled the covers up over his eyes and sank deeper into the bed. It occurred to her that he was trying to disappear.

A few weeks later, Steve was sitting in my office, sent to me by his internist. A complete physical workup had failed to show anything beyond some mild hypertension, which the internist was treating with diet. The symptoms that had brought Steve to me were ambiguous, but when he started to talk to me, I began to suspect that he was suffering from depression. His physical symptoms—weight loss; insomnia or excessive sleepiness; loss of interest in the world around him, especially his home life—and his psychological outlook fit the pattern.

Although he'd always liked his job—Steve was an accountant—he simply had lost interest. He was "down," he told me. And he frequently found himself, hand on his calculator, drifting off into space. He'd see the spreadsheets in front of him, but he couldn't focus. Worse, he couldn't make a decision, something that his clients expected him to do for them. The result, he said, was guilt, a feeling that his life had amounted to nothing and that he was totally worthless.

After hearing all of the above, I knew the answer to my next question.

"Yes," he said, "I have thought about suicide. First I thought about dying behind the wheel of my car. Later I found myself sitting at the kitchen table in the middle of the night spinning a carving knife. I wasn't sure what I was going to do with it, but all of a sudden, I realized that it might make sense just to end it all. Why not let Trudy deal with everything?"

Steve's vision of death and suicide, obviously, was the kicker, a red flag that he needed help. But what was interesting about his case was that it was so *obvious*. Rarely did I see a patient who presented me with all the basic symptoms of depression. Most people don't have "all of the above." That's why it's essential to probe deeper. I try to talk to other important people in the patient's life, to find out more about the way they interact. Even if patients are resistant, I try to talk to the spouse or to trusted friends to see if the symptoms they report are accurate and consistent.

Because it's possible—and even likely—to be suffering from some form of depression without all of Steve's symptoms, these interviews with family and friends are vital. Current treatment guidelines as laid out by the U.S. Department of Health and Human Services, Depression Guidelines Panel, suggest that even if only five of Steve's symptoms were present over a two-week period, then treatment is indicated. The key to his diagnosis was that his symptoms were consistent, present for most of the day, and were not going away.

TAKING THE NEXT STEP

After Steve's visit, I met with him and his wife to explain what the goals of Steve's treatment were going to be. If your doctor does not do this, or suggest this, then the likelihood of treatment success is diminished! Your doctor should lay out treatment priorities: eliminate the signs and symptoms of depression, get a patient back to a functional state at work and in the home, and reduce the potential for relapse. In Steve's case, I felt that his symptoms were so pervasive that they had to be my first priority. But, in general, depression is not going to recede as long as the patient can't get out of bed or, even worse, is expressing suicidal ideations.

Trudy's first question—"What can I do? I'm so worried about him"—was the one I hear the most. And I also knew that there was another question in the back of her mind: "How long is he going to be this way?" It's a normal and natural reaction. After all, Steve was very sick, and depression's symptoms can be very frightening.

My answer to Trudy and Steve was very direct.

"The treatment that I feel is most likely to work is the one that Steve can accept. That means a treatment that has the most likelihood of success with the fewest adverse side effects."

"What do you mean, adverse side effects?" Trudy asked.

"Steve's treatment, like all others, has to be realistic. I want to make sure that any side effects or medical complications don't make his depression worse. For example, many depressed patients are suffering from a substance abuse problem, and that has to be treated first. If the problem is an acute medical condition—high blood pressure, for example—I have to consider the effect of multiple medications that might be used.

"And not to be overlooked is the effect that treatment will have on the family. That includes not only the time and energy that has to be devoted to the patient, but also, unfortunately, the financial impact of any treatment decisions."

This conversation reflects one of the unique changes in psychiatry over the past decade. Treating the patient is not the only job we have. All of us who are treating a variety of depressed patients have had to develop other skills that treatment guidelines refer to as "clinical management." The days of dealing directly with a patient, administering medication and/or therapy along with an occasional therapy session with the family, are gone.

According to the Agency for Health Care Policy and Research, any practitioner today must see that "all treatments are administered in the context of clinical management, which refers to the education of patients and families, when necessary, regarding the nature of depression, its course, treatment options and costs of such. This clinical management is exceptionally important, especially with depressed patients, whose pessimism, low motivation and energy, and sense of social isolation or guilt may lead them to give up, not adhere to treatment, or even to drop out of treatment."

Next, I told Steve and Trudy about the complexities of developing a treatment program tailored to their lives. Trudy's next question is also common: "What's next? When do we start? I need my husband back, and the kids need a father who's the same dad they had a month ago."

This is the toughest question to answer. No two patients are the same, and recovery doesn't happen overnight. Still, treatment of first-time patients can be broken down into discrete phases. When I talk to patients and their spouses, I find that these phases, while somewhat artificial, help patients to understand clearly what the goals of treatment are. If I can involve them in reaching these goals, then treatment becomes more of a team effort.

For a patient like Steve, the first phase is acute treatment, a process that will take up to three months. No matter which treatment strategy I use, I will see him at least once a week, sometimes more often. Every four to six weeks, his treatment will be evaluated carefully. At this point, I'll examine symptoms, adjust his dosage, and determine my next step. This phase is the hardest of all, because I am searching for the combination of approaches that will reduce symptoms. If it appears that we've made real progress after four to six weeks, we'll stick with the plan for another month or two. The important factor here is to see that symptoms stay in remission for this period of time.

At three months I begin to consider how treatment should be continued. It's vital to remember that three months of success does not indicate a cure, even for a person who has never had a previous depressive episode.

I'd be reluctant at this stage to pronounce anyone cured, but an absence of symptoms for at least another four to nine months is certainly a good remission. Many factors that I'll discuss in detail later can threaten a patient during this crucial phase. For example, failure to take medication properly can lead to recurrence of symptoms, which is frequently followed by relapse. In fact, it's safe to say that the degree to which a patient complies with treatment recommendations is directly related to the success of therapy.

After a vigilant nine- to twelve-month period, if the patient is compliant and a strong family support system emerges, a long-term plan to prevent recurrent depression is established. My experience is that most patients who comply with a specifically tailored treatment program will be fine. But depression can strike again at any time, and psychiatrists can rarely predict which patients will have a recurrence, especially when treating them for the first time. We can minimize the risk of failure if:

- We make it clear to patients just what we expect
- We also make sure that they understand our instructions
- We encourage them to ask, "Why?" "When?" "How long?" "What can I expect from this drug?" and other questions that they may feel uncomfortable asking
- We make sure that a side effect is just that, and that an adverse reaction is dealt with promptly
- We make sure that they take their medication and come to therapy sessions
- We make sure that we know exactly what's going on in their lives and at work that may provoke new symptoms
- We are a source of hope and hopefulness for both patients and families
- We ensure that patient and family education continues so they understand just how important taking medication properly can be and what side effects can occur
- We recognize why a patient doesn't comply — for example, because of an underlying problem such as drug use, or even denial that there is a real problem. Frequently we have to be medical sleuths to figure out why a perfectly sound treatment program isn't working

Every treatment should begin with a properly recorded history, which would include questionnaires for the patient, an extended family history, and interviews with family members where possible. There would be a drug-free interim period before I prescribe medication, laboratory testing, and psychological testing to rule out the mimickers (underlying physical illness) and identify other psychiatric illness. Where necessary, patients are referred to an appropriate specialist or drug-treatment program. The lab tests (described elsewhere) would be completed and evaluated.

TREATMENT CHOICE

My clinical assessment, combined with objective data from the history, family pattern of illness, and laboratory results, all contribute to this critical decision.

When I sit with a patient like Steve and his family, I explain that the most common treatment alternatives include medication and psychotherapy. All recent evidence indicates that a combination of both modalities is better for major (biological) depression than either one alone. Positive neuroendocrine measures verify an active organic malfunction and may predict response to antidepressants. If I remain unsure that medication is appropriate, I might try another response-prediction test. Mood improvement following a single dose of amphetamine, for example, suggests that antidepressants will work.

Many psychiatrists hedge their bets and prescribe antidepressants to everyone, just in case they might work. Not me. Drugs are not the answer to everything, in medicine or in life. Comprehensive evaluation and testing are designed to help the psychiatric physician render a specific diagnosis that pinpoints a specific treatment.

The pharmacological treatment of the depressed patient can be one of the most rewarding aspects of psychiatric practice. When used properly in depressed patients likely to respond, it can help them resume a normal, healthy state of mind within weeks, with a minimum of side effects.

On the other hand, certain types of psychotherapy can benefit a great many people (more about this in the next chapter). Psychotherapy alone is the treatment of choice when the results of major-depression assessment and testing are consistently negative. (Note that negative test results do not imply that the depression has no biological basis. Tests tend to normalize just before symptoms disappear, or as a result of spontaneous remission or successful treatment.)

In the next section of this book we examine each of the treatment alternatives in greater depth, looking at the advantages and disadvantages of each of them.

CHAPTER 19

Treatment Alternatives: The No-Standard-Approach Approach

Patients often ask me, "What do you usually do in cases like mine?"

I wish I had the kind of clear-cut answer that, say, a cardiologist has for a patient with high blood pressure. After a careful evaluation and diagnosis, the cardiologist refers to standard protocols. In this case, the standard treatment might be, "Take this medication properly and regularly, alter your lifestyle, reduce your stress, improve your diet" — specific, straightforward instructions.

I suspect that for most people, being given a standard treatment would be somewhat reassuring. You may not be well, but at least you're not so sick that extreme or unusual measures have to be taken. But mental illness doesn't work that way. Depression is never the same in any two patients. In fact, one of the most important lessons we've learned in the past decade about treatment is that there is no such thing as a standard treatment. If you asked what I usually do, the only answer I have is that the treatment I select for you is the one that offers the greatest benefit with the least potential for harm *in your particular case*.

All physicians, no matter what specialty they practice, weigh the ratio of risks to benefits before instituting treatment. But for a psychiatrist, the difference in treating depression is that there may be several different treatments that all seem to work the same, but in fact do not.

Sounds confusing, right?

Think again about a person with heart problems. We know that certain medications, taken consistently at certain dose levels, will reduce blood pressure to a safe level. Other medications can reduce the symptoms of angina or help the heart pump more efficiently. Now, these drugs will do their job despite a whole host of psychosocial or environmental factors. Certainly our cardiologist considers the patient's stress or marital problems as factors that might affect his compliance, but we know that compliance with standard treatment programs for hypertension will almost always result in a successful outcome.

In the past decade psychiatry has moved closer to consistent treatment regimens, but we still are not quite where other specialties are. For our patients, this is both good news . . . and not-so-good news.

One of my favorite patients was Max, the tailor. Max was born in Russia and came to this country as a young boy in 1917. Settling in Philadelphia, he worked hard to overcome his Old World ways and, as all immigrants did in those days, sought a trade that he could always practice, no matter where he lived. "You never know," he would say, "when the Cossacks are going to come again." So Max apprenticed himself to a tailor down the street, and eventually opened his own shop, saved his money, and married Fanny, the beautiful brunette from around the corner. Max and Fanny flourished. They had three boys, who all went to college. One became an accountant, and the other two went into the carpet business together.

Max was independent. He never asked anyone for help. He could solve his own problems. One day while serving dinner, Fanny, then only sixty-five years old, suffered a massive, fatal stroke. Suddenly Max was alone for the first time in fifty years. But Max was a survivor. He found himself another wife within a year. Max told his surprised sons that he needed someone to take care of him and that Sadie Cohen was a good friend and a good choice. "She's a widow," he said. "She understands."

I saw Max two years after he remarried. He was referred to me by his cardiologist, who was actually treating Sadie for hypertension. She had confided that Max just didn't seem to have any zip left—wasn't really enthusiastic about life, was moody, and in fact had even turned down her brisket the other night. Somehow Sadie had gotten Max to come to see me. When we first met, my impression was that here was a tower of strength and mental health. But since the cardiologist's workup had been negative, we talked. Or Max talked to me, and it soon was clear that Max was suffering from a mild depression that was linked to grief over his first wife, grief that he had not fully dealt with. While he said he was only worried about his sons' business in the recession, it was clear that he'd never really come to grips with Fanny's death.

In the past, sorrow following a loss was never considered as something abnormal, and in fact, was put into a category called uncomplicated bereavement if symptoms appeared in the first three months after a loss. But in the past decade, we've learned that over 25 percent of all grieving individuals actually meet the criteria for major depression after sixty days and are still stuck in that state a year later.

Many psychiatrists treated grief with psychotherapy, occasionally adding a sleeping medicine or a tranquilizer, but few added an antidepressant medication, which we now recognize may be appropriate. What is most interesting is that grief is often a source of major, not minor depression, and also affects younger people, especially those who may already have had a bout with depression. But Max was a unique case, so I continued to look deeper just to see if, in fact, his depression was normal for someone his age.

The problems of the elderly are often misdiagnosed. In the aged, the signs of depression are not infrequently mistaken for the aging process itself. But, in fact, depression and physiological decline often are present *at the same time.* In Max's case, this still did not appear to be his problem. Since his physical evaluation had included a CAT scan and other relevant tests, and since he was not on any heart medication or other drugs that might cause depression, his problem seemed to be a moderate form of depression.

"You're saying it's all in my head. So Sadie's right—I'm losing my marbles?"

"No, no, Max, far from it. You are normal, and perhaps even a little better than normal, since most people who lose a loved one don't cope nearly as well."

"What does that mean—I'll get over it? You got a pill or something for me to take? Just give me what you give everyone and I'll be okay."

"Max, let me tell you straight. While your symptoms aren't too bad now, I'm concerned that they may get worse, and I don't want that to happen. So I'd like to have you take a medication that will get you back on an even keel—no more mood swings, and you'll be able to enjoy Sadie's brisket again."

"That's it, just take a pill?"

"Well, not exactly. You see, I need to see if this medication works well, then I need to adjust it if it doesn't. And then I'd like you to see a colleague of mine to help you work out some of your unresolved feelings about Fanny, and perhaps you may even want Sadie or your sons to come with you a few times. I'll see you again in a few weeks and we'll see how it's going."

He looked at me for a moment, and I could see that he was trying to decide whether to accept help—something that he rarely did.

"Okay, Doc. I'll give it a try." He moved toward the door, but stopped. "You know, Doc, you and me, we're in the same business."

"Really?" I said. "How's that?"

"Sure." He smiled for the first time that afternoon. "Mrs. Goldstein, she comes in with a new dress. She knows it's too tight, so I take a little off there, let it out a little more in another place. And she goes home. Then a week later she eats too much danish, and comes back, and I adjust it again. See, you're just like a tailor. You make things fit."

Max was right. Today psychiatrists are a little like tailors, who can take the same dress and make it fit a dozen different people's shapes and sizes. These people may all wear a size five, but how many size-five people look alike and have the same body shape?

In treating depression today, everyone's treatment *is* tailor-made, based on the expected benefits and potentially negative side effects. Perhaps there can never be, and never should be, a standard treatment for depression. By the way, Sadie is fine, and Max, now ninety, is "sort of" retired.

FOUR ROADS TO TAKE

So how do we treat depression if there is no standard treatment? There are really four main modes that we draw upon. Each has pluses and minuses, which are considered as we determine the best course. No matter which I choose, in my mind I'm looking to give my patients relief from their anguish first, get them back to work or at least some semblance of normality, and then try to prevent their depression from resurfacing in the future. In that order.

Over the past decade, we've also come to realize that tailoring treatment to each patient's unique needs can be a tricky balancing act.

For example, when medication is given as the only treatment, it requires close supervision, good follow-up, an eagle eye on side effects, and a careful evaluation of how the medication affects the symptoms being treated. While medication is a "simple" route because the patient is treated at home by himself, it can also be dangerous. Side effects can sometimes be severe. Overdoses of certain antidepressants have been used in suicide attempts.

A second option is, of course, psychotherapy, which has few adverse effects. Often, however, psychotherapy is not effective. Patients who suffer from major depression usually don't respond to psychotherapy alone, and unless the therapy is very targeted (i.e., marriage, job, stress reduction) by an expert therapist, it's also unlikely to affect depression. Psychotherapy can be expensive, inconvenient, and time-consuming. Usually it takes longer to be effective in those patients who do respond. In truth, the quality of psychotherapy varies widely, and, as in any other specialty, the experience and skill of the professional is an important element of successful treatment. Finally, there is very little evidence that psychotherapy alone can prevent a recurrence of depression.

Still, psychotherapy can be useful, especially in patients who do not respond to medication. There is new evidence that therapy aimed at changing certain behavior patterns can prevent relapse.

It would seem that the obvious choice is to pick the best of both worlds . . . but that's also not necessarily so. In some cases, such as Max's, I want to alleviate the patient's symptoms *and* get him past his trauma. Such patients are perfect candidates for both medication and therapy.

Like every other option, this too is a double-edged sword. Psychotherapy helps reinforce treatment and compliance with medication, and overall, the success rate of the combination approach is higher than that of each alone. Still, you are asking a patient for a double commitment to a form of treatment that may be very expensive and time-consuming.

The fourth approach—ECT (electroconvulsive therapy), better known as shock therapy—is far more controversial than it deserves to be. Most people have a very negative image of ECT. They remember scenes from the movie *One Flew Over the Cuckoo's Nest,* or the reports that Senator Thomas Eagleton was forced to drop out as a candidate for vice president in 1972 when it was learned that he had undergone ECT. There is also concern about the side effects of treatment, including temporary amnesia or memory loss. But ECT has a definite role in treating depression that does not respond to antidepressants or therapy, especially in patients whose physiological condition might make medication inappropriate. ECT must be used properly, in a facility that has experience with the procedure and an experienced medical staff to ensure proper care.

THE OPENING ACT

I see treatment for depression as a play in several acts, which, by the time the curtain drops, will bring a resolution to the drama. My job is to make sure that the show has a happy ending.

An accurate diagnosis is the prologue to the story. The first act is acute-phase treatment. During this period your doctor makes his first choices. The U.S. government's Clinical Practice Guidelines put it this way: "The practitioner must distinguish between major depression, severe enough to require intervention, and the sadness or distress that is a normal part of the human experience. If a formal mood syndrome is present, treatment is indicated."

Sounds pretty straightforward, right?

Actually, the first treatment may be no treatment at all.

In some cases I'll begin treatment of some sort immediately, but in others, such as a mild or even moderate depression with little impact on daily activities, I may wait a while, up to two weeks, so I can track symptoms. Often I may not need to do anything specific. Clinical management (that is, keeping an eye on things without treatment) may be enough, since in 20 to 30 percent of mild cases, symptoms may disappear by themselves.

So, even if I do nothing immediately, the first goal that I want to achieve when I decide on the treatment course in the acute period is full symptom reduction. If, as in many cases, this is the person's first episode, then I extend the evaluation period. This in itself becomes, in effect, a treatment. If symptoms continue to ease, treatment by observation continues, since it is also true that for every patient whose symptoms retreat, many more have a recurrence. The usual practice in these nonspecific-treatment cases is to continue with a close follow-up routine for six to twelve months. Unless there is absolutely no return of symptoms during this period, and the patient's life returns to normal, I take a different road. But the fact is— and many practitioners won't admit this—doing very little beyond close observation in mild cases of depression may be the right course.

I also wish that this were all that is needed for all my patients, but for the vast majority, some sort of immediate intervention is called for. Then I go back to the options mentioned above.

If I decide that observation alone will not work, I begin to craft a treatment program—the second act, so to speak. Working backward, I also begin to anticipate what factors may keep the treatment from succeeding.

Let me tell you about one case that succeeded in spite of the odds against it. It's a good illustration of the obstacles we sometimes encounter when deciding which treatment path to take, of how to meet treatment objectives, and of how we ultimately arrive at a decision on a certain course of action.

Gloria was a forty-five-year-old psychiatric social worker who came to this country from Cuba when she was five. Her father was a farmer who struggled to support his family by working in the orange groves across Florida. Her mother died about five years after they arrived. Gloria thought the cause had been cancer, but when I asked her what she remembered most about her mother's illness, she said simply, "She cried a lot." Gloria was not a typical psychiatric patient. She was a survivor, pulling herself out of the fields, getting an education, and finding a career.

She had also found a husband, Nick, who arrived here from Athens when he was in his twenties. Following in his father's footsteps, Nick worked twelve to fifteen hours a day in his father's restaurant. Ultimately, he went on to open his own very successful place: Nick's Greek Gardens. Although he was a decade older than Gloria, he was living proof that hard work is good for the body and soul. Nick loved to dance, to sing, to laugh. Gloria was smitten the first time she saw him, gracefully moving from table to table. A year later they were married, and in three years they had two boys.

Nick and Gloria were, in every way, the all-American success story, living the American dream: two immigrants, one with a successful business and the other with a successful career that afforded them a house on the water, a boat, and a sense of security that neither of their parents had ever achieved. Over the years they developed a comfortable lifestyle, each going in their own directions, but intertwined, and close.

One Saturday night, their sons out on dates and Nick away at the restaurant, Gloria tried to kill herself by taking thirty Valium tablets. Luckily, one of the boys came home early and found her sleeping. He also found her suicide note and called for help.

I saw Gloria a few days later. She was still hospitalized and under close observation, since she had refused to speak to anyone about her suicide attempt. When I arrived, I found Nick outside her room, pacing and fuming. It was not the same Nick I had seen at his restaurant. He was not distraught, as I had expected. If anything, he was angry.

"This is terrible," he said. "How could she do this to me?"

"She did it to herself, Nick."

"This is awful. What was she thinking?" Nick continued to mutter angrily. "She won't talk to me or the boys. She closes her eyes and pretends to be asleep!"

I examined Gloria at length, but at the end I found myself even more concerned by Nick's attitude. It was clear that she was going to need a lot of care, and the choices made at this point were going to have an impact on the family for a long time to come. Gloria was in need of acute care, and the chances of success in the current family atmosphere, no matter how good I was, were not looking promising.

I talked to Nick again. "Nick, Gloria is very sick."

"What do you mean, sick—like the flu?"

"No, she is suffering from a major depression. I'm not sure what caused it yet, but clearly she's a danger to herself."

"Oh, so she's not really sick—just crazy, right? She should pull herself together, get out of bed, and take care of her family!"

Nick meant what he said. Given his background and his own history in a family that learned to overcome problems by themselves, his attitude was not surprising.

"Nick, do you understand what has happened here? Gloria has tried to kill herself. She does not seem to have any underlying physical problems— no cancer, no hormonal problems—but she's just as sick as if she did. We have to get her back on her feet, and you have to help me. Your attitude will make a big difference in her treatment. If you don't understand exactly what's wrong with her, and if you don't work with me to figure out the best treatment options for her, the prognosis for her recovery is not great. Do you understand?"

Nick looked at me for a few moments, then said, "Okay, why won't she talk to me?"

"I don't know yet, Nick, but that's part of her illness—sort of a symptom. I'm going to have to put her on some medication that will stabilize her, and do some more tests—just to confirm my diagnosis."

"So what's the problem?" he asked. I still wasn't sure he was convinced that his wife was really sick.

"The best treatments are the ones that the doctor and the patient plan together—not the ones I impose. Patients and doctors working together have a better chance of success, but Gloria isn't cooperating, and our first goal is to relieve the depression—so I need your help, or at least your permission, to administer an antidepressant medication."

"And this is really necessary? I've heard bad things about those drugs. Won't she just calm down and get better? Then we can talk to her."

"I know this is hard for you to accept, Nick," I said. "But Gloria is very sick, and without help it's likely that she'll try to kill herself again before she improves. I think that Gloria needs care right now. It's urgent!" I could tell that I'd finally gotten through.

"All right—what's first? I'll . . . okay, let's start." And then he began to cry. "How could this happen, Dr. Gold? We have everything. She has everything. We have a great life. Maybe I work a little too much. . . ."

"Nick, this is not a question of who's at fault now. Let's get Gloria back up a little and then we'll find out the whys. The first thing we do is try the things that work best. In this case I'm going to put her on a fast-acting antidepressant medication because, from past experience, most patients respond well. It will take a few days to have any positive effects, and then we'll have to give it a little more time to see if it's going to work in the long run. This may take a few weeks. In the meantime, I'll see her every day, and I'd like you and the boys to come as often as you can. She needs to have something tangible to hold on to. Any questions?"

"One. What happens if it doesn't work?"

"There is no single treatment that works for everyone. The brain's chemistry is so complex and so individual that we often have to try several medications. Gloria didn't get to this point overnight—her illness must have been progressing very slowly—and it may take us some time to find the right treatment or combination of treatments that will help her. Try to be patient. If we don't have a good response at first, I'll bring in some consultants and see if there's something else that we're missing. And don't worry, I won't wait to do that, either."

I wasn't sure if he was convinced or not. It occurred to me that I was trying to change an attitude that was not only personal on Nick's part, but cultural. It was a common problem, and I always try to reassure people such as Nick by telling them one other thing.

"Nick, let me assure you that Gloria's care here will be the best that we can possibly find, and that if I need help from any other experts, they will be the best, no matter where I have to go to find them."

MAKING THE RIGHT CHOICES: THE ROAD TAKEN

Once a patient and the family accept the diagnosis, they simply want results. If they trust their doctor, they are willing to go along and accept whatever treatment the doctor chooses without questioning it too deeply. While this may be nice for some practitioners who don't want to be bothered with patient education, I want my patients to become educated consumers. In psychiatry, the best patient is an educated one.

In the case of Nick and Gloria, my first choice was medication. I've already touched on the pros and cons of different treatments, but let's examine my choices in a little greater depth.

Certainly there were some obvious reasons to use medication with Gloria. She was not only suicidal, but clearly suffering from a severe depression. Medication alone can also be an appropriate choice in some patients whose depression is mild or moderate.

As you'd suspect, however, there is some controversy about this among my colleagues. For example, in its 1993 Practice Guidelines for Major Depressive Disorder in Adults, the American Psychiatric Association says, "Most patients are best treated with antidepressant medication coupled with psychotherapeutic management of psychotherapy." In contrast, the U.S. Department of Health and Human Services Clinical Practice Guidelines says, "Patients with moderate to severe major depressive disorder are appropriately treated with medication, whether or not formal psychotherapy is also used."

I prefer my medication-first approach because I think that medication does the best job of getting a person back to some semblance of normality far more effectively than psychotherapy. Because it relieves symptoms, medication improves a person's frame of mind, thus helping the person make sense out of psychotherapy.

And there's another important point. Psychosocial problems sometimes arise as a result of the depressive episode. In such cases, the medication that relieves the depressive episode may allow the associated psychosocial problems to abate without additional therapy.

Put simply, we can eliminate the chicken-or-egg factor with medication in cases like Gloria's. I felt that once Gloria's symptoms were reduced, if not totally removed, I could consider other forms of therapy.

Now, this approach may sound pretty black-and-white for someone who has just said that all treatments are "tailored" and evolving. I should make it clear that I usually reserve this approach only for cases of severe or moderately severe depression, since I agree that it is the best way to find out whether or not there *are* underlying psychiatric problems that therapy can resolve.

Why, then, is this approach controversial? Why do various groups differ in their attitudes? Haven't we psychiatrists been able to make a clear decision in the past decade? There are several reasons for the ambivalence.

First, various studies of the use of these medications in moderately or severely depressed patients have not been conclusive in some ways. For example, some studies used only patients who had no other psychiatric or medical symptoms (such as panic attacks) and who were closely controlled in psychiatric hospitals. Such studies may be challenged because the results seen in such closely controlled patients do not always translate to real-world conditions, under which medications are not taken correctly.

However, the clinical evidence is clear to me. And if I feel the patient can tolerate the potential side effects, and if other medical conditions do not preclude it, the next act begins with an antidepressant. Later on, we'll discuss which ones I might choose.

Fortunately, not all cases are like Gloria's, and there is, in fact, a significant initial role for psychotherapy in the treatment of depression.

Again, let's look for a moment at what the two major acute-phase guidelines call for. The APA guidelines: "Some patients with mild to moderate degrees of impairment may be treated with psychotherapeutic management or psychotherapy alone, provided that it is not prolonged without distinct improvement before a trial of antidepressants is initiated (unless there is a specific therapeutic contraindication)."

The federal government's Clinical Practice Guidelines basically agree: "Patients with mild to moderate major depression who prefer psychotherapy alone as the initial acute treatment choice may be treated with this option. This option is not recommended for the acute treatment of patients with severe and/or psychotic major depression."

My experience is that psychotherapy has a very specific role in treating mild depression, and I employ it in a very targeted way. If my job is first to reduce symptoms, then it's also my job to get my patients back into the mainstream as quickly as possible. The problem is that I want to keep them there without a chance of recurrence, especially during this acute phase. Unfortunately, some studies indicate that, at best, psychotherapy can only delay relapse, not prevent it.

Therefore, if a patient is only mildly depressed, I will consider a wide range of therapies: cognitive therapy, behavior modification, marriage counseling, and even brief therapy for a few weeks instead of medication. Again, my aim will be to reduce symptoms, but in this case, I'll set limits. For example, I want to help the patient become aware of the conflicts or behaviors that may have led to the depression. At the same time, I want to accomplish this within a specific time period—four weeks, perhaps.

It's interesting to note that the APA guidelines do not set any limits to the use of psychotherapy alone, preferring to look at the different types of psychotherapy individually. They do indicate, however, that if the symptoms do not clear, then medication is in order. The CPG is a little more specific: "The therapy should be limited to 20 sessions, since efficacy research on longer forms of therapy is not available and since strong evidence for the efficacy of medication with clinical management is available."

One final word. There are studies that have looked at both medication and therapy in mild depression and found the results to be similar, but these studies, in my opinion, have not been carefully controlled and still have not convinced me that therapy alone is a good first choice in general.

We have looked at two specific roads to follow in the next act of this play. But there is also a third road, combining medicine and therapy for an even better result. Combined treatment is useful, albeit limited, especially for patients in whom medication and therapy are each partially effective.

Again, there is no conclusive evidence that use of a combined approach works for a patient with major depression, such as Gloria. Where it seems to work is in patients who do have recurrent depression (see page 311) and who need some support between episodes.

There was one other aspect of Gloria's case that I have not mentioned, and that's ECT. In fact, it is something we consider carefully in the acute phase of treatment. Because this method is so misunderstood, I devote part of Chapter 24 to it. It is one of the options that I looked at for Gloria but did not discuss with Nick. Since she was severely depressed, and she refused or was unable to communicate at first, I thought she might have been psychotic. But in the end, I felt that ECT was not appropriate because it was her first episode of any kind, and we certainly had not tried any other options.

One final question is also asked of me, especially by families: What do you do if the patient refuses all treatment? This has happened. The truth is that there is no easy answer. Some practice guidelines say that in cases less severe than Gloria's—those individuals who haven't tried suicide, for example—education can be tried. But for people who are suicidal or who are so depressed they can barely function, the family has to consider involuntary commitment very seriously. It takes a lot today to get someone committed to a mental institution—lawyers, judges, patients' rights activists, etc. But just leaving suicidal or severely depressed patients alone, allowing them to refuse treatment that they cannot understand is to their own benefit, is not acceptable.

So now the curtain falls on the first act. We've made a decision. We know what we want to do—medication, therapy, ECT. Now, let's explore in depth how we apply that treatment.

CHAPTER 20

Medication and Depression

Today, if you watch TV or read the newspapers, you could reasonably assume that the most important good news about depression revolves around the increasing variety of new medications we now have at our disposal.

That's almost the case. But something else is happening in neuro-psychiatry that will change treatment in the next decade even more radically.

The *best* good news about treatment is that we have begun to map successfully the chemical pathways in the brain. We understand more about the complex function of the numerous neurotransmitters that regulate our emotions and spread the word from nerve cell to nerve cell. This has opened up a new world for researchers, raising many questions yet to be answered, but also giving us many new—and very effective—medications.

In a way I find this ironic. After twenty years of clinical practice, I now find myself back where I was as a young resident: in the lab, looking at the brain and trying to figure out just why it works the way it does.

PAUL REVERE RIDES AGAIN

Basically, we have learned that the brain is an incredibly busy communications system, constantly sending a panoply of chemical messages to let us know how we're feeling. We know that a variety of neurochemicals and receptor systems, such as the dopamine system, are known to be involved in depression. We believe this communications system works in a cycle and that certain antidepressant medications called cyclics work within this cycle when they relieve depression.

Remember Paul Revere, riding through the streets of Boston, warning the colonists that "the British are coming"? He was spreading the message sent to him by a signal from a lantern: "One if by land, two if by sea." Well, the brain's cells do something similar. When they have a message, a chemical lantern is lit. For example, when the body has consumed food or drugs, or when the body should be experiencing an appropriate emotion due to fear or joy, the brain releases a certain amount of neurotransmitters. These chemicals roam the brain's pathways and are automatically sent to another waiting cell, where they bind to structures called receptor sites.

Just as each colonial home lit up when Paul Revere rode by, the brain cells turn on as they receive the neurotransmission, and react appropriately. The chemical might tell you to be hungry, or to feel wonderful after sex, or to feel bad because you're sick or because someone you love has died. The message gets through very quickly to the other nerve cells, which, in turn, tell you how to react.

Sometimes the neurotransmitters remain for longer periods in the synapses between the cells, providing more stimulation when needed. But usually, once the neurotransmitters have done their job, like Paul Revere and his horse, they return to the stable. That is, they actually go back to the cells that released them, in a process called reuptake. The neurons stop sending their signal when reuptake occurs. In the future, these neurotransmitters will ride again.

But Paul Revere's ride wasn't easy. He was constantly in danger of attack from the British. The brain's messenger system does not work all of the time because it too is in danger of "attack" from another chemical called monoamine oxidase. This enzyme breaks up neurotransmitters during their journey and disperses them. This causes their effectiveness to diminish. Too little neurotransmitter reaches the target cells or too little stays in the pipeline.

All of the above we know with reasonable certainty. And we have been able to put this information to good use in the development of the cyclic medications. to treat not only depression but substance abuse, pain, and other chronic medical conditions.

So the best news today for everyone is that we've finally begun to understand the system in the brain that enables antidepressant medications to work. And, along with this, the other great news is that we are beginning to know which systems and neurotransmitters, such as serotonin, are involved in other psychiatric syndromes such as obsessive-compulsive disorder [OCD]. We don't know everything. For example, we don't know why these drugs work so well in some people and not at all in others.

Why Some Drugs Work

We are reasonably sure that the neurotransmitters serotonin, epinephrine, and norepinephrine do play a key role in depression. Many psychiatrists believe that people with too little of these chemicals, for example, are more likely to develop major depressive episodes than people with normal amounts. These neurotransmitters actually function like a cut-off valve in the brain, keeping us from getting too high or too low. When the valve fails, the result can be depression or mania. What this implies is that when not enough neurotransmitter is released, or if it is not returned to the "stable" for future use, the result can be depression.

For a long time we believed that amitriptylene, imipramine, and other tricyclic antidepressants (TCAs) blocked the reuptake process, thus leaving plenty of neurotransmitter molecules swimming around in your brain. This seemed to reduce the symptoms of depression. So, by locking the stable door and keeping the chemical messengers out there all night warning the troops, you felt better. We also thought this theory was sound because antidepressants called monoamine oxidase inhibitors (MAOIs) prevent an enzyme from destroying neurotransmitters. And there was much clinical evidence that this theory was correct. People using "cyclics" and MAOIs did get better.

But in science we have a rule of thumb: As soon as we develop a theory such as the above, another study will come along to disprove it, or, more accurately stated, will add to the body of data filed under "what we don't know for sure." Our clinical experience with these two seemingly effective drug types has also raised some interesting questions that show us how much more we need to know.

For example, even though the cyclics and the MAOIs worked in many cases, they don't work immediately. It usually takes at least a week, and sometimes longer, for any therapeutic benefit to be noticed. If, in theory, they blocked the reuptake process immediately, why didn't our patients get better immediately? To add to this quandary, other medications, such as iprinidole, proved effective in treating depression but did not prevent specific neurotransmitter reuptake. Did this mean that blocking reuptake wasn't really the reason cyclics and MAOIs worked?

Maybe and maybe not. We knew that certain other compounds—cocaine and amphetamines, for example—do block reuptake of the same neurotransmitters as cyclic drugs, but they were not effective treatments for depression.

It all seemed so simple: If you block reuptake and provide more or higher levels of neurotransmitters, depression would wane. But the more we learned about the brain, the more we realized we didn't know about depression and the medications that treated it.

Scientists, however, love a good mystery, so they turned their microscopes to the other end of the pathway—the receptor sites on the target nerve cells. Researchers began to study what happens when the "alarm" reaches the "villagers." In colonial days, I am sure that most of the people leaped from their beds and charged out, muskets loaded, to fight the British. But I'll bet there were a few who slept through it all, or who were just a little slow in getting dressed, and missed all the action.

Well, we thought, that's probably what happens in the brain. For some reason, the message that the neurotransmitter receives doesn't sink in. Perhaps the "fit" isn't quite right; the molecular key doesn't fit the lock. It's also possible that external forces (early illicit drug use or disease, for example) or a naturally occurring genetic action can alter the receptor sites. If they become very sensitive, it is likely that depression will occur. If they are desensitized, mania might occur.

If Paul Revere had shouted a little louder or grabbed a few slowpokes from bed, they probably would have sprung into action too. The same method seems to work in the brain. Data from some research shows that if you can alter the receptor sites in some way, or add to the amount of naturally occurring neurotransmitters, you will have a greater antidepressant effect.

All of this information has led to the development of new cyclic drugs with different structures. These drugs are effective for people who don't respond to the older drugs. The newer drugs also have less risk and fewer side effects.

We still have a long way to go, but as you can see from the above, we're on our way. Not only do we know how and where some older antidepressant medications work in the brain, but we also know why. The newer information about receptor sites, we hope, will put us on the road to discovering drugs that are so targeted that effective ones may be found for everyone.

We think . . . we hope . . . we may know . . . How, you may be wondering, can doctors confidently prescribe a medication if they really don't know with certainty how or where these drugs work?

It's a fair question, and one that I get asked all the time. And if I'm not asked, I make sure that I raise the question myself. The patient, the doctor, and the family are all part of the treatment plan, and that plan can't work if everyone involved doesn't understand what the treatment is and what to expect.

Recently, I treated a patient who was, in fact, very knowledgeable about medications. She had taken the time to educate herself, reading some basic texts and many lay articles. Although her case was relatively straightforward, the dialogue she and I had about medication was not typical. I retell it as an example of the type of interaction patients should have with their doctors about medication.

Mary Beth was forty-seven years old, the divorced mother of a twenty-year-old boy, now in college, and an eighteen-year-old girl about to graduate from high school. She had been divorced ten years before, but was now in a relationship with Don, her high-school sweetheart. They had become reacquainted when she took a job as an art teacher in the school where Don taught history.

Creative and high-strung, Mary Beth had experienced several episodes of bipolar depression and described her life as a "trip through the mountains—ups, downs, twists, and turns." But she told me that she had mainly been on a rocket ride, driven by the need to support her children and a search for a relationship. She came to me after the family counselor she'd been seeing thought she needed an evaluation and "probably some sort of medication."

When Mary Beth walked in the door I knew this was going to be tough. Before she had her coat off and before she reached her chair she told me: "I am not taking any medications. I know all about them—they're chemical straitjackets, they have terrible side effects, and you guys have no idea what they really do to us."

"Well," I said, "I don't make anyone take medications if they don't want to. At this point I don't even know if you need them."

Mary Beth was wrong, but she was also right. The drugs we use today, contrary to what many people think, are not chemical straitjackets, and you won't feel high when you use them. An otherwise normal person, without depression, will not get high on low doses of these drugs. But she was right about side effects. Some medications have more than others. Side effects are a major consideration in choosing the right medication, but they are not a reason to avoid antidepressants.

"Slow down," I said. "You've reached a conclusion before I've even asked how you are. Let's talk about you before we even consider any type of medical treatment."

With that, Mary Beth relaxed. She loved her teaching job—and I could tell by the vivid images she used when she talked that she must be a wonderful teacher. We met three times before I was sure that medication would help her.

"Mary Beth, we need to think about the goals that we are trying to achieve here. I don't want you just to get better—I want you to stay that way. It seems that your life is entering a new phase—Don, the children leaving home. Why not enjoy it to the fullest? You deserve that.

"I think we both know that you have a bipolar disorder, probably one that used to be called hypomania, which means you have a lot more highs than lows. Interestingly, this disorder, which we now call bipolar II, is more common among creative people such as yourself. The fact that you have a family history of mood problems also indicates to me that your symptoms are not going to go away by themselves. You were most likely born with a predisposition toward this disorder. There are many studies of writers, composers, and artists that remind me of you. The good news is that bipolar II is becoming more easily recognized and better understood."

"But, Doctor, I seem to have survived all these years without drugs. Why can't I just continue like that?"

I told her about Kay Redfield Jamison's book, *Touched With Fire.* "One of the things she points out is that artists and writers especially may vary in their capacity to experience life, but also in their ability to tolerate extremes of emotions and live on closer terms with what she calls the 'darker forces.' Sound familiar?"

"I guess you're right. I certainly don't love the roller coaster all that much," she admitted with a smile.

"There are other reasons to consider taking medication. Like other people with this condition, you have probably noticed that you are more sensitive to the changes in seasons. You might not have a classic case of seasonal affective disorder, but many of your symptoms arise in the fall and the spring. Medication will help you smooth out those times. And you've told me that you've had long stretches where you just feel melancholy . . . not really depressed, but certainly not normal. Well, we can help stop that."

I could see that she was seriously considering what I had to say, but I wasn't sure that I was convincing her.

She said, "I know that I'm not van Gogh or any of those geniuses. But I have some talent. I'm afraid that the drugs will rob me of that ability. What if it messes up the chemicals in my brain that make me function and give me what creative abilities I have? Even you will admit that science doesn't exactly know why or how these drugs work."

"I guess the question you're really asking me is this: If van Gogh had been on lithium or some other drug, would he have still painted *Starry Night* or *Sunflowers?* My answer is yes. But, even more important, if he had the medications we have now, he probably would not have committed suicide and might have painted many more masterpieces."

"Okay." Mary Beth was serious now. "Let's say I decide to take medication. You still haven't told me how you know it's going to work and which drug and why."

"Both of those are fair and appropriate questions. I wish all of my patients were as interested. The more you know, the better you comply with the treatment, and the more you are aware of how well the drug is working.

"As to which drug, the short answer is that to some extent we decide together.

"As to how they work, that's a little more complicated. One thing we do know is that all of the drugs seem to work about the same—that is, they help about the same percentage of people who have similar types of depression. But since these groups of people are usually very dissimilar, we can't predict who will respond best or who will experience the fewest side effects."

"So you'll just choose something and hope it works?"

"Not at all. I'll gather all the evidence I can, and then, following a protocol developed through experience, together we'll choose what appears to have the best chance of working *for you*."

"Well, I'm glad to hear that. At least you have some reasons for what you do."

"Absolutely. I want you to feel comfortable and confident about taking any medication I prescribe. First, tell me whether or not you've had any other antidepressant medications, at what dose, for what length of time, and to what effect. Or if anyone else in your family—your mother or father, for example—responded to a specific drug."

"I've never taken an antidepressant, and, as far as I know, neither have my parents," she said.

"Do you have any other emotional problems? Are you taking anything for, say, anxiety, phobias, or more serious problems? I need to know, since there can be interactions or an increased risk of side effects."

"I take a Xanax on occasion for anxiety. And I have taken some sleep medication that my gynecologist gave me. Did I tell you about that?"

"I saw it in your record. So already you're ahead, because you probably won't need those medications at all when you switch to an antidepressant. What about other medications—contraceptives or anything for high blood pressure, for example? If so, I can suggest an antidepressant that's safe for you if another medical condition is present. For instance, Prozac can be taken safely along with heart and blood pressure medications."

"No, no other medications."

"How about over-the-counter meds? In years past, we often mistook side effects of those drugs for depression itself. Luckily, most of the newer drugs have fewer side effects."

"Nothing more than the occasional antacid."

"Great. Now, I have a whole laundry list of other factors to consider: how well you comply with medication instructions in general, the specific diagnosis I've made, does this medication come in a single dose, is it available as a generic, how often will I have to see you for follow-up or blood work—I don't want this to become your life. There are two other factors as well: my own experience with the drug, and, to some extent, what you feel works best after you've taken the drug for a specified period."

"I notice you've omitted one thing, Dr. Gold."

I knew what was coming next, because it's the one question that we can answer only after the fact. "Let me guess: side effects."

Mary Beth just smiled at me.

"If I told you there was no risk, I'd be doing you a disservice. For every group of patients, some will experience side effects—both long- and short-term—and we can't predict who those people will be. In fact, even when I consider all of the factors I mentioned before, I can't predict exactly what the effect of a medication will be on you. We have to adjust the dosage levels, and we have to check the levels of the drug in your bloodstream as we go along."

"Just as I thought—I'll be a guinea pig."

"No. Absolutely not. Side effects are one of the most misunderstood aspects of medications. Almost every drug, even aspirin or a placebo, has them in one form or another. And most people confuse them with what we call 'adverse effects.' I don't want you to think that side effects are unimportant, but they are not the reason to avoid medication. Too many people forget that with every benefit, there may be a down side—but in this case the benefit to you is very high compared to what I am sure will be only a temporary down side."

"I'm not sure that I understand what you mean. Aren't side effects the reason why some people can't take these drugs?" Mary Beth was clearly concerned. And she had a right to be.

"Actually, it's true: The reason many people stop taking the medication or don't take it properly is that they quit as soon as the side effects appear. If this happens, it's my fault—not yours.

"First of all, I expect side effects to occur. Usually they show up when you first begin taking a medication, and they disappear as soon as your body adjusts. For example, many people may feel lethargic when they begin taking a heart medication or high blood pressure drug, but soon afterward they feel much better than they did before the drug. The side effect is predictable and expected, and it is short-term. Psychiatric medications work in a similar fashion—the patient adapts.

"It is true, however, that medications in almost every class have long-term side effects—for example, weight gain is a common one, or a rash, or stomach upset. There are two ways to deal with this. One is to try to change the dosage—reducing it so that the side effect is tolerable and so we don't lose antidepressant efficacy. Or we can change the medication . . . but only after we've determined that the side effect is not going to go away. If you report a side effect to me and I say, 'Well, just live with it,' I've done you a disservice. You have the right to expect your doctor to respond in some way. But I probably won't discontinue the medication immediately if I think what you are experiencing is a common reaction and will soon disappear.

"Side effects will influence the choice of medication as well as the manner in which I prescribe. For example, giving a corporate executive a heavily sedating drug is asking for failure, especially if prescribed at intervals throughout the day. On top of the depression, any further inability to function may be the last straw; the patient may become even more depressed and possibly suicidal, or will quit treatment.

"A psychiatrist must be fully aware of how these drugs work and of their side effects, so that patients will continue taking their medication and so that their health is safeguarded. Side effects can sometimes be used to advantage. Prescribe a sedating drug in a single large dose at bedtime, and the insomniac executive will finally begin to get some sleep, yet be alert during working hours. After the first week of real night-long sleep in months, the patient may even think there is something to this treatment after all.

"This is why communication between doctor and patient is so important. I don't really worry too much about initial side effects, and I will tell you what to look for, and what to expect. Most drugs have very similar, common side effects. They also have less-common or rare side effects, but again, that is not a reason to stop using the drug. These rare side effects usually occur in less than 1 percent of all people taking the drug. Sometimes we might add a second medication to help reduce the side effects you experience."

"I understand that, Doctor, but what are 'adverse effects'?"

"These are something we are very concerned about. They are unexpected effects or an effect that could be life-threatening. For example, if a drug causes you to pass out or feel faint when you stand up, it's having an adverse effect. But drugs also can cause adverse effects that you can't see—for example, changes in blood chemistry or other problems that can be picked up only through medical testing and screening. That's another reason why we draw blood. The reason I asked you about other drugs before was because an interaction with another drug can create both common and adverse side effects."

"You make it sound rather simple," Mary Beth said, "just pick a drug and let it have an effect."

"No. In fact, every time I treat someone I actually learn something new. And as a profession, psychiatrists are always asking themselves the same questions over and over." At that point I showed Mary Beth a page from the most recent Clinical Practice Guidelines.

> Which treatments are most efficacious in the initial phase of treatment? Which treatments are most effective in preventing relapse? Should multiple forms of therapy be used, and if so, should they be given conjunctively or sequentially? What is the optimal frequency of psychotherapeutic contacts, for the various forms of treatment, in the acute, continuation, and maintenance phases? Despite notable clinical progress in predicting a beneficial response to antidepressant medication treatment, many issues continue to require clarification.

"The truth is, we are always on a search, because the brain is the last frontier of medicine. Today, we can tell you much more than we could a decade ago, but no one in any branch of medicine, especially psychiatry, can say, 'This is a firm prognosis.' There are too many individual variables. But we have so many different choices now, and what we can do is give you much greater hope that your problem will not recur."

Mary Beth's was a relatively simple case. It was clear from her constellation of symptoms that medication was indicated. That medication was probably going to be lithium, since it is the best drug for a new bipolar patient. And so after at least answering her questions, if not satisfying her curiosity totally, I developed a treatment program she felt she could live with and comply with.

Today, for the most severe, major depressions, I try tricyclic antidepressants first. I use the SSRIs first for outpatients and other depressive syndromes. Treatment with tricyclics is complicated by side effects, choice of medication, and dosage. Additional testing can dispel the which-one-will-work-and-at-what-dosage? quandary. Here the MHPG urine test comes in handy. Patients who excrete the least amount of MHPG (a substance produced when neurotransmitters are broken down by enzymes) respond better to noradrenergic antidepressants. These include nortriptyline

(Aventyl, Pamelor), desipramine (Norpramin, Pertofrane), and im- ipramine (Tofranil). The highest MHPG excretors may respond to a broad spectrum of treatment if continued over a long term. The intermediate group is treated most successfully with serotonergic antidepressants, in- cluding amitriptyline (Elavil), trazodone, tryptophan, or SSRIs.

The tricyclic dose-prediction test ascertains how a patient metabolizes the selected medication. We give a test dose of nortriptyline and twenty- four hours later measure how much of it remains in the blood plasma. From this measurement we can predict the therapeutic dosage and thus minimize dose changing and unnecessary side effects.

One important change that has affected how I make decisions are the many new tricyclics (TCAs) and other antidepressants available. These new medications have become the largest group of antidepressants and are effective for both unipolar and bipolar depression. TCAs such as amitriptyline, imipramine, and others with different ring structures, such as nortriptyline, or even new drugs such as Prozac (see Chapter 22), are basically similar and seem to have about a 70 percent success rate in patients with depression, but have an even higher success rate—up to 90 percent—in patients with melancholy.

Nortriptyline, which I usually use first in the most difficult cases, is the one medication that has the best-established blood levels for our own testing purposes and the one we know the most about in regard to toxicity. The desired blood levels, especially in patients who previously did not respond to a medication, is well known: 100mg/ml in blood for four to six weeks. No response means no response . . . period . . . the end.

If these drugs don't work, however, I can also be flexible. For atypical cases I might consider switching the patient to an MAO inhibitor (MAOI). MAOIs, including phenelzine (Nardil), isocarboxazid (Marplan), and tranylcypromine (Parnate), function somewhat differently from tri- cyclics, although they work just as well. Years ago MAOIs developed a reputation for being extremely dangerous, so many psychiatrists stopped prescribing them. As it turned out, though, the dangers of these medica- tions were exaggerated. There is one serious risk, because these drugs can interact with certain foods, drinks, and other medications. Aged cheese, red wine, and cold medications are among the substances that can trigger a loss of blood pressure control and a potentially fatal hyper- tensive crisis. Patients who follow certain dietary restrictions will avoid this uncommon consequence. It is also possible to take a fatal overdose. MAOIs can work well, but the psychiatrist has to be sure the patient will follow the rules.

Let's look at the classes of antidepressants a little more closely.

The drugs known as cyclics get their name from the circular shape of their molecular structures. The tricyclic antidepressants, or TCAs, have three rings, and the heterocyclics (HCAs) have five. All of the cyclics are similar in certain respects. However, the tricyclics (amitriptyline, clomipramine, desipramine, doxepin, imipramine, nortriptyline, protriptyline, trimipramine) tend to affect selectively the release or reabsorption of chemical messengers. In contrast, the heterocyclics (such as amoxampine, bupropion, maprotiline, and trazodone) appear to work exclusively by preventing reabsorption. Some of the tricyclic medications are classified as secondary amines (examples include desipramine and nortriptyline) and some as tertiary amines (for example, imipramine and amitriptyline). Basically, all the TCAs work equally well, but those in the secondary amine group tend to produce fewer side effects.

All drugs pose some risks. The MAOIs, for example, have been used in accidental and intentional suicides. If I believe there is a risk for a particular patient, I prescribe only a limited supply of the drug, schedule regular, short office visits, talk with the family, and make sure that the patient is closely monitored.

For elderly patients I usually start with SSRIs like Zoloft or Paxil or a tricyclic. One advantage with the secondary amines is that I can monitor the blood levels in these patients more carefully. Interestingly, most studies show that antidepressants are about as effective in older patients as in younger ones, which would seem to reinforce some of our theories about how these drugs affect neurotransmitter systems.

The even newer cyclic antidepressants (e.g., bupropion, fluoxetine, paroxetine, sertraline, trazodone) may not be better in absolute terms than the older tricyclic drugs but they are easier to prescribe and seem to have fewer long-term side effects, such as weight gain. For patients who have depression with obsessions, compulsions, or eating disorders, I prefer the newer medications, which seem to be effective for both conditions. These would include clomipramine and fluoxetine. We have also had very good success in treating major depression with bupropion, fluroxamine, paroxetine, sertraline, nefazodone, and venlaflaxine. But not always. For example, in treating what we call atypical depression, the MAOIs appear to be more effective than the cyclic medications.

Let me explain what I mean by *atypical*. In most cases, depressed people sleep less than normal individuals. This often involves early morning waking and an inability to return to sleep. Also, they are unable to snap out of their low mood. Positive or happy events don't make any difference to them. Depression robs them of their sense of pleasure, which usually translates into a loss of appetite for food and subsequent weight loss. A certain group of patients, however, will exhibit atypical symptoms. Atypical depression is marked by excessive sleep—ten to twelve hours or more per day. Another symptom is mood reactivity, which means that cheerful or positive events, such as a visit from children or a compliment from others, can work to lift the person's spirits. People with atypical depression often report increased appetite and weight gain. Other symptoms include leaden paralysis (heavy feeling in the arms and legs) and a pattern of extreme sensitivity to feelings of rejection by others, resuting in the inability to function on the job or within society as a whole. As I noted, people whose depression has some or all of these features usually respond better to an MAOI antidepressant. And recent studies seem to indicate that a depressed patient with some symptoms of psychosis will do better on a cyclic antidepressant plus a neuroleptic drug.

Before an antidepressant is prescribed, it is essential that a complete history be taken and a physical exam and neurological assessment be performed. Tests that I give before prescribing include urine and blood tests that check for toxins in the system, for substance abuse, and for liver, thyroid, or heart malfunction. No one should take an antidepressant without a thorough exam and, at the very least, these tests.

One final thought that I often share with my patients is this: The main reason I choose tried-and-true medications such as the older tricyclics first is that we have more experience with how they work. There are more studies on more actual patients—rather than just lab studies—and these drugs have a good track record. We know how to determine if they are working properly and we know what the early warning signs for dose adjustment are.

MONITORING ANTIDEPRESSANT BLOOD LEVEL

Tests to monitor the level of medication in the blood replace the guesswork that can drag treatment out for months. They are among the most valuable tests in the biopsychiatrist's bag of tricks when faced with a patient whose treatment with other medications has not been successful.

All antidepressants are ineffective below a certain concentration in the blood plasma. We now know, too, that some of them are nothing but trouble if their levels are too high: Effectiveness decreases and side effects multiply, endangering patients, especially those who have cardiovascular disease. The psychiatrist must prescribe sufficient medication to hit only within this narrow range, which we call the therapeutic window. Unfortunately, we do not know the blood-level response relationship for every drug. Blood-level tests at last make this target visible. Performed one or more times during treatment, this simple procedure reassures us that the medication is being taken and that we are prescribing correctly, with the least risk and discomfort to the patient. If the medication fails to work, we can change treatment strategy without having to agonize over whether the dosage was right.

TRACKING COMPLIANCE

Monitoring antidepressant blood levels also reveals whether the patient is taking the medication as prescribed. A quiz: How many people taking antidepressant medication neglect to follow the treatment regimen accurately? More than half? About half? Less than half? You'll find the correct answer along with a discussion of noncompliance at the end of this chapter. Suffice it to say here that not following the doctor's orders—increasing or decreasing dosage, altering the timing, even failing to take the medication altogether—can lead to treatment failure.

ALTERING TREATMENT

Sixty to 85 percent of my patients will improve within about three weeks of taking medication and maintaining it at the target level. Including the diagnostic phase, about four weeks will have elapsed since the time they despondently set foot in my office.

For nonresponding patients, at four weeks it is time to alter treatment. Supplementing the medication rather than changing it will quickly do the trick for many. Antidepressant effects may be triggered by adding small amounts of thyroid hormone, tyrosine (a naturally occurring amino acid, especially effective with patients who secrete low levels of MHPG), tryptophan (another natural amino acid, by itself a possible treatment for depression, pain, and insomnia) or even lithium. For depressed patients who are already taking lithium, thyroid hormone can have profound results, largely because lithium slows down the thyroid gland. Treatment supplements generally work within a week or two. If not, I discontinue them and try something new.

CREATIVE PRESCRIBING: HARD-TO-TREAT PATIENTS

The rare person will remain depressed despite all these efforts. A psychiatrist may recommend ECT, but even if the patient refuses it, there is no reason for either the patient or the psychiatrist to throw in the towel. The psychiatric literature of innovative treatments grows fat as practitioners report novel treatments that work with individual patients. Innovative uses of drugs such as anticonvulsants or combinations of medication stimulants with MAOIs can pull the rug out from under a tenacious chronic depression.

Let me share with you a note from my colleague Jerrold G. Bernstein, M.D., director of the Boston Psychopharmacologic Institute.

Since many of my patients suffer from what has been called refractory depression—that is to say, depression which is difficult to treat—I have to be flexible. If necessary I will try a variety of medication regimens, combining two, three, even four medications simultaneously. Oftentimes, small doses of antipsychotic medications, even for patients who are not psychotic, will spell the difference between a satisfactory response and utter incapacity. Some depressed women approaching menopause experience a considerable improvement in their mood when estrogenic hormones are added to the antidepressant regimen.

We must remember that each patient is an individual and that no particular treatment works for everyone. The difference between a favorable and unfavorable outcome may be directly proportional to the willingness of the physician and the patient to experiment with changing treatment regimens or with more complicated regimens involving the administration of multiple medications simultaneously.

The good news is that most depressed patients will be better if they and their physicians persist long enough, and if they are willing to be flexible and try different approaches to treatment.

YOU

As much as practitioners try, patients are themselves responsible for treatment failure more often than one might imagine. The majority of persons do not take their medicine as prescribed, and not just psychiatric patients. Here we doctors are, scratching our heads over why treatment is not working, and it turns out the medication is not entering the mouth, let alone the brain.

The problem pervades all of medicine today and accounts for a substantial number of treatment failures. Twenty to 25 percent of all hospital admissions for depression result from noncompliance. Among psychiatric patients who end up labeled treatment-refractory, 12 percent have not followed the treatment regimen.

Many people adjust their own dosage, usually by increasing it, in the mistaken belief that more drug will yield greater benefit. They may decide to supplement their medication with other drugs they have around the house, which may throw off antidepressant effectiveness, cause serious side effects, or both. They may take their medicine only when the mood begins to worsen, even though the instructions clearly say to take one or two times a day, every day. Many people stop taking their antidepressants because they are feeling a little better and begin again when they start to feel worse. They do not understand how antidepressant therapy works. Often the prescribing physician is at fault for not making sure they understand that medication has to be taken as prescribed, even if symptoms have abated, to prevent the problem from recurring.

Many persons stop or reduce the dosage of the drug because of side effects. Some of them do not wish to hurt their nice, caring doctor's feelings by admitting they cannot tolerate the drug the doctor assured them would be so wonderful. Others become angry at the doctor for their discomforts, so they just quit taking the pills. It's always up to the practitioner to inquire about the side effects. A little reassurance can go a long way: Many of the side effects in time will pass, and isn't just a little discomfort worth the eventual payoff? On learning that side effects are a problem, the doctor may wish to adjust dosage or switch the patient to another drug that he or she can tolerate better.

Here's an example of how being sensitive to the patient's individual experience can help that person remain compliant. An eighty-year-old woman presented with a five-year history of depression. Her husband was an invalid, and her mother, in her late nineties and living in a nursing home, was demented. Six months before she came for treatment, one of her two sons, who was in his fifties, was killed in a car accident. She became extremely depressed. All attempts to treat her with antidepressants failed because of a lack of response or difficulty with side effects.

When Parnate, an MAO inhibitor, was prescribed, she began sleeping and eating well. Her energy level increased markedly, as did her sexual interest. But because she felt "very sexual," she stopped the medication. She said that her husband was not sexually interested in her and that she believed masturbation and extramarital affairs were wrong." So the treating psychiatrist cut the dosage in half. The patient agreed to give it another try. The lower dosage worked without the side effect that this particular patient could not tolerate.

Noncompliance can be a kind of symptom of depression. The illness creates a what's-the-use attitude: "Why bother with this miserable stuff? Nothing's going to help me anyway, ever." Forgetfulness, the result of depression or a side effect of the medication, also contributes: "Did I take my afternoon pills? Well, I'll take two more, just to be sure." Family members can help out immeasurably by encouraging compliance with the doctor's orders and by keeping track.

Finally, some persons resent being dependent on pills, especially those who believe that they should have psychological control over themselves. One of my patients went off on a two-week vacation to a tiny Caribbean island and "forgot" the medication that had brought him out of the pits and enabled him to go off to have a good time. He felt that his biological depression was the "fault" of his neurosis. He returned in pretty bad shape. He was lucky, though, that he did not suffer any adverse physiological reactions from going off the medication so abruptly (if one must discontinue antidepressant medication, the best way is to do so a little at a time). This patient told me he had not taken his pills; most people do not bother to inform their doctors. They get classified as nonresponders when in fact they respond quite well—when they take their medication.

I never completely rely on patients to tell me whether they are compliant. The family and blood-level testing give me all the information I need to monitor—and correct—this curious, complicated, and utterly human reaction. A couple of blood tests during treatment protects patients from nonresponse—and keeps psychiatrists from getting too depressed over the patient's perplexing inability to get better.

In the next section we take a close look at each one of the medications that are used to treat depression. The profiles of the drugs and drug classes will give you a good idea of the indications and the potential side effects, adverse effects, and dosages used.

CHAPTER 21

The Antidepressant Arsenal

This chapter contains a description of commonly used antidepressant drugs and how they work. I've tried to remove the jargon and leave the basic, bare-bones information.

ANTIDEPRESSANT DRUG CLASSES

For our purposes, there are three different types of antidepressants:

- The cyclic drugs
- MAO inhibitors
- Lithium salts

The Cyclic Drugs

The cyclic drugs are the largest class of antidepressant drugs, the ones we usually turn to first when we begin our assault on symptoms. They are the classic front-line treatment for unipolar depression and they have the best-established results—the Old Faithfuls of antidepressants.

We refer to them as cyclics because of their distinctive interlocking ring chemical structure. Cyclics are divided into two categories:

- The older tricyclics (TCAs), including:

  Amitriptyline (Elavil, Endep)   Imipramine (Tofranil)
  Clomipramine (Anafril)   Nortriptyline (Pamelor)
  Desipramine (Norpramin,   Protriptyline (Vivactil)
    Pertofrane)   Trimipramine (Surmontil)
  Doxepin (Adapin, Sinequan)

270

- The newer heterocyclics, which include:

  Amoxapine (Asendin)   Fluvoxamine (Luvox)
  Maprotiline (Ludiomil)   Venlaflaxine (Effexov)
  Trazodone (Desyrel)   Nefazodone (Serzone)
  Bupropion (Wellbutrin)
  Fluoxetine (Prozac)
  Paroxetine (Paxil)
  Sertraline (Zoloft)

The good news about these drugs is that they work fast and they work well. The vast majority of people who use this type of antidepressant will get better with the first cyclic we try. Seventy to 80 percent of people with a serious depression and as high as 90 percent of people suffering from melancholy report a reduction of symptoms.

All of the tricyclic antidepressants (TCAs) block reuptake of nor-epinephrine. Norepinephrine is involved in regulating a number of body systems. It causes blood vessels to contract and blood pressure to rise. It also affects breathing and is believed to relax the muscles in the intestinal tract. Within the brain, it regulates feelings of panic and anxiety, and it affects the changes in respiration, pulse, and blood pressure seen in response to fear or during drug withdrawal. In addition to blocking nor-epinephrine, some of the other TCAs block reuptake of several biogenic amines, including epinephrine, serotonin, and dopamine.

The heterocyclic antidepressants generally work by blocking reuptake of one specific neurotransmitter more than others. Most of these work on the serotonin system and are sometimes referred to as selective serotonin reuptake inhibitors, or SSRIs. (One relatively new drug, bupropion [Well-butrin], seems to block reuptake of dopamine, not serotonin, but is still classified with the heterocyclics.) The SSRIs prevent serotonin from being reabsorbed by the neuron; thus more of the neurotransmitter remains in the synapse so it can attach itself to receptors and keep sending its message. Serotonin, found in many tissues throughout the body and especially in the brain, was originally thought to be involved in aggression, obsessive-compulsive disorder, suicide, and irritability. Serotonin receptors in nerve cells are the landing sites for the hallucinogen LSD. Serotonin acts on the blood vessels and intestines in ways similar to norepinephrine. Serotonin's ability to control mood, attitude, and consciousness make it a key player when depression is present. The SSRIs include fluoxetine (Prozac), parox-etine (Paxil), and sertraline (Zoloft). Because these drugs are so important, we discuss them in more depth in Chapter 22. They have had a major impact on the treatment of depression, the way many physicians use antidepressant drugs, and how researchers conceptualize the biology of depression. The SSRIs have changed our thinking about the mechanism of depression, and may even change how we define a depressed person. These drugs herald a new age in depression treatment.

Although many of the antidepressants have very similar chemical structures, and although as a rule they are equally effective in treating depression, there are some important differences. One critical difference is the number and types of side effects that may result.

Side effects can be a big problem, one that prevents people from staying compliant with their treatment program. Unfortunately, virtually all drugs cause side effects in at least some people. When we say that one drug causes fewer side effects, we don't mean that it causes fewer different *kinds* of effects, but that these effects, whatever type they are, occur *less frequently*.

The cyclic antidepressants often interact with another neurotransmitter, acetylcholine, which operates on the neuron pathway called the cholinergic system. Acetylcholine helps regulate the actions of muscles and nerves. If molecules of antidepressant attach themselves to acetylcholine receptors, like rude drivers hogging someone else's parking space, then side effects usually occur. Chemicals that block the actions of acetylcholine are called anticholinergic agents. Anticholinergic side effects generally seen with cyclic antidepressants include dizziness, constipation, fainting, difficulty urinating, dry mouth, confusion, visual problems, irregular heart rhythms, muscle spasms, sedation, and weight gain. Some cyclics are more likely to cause these side effects than others (see chart, page 273).

Why do side effects occur at all, and, more important, why do they vary from medication to medication and individual to individual? As new drugs appear on the market, and as data accumulate on the use of these products in patients, we learn more about the effects they have at the receptor sites. Each new medication has different side effects because it affects binding of different neurotransmitters. It is possible, we think, that every receptor can cause a different positive reaction or negative side effect, which is why there is such a wide variety of reactions to the different drugs.

One advantage of the newer SSRIs is that they seem to produce side effects less frequently, as well as having a much lower potential for overdose. Some of their side effects may actually enhance the antidepressant effect: For example, they disrupt the REM (dreaming) phase of sleep, which we believe may help to elevate mood, at least in the short term.

Differences among the Cyclic Antidepressants

	More	Less
Sedation	amitriptyline	desipramine
	doxepin	protriptyline
	trimipramine	
Anticholinergic effects (dry mouth, constipation, etc.)	amitriptyline	desipramine
	doxepin	nortriptyline
	fluoxetine	protriptyline
	imipramine	
	trimipramine	
	trazodone	
Weight gain	amitriptyline	bupropion
	imipramine	desipramine
	nortriptyline	fluoxetine
	trimipramine, etc.	protriptyline

The SSRs seem to be safer in patients with medical problems, especially heart disease, strokes, Alzheimer's, and other diseases associated with cerebral vascular deterioration. This safety profile is one reason they are more often prescribed by physicians who treat elderly patients.

MAO Inhibitors (MAOIs)

The MAOIs are commonly prescribed but widely misunderstood by both patients and practitioners. As I mentioned before, MAOIs prevent the enzyme known as monoamine oxidase from dissolving serotonin, epinephrine, and norepinephrine. When the MAOIs work, increased amounts of the neurotransmitters remain in the system, elevating mood and controlling depression.

It is my experience that MAOIs can reduce the symptoms of major depression as effectively as the cyclic drugs. In some people they may even be more effective. In general, I use MAOIs when the cyclics don't

---

Multifaceted Medicines

Somewhat surprisingly, the side effects experienced by patients have led to treatment of other medical and psychological disorders. For example:

- A variety of phobias and panic attacks and chronic bedwetting in children have been treated with imipramine (Tofranil)
- Relief of peptic ulcer in depressed patients has been attained by using doxepin (Adapin) and trimipramine (Surmontil)
- A variety of allergic reactions and skin rashes have been treated with doxepin, trimipramine, amitriptyline (Elavil), and maprotiline (Ludiomil)
- Protriptyline (Vivactil) has been used in treatment of two sleep disorders: hypersomnia (too much sleeping) and sleep apnea, which occurs when you stop breathing for a few seconds while asleep. This drug, when taken in the morning, seems to decrease the excessive sleeping, prevent sleep apnea, and also help keep the heart better regulated
- Eating disorders such as bulimia have been treated with fluoxetine (Prozac) and desipramine (Norpramin)
- Substance abuse, specifically cocaine dependence and craving, has been treated with desipramine
- Imipramine has been used to treat narcolepsy, a condition that causes people to fall asleep often during the day
- Relief of certain types of chronic pain syndromes and migraine headaches has been found with trazodone (Desyrel) and amitriptyline
- Attention-deficit disorder has been treated with imipramine (Tofranil)
- Obsessive-compulsive disorder has been treated with clomipramine (Anafranil) and with fluoxetine (Prozac) and other SSRIs.

---

seem to be working, which happens in perhaps 20 to 30 percent of all depressed patients. MAOIs may, however, be less successful in treating some cases of atypical depression or when a panic disorder is also present.

The MAOIs have some distinctive properties that have made them controversial. In some people they may induce euphoria—a feeling of being high. There is some risk that they promote hyperactive behavior in people with manic depression. Generally, though, MAOIs are safe and effective and have little potential for abuse or overdose.

A concern about MAOIs is that they prevent the enzyme from doing its other main job, which is to break down a molecule called tyramine. Tyramine helps to regulate blood pressure. You consume a lot of tyramine when you eat such foods as aged cheese, beer, wine, pickled herring, chicken liver, yeast, coffee, broad beans, and canned figs. After you eat these foods, tyramine molecules swarm into the brain. Normally the MAO enzyme keeps the levels of tyramine in check. But if you take MAOI antidepressants, you knock the enzymes out of commission. The tyramine level stays too high, and there is a risk that blood pressure will shoot up to dangerously high levels. Some of the symptoms of this problem, some-times known as the "cheese reaction," include fainting, lightheadedness, dizziness, headaches, neck pain, heart palpitations, extremely high blood pressure, and brain hemorrhage. These problems are potentially life-threatening. People taking an MAOI antidepressant must avoid foods con-taining tyramine. If they do, there is very little risk of serious adverse events with these medications. I believe that MAOIs have an important role in the treatment of depression and that they are underused in this country. In my experience, most patients, given careful education and support, can easily adjust to the necessary dietary restrictions they must follow when taking MAOIs.

Lithium

Lithium is the only drug that over the years has been proven effective in controlling the vast mood swings and roller coaster–like behavior of the manic-depressive patient. Its primary action is the control of the manic highs of bipolar disorder.

Lithium is a metallic alkali element that has been used for over thirty years and has been found to be safe and effective for the vast majority of bipolar patients. Even though we are not quite sure why it controls the wild manic behavior of some people, we believe it acts on the same neurotransmitter systems as other antidepressants.

Whatever its mode of action, lithium works, and it works well in up to 60 to 70 percent of all patients. Literally hundreds of thousands of people who could not control their aggressive and out-of-control behavior have returned to normal lives because of this drug. Doctors have learned, over the decades, to change the dose by monitoring blood levels carefully, so that the optimal effect is achieved quickly. Most people respond to lithium within four to six days.

In general, lithium will not make you tired, dependent, or "doped-up" if the dose levels are correct and checked at least every three months after you are stabilized. However, too much lithium in your system increases the risk of tremors, muscular rigidity, seizures, and coma.

In the early stage of lithium treatment, side effects can include thirst, fatigue, weakness, hand tremors, nausea, vomiting, and excess urination. Often thirst and urinary problems will remain after the drug dose is stabilized. Lithium may not be indicated for patients on a low-sodium diet; if such patients do take it, dose levels may have to be adjusted more frequently.

So far, lithium has been found to be effective only in the treatment of manic-depression. In some cases it helps enhance the effects of anti-depressants in patients who haven't responded to a medication. Research is under way to see if lithium might work as a treatment for migraine and cluster headaches, alcoholism, substance abuse, some forms of aggressive behavior, and certain blood disorders.

CHAPTER 22

Prozac—Hype or Hope?

In an age of wonder drugs, the selective serotonin reuptake inhibitors, or SSRIs—Prozac, Zoloft, and Paxil—are perhaps the most amazing of them all. Hearing Prozac, the first SSRI, described as the cure of the '90s is not all that surprising to me.

- Within two years after its introduction in 1988, Prozac was *the* drug that everyone was prescribing. Today, five million Americans and another five to ten million people around the world have used Prozac.
- The media hailed Prozac as the wonder drug for everything from weight loss to eating disorders to PMS. It seemed too good to be true! Multiple investigations of the drug were undertaken to prove or disprove the claims of Prozac. TV talk shows, tabloid-news programs, and negative PR (much of it generated by the Church of Scientology) brought the Prozac debate to the attention of everyone.
- The FDA and Congress held hearings on Prozac in late 1991. The hearings, widely covered, featured lurid tales of patients who allegedly had committed suicide, attacked their spouses, or committed other violent acts while taking Prozac. But in the end, the FDA ruled that Prozac was indeed safe.
- Today, the negative publicity seems to be a distant memory. Almost one million prescriptions are filled for Prozac each month in the United States alone. Prozac is one of the twenty most prescribed drugs in America.
- Even *Consumer Reports* vouched for its safety in response to a letter from a consumer. It replied: "Studies have shown that a small number of people who have committed or attempted suicide while on Prozac generally had suicidal tendencies before they started taking the drug. An analysis of statistics from poison control centers and emergency rooms has also shown that Prozac is much less toxic than older antidepressants. . . . Prozac poses relatively little risk. . . ."

After two decades of treating people with psychiatric illness, I can easily see why this medication sparked such heated debate. The often overwhelming emotional toll of even relatively mild emotional illness—stress, anxiety, panic—has made virtually every new psychotropic medication a "wonder drug."

Only a few decades ago, news of the miracle of Valium (a benzodiazapine tranquilizer) was the hot topic of conversation. Valium became so popular—it was the most prescribed drug in America in 1977—that it became a running joke in movies, talk shows, and books. It was even the subject of rock songs ("Mother's Little Helper," by the Rolling Stones). People thought of it as a panacea, a cure-all, which it was not and was never intended to be.

I doubt whether even the original Panacea, the ancient Greek goddess of healing, would have embraced an elixir as powerful as Valium the way we did in this country. It remained one of the top five prescription drugs for several more years. But it was not the cure for the things in life that produced stress and dysfunction.

Popping a Valium every time life became difficult not only didn't work, but proved to be dangerous. Like many psychotropic medications, the drug had dangerous interactions, especially with alcohol, and had to be prescribed and withdrawn carefully. Several bestselling books, such as *I'm Dancing as Fast as I Can*, chronicled their authors' addiction to Valium. Today, Valium is still among the one hundred most prescribed drugs, although it has been replaced in the top ten by another tranquilizer, Xanax, at number seven.

Valium, however, is only a metaphor for the age-old search for something we can take that will calm us down, help us cope, make us feel better, enable us to be productive; ideally, such a medicine will have no serious side effects. Many medications in all different classes have appeared to come close to this ideal. Some have failed and been withdrawn from the market, but others have actually redefined the illnesses they treat. The classic example is penicillin, which turned a whole range of fatal infections into simply annoying inconveniences.

Psychiatry has also had its share of medications whose surprising results have catapulted them to wonder-drug status. Initially, lithium was widely prescribed to allegedly schizophrenic inmates in state mental hospitals. Remarkably, it appeared to work on large numbers of people whom we had thought were untreatable. Only later did we discover that the people we had labeled schizophrenic were actually manic-depressives whose symptoms or disease state closely mirrored schizophrenia.

Thorazine was another drug that changed psychiatry, not by changing our understanding of psychosis but by relieving symptoms for thousands of people who would otherwise have spent their lives in an institution.

While it's not surprising that Prozac has become the subject of countless cover stories and even a few bestsellers, the final judgment is still not in.

First, whether we're talking about an antidepressant or an antiulcer drug, long periods of time are necessary to fully appreciate the limitations of any drug treatment. Many times the treatment is ultimately found to work well or even be more successful than had been anticipated. A decade's worth of field testing usually tells us what happens if you mix the drug with alcohol, marijuana, antihypertensives, allergy medications, and so on. Is it lethal? Can it be used in suicides? Does it impair driving or operation of equipment? What happens when you take the medication for months as prescribed and then suddenly stop, or go on a crash diet before a wedding and lose twenty pounds, or drink ten cups of coffee a day? What happens if you're elderly?

The second lesson is about expectations, which, by the way, is really what the Prozac story is about. How we treat an illness, how we view the dangers of an illness, can change over time. Until the 1950s, polio was one of the most feared diseases in the world. Today, a routine childhood vaccination has removed the threat. Another example is high blood pressure—we now know that if you take your medication, you should do just fine.

What, then, will be the fate of the new wave of psychiatric drugs, such as Prozac, after they've had a decade of field testing? Will they be an important part of the regular arsenal biopsychiatrists have at their disposal? Or will they be another false hope?

Before we look into the crystal ball and answer that one, let's remember the most important medical lesson of the last decade for those of us who treat depression.

The previous section of this book discussed the prevailing theories of depression and how they relate to other psychiatric illnesses. If successful antidepressant drugs block the reuptake of a certain group of neurotransmitters known as the catecholamines, thereby increasing their availability to the system, then it would seem that depression is due to a lack of these chemicals. But, as we've also seen, these medications don't provide immediate relief of symptoms, and they are involved in changes in the sensitivity of the receptor sites over long periods of time.

These contradictions, as we've discussed, led us to look at a different neurotransmitter as a possible culprit. One theory was that serotonin deficiency or some other mechanism related to this neurotransmitter was responsible for depression or other psychiatric responses. Scientists looked for the answer, and decided it was indeed serotonin.

To recap my previous science lesson, serotonin is a neurotransmitter that the brain stockpiles in vesicles, or minute sacs, found in specific nerve cells (also known as neurons). A trigger, or impulse, either environmental or physiological, provokes the release of serotonin, which quickly binds to and stimulates another neuron that has been designed to receive it, known as a receptor. The receptor cell sets off its own impulse, which, in the case of serotonin, can mean many things. We believe that serotonin is one of the most important of all mood-relevant neurotransmitters, playing a role in a complex set of activities that control sensory and behavioral activities. For example, we believe that not only does lack of enough serotonin affect depression, but it also is somehow involved in obesity, aggression, obsessive-compulsive disorder, eating disorders, and substance abuse.

Serotonin activity peaks during the time when we need it the most — our waking hours. It also appears that it has a role in controlling impulses that cause us to be overly aggressive, deeply unhappy, or suicidal. Once it has done its job, serotonin is then sent back to its home cell through a mechanism known as an uptake pump. It is either stored for future use or dissolved by the monoamine oxidase (MAO) enzyme. Prozac and the other SSRIs block that reuptake to keep more serotonin working in the system. It's important to remember this science lesson when I explain how Prozac saved a patient whom I thought I'd never be able to help.

If his chart hadn't said *accountant* next to *profession,* I'd have guessed that Roger was a homeless person who had stumbled into my office by mistake.

But, in fact, he was an Ivy League graduate with an MBA, and was now virtually nonfunctional. He had failed his CPA exam twice, which on the basis of his education should have been a no-brainer for him. Actually, the third time he had failed even to show up for the test. He gave me the impression that he was the proverbial time bomb waiting to go off. Even though he was outwardly meek, he provoked in other people the same feelings of uneasiness that you get when you encounter a vagrant on the street.

Roger was referred to me by a psychologist he'd been seeing, who had convinced him to join a therapy group. Roger had presented my colleague with a long account of his fears of virtually everything, especially a fear of women and of failing. His fear of failing was obviously being reinforced by his inability to concentrate on work. When it came to dating, his life was a real disaster. He was thirty years old, unemployed, and, in his own words, "unloved, unwanted, and unworthy."

He soon revealed to me that, yes, he was very interested in women, but he "could not perform." That problem, he said, was due to the fact that he had "nothing going for him" and, as a result, women were not interested in him.

In fact, in everything he tried, he failed. He joined a health club to lose weight because he had no life and had become a couch potato. That effort failed because he had trouble motivating himself to go to the club.

Nothing worked for him. Roger was adrift on a sea of negativism. His psychologist was now seriously concerned because nothing he had done had changed Roger's outlook. As this downward spiral continued he feared that Roger might become so down that he'd harm himself.

To me, Roger's history said tumor or, at the very least, some sort of hormonal problem that hadn't been picked up in superficial physical exams. I sent him for a battery of tests. I did brain scans, which were negative, and I even had him checked out at a sleep lab that, by monitoring his nocturnal erections, showed his impotence was not physiological.

My second thought was substance abuse. Wrong again. He didn't even drink!

Most disconcerting was that he really didn't fit the profile of someone with major depression, at least when I considered the standard criteria. He was negative, but he hadn't lost interest in life. He had a good appetite, had no suicidal ideations, and, beyond significant weight gain, didn't seem depressed in the classic sense. But he was unhappy, not functioning, and certainly not getting any better.

But there was one thing that kept me searching for a psychiatric diagnosis. He had a family history of psychiatric problems. His older sister, a successful real-estate broker, had taken an overdose of sleeping pills several years before and had been successfully treated with imipramine.

When I learned this, I thought the rest would be simple: His sister had responded to a tricyclic antidepressant, so Roger would too.

Wrong again. I tried three different medications with Roger, and although blood-level tests showed each time that the drug was in his system at supposedly therapeutic levels, and that he was taking the pills properly, the clinical response was zero.

Roger, in the meantime, was becoming more and more fearful. He wasn't having panic attacks, but he was afraid to try anything new, convinced that his inability to find work or succeed confirmed that he was a "failure."

After one particularly frustrating session, I came to the conclusion that Roger fit a pattern that was becoming more of a norm among certain groups of patients, especially men. Maybe Roger is actually depressed, I thought. The fact that he is a man makes it harder for him to express his depressed feelings. What's more, his condition is chronic, which means that what would normally be acute symptoms have blended together to make him dysfunctional. The pieces of the puzzle were there, but just not as clear-cut as they were in other depressed patients. I had, in fact, ruled out everything, but with the family history considered, I decided that Roger was a candidate for Prozac.

You can guess the rest of the story. Roger is not only better, but a true success story. He is now a bank vice president, is married, and, as he puts it, "I finally have a life." I watch Roger closely: I see him every three months, and give him a physical twice a year. Roger has slimmed down and he exercises regularly.

But this is not a simple story with a classic happy ending. After Roger had been on Prozac for nine months, I tried to withdraw him from the drug. Within a week he called me, very concerned. He had begun to feel fearful again. He'd lost confidence in himself, and he was sure that his co-workers would see that he wasn't pulling his own weight. I wanted to put him back on the drug at his previous dose, but I had some concerns. At this early point, in Prozac's history, there wasn't much information about the effects of using the drug on a long-term basis. Roger and I talked about side effects that we know about, and those that we don't. But he chose to stay on the drug. Within a few days Roger was back on track.

What have I learned from Roger? Well, he didn't meet the standard criteria for depression, but I had treated him with three antidepressants that didn't work, and then finally one that did.

Does that mean he was depressed? I choose instead to say that he had Prozac-reversible disease. This drug, which has a targeted effect on se-rotonin, worked very well for Roger, and my experience with it in many patients has been very similar. Cases such as Roger's seem to be leading to more good news, since we will once again begin to see our role as diagnosticians differently. To some extent, diagnosing the illness partly by seeing if a patient responds to a certain treatment is the message of Prozac—no two depressed people are alike. Ultimately, the goal is to be able to learn from patient interviews, histories, and physical examinations the characteristics that identify the group of patients who all share an important biological feature: specific response to a specific treatment.

For me, the question is not whether or not Roger met standard criteria and was a "person suffering from depression." That description does not predict whether he will respond to use of an antidepressant drug, nor does it tell me which drug to try.

The *real* questions are: Why do these drugs work on certain people, and are they safe to use in long-term treatment, especially in the group of people with recurrent depression? It's also about expectations, as I said earlier. Doctors often expect someone who is depressed to be "typical." We expect a "wonder drug" to work wonders on everyone. Well, the real world is not like that, so sometimes, as in Roger's case, we have to try many things before we come to the right conclusion. Prozac is a drug that seemingly works so well on a variety of people and appears at this point to be so safe, relatively speaking, that the boundaries of our diagnosis can be expanded.

Roger is the classic case of a person waiting for a specific type of drug, in this case an SSRI, to be invented. So let's look at the pharmacology of these drugs just a little more closely.

SSRIs Up Close

Since the advent of Prozac in 1988, two other SSRIs have appeared on the market: first sertraline (Zoloft) and then paroxetine (Paxil). Still others, such as citalopram, nefazodone, fluvoxamine, and zimelidine, are in the pipeline (and may even be available by the time you read this book) or are approved for use in other countries. I'll discuss these drugs as a group because, as one researcher put it, "the similarities between the SSRIs are more obvious than their differences."

The SSRIs typically begin to work relatively faster than the TCAs. I usually caution patients that a tricyclic may need about three weeks to produce antidepressant benefits. Most doctors give patients the same warning about the SSRIs, especially Prozac, but many people report noticeable improvements in their mood within a few days. (It's not uncommon for patients to tell me they feel something positive within twenty-four hours.) Research shows that Paxil reaches steady-state concentrations within four to fourteen days. In other words, at the two-week mark, the level of drug circulating in your body is high enough to produce its effects (without additional dose changes), and the dose you take each day is roughly the same as the amount that gets eliminated. Prozac usually takes longer to reach steady state than the other SSRIs.

The body metabolizes (breaks down) a drug as part of the process of elimination. The molecules that result from this process are called metabolites. Sometimes metabolites themselves can act like drugs by producing their own effects (usually unwanted) on tissues, but often they don't do anything at all. Studies show that the metabolites arising from Paxil are less active within the body than the metabolites from Prozac and Zoloft.

Researchers have not yet determined, however, whether that difference has any clinical significance, such as a lower incidence of certain side effects.

The half-life of a drug is the time it takes for half of a dose to be eliminated by the body. Everything else being equal, shorter half-lives are safer and better. If a patient has an unwanted reaction, drugs with a shorter half-life leave the body more quickly, leading to a faster return to normal. Prozac has an elimination half-life of two to three days, while its younger relatives have a half-life of about a day.

A drug's potency (sometimes called its bioactivity) depends on a number of factors: how rapidly it enters the circulation; how efficiently it passes out of the bloodstream and into the brain; how strongly it affects the brain cells and their receptors; and how able it is to resist the action of enzymes during metabolism. Each new generation of SSRIs seems to have greater potency: Paxil, the new kid on the block, is more potent than Zoloft, which in turn is more potent than "grandpa" Prozac. That doesn't mean new products are necessarily better; sometimes I prefer not to give patients more potent medications, just as you may not always want to take an extra-strength pain reliever. Good medical practice requires doctors to give the lowest doses of any medication that will produce the most benefit at the lowest risk of side effects.

No drug will work if it sits in a bottle in the medicine cabinet. Compliance is always an issue. The easier a drug is to take, the more likely it is that the patient will take it. Medications with once-a-day dosing are more convenient than those that have to be taken twice or more each day. All of the SSRIs now on the market can be taken once a day. If patients notice troublesome side effects, such as a "speedy" feeling or sleepiness, I may recommend that the patient take half the dose twice a day, or take the full dose at bedtime.

Of course, safety and effectiveness are always the main concerns with every drug. Although many people regard Prozac and its relatives as wonder drugs, the truth is these antidepressants are, in general, no more effective than the tricyclics that have been around for years. The advantage, though, is that the serotonin drugs are less likely to interact with the central nervous system in the way that the TCAs can. TCAs apparently have a kind of shotgun effect within the brain, affecting a number of different neurotransmitter systems. The first *S* in SSRI stands for *selective*, which underscores the fact that these drugs target one particular chemical pathway. (Evidence suggests that SSRIs do affect other neurotransmitter receptors, but to a much less significant degree.) SSRIs are less likely to cause the typical troublesome side effects seen with tricyclics, such as dry mouth, nervousness, sedation, and so on. They also pose less of a threat to heart function.

Another real advantage of SSRIs is that they are much less likely to cause weight gain, a common problem with TCAs. That feature is important in depression for a number of reasons. Weight gain is one of the main reasons patients fail to comply with their prescriptions; that, in turn, increases the risk that their depressive symptoms will worsen. Another problem is that depressed people already struggle with feelings of hopelessness, low self-esteem, and the sense that they are unlovable. Extra pounds can further undermine their already shaky view of themselves. When Prozac first appeared, some people believed—inaccurately—that it would work as a weight-loss pill. That speculation was fueled by the fact that some studies showed that people taking Prozac did in fact lose some weight. That theoretical benefit evaporated, however, when long-term studies found that weight loss was minor, and that after eight weeks or so, the lost pounds came back.

Of course, no drug is perfect. To some extent, SSRIs trade one group of side effects for another, but most patients seem to find those problems more tolerable than the ones encountered with TCAs. About one in five patients taking an SSRI experiences gastrointestinal symptoms, especially nausea. Other related side effects include diarrhea or loose stools or, paradoxically, constipation. As a rule, though, these problems are mild and short-lived. I counsel patients who notice these side effects to try to bear with the treatment for a while and see what happens. In most cases these problems disappear within a few days or a week. If not, I might adjust the dose or suggest that the patient take the medication at a different time of day. Another option is to switch to a different SSRI, or try another type of antidepressant altogether. One potential risk involves the fact that, like many drugs, the SSRIs are metabolized in the liver. Patients with impaired liver function may not be able to use these antidepressants.

There are two side effects that my patients often mention but that, oddly enough, haven't received a lot of attention in the medical literature. The first is relatively benign: vivid dreams. One patient described his dreams as being like "cable television" with colorful programs containing complex plots, lifelike characters, and dynamic action. In some instances, however, such dreams can turn into intense nightmares. If this problem disrupts the ability of the patient to get a good night's rest, I don't hesitate to try another SSRI or another type of antidepressant entirely.

The second side effect is one of potentially great concern: a significant reduction in sexual performance. In both men and women this often translates into difficulty achieving orgasm. For a large group of patients, it can mean that orgasms disappear entirely. In men, sexual complications might involve trouble achieving or maintaining an erection, but mostly it's failure to ejaculate. An informal survey suggests that perhaps 40 percent of people taking Prozac have noticed some impact on their sexuality. It's a topic that comes up at social gatherings where the talk so often turns to who is taking what modern miracle drug. A number of my patients have been so upset by the problem that they have asked to be taken off the medication. Some others, however, don't necessarily regard this *side* effect as an *adverse* effect. For example, their improved mood may seem an acceptable trade-off for the decline in sexual appetite. People who are not currently in an intimate relationship may not mind as much if their sexual desire is curbed to some degree. And some men who in the past may have reached orgasm too quickly are actually happy to have delayed orgasm and greater endurance (provided, that is, that they can get an erection). In fact, a number of physicians who treat sexual problems are experimenting with the use of SSRIs as treatments for premature ejaculation. There is some evidence that these drugs may help to reduce sexual cravings and behavior, which may improve the treatment of sexual addiction or criminal behavior by sex offenders. Still, the sexual impact of these medications is an underrecognized problem, and more research is needed to find out why it happens—and to help us discover drugs that don't have this feature. A new type of antidepressant, bupropion (Wellbutrin), apparently avoids sexual side effects. Because bupropion works on a different neurotransmitter system (dopamine), it does not have the orgasm-inhibiting property of the SSRIs.

The SSRIs are often a good choice for the elderly, whose bodies are often less able to process drugs as well as they did in their younger years. Often older patients experience a number of other medical complications and are taking other medications. SSRIs generally seem to have less capacity for causing interactions with other drugs, although there is a risk that they will interact with MAOI antidepressants, phenobarbital, and phenytoin. Zoloft and Paxil are less drug-interactive than Prozac. We need more studies, however, before we have definitive answers about the use of these medications in older patients.

Nursing mothers are usually withdrawn from any medications to reduce the risk that drugs will pass into their breast milk and thus be consumed by their infants. It may be, however, that antidepressant treatment is important for a seriously depressed new mother. In such cases the advantages of breast-feeding need to be weighed against the medical needs of the mother. Studies indicate that small amounts of Prozac, but larger amounts of Paxil, are secreted in breast milk.

It often happens that a drug found effective for one purpose is found to work in other areas as well. Some studies on lab animals demonstrate that SSRIs can decrease appetite, reduce body weight, and even lower the desire for alcohol. Such results suggest that these drugs may have a role to play in managing other psychiatric and physical problems, such as obesity, obsessions, and compulsions, common to substance-abuse disorders. Other potential uses of drugs that affect the various components of the serotonin system include treatment of panic and anxiety; reduction of nausea and vomiting associated with cancer treatment; and treatment of obsessive-compulsive disorder, eating disorders, atypical depression, premenstrual tension, chronic pain, dementia, and personality disorders (especially those involving aggression or impulsive behavior).

LONG-TERM SAFETY

Because the SSRIs have been on the market for only a few years, carefully designed long-term studies have not yet been conducted. Some studies have been done that have lasted up to four years. According to the manufacturer of Prozac, such open-label studies—in which the name of the drug is known to everyone involved—demonstrate that Prozac maintains its effectiveness and safety over time. About 15 percent of patients stop taking Prozac because of adverse effects, compared to about 30 percent of patients taking TCAs. What we don't yet have, however, are the results of studies in which neither patients nor their doctors know the name of the medication or whether the pill being given is actually an inactive placebo. Such double-blind studies help eliminate the effects of bias that can creep into the results if people know which drug is being used.

As time passes it appears that the reports suggesting Prozac causes suicidal or violent behavior often ignored important evidence that the underlying disease or other factors were involved. For example, in some of the cases, the person involved was actually taking multiple medications, and it was not possible to sort out which drug might have caused which reaction—if, indeed, any cause-and-effect relationship could be identified. In other cases the person might have been taking huge quantities of the medication. An investigation by the TV news program *60 Minutes* examined the question and found that despite people's claims that Prozac had made them violent or suicidal, many of these individuals had in fact had histories of such behavior or other serious medical or emotional problems stretching back as long as twenty years.

Prozac's maker received so many queries about safety that it issued the following statement:

> In a retrospective review at two poison control centers of 44 cases of overdose with Prozac (fluoxetine) alone and with other drugs, followup was available on 33 cases.
>
> The investigators concluded that "overdose with fluoxetine presents minimal risk of serious cardiovascular or neurological complications. . . . Among 48 cases in a prospective study of fluoxetine overdosage at 5 poison control centers, 19 patients ingested fluoxetine alone or with alcohol in amounts ranging from 140 mg to 1500 mg [the standard dose of Prozac is 20 mg a day]."
>
> The investigators concluded that, based on their limited experience, fluoxetine in overdose appears to be relatively benign.
>
> A retrospective study of 1,017 depressed patients showed no statistically significant differences in the rates of emergency of suicidal ideation across five classes of antidepressant therapy: tricyclics alone and tricyclics with lithium; fluoxetine with tricyclics; monoamine oxidase inhibitors; other agents, and fluoxetine alone.
>
> In U.S. clinical trials, suicidal thinking emerged less often during therapy among patients treated with Prozac than among those receiving TCAs or placebo.

As someone who has practiced psychiatric medicine for over two decades, and based on my experience with a number of so-called wonder drugs, such as Valium, I'm inclined to be skeptical about accepting a manufacturer's claims at face value. Having said that, I honestly believe that Prozac and the SSRIs were developed carefully. Prozac was tested in human trials for a decade before it received FDA approval. I monitor the scientific literature carefully, and I know that Prozac is under tight scrutiny by both the medical profession and the public—as well it should be. I hope the drugs live up to our expectations. Only time will tell. I know for certain, however, that the story is not over. Newer, even more well-designed products will enter the market and will offer even greater benefits with less risk of side effects.

In his bestseller *Listening to Prozac,* Dr. Peter D. Kramer puts the arrival of Prozac into perspective:

> Prozac stands in marked contrast to lithium. Whereas lithium is the simplest of chemicals, an element, unpatentable, its usage discovered by a solitary practicing doctor with no eye toward profit, Prozac is a designed drug, sleek and high-tech. It comes from a world even most doctors do not understand. I sometimes wonder whether this "feel" of

Prozac—so different from that of lithium—has had some subtle influence on its reception, as regards both the sense of wonder and the sense of discomfort at its (alien) power.

The story of Prozac is typical in another way as well. Chemists working today to develop drugs for the mind start not so much with diseased patients as with models of nerve transmission, and they tailor molecules to affect that basic process. The goal is clean drugs—drugs that are ever more potent and specific in their effects on nerve transmission. The likely result of this form of research is not medicines that correct particular illnesses but medicines that affect clusters of functions in the human brain, often in both well and ill persons.

For me, the story of Prozac will always be Roger and my preconceived notions. I began by thinking Roger was either x, y, or z. But when I found he was none of the above, and in fact turned out to be Prozac-responsive, it didn't matter what I thought he was. He was remarkably better. That's what really matters.

And as Prozac's promise holds up in the coming years, it will give me hope that the next step, an even better Prozac, is around the corner.

Prozac and the Politician

After the devastation of Hurricane Andrew in 1991, Florida's governor, Lawton Chiles, was the ultimate hands-on governor, helping individuals restore their lives and overcome the anguish of this disaster. When Florida's tourist industry was threatened by a series of violent crimes, Governor Chiles was in the streets again, even riding with police to help reassure the people. He is to many Florida residents a hero, having restored the state's economy and revived its morale. However, only a few years ago, Chiles was not known as a hero, but as the "Prozac candidate."

Recent educational campaigns by self-help groups, the NIMH, and the American Psychiatric Association are finally cracking the mental-health barrier. One sign that the stigma of mental illness is fading is the election of former U.S. senator Lawton Chiles to the governorship of Florida and the transformation of public opinion.

"Talkin' Lawton" Chiles, a sixty-year-old self-proclaimed populist, is the first national politician to be elected while openly being treated for depression. Further, Florida's voters overwhelmingly elected Chiles, knowing that he was taking the controversial medication Prozac.

In 1987, after Chiles underwent quadruple heart bypass surgery, his wife, Reah, noticed that he seemed depressed, so she spoke with a

continued

congressional doctor. But it was only when his lack of appetite and inability to sleep or concentrate persisted that Chiles agreed to meet with the chief of outpatient psychiatry at Bethesda Naval Hospital in Washington, D.C., and the diagnosis was confirmed.

Depression is fairly common in heart surgery patients. Chiles's depression lifted with the help of antidepressant medications and psychotherapy.

Karl F. Hempel, M.D., the doctor who treated Chiles for depression in December, 1989, noted that Chiles's symptoms were typical and that he responded well to medication. It was Dr. Hempel who prescribed Prozac, the antidepressant that had already helped over one million people since its introduction in the marketplace in 1988.

According to Chiles, after eighteen years as a U.S. senator, he found himself in the same position that many others do—burned out on the job, almost unable to keep up with the daily demands of his office.

As head of the Senate Budget Committee, Chiles was in a job that "almost killed" him. He told reporters during his gubernatorial campaign that his frustration and feelings of worthlessness grew as he attempted to convince his colleagues that the U.S. budget was out of control. Some mornings Chiles couldn't decide whether to shave or shoot himself. Citing burnout, Chiles reluctantly retired from the Senate in 1988.

Chiles, long known for his quirky style of politics, decided to come out of retirement in 1990 after accepting treatment for what he called "the blacks." "I wish I'd known about Prozac before," Chiles said, "because it helped me."

No stranger to a tough political campaign—he once walked a thousand miles while campaigning in 1970—Chiles began running in the primary as an underdog with far less of a war chest than his opponents. Yet his candor about his depression helped him rather than closed the doors to him, as happened to Senator Thomas Eagleton when his ECT treatments were revealed during the 1972 vice presidential race.

When Chiles's opposing Democratic candidate, Representative Bill Nelson, called for the release of Chiles's medical records, the Senator saw his thirty-six-point lead in the opinion polls shrink to twelve points. At a public meeting, Tom Gustafson, Nelson's running mate, hinted that the pressures of the election for the governorship might conceivably drive Chiles to suicide. Gustafson later made a public apology for his statement.

Chiles released his medical records and spoke frankly about his depression, saying he felt so much better since treatment that he wanted other people to know about it. Happily married with four children and eight grandchildren, Chiles said that no member of his family had ever

continued

suffered from depression, even though the illness tends to run in families. Unlike most people, Chiles sought help.

With his depression under control, Chiles's story had a unique and happy ending. He won the primary with 69 percent of the vote and went on to win the governorship against the Republican incumbent, a victory not only for him, but for all people who have been victims of the stigma of mental illness.

Mental health experts say Chiles's political success represents an acknowledgment by the American people that depression can be successfully treated—by medication or other means—and that a mental health problem, like any other health problem, should not be a cause of discrimination.

Chiles's 1990 election campaign, and his open approach to his depression, has given hope to millions of Americans who suffer in silence, or who go untreated for fear of losing their jobs or because they are afraid of the impact it may have on their family. It is significant that almost no one remembers Chiles for his fight against mental illness, but for his stability and healthy mind in the face of all sorts of adversity.

CHAPTER 23

More Good News:
A Lifetime of Relief
for Recurrent Depression

The best news of all about depression is that once we have relieved your symptoms, the odds are very good that we can keep you symptom-free for life.

Recently I saw one of my patients again, two years after I had treated him for a severe depression. Fred was fifty years old and was recovering from an attempted suicide when I saw him the first time.

Fred had worked for the government all of his adult life. In the 1960s he'd been an engineer with NASA, a civilian troubleshooter for the Navy working on carriers during the Vietnam War, and had been installing computer systems in jets for a defense contractor ever since. His future seemed secure. Then, in the late 1980s, the Berlin Wall fell and the cold war ended. When peace broke out and the Defense Department cut back, Fred was out of work for the first time since he got out of grad school in 1960. But that didn't stop him.

For two years, Fred lived off his severance pay and did some consulting work on the side. His daughter had been out of the house for years, and his wife, Francine, was still teaching Spanish to middle-school students. Fred used to say, "I've got it all."

Two years ago, Fred and Francine took advantage of her summer vacation and his frequent-flier miles to spend the summer in Europe. They went to Costa del Sol in Spain for a month, and then toured Italy and France. One day, Francine woke up and discovered that Fred was gone. Vanished. Three days later, he was found sitting in a small village, curled up in a doorway, crying and virtually unable to communicate. With the help of the local American consul, Francine got him home and into a hospital, where he eventually was diagnosed with both depression and post-traumatic shock related to his career decline.

"How could he be so sick," Francine asked, "without my knowing it? He was depressed sometimes, but nothing that seemed unusual." But one thing I've learned in my years as a doctor: Depression doesn't occur out of the blue. Once Fred's doctors began to probe, they found some signs that indicated the direction Fred had been headed in since he lost his "real" job. They discovered some evidence of a family history—a brother had bouts of alcoholism that probably masked depression. Fred had been expressing melancholy thoughts, which Francine had dismissed as middle-age blues and boredom. He had cut back his consulting, and while in Europe had quickly lost his enthusiasm for touring castles and museums. Finally, he told his doctor, he got up one day and just had no idea where he was or why he felt so bad. He took a walk and never went back.

Fred was sick, no question, but once he was on medication and had spent some time talking to a therapist, he bounced right back. For two years life returned to normal. Fred split his time between consulting and working part time in a computer store. He had been off medication for a year when his life came apart again. He began to have problems concentrating at work. Soon he was also having trouble sleeping and eating, and he started losing weight. Then . . . déjà vu! This episode of depression was far more severe, and he knew what was coming, but he couldn't stop the avalanche. In despair, he took what was, at first, thought to be an accidental overdose of sleeping pills and alcohol.

I didn't think the overdose was accidental. In looking at Fred's family history and the progression of his life, it was clear to me that this new bout of depression was the same as the last one, triggered by the same type of incident but more severe.

But this time I had some good news for Fred. "I can relieve your symptoms and keep you symptom-free for life. We've learned a lot about recurrent depression in the last few years," I told him, "and also how to treat it, but the method is still controversial." When I told him the rest of the news, he was not so sure that it was good.

I said that he was just like a heart patient, or a diabetic, or a person with hypertension. He had what was, in effect, a recurring disease that would be with him all of his life. And, like people with high blood pressure or an irregular heartbeat, the best treatment was medication, taken every day for the rest of his life. It wasn't a question of "When will I be cured?" or "When can I stop taking antidepressants?" but rather, "Why risk the chance of becoming depressed again?"

Fred said that other doctors had told him it was common practice for a patient to go off medication after a symptom-free period, and that medication was not needed unless the depression came back.

Well, that's true. It has been common practice to discontinue medications after four to nine months of continuous treatment. In fact, the government's Clinical Practice Guidelines recommend that approach. The guidelines say medication should be stopped, "since only 50 percent will have another episode of major depressive disorder. Even then, the next episode may be years hence."

But over the past decade, I have learned something very important about depression that has changed my approach to treatment: For a certain segment of the population—upwards of two-thirds of all patients—*depression is forever.* But its symptoms may not be. Just like high blood pressure, the illness is there, even though you feel fine. In using our laundry-list approach to diagnosis, we've never really looked at patients over the long term, especially those who develop depressive illness in middle age. It is clear now that the symptoms of depression may subside, but the disease will always be there, a silent threat, unless it is treated continuously.

"Prevention is the best treatment"—it's as true for mood disorders as it is for drug addiction or polio.

Like many of my colleagues, I am convinced that many, many depression patients have to be on medication for life. I recommend that, even if treatment has alleviated symptoms, medication dosages should remain at the same level used when symptoms were full-blown. This is not only a very new approach to treatment of depression but a controversial one: It suggests that failure to stay on the medication may turn a somewhat benign depression into a malignant, rapidly relapsing, harder-to-treat disease!

Why, Fred wanted to know, had I come to this conclusion? What had changed my view?

The answer comes not so much from the new understanding of the biology of depression, but from the results of longitudinal studies. Such studies follow patients over time to see how they progress after symptoms dissipate, and how discontinuing medication affects that progress over the years.

Recent studies from the National Institute of Mental Health (NIMH) and the National Institutes of Health (NIH) have demonstrated that depression, mood swings, bipolar disorder, and other similar mental health problems recur far more frequently than was previously thought.

Studies done at several major university teaching facilities showed that 50 to 85 percent of patients who were diagnosed as suffering from a major depression will have at least one more bout of depression in their life-times. In fact, concluded the researchers, depression should be considered a recurrent lifetime disease in most cases. By looking back and reviewing cases carefully, other studies have shown that patients with major depression usually have, on average, five recurrences. Bipolar patients may find themselves combating their severe mood swings eight different times.

Fred's case was, in some ways, slightly different than most. For example, his disease didn't break through until he was middle-aged. Usually, major depression surfaces years earlier, giving us early warning of a lifetime pattern—especially if the first occurrence is during childhood or adolescence. And his family history wasn't known until his brother's problems came to light.

But still, what we've learned made me believe that, even after only one recurrence, Fred should be on medication for life. In fact, Fred was lucky because he came to me at a time when the evidence that supports this approach is becoming stronger. The data we have now adds up to a somewhat startling conclusion: The more episodes a patient has, the more likely it is that future episodes will occur.

We have learned that the patients who will benefit from lifetime treatment follow one of several patterns. Their depression:

- has recurred several times, with the occurrences separated by several years without symptoms
- never really subsides, but continues for lengthy periods without proper treatment
- returns several times, then subsides into a period of euthymia (hyper behavior)
- returns frequently, with the gap between episodes shortening each time. This so-called cycle acceleration has been tracked in over 50 percent of all depressed patients

The evidence is becoming clearer and clearer. Each time depression reappears, the chances that it will be back again, more quickly and with increasingly severe symptoms, are greater. It appears that the recurrence itself is a risk factor for more episodes.

How many patients does this happen to?

Several investigators have identified a recurrence risk of more than 50 percent following the first episode and a 70 to 80 percent or more risk after the second episode.

Such results are why I was concerned about Fred, and why I was recommending a lifetime of antidepressant medication. But there are other reasons why this type of treatment may be the best route for patients like him.

One is his age. The later in life depression occurs, the higher the risk that it will return. There is strong evidence that if you become depressed at or around fifty years old, you are more likely to have a recurrence of depression.

Although Fred is just barely in this category, aging itself can be both a risk factor and a risk in itself for more severe depressions. Aging becomes sort of a classic Catch-22. As you grow older your brain's capacity or reserve is diminished. The level of mood-active neurotransmitters decreases and the ability to recover from changes to the neurotransmitter systems slows. Depression may cause difficult-to-reverse changes in the brain's normal function, specifically in the ways that the nervous and endocrine systems function and in the levels of hormones secreted by endocrine glands. When depression reappears, not only is the altered brain less able to combat it on its own, but the neural structure of the brain is altered once again. In effect, the brain's capacity to make and store the vital neurotransmitters that can offset depression is permanently diminished and then weakened again. This leaves the patient at higher risk each time for more and more devastating episodes of depression.

The one category where Fred did not fit in terms of risk factors was gender. One of the constants about depression is that it occurs more frequently in women than men. Data shows that women are three times more likely to become depressed, and this statistic carries over into recurring depression. There is some evidence that developmental changes in the brain at puberty may put women more at risk for depression.

We also believe that other gender-specific effects, such as neurological responses to seasonal shifts, menstruation, and menopause, also are risk factors. These are what we refer to as chronobiological factors: processes that influence the body's natural biological rhythms. They seem to figure somewhere in the equation that leads to recurrences of depression in middle age.

Another reason for our shift in viewpoint about long-term treatment is work being done by research psychiatrists at the NIMH on the biological effects of depression on the brain. There are two specific theories being explored to explain why the increased recurrence of depression can lead to more frequent and severe episodes.

One theory is called behavioral sensitization. This is an idea that also relates to some of my studies of the addictive process. We know that if someone takes cocaine or other drugs of abuse frequently, a consistent biological response occurs with each use that makes additional use more likely. It would appear that the brain's response to the stimulation of the drug is both psychological and physiological. The same type of repeated response seems to occur when depression strikes. A certain behavior or event that results in depression can make a person even more vulnerable to mood disruption the next time a similar behavior or event occurs.

A second concept, which is known as kindling, is a little more esoteric, but also applies to drugs such as cocaine. If cocaine causes a seizure once, it is more likely to leave the person with a seizure disorder that can be activated by cocaine or another stimulus. Kindling is similar to behavioral sensitization in that it may also be related to the results of stimulation. Some researchers feel that when the brain is repeatedly stimulated, an electrical response occurs that becomes more pronounced each time the stimulation occurs. If, for example, you continue to use a drug such as cocaine over and over, this discharge will eventually change the brain's structure, making it more sensitive to the next application. The same kindling effect may be a contributing factor in recurring depression.

The bottom line: The brain will "learn" from previous episodes of depression. This learning results from the fact that depression can change the brain structurally and physiologically. Therefore, not only will it take less of a trigger or stressor to set off a response such as depression each time, but the brain may be so altered that it can actually begin to produce spontaneous episodes of depression.

So that's why Fred is taking medication. Despite the fact that he hasn't had more than two episodes, and he's not female and he's just fifty years old, he is actually the ideal candidate for lifetime treatment. He *can* be spared from—what is very clear to me and other scientists—a lifetime of depressive episodes. Fred is the patient for whom medication becomes more than a treatment—it is the classic preventative measure that we are reasonably sure will work! Knowing what we know now, I keep patients like Fred on a high dosage level for at least the first year after their initial depression, rather than taper them off or remove them from treatment whether they are symptom-free or not.

The theories about behavioral sensitization and kindling may one day explain some of the things that we still don't understand about depression and relapse. For example, why do all forms of depression—not just seasonal affective disorder—seem to worsen in the winter? Why do suicide rates increase in both the spring and the fall, and why do bipolar patients tend to become more manic in the spring? And we also want to know why some feel worse in the early part of the day rather than at night. Why does staying up all night temporarily relieve depression? Why does exercise improve mood? What about the effects of time changes, the location of the person relative to the equator, and other unknown factors that increase the likelihood of recurring depression as we grow older and if we've had an episode of depression that began in middle age? The answer to all of these questions may lie in the aftereffects of the biology of depression.

What then, in my opinion, should standard practice be for long-term treatment of depression?

To date, no authoritative body has published specific parameters that would enable us to simply say, "Okay, you're a person who should take antidepressants for life." But there are some general signals that will tilt me in that direction. These have been summed up succinctly by Dr. John Greeden, chairman of the Department of Psychiatry at the University of Michigan Medical Center, and appear in the box below.

When I finished explaining a lot of the symptoms to Fred and Francine and had also given them some literature to read, they had the same reaction.

"I don't know whether to be happy or unhappy. On the one hand, never having to feel the way I felt this last time would be wonderful. But on the other hand, the idea of being dependent on medication for the rest of my life — well, it's hard to feel good about that," said Fred.

Signs Calling for Long-term or Lifetime Treatment for Depression

- Three or more episodes, regardless of patient's age
- Two or more episodes of major depression in a person age forty or older
- First depressive episode occurring at age fifty or older

Others who should be considered for lifetime maintenance therapy include:

- Those whose prior episodes, even if only one or two, were extremely severe and disabling
- Those whose prior episodes were associated with severe suicidality
- Those who would be personally devastated by recurrence of depression or mania, e.g., individuals who are self-supporting or the primary providers
- Those in whom discontinuation of medication in the past resulted in distinct, prompt, and severe relapse

Note: Even when lifetime therapy may not be selected, it is important to treat an initial episode for an adequate period of time—at least twelve months after full recovery—regardless of the severity of the episode.

Francine added, "The pills Fred had before were really powerful—they had some very unpleasant side effects. You know," she said, chuckling, "sometimes I suffered as much as Fred."

I knew what she meant. Recovery from depression involves the entire family, and, as we've discussed elsewhere, some side effects can affect others, especially spouses. Still, I feel that all patients should be told that they are probably going to be on medication for life and given straight information about their risks.

I explained that because we think depressive episodes may cause permanent brain chemistry alterations, the sooner we get on with treatment the better. I knew also that Fred's current phase of recovery could end up being just that—a phase—if I didn't reduce his risk as quickly as possible. In fact, if Fred had been treated quickly when his second episode began, it's likely that his suffering would have been stopped before he made his suicide attempt.

I prescribed one of the new SSRIs that have to be taken only once a day, and that have significantly fewer side effects. I told Fred that he would be taking the same dosage level for several months. There was a possibility that it could be lowered, but, frankly, that was not likely.

I also told him that I would be monitoring his response closely. Not only did I expect him to report to me on how he was doing between visits, but it might be a good idea to keep a diary or journal to ensure that symptoms were not recurring. I also made sure that he was familiar with the medication's effects. I reminded him that depressive episodes could be triggered by use of drugs including alcohol, illicit drugs, or various prescription or nonprescription medications, or by consuming certain foods or beverages. And I stressed once again how important it was to communicate with me if any problems should arise, whether of a medical nature or not.

Long-term treatment of depression with medication remains controversial. There are many obvious reasons to put Fred on medication for life, as I've discussed above. More evidence supporting this approach will emerge in the future. Already there are studies that indicate that the more times treatment is interrupted and then reinitiated, the more likely it is that sensitive brain functions will be disrupted and cause changes in the way medications work. We may find that the antidepressant medication that worked the first or second time is totally ineffective unless the patient takes it for life!

It's important to make one other point. Obviously, treatment of recurrent depression is not simply "take a pill and you'll be better." In Chapter 24 I discuss psychotherapy in depth. Although studies have shown that there is a role for psychotherapy as an adjunct to drug treatment, medications are the most effective way to treat recurrent depression.

Another part of the good news for Fred, as we saw in the previous chapter, is the development of certain medications that are well suited for use over the long haul. These are primarily the SSRIs. Easy to administer, possessing few side effects, the SSRIs have revolutionized both the diagnosis and the treatment of depression.

PART V

TREATMENT TODAY
Beyond Medication

CHAPTER 24

More Tools in the Arsenal

Today, the "new kids on the block," SSRIs, are getting all the front-page press. But that doesn't mean that they are the only good news. More traditional means of treatment—ECT (shock therapy) and psychotherapy—remain valid.

Another part of the good news is that over the past decade, the controversies surrounding such issues as when to use ECT, when to use medications, and when to use psychotherapy have disappeared. Today, we have a greater understanding of the values and efficacy of these treatments, and of how they can be used together. The end result is that the various forms of treatment of depression are like strands that have been braided together and are much stronger than before.

SHALL I SHOCK YOU?

For the actively suicidal or homicidal depressed patient, or for the patient whose physical condition precludes medication, time may be running out. It is entirely appropriate today to forgo another medication trial and instead choose electroconvulsive therapy (ECT).

Shock therapy has had an awful reputation, to a large extent well deserved. Since its introduction in 1938, it has at times been used indiscriminately, punitively, and dangerously.

Today, the federal government's Clinical Practice Guidelines are very clear. ECT is indicated in "the treatment of severe depression when the symptoms are intense, prolonged, and associated with severe vegetative symptoms and/or a marked functional impairment, the presence of psychotic symptoms, or failure to respond fully to several adequate trials of medication."

303

In addition, ECT is used today for those who cannot take antidepressants due to a medical risk and those who have mixed manic episodes, catatonia caused by another medical condition, neuroleptic malignant syndrome (NMS), hypopituitarism, intractable seizure disorder, and certain forms of Parkinson's disease.

During ECT, electricity passes through electrodes attached to the patient's head. The shock to the brain causes a convulsion, or seizure. The seizure is essential to the treatment, not a side effect (although some physicians bill patients for "nonconvulsive ECT"). Research shows that depression lifts after a series of treatments if the technique is applied correctly. The reason for ECT's terrible image is that in some cases prior to recent medical protocol changes, psychiatrists zapped patients' brains with high-energy currents while they were fully awake. Patients had to be tied down because their whole bodies went into horrific convulsions; vertebrae sometimes snapped from the violence of the seizure. Sometimes the patient's heart stopped. Often people were forced to endure this treatment; no one bothered getting their consent, because they were neurotic or psychotic or had a behavior problem.

Today, low-energy electrical currents are briefly aimed at one or both sides of the brain. (There is debate about which method works better and causes fewer side effects.) The patient, who receives oxygen, is relaxed and asleep, courtesy of muscle relaxants and several new, short-acting anesthetics. Monitors are used to check vital signs. The major known side effects of ECT are confusion and memory loss, which is usually short-term but which sometimes is long-lasting. Damage to the brain may result, especially for the patient who undergoes numerous courses of treatment. And use of general anesthesia carries its own risks. However, several new studies show that brain abnormalities do not usually result from ECT.

There is some evidence that one reason ECT works is that the shock affects important parts of the brain normally involved in mood (specifically, the locus ceruleus, raphe nucleus, and hippocampus). It appears too that ECT may stimulate the production of certain essential amino acids, such as tyrosine, that are the first step in the production of the major neurotransmitters.

Electroconvulsive therapy is no longer the torture it once was, although that image persists. ("It may be hard for the average person to separate the image of the therapeutic electric-shock device from the torture of the electric chair," wrote one journalist. "Correcting a malfunction of the brain with a jolt of electricity may sound too much like kicking a television set to adjust its fine tuning.") The fact is, ECT works to relieve the symptoms of depression faster than any other treatment we have. A series of treatments, perhaps three a week for two to three weeks, will jolt the depression out of existence. But the effect may be temporary. For this and other reasons, I seldom recommend it for the people I treat.

Recently, however, ECT did work splendidly for one of my patients. This man in his late fifties, a Washington politician, was convinced he was emanating an odor that was poisoning the nation's capital. He believed he had to kill himself in order to save the country. For the previous several months this man had received excellent care from qualified biopsychiatrists. He was one of the people who did not respond to any antidepressant medication. ECT had not been tried; when I was brought in on the case we had to work fast because he was actively suicidal. To make a long story short, ECT worked. Within six weeks he had returned to the business of government, where he remains, free of relapses, to this day.

ECT is enjoying a new surge of popularity among psychiatrists, including some biopsychiatrists. In a certain group of patients it may be the treatment of choice, but more often it is used as a last resort. We have been shocking patients for half a century, but we still know too little about why it works or how the treatment changes the brain for better and for worse.

PSYCHOTHERAPY FOR DEPRESSION

Without a doubt, psychotherapy for depression can help a great many people. While we are unable to show that psychotherapy in general effectively *cures* depression, we have proof now that, in some cases, at least three forms of psychotherapy—behavioral, cognitive, and interpersonal—work almost as well as medication alone (prescribed traditionally and without blood-level measurements).

The government's Clinical Practice Guidelines emphasize, however, that psychotherapy is to be used by itself only as a first-line treatment, and then only if the symptoms are mild to moderate and if the patient desires psychotherapy as a first-line therapy. I'll go the government one better and say that, in my experience, one or another of these forms of psychotherapy, combined with medication, treats depression better than medication alone, even when the patient's illness is severe.

As is true of all treatments, psychotherapy must be closely monitored. If results aren't good enough, other steps must be taken. As the new guidelines emphasize, "If the psychotherapy is completely ineffective by six weeks or if it does not result in nearly a full symptomatic remission within twelve weeks, a switch to medication may well be appropriate, since there is clear evidence of its specific efficacy."

Not everyone in the psychiatric establishment is willing to be as specific as the U.S. Department of Health and Human Services, which issued these guidelines. In fact, a supplement to the *American Journal of Psychiatry,* the official publication of the American Psychiatric Association (APA), contained treatment-practice guidelines that cover behavioral, cognitive, and interpersonal therapy and that also consider the role of marital therapy, brief (ten sessions) therapy, family therapy, group therapy, psychodynamic therapy, and even psychoanalysis as possibly useful in treatment of depression. The APA guidelines do not make a specific recommendation. Instead they note that "patient preference plays a large role in the choice of a particular form of psychotherapy. . . . [A]nother factor influencing the selection of psychotherapeutic treatment is the stage and severity of the depressive episode."

How Modern Psychotherapy Works

In psychoanalysis—the dominant form of psychiatric treatment throughout much of this century—the patient talks and relates to a trained professional in conditions of utter privacy. The therapist listens and observes with empathy, slowly and appropriately aiding the patient to understand thoughts, feelings, ideas, and actions in terms of unconscious patterns that extend far into the past. This deepening intellectual and emotional awareness of self allows the individual to become free of the grip of the unconscious and to establish new, healthier, and more adaptable patterns. In this way the person undergoing therapy unlearns old ways of behaving and learns new ones to take their place. As one doctor put it, psychoanalytic psychotherapy "adds insight to injury."

Today's approach to psychotherapy contains some of these same elements. But instead of focusing on unconscious motivations arising from deeply buried traumas of the past, modern therapy emphasizes practical strategies that apply to daily life here and now. Nonanalytic therapy teaches new patterns, but it does so by directly addressing the person's current thoughts, behavior, and relationships.

Is there a connection among the way we think, the way we feel, and the way we act? Without a doubt. To illustrate, let me tell you about Eric and his friend Tim.

Tim was my patient, a screenwriter in his late thirties who felt depressed and who came to me for treatment. His eight-year marriage had broken up some months before. During this time—at least, until recently—he found a lot of support through his friendship with Eric. Eric was about to be married a second time. Tim found his friend's happiness hard to bear, because he was deeply depressed and feared that he would never again have a close relationship with a woman. Tim had loved and admired his wife, Jeanne, but once he found out about her long history of affairs, he could no longer tolerate her presence. Unspeakably wounded and privately convinced that were he the man he should have been, she would not have cheated on him, Tim had moved out.

He had dated lots of women lately, so many he could hardly remember their names. Once out of bed, though, all of these women bored him. No one came close to having the qualities he had so loved in Jeanne.

His buddy Eric, a sensitive guy, tried to reassure Tim that everything would work out in time. "Eric told me that after his first marriage broke up he was one hundred percent certain that he'd never find a woman," Tim said. "He went to bars and picked up women, but the next morning he'd wake up and find these strangers in his bed. She'd be warm and affectionate, and he'd be hung over and cold. He hated the parting scenes, when she would be hanging around waiting for some sign that he wanted to see her again. Eric felt nothing but contempt for them. When the door closed behind them, he'd go back to bed, knowing he would never be happy again."

Tim told me, with horror in his voice, that Eric had been so despondent that he even considered killing himself. One Sunday morning Eric had woken up alone and in such anguish that he felt he couldn't go on. He had a stash of sleeping pills and pain pills left over from when he was recovering from a knee operation. All he had to do was get up, take the pills from the medicine chest, and wash them down with the bourbon left over from his binge the night before.

"But Eric realized what he was thinking—that he was actually planning to end his life—and was jolted back into reality. Just like that, he said, the fog in his head cleared." I asked Tim what it was that Eric had suddenly realized. "He understood that he'd been through painful endings of relationships before his marriage, that he'd always gotten over them, and that he'd recover this time too. He'd fall in love again, the way he always had before."

As it turned out, once Eric believed things would get better, he'd begun to take care of himself again. He'd realized his frequent nights in bars had been the sign of a growing drinking problem, for which he sought help. He began treating women with renewed respect. Six months later Eric met Tina, the woman he was now about to marry.

Tim's story about Eric shows how the way a person thinks influences what he does and how he feels. Eric believed he would never fall in love again, so he treated women badly, thus virtually guaranteeing that his prophecy would come true. In time he felt so bad that he began to want to die. The story also demonstrates that once Eric realized that his basic assumption was illogical ("Of course I'll fall in love again; I always have before"), he could act differently ("May I call you again?") and feel a lot better about his life ("I love Tina and I know we'll be happy together").

Because Tim was depressed, though, he couldn't see the positive lesson to be learned from his friend's experience. His depression distorted his thoughts. "Lucky Eric," he said gloomily. "He had a good love life before he met Tina, but I didn't. All my relationships were terrible. It's because I'm such a loser." All Tim could remember about his relationships were the painful endings. His depressed mind couldn't recall the simple reality that after each relationship ended a new one always followed, eventually.

Tim didn't need psychoanalysis. What he needed was help changing the tangled connections among his thoughts, feelings, and behavior. He was a good candidate for modern psychotherapy.

"If we see things as negative we are likely to feel negative and behave in a negative way," says psychiatrist Aaron Beck, M.D., founder of cognitive therapy.

As both Tim and Eric discovered, mildly or moderately depressed people perceive themselves and the world darkly: "No matter how hard I try, I never do well enough." "It's no use; no one will ever understand me." "If only I had worked harder fifteen years ago, I would be a success today." "I don't have what it takes to be happy in life." These are the kinds of frustrations that patients tell me about all the time. When depressed people measure their experiences, they see only the failures, never the successes. No matter how vehemently one might insist, "Stop talking like that, it's not true," depressed people are convinced that their convictions are correct.

Bad feelings accompany negative thoughts. What anguish to see yourself a failure after all the effort you have put in! A future without hope of change is a nightmare. And the behavior that results from such a dark, pained view of the universe can be nothing short of self-defeating. If you're such a rotten egg, why bother to try again? If the future stretches on in unremitting agony, why go on? If you cannot see the alternatives, of course you have no hope.

Thoughts, feelings, and actions all feed upon one another and can indeed make life worse, confirming the depressed person's certainties. True to their perceptions, depressed people have nowhere to go but down.

But the depressed perception of the world is the product of a diseased mind. What the depressed person sees arises from faulty information-processing that is symptomatic of depression. Given this way of thinking, depressed behavior is a natural result, and shattered relationships are the fallout.

Changing Your Mind: Cognitive Therapy

Cognitive therapists set out to correct their depressed patients' thinking style. They aid them in identifying their false assumptions and the feelings and behavior that result from them. Then they work with the patient to replace the mental distortions with a more balanced view that allows them to function, achieve, feel confident, and have faith.

Recent research has not verified Dr. Beck's theory that the negative thoughts themselves can cause the depression. Still, certain types of depression are commonly associated with negative thoughts. For many people, the therapy he developed can provide a relatively swift return to reality. And learning to distance oneself from the symptoms of illness proves useful in dealing with any recurrences of the darkness. Once you know that hopelessness is a symptom of the illness and not the inevitable fate of your life, you can work against the temptation to succumb to such a deadly assumption. You can change your emotional response.

In a typical course of cognitive therapy, patient and therapist work hard for sixteen to twenty weeks. Without vigorous effort and cooperation with the therapist, treatment cannot work. (Becoming physiologically normal and able to concentrate on the work is the job of medication, about which more follows.)

A cognitive approach explores the thought processes that may be contributing to the problem. Take the case of a man whose boss is constantly berating himself about his job performance. Thinking he is powerless to fight back against the person responsible for his paycheck, this man convinces himself he is an utter failure: "The boss is right—I am doing a lousy job. That's because I have no skill at all. I'm a loser. This department would be better off without me—the whole *world* would be better off without me." Clearly, such a thought pattern is a spiral into misery. Unless he gets help, a man who thinks this way is at risk of serious harm, perhaps even suicide.

A cognitive therapist would help him identify the thought patterns that contribute to his depressed mood. In the process they would discuss how to replace those patterns with other, healthier ones. For example, in response to criticism, the man may learn to think, "Well, the boss is right. I did make some mistakes. But I don't think they were as serious as he made them out to be, and most of them can be fixed pretty easily. And I've talked to some of my co-workers, and they've told me I do a pretty good job. I think the boss may be upset at me because he's under pressure from the guys upstairs. When he's a little calmer, I'll go in and show him a few of the ways I've found to fix some of the problems he's concerned about."

Behavioral Therapy

As you can see, thoughts and actions are closely connected. When we learn to think a new way, new behavior usually follows. Conversely, when we "rehearse" new behaviors, new thoughts are often the result. Behavioral therapy (also called behavior modification) uses rewards and punishments to condition, or train, new habits and patterns. The therapist does not explore the psychological origins of, say, a person's feelings of failure. Instead the therapist helps this person identify situations that evoke those feelings and discover alternative ways of dealing with them.

Take again the man whose boss berated him about the quality of his work. In therapy this man might learn how to act more assertively to let his boss know that his criticism is having a negative and counterproductive effect. Similarly, he might learn practical steps he can take to remove himself from this unpleasant situation, such as transferring to another department or looking for another job entirely. Rewards can be implemented to reinforce the lessons. For example, every time the man takes some action that improves his situation, the therapist encourages him to reward himself. He may buy that new compact disc he's been wanting, or he might simply allow himself an extra five minutes during his morning shower. Eventually his body and his mind will get the message: Behaving in a healthy way makes me feel good, so I guess I'll keep doing it.

Because the link between thoughts and actions is so tight, many caregivers don't make a distinction between the two methods of therapy. Instead they may identify themselves as cognitive-behavioral therapists.

Interpersonal Therapy

Depression distorts all aspects of a person's functioning, including relationships with other people. Troubled relationships with spouses, lovers, friends, bosses, co-workers, parents, and children are the rule for almost every depressed person during the illness, and often before. Indeed, the symptoms—moodiness, withdrawal, irritability—are often most noticeable in the way the person interacts with others. The pioneer psychiatrist Gerald Klerman and epidemiologist Myrna Weissman discovered a form of short-term therapy that helps patients identify and resolve their here-and-now problems with other people. This approach, called interpersonal therapy, assists in the recovery from depression. They published their techniques in a procedural manual for therapists. Studies have shown that interpersonal therapy is as effective as cognitive therapy.

Whether the disturbed relationship triggers the depression or the depression gives rise to the interpersonal problem is unimportant. As Tevye the milkman said, "Whether the stone hits the pitcher or the pitcher hits the stone—either way it's bad for the pitcher." The interpersonal therapist helps determine the nature of the relationship problem, then sets out to find solutions.

Most often, interpersonal problems involve role transitions or role disputes. Transitions from being single to being married, or from being married to being single or widowed, from having children at home to seeing them leave the nest, from having day-to-day relationships with co-workers to being home alone retired—depression can arise from many such profound changes.

Role disputes commonly involve differing expectations of the relationships between lovers, spouses, and family members. The depressed person will be at a loss to change the nature of the relationship. She wants him to share the child care and housework so she can devote more time to her career; he says, "No way!" She's convinced she loves him more than he loves her. She's stuck; she doesn't want to leave him, but she can't go on this way. There's nothing she can do. Her future is bleak. The interpersonal therapist treats both people involved in role disputes, helping them to communicate, negotiate, and see things as they really are. There are always alternatives, even though depression blinds us to them.

Interpersonal therapy also helps the isolated person who lacks the self-esteem and social skills necessary to establish a relationship with another human being. The dependent person who can't break away is a candidate for interpersonal therapy too.

Combination Cures

For the largest number of severely depressed persons, a combination of pharmacological and psychotherapeutic treatments produces the best results. The order of treatment is important. Every depressed person requires some supportive therapy. The psychiatrist immediately establishes a trusting, accepting, and encouraging relationship with the depressed person: "You're not alone in this. I'm here to help you. You are suffering from an illness; you have done nothing to deserve this. We will work together and everything will be okay."

The patient can now begin active pharmacotherapy or psychotherapy—or both—in a comfortable, mutually honest partnership with the psychiatrist. Most important, the biologically depressed person will now have a reliable person to turn to should side effects of medication threaten to sidetrack treatment.

Once the medication begins to work, confusion lessens, energy improves, and sleeping and eating patterns return to normal. The individual can then move into an active problem-solving psychotherapy, be it cognitive, behavioral, interpersonal, or some mix of the three. Psychotherapy that begins before the patient can think straight is almost guaranteed to fail.

Nondirective therapies, in which the therapist mostly listens instead of actively working with and supporting the patient, can be dangerous. Severely depressed persons misinterpret the therapist's attitude as profoundly rejecting. Self-esteem dips below zero, and helplessness overwhelms. In studies assessing the benefits of psychotherapy and medication, patients who receive nondirective psychotherapy fare worse than the control group, who receive no treatment at all. But when the therapist actively directs the patient's returning energy into accomplishing specific goals, the resulting self-mastery can feel wonderful. After being utterly at a loss for months or years, it's a godsend.

The newfound strength that can result from short-term psychotherapy complements medication therapy and, as studies are beginning to show, helps prevent relapse. People who are better able to control their emotions and who are better adjusted socially by the end of all treatment are significantly less vulnerable to a return of the depression. This is important since, as researchers have learned recently, having one bout of depression increases the risk of having others.

Patients on medication will probably continue it after short-term psychotherapy concludes. As I stated in the previous chapter, many patients will benefit from a lifelong course of drug treatment. They will appear and feel normal; they will not be suffering, and they will have learned how to cope for the present. For those who wish to go on to a longer-term, deeper type of psychotherapy, now is the time.

Long-term Psychotherapy

Because the stresses that trigger depression are so complex and varied, for some individuals additional therapy may insure more lasting protection. It is important to understand that although it is difficult to design studies that demonstrate the effectiveness of long-term therapies, clearly they offer help to many people.

An article by an anonymous recovering patient that appeared in the *American Journal of Psychiatry* underscores the value of psychotherapy when used along with medication in the treatment of severe mental suffering. The article was written by a recent Harvard graduate who said he had spent half his college life at a private psychiatric hospital. Although this person had schizophrenia, many of his words apply equally to anyone who has battled with depression. I will substitute *depression* for *schizophrenia* as I quote a few paragraphs from this article, which explains the reasons for—and rewards of—psychotherapy from this patient's point of view.

> Even if one adheres to the belief that psychotherapy lends itself more to emotionally oriented problems than to something that appears to be more biochemical, one must take into consideration the emotional aspects of depression. Besides the day-to-day stress of contending with what often seems to be a monster raging inside one's mind, there are emotional problems that have evolved and accumulated over the course of the patient's life. Assuming that a person is biochemically predisposed to the illness, there are certain problems that appear before its onset. I believe that several incidents during my lifetime occurred because of something "different" about me; perhaps I was physically and emotionally abused because my abusers sensed some vulnerability in my nature. I have learned that some of the basic elements of my illness may have been present since early childhood, in which case the way I related to my family and early acquaintances must have been affected and probably influenced the way other people related to me, even on an unconscious level. . . .
>
> Even if medication can free the depressed patient from some of his torment, the scars of emotional confusion remain, felt perhaps more deeply by a greater sensitivity and vulnerability. . . .
>
> I was once told that I had a very strong observing ego, and I was fascinated and encouraged to think of my mind having that power to step away from the depression, to look at it and understand it. Perhaps that is why therapy has worked so well for me. This capacity and a strong motivation to develop it have driven me to uncover what it is about my mind that makes me retreat into depression when the stresses of my life, real or imagined, become unbearable. I do not believe I had this observing ego when I began therapy. It took me time to develop and, more importantly, it took the skill and patience of a therapist who was willing . . . to work very hard. . . . I know I have a long road ahead of me, but I can honestly say that I am no longer without hope.

Is Psychotherapy Effective?

Cognitive and interpersonal therapies are my recommendation for patients who come to me with only mild or moderate symptoms and are adamant about avoiding medications.

I remember one case specifically. A talented commercial artist named Bill had gone through a very rough time before being referred to me. He'd lost his job at an ad agency, his father had died unexpectedly, and he had been diagnosed as a hypertensive when taking an insurance physical. He'd been hit from all sides in a period of six months, and was, understandably, unhappy. And when things didn't turn around, he got lower and lower.

Although he never did anything self-destructive, and in fact continued to try to find work, he said he felt like he was "fading from life." His wife and kids reported that he was distant, distracted, and depressed.

I suggested that an antidepressant, or at least some sort of stress-relief medication, might be helpful. His refusal didn't surprise me. Although Bill was a bright and informed guy, he was convinced that any medication or drugs would alter his talent. Despite my reassurances, he was sure that any chemicals would change his special gifts. This is not an uncommon reaction among creative people who don't really understand why they can do what they do.

This type of patient, who is verbal and intelligent, can do well with psychotherapy. But Bill's personality and gifts were not my deciding factor. My judgment call in this case—the decision to refer him for psychotherapy—was based on the same guidelines that I always use: relief of symptoms. Fortunately, I was right, and the therapist I found for Bill helped pull him up and restore his enthusiasm.

For a patient like Bill, cognitive therapy, behavioral therapy, and interpersonal therapy have a high success rate because they were originally developed to treat certain depressions only. These methods are practical, focused attempts to deal with the mental and behavioral components of depression: the way you think and the way you act. They focus on present difficulties, paying little heed to past problems. And they are short-term approaches, rarely lasting more than half a year. Deeper, underlying difficulties may remain after the conclusion of therapy, at which time psychoanalysis or other extended types of psychotherapy may be appropriate. But usually you won't be depressed, and that's the result you came for.

Recent studies show that cognitive, behavioral, and interpersonal psychotherapy can indeed assist recovery from as serious a mental health problem as depression. Over 50 percent of all patients in several studies did very well with these methods. It is important to note that such treatments emphasize precise diagnosis, targeted treatment, and administration of the treatment by specially trained practitioners according to a preexisting protocol.

How Do You Pick a Psychotherapist?

Here's another question I am asked a lot: Who is the best psychotherapist?

Only a biopsychiatrist has the training and experience necessary to provide a complete diagnostic evaluation and to determine the best type of treatment for a depressed person. While any M.D. can legally prescribe medication for depression, not every physician—indeed not every psychiatrist—has the expertise to provide the most up-to-date pharmacotherapy and laboratory testing.

Which mental health specialists are best equipped to provide psychotherapy is a far more difficult question to answer. One does not need to be a biopsychiatrist, or even a psychiatrist, to practice psychotherapy. Psychologists (Ph.D.s), social workers (M.S.W.s), and nurses (M.S.N.s) may be equally competent, sometimes even better-trained in certain psychotherapeutic techniques. The training, competency, and ethics of each practitioner must be judged individually. Since psychotherapy is one piece of the total evaluation and treatment of the depressed person, the biopsychiatrist is probably the best source of information on qualified psychotherapists in the community, particularly those practitioners who offer depression-specific therapies. Remember, though, not to "take the cure" before you know the actual nature of your depression. It bears repeating that complete medical and psychiatric evaluation and diagnosis must come first.

Curing Yourself of the Blues

You can treat a mild depression on your own, even help a severe depression heal faster, by using some of the techniques of cognitive, behavioral, and interpersonal therapies. Stress-management strategies also help. Here are some examples:

1. Observe yourself when you are depressed. Listen to the self-critical language of your thoughts. Do you find yourself thinking, "I can't . . ." "I'll never . . ." "If only I had done such and such . . ." "I'm not good enough or smart enough or attractive enough, or a good enough friend, parent,

spouse, sibling . . ."? How do you talk to yourself? If you make a mistake, do you silently curse yourself or call yourself a jerk, a dope, or a fool?

Do you have a hard time thinking of alternatives? Do you think in black-and-white terms, such as "If my wife dies before I do, I won't survive," or "If I don't get this promotion, I will be a failure"?

The point of self-observation is to establish distance between you and your depressed thoughts. You will weaken the grip of depression once you are able to accept (even if you can't fully feel) that you are perceiving the world through depressed eyes. You are not a jerk or a failure or a worthless human being; you're depressed. Techniques of meditation make self-observation easier.

2. Distract yourself. Depressed thoughts feed upon one another. If you retreat to your bed and stare into space thinking about how awful things are, you will feel worse and worse. Trick your mind by occupying it with other things, especially with other people. Do not retreat from social activities, no matter how much you may want to and despite your feelings that you're a real drag.

3. Exercise. Most people find it impossible to be depressed while they are actively exercising. Aerobic exercise, which increases oxygen intake, counteracts depression even in severely depressed people. Jogging, aerobic exercises or dancing, distance swimming, weightlifting, brisk walking—any exercise that keeps you moving for at least twenty minutes, practiced three times a week or more, is sufficient to keep depression at bay temporarily. Some experts believe that aerobic exercise alters the release of brain neurotransmitters. Aerobically fit individuals respond better to stress overall and have less anxiety and depression. If you have trouble motivating yourself, enlist a friend to come over at 7 A.M. and get you going.

4. Avoid drugs and alcohol. While they may help to lift your spirits briefly, they make matters much, much worse in the long run. Indeed, the depression you feel may have more to do with the drugs you take to relieve it than the blues you felt in the first place. Do without the drugs and see how you feel.

5. Stay up all night and see if you feel much better in the morning.

6. Seek help. The best way to help yourself may be to admit that you can't do it alone.

7. Join the National Depressive and Manic-Depressive Association (NDMDA), a rapidly growing organization of self-help, education, and support groups throughout the United States and Canada. For a list of local chapters, write or call: NDMDA, 730 N. Franklin Street, Suite 501, Chicago, Illinois 60610; (312) 642-0049.

CHAPTER 25

The Chosen: Depression in Groups

In this book I have focused on depression as a disease that strikes individuals with certain vulnerability factors. Depression also strikes groups. Women are depression's favorite sex, children its newest victims, older persons its chosen age group. It seems fitting to conclude this book by looking at the needs of these groups, since to make an inroad on this widespread disease we must successfully diagnose and treat people by the millions.

The special needs of women, children, and the elderly have in the past been largely overlooked or disregarded. The good news is that bio-psychiatrists are beginning to identify the diagnostic and treatment issues particular to these groups in order to stem the tide of the epidemic of depression in our society.

DEPRESSION IN WOMEN

Women are two to three times as likely as men to be depressed. They go to doctors more often than men do, for many reasons. Physicians long believed that women had "weak constitutions." As one doctor expressed it in 1827, the female "is far more sensitive and susceptible than the male and extremely liable to those distressing affections which for want of some better term have been determined nervous, and which consist chiefly in painful affections of the head, heart, side, and indeed of almost every part of the system."

In the late twentieth century, actions speak more powerfully of a similar bias: About 75 percent of all prescriptions for mood-altering drugs are written for women, who represent only 60 percent of the patients

317

physicians see daily in their offices. Many of these prescriptions are for addicting tranquilizers.

Medicine still clings to the notion that "the remorseless biological demands placed by nature on womanhood" explains the higher incidence of depression and other "nervous affections" among this group. We have not progressed far in the objective understanding of the psychobiological functioning of women. Even though medicine has lately recognized the medical validity of the set of symptoms known as premenstrual syndrome (PMS), its diagnosis and treatment have been fraught with partial understanding and downright error.

A joint panel of the American Psychological Association, the Women and Health Roundtable, and the Federation of Organizations for Professional Women concluded that women's mental health needs are not being met. The panel reported that research, training, diagnosis, and treatment are all oriented toward men.

Biopsychiatrists are beginning to devote serious attention to the study of women. One thing we have learned so far is how much we don't know. Here are some other recent lessons.

PMS

We know that women's suicide attempts and threats, as well as their admissions to psychiatric hospitals, increase in the days before the onset of menstruation.

We know that over two-thirds of women with a history of severe depression have significant premenstrual lows.

We know that women with premenstrual mood problems are likely to have a family history of depression.

We also know that there seems to be a biological connection to PMS that recent studies of ovarian function are just now confirming.

In other words, there is a strong relationship between the menstrual cycle and depression. But despite the increasing frequency of the PMS diagnosis (and self-diagnosis) for women who become depressed premenstrually, we don't know whether a woman who suffers from depression in the premenstrual phase of her cycle indeed has PMS. A differential diagnosis, which few doctors perform, might reveal instead that she has a thyroid deficiency; hypothyroidism, as I pointed out in Chapter 9, is by far more common among women, and some studies show that hypothyroid women almost always suffer from premenstrual depression. A good diagnosis might show a premenstrual exacerbation of a chronic depression problem, so that it is most noticeable at that time of the month. Or it might turn up dysmenorrhea (painful menstruation) or endometriosis (a disorder in which tissue from the lining of the uterus, the endometrium, becomes detached and grows elsewhere in the abdomen). Appropriate, safe treatment follows a correct diagnosis.

WHAT IS PMS?

The answer to this question is complicated. Probably PMS (also called premenstrual changes, premenstrual tension, or premenstrual stress) comprises a number of different subtypes that occur in the luteal phase of the menstrual cycle, a week to ten days before the onset of the menstrual flow. "Premenstrual syndrome has come to include any of a number of different symptoms, both physical and emotional, which occur in a cyclic fashion just prior to the menstrual flow," write Steven J. Sondheimer and colleagues. "These symptoms should begin to abate with the menstrual flow. Individual patients may have some symptoms and not others. Many patients have predominantly affective symptoms with very mild somatic symptoms, while other patients, particularly in an outpatient general gynecological practice, may have physical symptoms with few affective symptoms. It is not known whether these different groups have similar etiologies."

We should note that not all the reported symptoms are unpleasant or uncomfortable. Ten to 15 percent of women actually feel better premenstrually.

Uriel Halbreich, M.D., a prominent PMS researcher at the State University of New York at Buffalo, suggests that to merit a diagnosis of PMS, the symptoms must be markedly more severe in the twenty-first through the twenty-eighth day of the cycle (counting from the first day of menstrual flow), compared to the sixth through the twelfth days, when symptoms should be virtually absent. Also, the symptoms must recur for at least two consecutive cycles. PMS studies and specialists often require that patients keep a daily mood diary to determine whether they meet these two criteria.

Meeting the criteria establishes the diagnosis of premenstrual syndrome, but it does not explain what it is or where it comes from. Most important, as far as the woman herself is concerned, the diagnosis does not indicate treatment. While over three hundred possible treatments for PMS have been reported, none has proved more effective than placebos. Some treatments work for some women, others work for other women. None is a cure-all, no matter what you may read.

And some treatments are dangerous. Many self-help booklets currently recommend doses of vitamin B_6 that may be neurotoxic. Others suggest taking doses of progesterone that exceed those currently approved by the FDA or being tested in controlled trials. As with all treatments, possible side effects of progesterone (e.g., headache, exhaustion, lightheadedness, uterine bleeding) must be clearly weighed against possible benefits.

A CALL FROM A FRIEND OF A FRIEND

Susan T., thirty-four, read a popular book on PMS and recognized many of her own symptoms. She too became painfully bloated and irritable almost beyond measure. "I feel like Dr. Jekyll and Mrs. Hyde," she told her gynecologist. "I really worry that I'm going to kill somebody—most likely my kid. Then I get my period and the next day I'm normal and nice." She was relieved to discover that she was suffering from an extremely common physiological disorder that could be treated. The book spoke well of treatment with the hormone progesterone. Susan asked her gynecologist to prescribe it for her.

Her doctor refused. He said, "I do not know that you have PMS. That is a difficult diagnosis to make, far more complicated than your book suggests, and I don't want to start prescribing hormones for you unless I am absolutely certain you need them. In fact, Susan," he told her, "we don't really know what PMS is. The symptoms you have could be caused by a number of different disorders. I understand you want to get to the bottom of these mood changes. They're awful for you and for your family. Here's the best way I can help you." The doctor advised Susan to undergo a thorough examination at a PMS evaluation clinic at a nearby university hospital. He said he would be glad to call and set up an appointment for her, but Susan was miffed that he would not give her the medication she was certain would cure her. Without another word she put on her coat and left his office.

Susan is a friend of a friend, and when she got home she called me. She believed that her gynecologist had mistreated her by refusing to prescribe progesterone. Although it sounded to me that he had behaved responsibly, I said I'd call and talk to him. We ended up having an interesting conversation about diagnostic issues related to PMS. He told me about the work being done at the clinic he had recommended to Susan. I called her back and explained, too, that progesterone could have serious side effects, including uterine bleeding. I told her that the PMS clinic sounded like a good idea. Or, I said, she might want to come to me and be evaluated for depression.

"Well, I'll think about it," she said, now disappointed with me too. I heard several weeks later that she had found a gynecologist who "took her seriously" and prescribed progesterone for her. As far as I know, she still suffers bouts of depression premenstrually, the cause and the treatment of which have never been determined.

OR IS IT DEPRESSION?

Given the stigma that continues to be associated with mental suffering, "it may be more socially acceptable for women to think of their mood problems as a premenstrual phenomenon rather than a more generalized disorder, and consequently they present their difficulties in this context," observe Wilma M. Harrison, M.D., and colleagues.

As mentioned previously, most women who suffer from severe depression have a worsening of symptoms in the days just prior to their periods. Women with milder mood problems also tend to have premenstrual mood changes. At other times of the month the depression may not be so intrusive. A woman may become more aware of the unpleasant symptoms only when these symptoms worsen in the premenstrual phase. Before being evaluated for PMS, she may be unaware that she has a chronic mood problem.

Harrison and colleagues discovered that the large majority of women who volunteered to participate in a PMS treatment study did not in fact have the disorder. Even many of those who passed the initial screening were later excluded when closer evaluation revealed that their distress could just as well be caused by another psychiatric or medical illness (58 percent) or by use of a drug or medication (31 percent).

"The most frequently reported premenstrual mood symptoms are irritability, tension, anxiety, depression, and mood swings, which not only are not specific to premenstrual syndrome but may characterize any number of . . . disorders," they note.

Postpartum Depression

We may not know all that much about PMS; we know less about postpartum depression—the blues of the birth—which in its mildest form affects an estimated 70 to 80 percent of all women following the birth of a child. From 10 to 20 percent of new mothers experience a full-blown clinical depression. A far smaller number, approximately one in a thousand, develop a postpartum depressive psychosis. Despite the high incidence of depression following childbirth, the often desperate new mother may receive inappropriate or inadequate treatment or, most likely, no treatment at all. Psychiatrists, notes a commentator in the *Journal of the American Medical Association,* are not taught to differentiate these mood disorders from others unrelated to childbirth; psychiatry training programs and texts refuse to separate them from nonpostpartum conditions, or recognize them as distinct disorders.

And even if psychiatrists are aware of this type of illness, comments the writer, the people most likely to encounter it firsthand—obstetricians, general physicians, nurses, and husbands—are even less likely to know anything about it. Because postpartum psychiatric problems fall somewhere between obstetrics and psychiatry, these problems often fail to receive the attention of specialists in either field.

It is vital that we understand this set of disorders, for the sake of the mother and for the infant as well. Recent research has revealed that a mother's depression in the baby's first years may affect the child's subsequent emotional and cognitive development (more about this later in the chapter). "This doesn't mean a child's future is profoundly determined," says British psychiatrist Harold L. Caplan, M.D., "but there now seems sufficient evidence in terms of the development of the child . . . to justify strenuous efforts to detect and treat maternal depression."

MAKING THE DIAGNOSIS

The research effort is accelerating. Throughout the world, scientists are attempting to determine the connections that must exist between the many hormonal, metabolic, and psychological changes that take place at childbirth and the high incidence of depression. Differential diagnosis is, of course, essential. What may result from a thyroid insufficiency in one woman might in another be caused by a combination of sensitivity to hormonal shifts and the stress of giving birth and adjusting to a new role. As always, appropriate, effective treatment depends on pinpointing a diagnosis.

Identification of vulnerability factors will help identify and ultimately prevent this type of suffering. As with premenstrual depressions, a history of depression increases the risk of postpartum depression. Since the postpartum depression for some women is the first in a long series of depressive episodes, the discovery of biological markers and other risk factors would be a boon. Hypothyroidism commonly develops in women following childbirth; autoimmune thyroid disease can be detected by the existence of antibodies early in pregnancy in time to treat it and prevent its severe emotional consequences.

THE SUBTYPES

For most women, postpartum depression is temporary. Treatment, if any, consists of relief of symptoms, which themselves depend on the type of postpartum depression the woman has. Whether a woman receives medication may depend on whether or not she is breastfeeding her infant.

The vast majority of women endure "maternity blues." Frequently on the third day following delivery, the new mother becomes tearful, sleepless, tense, and angry. Episodes come and go for twenty-four hours to a week, then they lift.

Ten to 20 percent of new mothers will move from the blues to a full clinical depression. The depression may last two to eight weeks, but sometimes it may continue for as long as a year. Some psychiatrists and obstetricians refer to this type of depression as *postpartum neurotic depression* because stress factors, including changing family roles and insufficient preparation for motherhood, often are prominent. Since the biological mechanisms of postpartum mood disorders have not been identified, we should be wary of jumping to conclusions.

A small number of women have to be hospitalized with a full-blown postpartum depressive psychosis. Although most recover, the separation of mother and infant at this time threatens that most important bond.

A BETTER START

A postpartum clinical depression is not natural or normal, no matter what anyone might tell a suffering new mother. "Most obstetricians don't have great insight into the emotional problems of childbirth," admits David N. Danforth, M.D., Ph.D., professor emeritus of obstetrics and gynecology at Northwestern University School of Medicine in Chicago. The mother deserves help as soon as possible so that she and her new baby get off to a good start, and so that she can be sure to prevent future episodes. To be on the safe side, if you experience any form of postpartum depression, seek a biopsychiatric evaluation, which includes a medical and psychological workup and the most advanced types of treatment. If the depression begins during pregnancy, get help right away.

The Future of PMS and Other Mood Disorders among Women

We do not yet fully understand a woman's normal hormonal cycling, much less the abnormal. The more we discover about the neuroendocrine links among mind, brain, and body in depression, no doubt the more we will understand how sex hormones specifically influence depression and behavior. Researchers are finding evidence of the influence of sex hormones on neurotransmitter functioning in men as well as women. Men, however, do not experience a similar periodic hormonal cycling; nor do they experience the reduction of hormones that women undergo at menopause (and which may be responsible in part for the depression some women must deal with at that time). The desynchronization of monthly and other periodic hormonal cycles in relation to other biological-clock variables may be the key to understanding cyclic depressions in women.

We can expect most progress to be made in the diagnosis and treatment of PMS. As with depression itself, research is likely to reveal specific, identifiable biological subtypes and biological markers for PMS. The next step will be treatments that are actually effective, which cannot be said for present-day approaches. Remember, PMS has only recently become a legitimate area of medical investigation; much work remains to be done. One new approach is to turn off the ovaries chemically and see if the PMS really disappears. Certainly, PMS complaints appear less common in non-menstruating female athletes and in women who have had their ovaries removed.

Menopause

In the early editions of the DSM, there appeared a disorder, first identified in the early nineteenth century, called *involutional melancholia.* Translated, this term means "menopausal depression." There it was in black and white, inscribed in the bible of psychiatry: Menopause was not a natural process of aging but a diagnosis—a sickness. I am happy to report that over the years, belief in involutional melancholia has faded into the mists of medical history—along with the belief that the pattern of bumps on our skulls reveals profound truths about our personality. The (relatively) enlightened authors of the DSM-IV have banished this archaic diagnosis from their modern list of depressive disorders.

Still, one of the hottest debates in medicine right now is whether the hormonal changes of menopause contribute in some way to the incidence and severity of depression. Most of a woman's supplies of estrogen and progesterone come from the ovaries. When ovarian function ceases at menopause, estrogen levels decline. Some estrogen continues to be produced in other tissues, but the overall drop is 50 percent or more. For many women, a significant symptom of menopause is mood fluctuation. It's natural to wonder, then, if loss of hormones, particularly estrogen, can lead to clinical depression.

The question is very complex. For one thing, as we saw in Part II of this book, a number of medical conditions can cause the same symptoms as depression without actually meeting the criteria for a textbook diagnosis of depression. Just because a woman experiencing menopause might feel blue for a while does not mean she is clinically depressed, or that her mood symptoms require (or will respond to) antidepressant therapy. The standard approach to treating menopausal symptoms calls for oral doses of estrogen (or estrogen plus progesterone) to replenish the supply of hormones previously contributed by the ovaries. Hormone replacement therapy, or HRT, can provide a number of benefits, including the reduction of troublesome symptoms such as hot flashes. It can also work to stabilize mood.

In some cases it is possible that a woman who is experiencing menopause can also have a depressive illness at the same time. That the mood disorder emerges at this stage of life may be a complete coincidence. Or it may be that the stress of menopause and the enormous physical and emotional upheaval it can produce in a woman's life may be enough of a trigger to activate depression. If she has one or more of the risk factors, such as a family history or a history of previous bouts of depression, she may be especially vulnerable.

The hallmark symptom of menopause is the hot flash: a feeling of intense heat, especially in the face and chest, that erupts suddenly and that may last anywhere from a few seconds to nearly an hour. We don't yet know why hot flashes occur; they appear not to be the direct result of estrogen loss but may be the result of other hormonal influences on the body's internal thermostat. In this country, up to 85 percent of menopausal women report experiencing hot flashes. The range of hot-flash symptomatology is very broad. Some women have many severe hot flashes a day for a period of years; some have only a few mild ones that disappear over the course of a few months. Frequently hot flashes are accompanied by severe sweating, in some cases necessitating changes of clothes several times a day. One of the most annoying problems of hot flashes is that they often occur at night. When they do, the woman's sleep is disrupted. Often she wakes up drenched in sweat and must change her nightclothes or the bedding. Not surprisingly, the next morning she awakens exhausted, not having been able to savor the benefits of restful sleep. If she does not get relief for her hot flashes, she is at risk of becoming chronically sleep-deprived. Women in this situation are naturally prone to depressed moods—part of the domino effect caused by hot flashes. But as I hope I've made clear, these moods may be the result of lack of sleep and other menopause-related stress, not necessarily because the woman has a bona fide depression.

The average age of menopause is about fifty-one; most women will experience menopause roughly between the ages of forty-seven to fifty-six. This stage of life is marked by many changes. With the loss of ovarian function, women can no longer have children (unless, of course, they undergo some kind of assisted reproduction). Understandably, many women experience this transition with a sense of loss. If they have never had children, they may feel profound regret that now they never will. If their lives have revolved around the bearing and rearing of children, women may feel that they have lost their most important function in life. This is often the time of life when their children leave home. The empty-nest syndrome can cause some women to feel lonely and blue.

Another complication is that our society places such enormous value on youth and beauty. Women in menopause may pick up cultural messages—erroneous, but nonetheless quite powerful—telling them that they are old, over the hill, unattractive, undesirable. No wonder women in this stage of life are prone to feeling a little down!

These negative messages are reinforced by another common and troubling symptom of menopause: vaginal dryness. One of the jobs of estrogen is to maintain the thickness of vaginal tissue and its ability to produce lubricating fluids. As estrogen supplies dwindle, the lining of the vagina becomes thinner. During sexual activity it can take longer for women to become aroused to the point where they are sufficiently lubricated. Intercourse becomes a painful experience rather than a pleasurable one. Although HRT or moisturizing lubricants can help women stay sexually active, some may feel—inappropriately—that menopause means an end to their sexuality.

The good news for many women is that, properly managed, the onset of menopause does not automatically mean a depressed mood is in their future. For one thing, many women welcome the fact that they no longer have to worry about becoming pregnant. They discover that sexual relationships can once again be full of spontaneity, without the need for the Pill or cumbersome contraceptive devices. And contrary to the empty-nest stereotype, studies find that most women are actually happy to see their children grow up and leave home. After all, the successful parents are the ones who train their children to be independent and well-adjusted; the kid who strikes out on his own is a tribute to a parenting job well done. Now free of many family responsibilities, women in this stage of life often find the time they lacked to pursue new interests. Often they return to school to further their education, or take advantage of advancement opportunities, or begin entirely new careers.

The point is that menopause does not routinely cause depression. Some women may experience low moods; some may have other symptoms, such as difficulty concentrating, memory impairment, loss of self-esteem, or feelings of unworthiness. And some may indeed have a diagnosable depressive disorder. But there is no direct, inevitable link between the two.

In fact, studies show that women are more likely to experience depressive symptoms in the years *prior* to menopause, as the ovaries begin to lose their hormone-secreting powers. Experts interpret this to mean that it is the *changes* in hormone levels, rather than low levels per se, that affect mood. This conclusion is supported by evidence that premenopausal women whose ovaries have been removed—that is, who have undergone surgical menopause—are more likely to be depressed. Apparently this results from the immediate loss of hormones, as opposed to the gradual loss that occurs in natural menopause.

After menopause, when hormone levels stabilize again, the incidence of depressive symptoms declines. A number of studies of menopausal women find no higher incidence of depressive episodes, no higher rate of new depressions, and no clear difference in symptom patterns than are reported by women of other age groups. The same holds true in studies of women with bipolar disorders: the incidence, severity, and symptom patterns are no different before, during, or after the menopause.

Intriguingly, there is some evidence to suggest that the physiological changes of menopause may have some impact on the body's serotonin systems, resulting in lower levels of serotonin or changes in serotonin receptors. Researchers are looking into the possibility that decreased serotonin during menopause temporarily makes women who are depressed more susceptible to suicidal thoughts or behavior. Estrogen also appears to play a role in regulating levels of MAO enzymes. Falling estrogen levels mean more enzyme is available to break down neurotransmitter molecules. This may account in part for the changeable moods reported by many women during the menopausal years.

The question naturally arises: If changing estrogen levels affect mood, might estrogen work as a treatment for depression? It's a controversial topic, but preliminary evidence offers some tantalizing clues. Some studies have found that estrogen acts on neurotransmitters and receptors in a way that is similar to antidepressants. In fact, in some patients, estrogen apparently enhances the effects of some antidepressants. And one study found that very high doses of estrogen (up to twenty times the dose used in HRT) provided relief to severely depressed inpatients who had not responded to other antidepressants, psychotherapy, or electroconvulsive therapy.

That Sex Difference

A few years ago the federal government mandated that women and women's health issues be included in all relevant studies. Overall, the greatest progress for women may stem from the design of better research studies, which may help us determine more accurately the causes for the sex differences in depression. That a woman's biological differences determine her vulnerability to this disease advances the old anatomy-is-destiny argument.

In an attempt to explain sex differences in the incidences of depression, British physicians Rachel Jenkins and Anthony W. Clare took a hard look at epidemiological studies. They determined that most epidemiologists have not studied a homogeneous sample. The men and women included in the studies that found a preponderance of depressed women have differed in terms of social variables such as occupation and status. The few studies Jenkins and Clare found in which men and women were equivalent on all variables revealed no sex difference in the incidence of depression. We need more homogeneous studies to confirm these findings. For now, conclude Jenkins and Clare, "All claims that the excess of depression in women is explained by their reproductive biology, or indeed by their constitution in general, should be treated with grave caution."

WHEN DEPRESSION AFFLICTS A CHILD

What can be more tragic than illness in a child? And what can be worse than mental illness in a child? One of the things that always struck me when I visited the adolescent unit of the hospital was that the kids looked normal on the surface, but once I peeled away a layer I saw just how sick they really were. Despite the fact there has been some controversy in the diagnosis and hospitalization of children, there is clear evidence that we can help children who are suffering from the terrible symptoms of depression.

Twenty years ago psychiatrists believed that depression in children did not and could not exist. Now experts in child health are sounding a much louder alarm. Some claim that between three and six million American children suffer from depression, much of it unrecognized and untreated. This terrible truth has caught psychiatrists and pediatricians by surprise.

Depression in children can result in learning problems, school failure, drug abuse or addiction, disturbed relationships with other people, tendency to illness or psychosomatic disorders, even homicide. If depression in a child is not detected and treated, the child may be in for a lifetime of suffering. Often it takes a child's attempt at suicide for the parents to get the message. For the families of the five to ten thousand children who succeed in killing themselves each year, that message comes too late. If a suicide attempt fails now, another may succeed later.

Depressed kids need help. But kids can't get that help on their own. An adult first has to recognize the problem and take it seriously. That's the hard part.

Diagnosis and Misdiagnosis

Depression in adults and children is remarkably alike, from its incidence to its biological subtypes. While the symptoms are similar (sleep and appetite disturbance, bodily complaints, hopelessness, guilt, lack of self-esteem, loss of ability to experience pleasure, confusion, fatigue, and so on), kids do not always express these symptoms in the same way as grown-ups. The child's facial expression, posture, and tone of voice may present an eloquent picture. But ask what's wrong, and the little one may only shrug and pout. The older child may not wish to share his or her feelings. If parents have other things on their minds, they may not notice that anything is particularly out of the ordinary. The extremely well-behaved child who always tries to please is being good, right? As for that sulky and sloppy and irritable one who's not eating or doing his homework, he's just a normal rebellious teenager. He'll grow out of it. . . .

The sudden effort to comprehend the recent increase in adolescent suicide has led to a discovery about adolescence: Private anguish and unpredictable, downright obnoxious behavior are not necessarily a normal part of growing up. They are often symptoms of depression.

Masks

As in adults, masked depression in children is common. Depression in adults is often cloaked by physical complaints. Children, too, may be treated for headaches or stomach problems when depression is the real problem. Other kids tend to mask their symptoms with behavior problems, including disruptiveness, fighting, delinquency, school difficulties, bedwetting, alcohol and drug abuse, and so on. Many kids end up being treated for hyperactivity and learning disabilities, punished for laziness, or even placed in detention for aggressive, destructive behavior, when what they really have is depression.

Mimickers

By the same token, kids may seem depressed and get hauled off to therapists or school counselors when they are in fact physically ill. "When a
nine-year-old suddenly can't function in his environment, refuses to go to
school, or becomes very aggressive, you also have to look at whether
something is going on organically," says child psychiatrist Nancy Roeske,
M.D. "Every child with a problem needs a thorough physical examination.
For example, at nine and ten the child is entering an age where diabetes
or epilepsy may begin to show up. . . . And, unfortunately, you also need
to think about whether the child has become involved with drugs or
alcohol."

Drug and alcohol abuse is by far the major mimicker among apparently
depressed children. Thyroid deficiency is also common, particularly
among adolescents. Not long ago, my colleagues and I evaluated twenty-
eight adolescents who were being admitted with symptoms of difficult-to-
treat depression and lack of energy. After a comprehensive thyroid evaluation, we discovered that 11 percent were also suffering from subclinical
hypothyroidism.

A host of other diseases that appear with emotional symptoms can also
strike children, from lead poisoning to cancer. A New Mexico child psychiatrist tells us of an eight-year-old boy, Paul, whose mother brought him
in for treatment of depression. The mother, a young widow, had moved to
the Southwest from Pennsylvania after her husband's sudden death the
previous year. Paul had been deeply depressed the whole year, and the
move appeared to worsen his symptoms, which included pains in his leg.
In Pennsylvania, Paul's mother had taken him to a pediatrician, who found
no signs of physical illness. He recommended a child psychiatrist, who
treated Paul with no apparent success. Paul had had another physical
before entering his new school in New Mexico. His mother had told the
pediatrician that Paul had been having leg pains off and on since his
father had died. Again the pediatrician noted nothing unusual and recommended a local child psychiatrist.

Paul's new psychiatrist was concerned about the boy's physical symptoms. They did not seem to conform to the usual pattern of psychosomatic
aches and pains. After working with the boy for a few weeks, he did not
think that a psychiatric condition was at the root of Paul's problem. He
referred Paul's mother to a pediatric specialist for a thorough medical
workup. Paul's mother refused; she'd been to two pediatricians already.

The Christmas holidays came, and the psychiatrist left town on a weeklong ski trip with his family. When he returned, Paul's mother called to

cancel her son's next appointment. Paul had fallen and badly twisted his leg. It was his right leg, the one that had been giving him so much trouble. At the emergency room where she took him, the doctors x-rayed the leg and discovered bone cancer.

Paul was operated on three days later. He lost the leg, but he survived. Four years have passed and the psychiatrist still wonders whether there wasn't some way he could have convinced Paul's mother to take her boy for evaluation earlier—and thus saved the boy's leg.

Depression in a Family

Depression is a family affair in more ways than one. The predisposition to develop depression can be inherited, as we discussed in Chapter 14. Many investigators now believe that children who experience depression before puberty are probably genetically driven into such an early expression of the illness.

Relationships within the family can also trigger depression. Children whose parents abuse them are at great risk for depression. So are kids whose parents are overly critical and who focus on their child's inadequacies. Depression is common in kids whose parents don't pay them genuine, thoughtful attention. A parent may dismiss as trivial an anxious, striving teenager's crisis over a failure to get a grade he wanted, then claim that the suicide attempt "came out of nowhere."

Not that parents necessarily understand the harm they are doing, or that they intend to do it. The struggle to get by financially, to endure a separation or divorce, or to deal with kids in a violent world of drugs, sex, and crime may overwhelm a parent. Sometimes, though they may be reluctant to admit it, parents who have too much to deal with in their own lives, just don't want to know about their kids' problems. When the parents are themselves depressed, they can hardly take care of their own needs, much less their kids'. They may not recognize that depression in kids is not normal, since they themselves were depressed as children. Conflicts and difficulties mark the families of most depressed people.

Kids take it personally when a depressed parent withdraws, or becomes suddenly angry, irritable, critical, and punishing. They think, "I'm bad," or "There's something wrong with me." Mommy gets depressed and turns from warm and nurturing to icy and impatient. The child may try desperately to please, not understanding that Mommy can't be pleased until she feels better.

Even infant children of depressed mothers become depressed, we now know. The effects can be devastating. Some withdraw and slow down,

often failing to make eye contact or smile. They develop digestive problems, such as colic. They may grow and develop much more slowly than
normal. The future is cloudy for these kids unless someone intervenes. In
the past, when extended families were the rule, the baby would be able to
make a good attachment with a grandmother or an aunt. Today infant
psychiatrists and other specialized health care workers step in to correct
the mother-child interaction if the mother comes for help.

Mostly, however, children in depressed families continue to fall through
the cracks in the health care system. Studies reveal a 40 to 45 percent rate
of psychiatric disorders, mostly depression, among children of parents
with mood disorders. "Early infancy and adolescence seem to be the
stages in which children are particularly vulnerable," report psychiatrists
William R. Beardslee, M.D., and colleagues. Nonetheless, even when the
parents are in treatment, the physicians and therapists rarely stop to think
that the patient's children are probably affected. "The seriousness of the
impairment and the finding that few of these children received any treatment at all strongly suggest the need for heightened awareness among
clinicians about the seriousness of depression in children whose parents
have affective disorders," they state. Likewise, parents of depressed kids
should be evaluated and treated for depression.

Good Treatment for Depressed Kids

Provided that they receive a thorough biopsychiatric evaluation, many
types of treatment are available to children too. Antidepressants are often
prescribed for teenagers; increasingly they are being given to seriously
depressed younger children, despite the fact that the FDA has not approved these medications for use in children at the doses needed for
effective treatment of depression. Medical management of kids taking
antidepressants is essential, since they metabolize these drugs differently
than adults and are much more at risk of side effects. Experts recommend
that antidepressants be used carefully in children with depression who did
not respond to psychotherapy or changes in their situation at home.
Careful monitoring of side effects and proper dosage as reflected by
medication blood levels are definitely indicated. Blood pressure, blood
levels, pulse, and heart rhythms should be screened regularly.

The risk of hypersecretion of the hormone cortisol tends to increase
with age. Even in adolescence the dexamethasone test can detect this
biological abnormality of depression. Younger biologically depressed children often oversecrete growth hormone during sleep; tests for this hormone may confirm the diagnosis.

Psychotherapy is the traditional treatment approach. Child psychiatrists and psychotherapists are trained to speak "childese"; they understand the meaning of children's behavior and feelings. They can find out what is really disturbing the child in a supportive, trusting environment free of parent-child conflicts. Then they can help find solutions. Sometimes that means the parents must recognize their own problems and the effects they have on their children. Child psychotherapy, especially with younger children, must involve the parents, who are the only people with the power to make the changes that the child requires. A child may benefit from changing to a different type of school, for example. Perhaps the child is suffering from the loss of a grandparent; the parents may need to talk more openly about death with the whole family. Or the parents may need to learn that they are putting too much pressure on the child to achieve. When the whole family is in crisis, family therapy can be extremely effective in helping all members understand their effects on one another.

Cognitive therapy has been adapted for kids, and group therapy can be very helpful, since depressed children almost always have trouble relating comfortably to their peers.

Drug rehabilitation is essential for depressed kids who use alcohol or drugs or both. Kids may take to drugs to try to escape their pain. Or they may become depressed as a result of the drugs. In either case the depression will recur if drug use continues or resumes. And in all cases, therapy for drug or alcohol problems must begin immediately; treatment for depression is secondary.

WHEN GRANDMA OR GRANDPA IS DEPRESSED

Twentieth-century medicine continues to indulge Americans in their wish to live longer. The improvement in diagnosis, treatment, and prevention of formerly deadly diseases has resulted in a huge increase in the number of older people in this country. Today, the fastest-growing segment of the population is over eighty-five. Evidence suggests no halt to this trend. At present about 12 percent of Americans are over sixty-five. Within fifty years that percentage will approach 20 percent. By the middle of the next century, life expectancy will be in the nineties.

But, in the words of T. S. Eliot, "As we grow older/The world becomes stranger, the pattern more complicated."

Living into old age means contending with loss: loss of health, vigor, opportunities, strength, physical and mental prowess, friends, spouses, siblings, work, earnings, independence, residences, and support networks. Loneliness, boredom, and helplessness threaten. Esteem diminishes in a society that does not respect its elderly. The longer we live, the more pain we have to contend with. To live long requires a continuous expenditure of energy simply to survive. Canadian psychiatrist H. E. Lehmann, M.D., perceives that "the elderly are in double jeopardy, as the aging process invariably reduces a person's ability to adapt and to cope at a time when this is most needed, as life stresses increase."

The risk of depression increases as the ability to tolerate biological and psychosocial stressors declines. Thus the incidence of depressive illness is highest in old age. Depression is four times more prevalent among the elderly compared to the general population. The rate of suicide is fifteen times higher. While persons over sixty-five account for 12 percent of the population, they commit 25 percent of all suicides. Ninety percent of all their suicide attempts succeed.

The view persists that the loneliness, isolation, difficulties in sleeping and eating, loss of energy, decline in sexual interest and ability, deficits in mental function, loss of peace of mind, constipation, and other physical and emotional discomforts that accompany depression are normal to this phase of life.

They are not.

In fact, studies and reports indicate that the psychiatric problems of the elderly cannot be ignored or written off. The government's Clinical Practice Guidelines have reemphasized this: "Depression in the elderly should not routinely be ascribed to demoralization or normal sadness over financial barriers, medical problems, or other concerns. The general principles for treatment of adults with major depressive disorder apply as well to elderly patients."

Years ago when living to an advanced age was not a realistic expectation, no one paid much attention to the quality of life in the late decades. Now, however, we are witnessing a massive medical effort to deal with the aging of America. Biopsychiatry has played a major role in this turnaround. Its practitioners have contributed to research in the physiology and psychology of the aging mind and body. We have determined that the quality of mental life can be restored to a depressed person. With treatment, even a person of advanced years can recover sufficient energy and coping ability to lead a dignified life.

Many elderly people with depression do not receive treatment. They either deny their symptoms, accept them as normal and do not come for treatment, or receive an incorrect diagnosis when they do seek help.

Differential diagnosis of depression in this age group is tricky for even the most skilled clinicians.

In addition, treatment may often be unsuccessful because the side effects of medication may reduce compliance. Often there is inadequate family support to ensure compliance, or elderly patients may change their dosage without telling their doctors.

The Masks of Depression in Older Age

H. E. Lehmann teaches physicians that "frequently, clinical depression is missed in a person over sixty because the affective disorder is masked by a host of physical symptoms and somatic complaints. The physician may find in his depressed patient hypertension, emphysema, diabetes, or a chronic urinary infection, and may then miss the associated depression which, in its own right, may have become the most important and most urgent pathological condition." Sometimes, too, the physician will diagnose a disease such as Alzheimer's and ignore the patient's depression, thinking that it is inseparable from the illness and in itself untreatable.

Or, says Dr. Lehmann, the depression may be cloaked entirely in complaints about bowel functions, urinary frequency, dizziness, peculiar taste, burning on urination, or various aches and pains without organic basis. The individual receives treatment that he or she does not need, increasing the likelihood of drug interactions that worsen both the psychiatric symptoms and the risk to the patient.

The Mimickers

In part because physicians accept, even promote, the usual stereotypes of old people, they often leap to psychiatric diagnoses when a patient is grouchy, complaining, apathetic, confused, and annoying. In the absence of obvious signs of physical illness, or when a patient is unable to provide a complete and lucid history, doctors may not investigate thoroughly. They will proceed to overlook the medical diagnosis to which the psychiatric symptoms should have provided clues. Because susceptibility to disease increases with age, the elderly are the most vulnerable to most of the mimicking illnesses that we discussed in detail in Part II. Brain tumors, pancreatic cancer, thyroid disease, rheumatoid arthritis, and cardiovascular disorders, for example, are much more common in this age group. A combination of gastrointestinal illness and poor diet may produce malnutrition and weight loss—a common symptom of depression.

Medications

The elderly take more than 25 percent of all prescribed drugs. Not surprisingly, a much-overlooked medical condition that mimics depression in older persons is adverse reactions to prescribed drugs. A large majority of persons sixty-five and over take an average of seven or more medications regularly. Many of these drugs, separately or in combination, can cause symptoms of depression, among other, often dangerous, reactions. Some physicians multiply the suffering and the dangers by neglecting to ask about other medications, forgetting to discontinue unnecessary drugs, failing to substitute more tolerable formulations, or prescribing still more drugs to counteract the symptoms.

A Florida physician asked psychiatrist David A. Gross to look in on his father. The seventy-three-year-old man had retired the previous year and had been looking forward to the good life in a new home in another state. No sooner had he arrived than he had to be hospitalized with an acute ulcer. The man did not recover his health. He became so depressed and confused that he was unable to take care of himself. His son brought him back to Florida and placed him in a nursing home, where he would be able to receive the constant care and attention he now needed.

Antidepressants provided no improvement and were discontinued. The man's condition grew worse. He developed tremors and other neurological symptoms, which led to a diagnosis of Parkinson's disease in addition to depression. When Dr. Gross first saw him, the man could not maintain a train of thought or even stay awake for long periods. He barely moved or spoke spontaneously. His face was devoid of expression.

Dr. Gross recognized the problem. He suggested a change in the man's blood pressure medication and the elimination of one of his ulcer prescriptions. Gradually but steadily the physician's father recovered his spirits, his mind, and his happy interactions with other human beings. He left the nursing home to return once more to the pursuit of the good life.

Alcohol, Etc.

Abuse of drugs and alcohol is not confined to youth. Years of use can produce a pattern of symptoms that will seduce an unsuspecting physician into the wrong diagnosis.

"I was recently consulted by an internist to see a ninety-four-year-old woman who had been diagnosed as having mild to moderate Alzheimer's disease," Philadelphia psychiatrist Troy Thompson recently told me. Despite her confusion, memory loss, and other symptoms of dementia, the woman managed to live on her own. She had been thoroughly evaluated, including a CAT scan of the head, which revealed brain changes that Dr. Thompson considered unremarkable in a patient of this age. Her internist and neurologist had found no specific cause for dementia, so as a diagnosis of exclusion she was thought to have Alzheimer's.

"But she didn't seem so demented to me," he says. "She had a devilish gleam in her eye, unlike anything I have ever seen in a truly demented patient. So I asked about her drug and alcohol use. She freely admitted to 'nipping a little Scotch to take off the chill.'

"I asked her how often she felt the chill. She smiled and said, 'All day, every day.' She'd been drinking over half a fifth a day since her second husband died, back before World War II. To help get to sleep she also took two or three over-the-counter sleeping pills nightly. 'If one is good, three should be better,' she said."

Dr. Thompson disagreed. He suggested that she cut back to two jiggers of Scotch a day, and he prescribed a sedative-hypnotic for sleep that would be more effective and that would clear out of her system faster.

She followed the doctor's regimen, and her "Alzheimer's" improved markedly over the next month.

Pseudodementia

The worst misdiagnosis for a depressed person to be stuck with is Alzheimer's disease, or senile dementia.

The diagnosis of Alzheimer's can have horrifying consequences for a depressed person. Dr. Thompson's patient fortunately had sufficient wits about her to insist on taking care of herself. Most Alzheimer's patients, whether correctly or incorrectly diagnosed, are considered incurable; they end up in nursing homes, sometimes for many years, until finally they die. Confusion, loss of memory and intellectual functions, and inability to recognize familiar people characterize depression or alcoholism as well as Alzheimer's. Everybody used to think that *old* and *senile* were synonymous. Nowadays, as Alzheimer's becomes more recognized, *senile* means Alzheimer's; sometimes it is diagnosed with reckless abandon. More older persons with these mental symptoms are depressed than have Alzheimer's—so many, in fact, that the syndrome has been given its own name: depressive pseudodementia.

In one study, a total of 213 patients were treated and discharged from the geriatric service of New York Hospital–Cornell Medical Center at White Plains. Sixty percent of them had pseudodementia. Correctly diagnosed and treated for depression, they recovered.

They were lucky. When Alzheimer's is misdiagnosed instead and the depression not treated, the condition becomes chronic and can lead to true, irreversible dementia.

Because depression and dementia can coexist, and because the symptoms of depression may mask a true dementia (see the case of Mr. R. in Chapter 6), the physician must perform a thorough diagnostic workup. The depression that frequently accompanies Alzheimer's can often be treated with antidepressants, making the dementia somewhat less intolerable to the sufferer, who in the early stages is usually aware of what's happening.

Biological Depression

We are discovering some reasons why older persons are so much more prone to biological depression. It seems that with age, the supply of crucial brain neurotransmitters decreases while the monoamine oxidase enzymes, which metabolize these neurotransmitters, increase. The maintenance of mood and motor function depends in part on the steady, balanced supply of these brain chemicals. Also, aging brain cells become less able to maintain function in the face of stresses, alcohol, medication and combinations of medications, and the deterioration of body systems. The body's timekeepers also tend to slow down and possibly to go out of sync with one another. In the face of these biological stresses, depression may develop for the first time. In people who have had previous depression, episodes of depression increase in frequency and severity.

Tests for biological depression can be used in this age group, in which biological signs are often very evident. For example, the day/night pattern of cortisol secretion is often absent, and oversecretion of cortisol is highest among depressives of this age group.

The Treatments

The aim is to save precious time. Older patients benefit least from traditional trial-and-error approaches to treatment. They haven't time to wait and see if they are going to feel better and get a little enjoyment out of life. Therefore the biopsychiatrist will use all available technology to determine which is the most appropriate, safest, and by all means fastest way to effect a cure. Because it can work so quickly, some clinicians more readily consider electroshock for patients in this age group, particularly those for whom medication may prove too dangerous. However, the clinician must exercise caution in its use in order to minimize any risk of temporary confusion and memory loss.

ANTIDEPRESSANT DRUGS

Antidepressants can work wonders, but they are not without risk. They can cause low blood pressure on standing and other side effects that may inflict suffering, permanent damage, or death. The difference between cure and disaster hinges on the knowledge and skill of the prescribing physician.

The aging body absorbs, metabolizes, distributes, and excretes drugs differently than it did when young. Generally, older persons end up with much more of the drug in their systems. They overdose on amounts that a younger person wouldn't even notice. This age group is more vulnerable and sensitive to drug effects and side effects overall. People over seventy have approximately twice as many adverse drug reactions as people under fifty.

Many antidepressants can be deadly to a weakened heart, but that is only one of their potential dangers. The physician has to know the positive and negative effects of each antidepressant drug as well as their potentially dangerous interactions. Which drug is likely to cause such a drop in Mrs. Blum's blood pressure that she may faint, fall, and break her hip? Which ones will be so sedating as to throw Mr. Jones into utter confusion? Can I trust Miss Brown to follow the dietary restrictions if I prescribe monoamine oxidase inhibitors? Is Ms. Cruz really going to remember how many of these pills she's already taken? Do I dare prescribe these pills to Mr. Eklund following his heart attack? Which drug will block the effect of Mr. Yamamoto's blood pressure medication and throw him into a hypertensive crisis? If I prescribe these pills to Mrs. O'Malley, will she use them to kill herself?

Too many physicians, psychiatrists included, who prescribe antidepressants to their aging patients would fail this test. And too few of them monitor medication blood levels to be sure they are prescribing a safe and effective dosage.

PSYCHOTHERAPY

For young and old patients alike, a combination of medication and psychotherapy provides the best results. The short-term therapies are just the thing, with their emphasis on immediate problem-solving and coping skills. Sex therapy too can do a world of good. When depression lifts, the recovered patient is probably going to feel sexy again, perhaps for the first time in years. The therapist can help the man or woman overcome inhibitions against behaving sexually at this age. Interpersonal therapy can help older people out of their isolation. Marital therapy helps couples meet the needs of this stage of life.

One study indicates that a combination of interpersonal psychotherapy and nortriptyline plus supportive psychoeducation is successful in about 75 percent of elderly people in the acute phase of the illness.

When they can, some geriatric psychotherapists involve the families of their older patients, who may themselves be having difficulty dealing with the individual's symptoms. Sometimes patient and family can work with the therapist to help each other. Most older people feel better about themselves when they can have something useful to do. As Dr. Lehmann puts it: "Examples of activities I have found useful for this purpose are photocopying papers, polishing silverware, feeding and walking pets, and watering, repotting, and otherwise caring for plants, not only for the patient's family, but also for others who would appreciate help with such chores." The activities, of course, depend on the health and vigor of the older person. Once energy and interest return, a recovering person may reap great rewards from volunteer work.

Increasingly, psychotherapists treating older people recommend exercise, from walking to supervised aerobic programs.

Because of the interrelated medical and psychosocial considerations involved in treating older individuals, a biopsychiatrist who also practices psychotherapy may be the best choice. Nonmedical therapists must be medically aware and willing to work closely with physicians. In every case, the practitioner must be particularly sensitive to people at this stage of life. Not everyone can work with the older patient. Sometimes a clinician's own fears of getting old, difficulties dealing with his or her own aging parents, or attitudes about investing time in patients who have little life remaining can get in the way. If you are seeking treatment for yourself or someone you love, make sure you find someone who shows warmth, caring, and understanding.

Dr. Troy Thompson writes: "A refined elderly gentleman consulted me regarding memory problems. He detailed exactly when and how his memory had failed him over a period of months, so much so that there was little question in my mind that his memory was excellent. He somewhat sheepishly explained that he did well with 'numbers, presidents, and the news items,' the types of memory gaps we check for in mental-status exams, but that he continually forgot things around his apartment.

"I sensed there was a hidden agenda, so I asked what he thought would help him most. He related that he had read about a tablet that improves memory and that must be taken three or four times daily. But, he added, since his memory was so erratic, he would have to have someone remind him several times a day to take it.

"I asked who he had in mind. He mentioned a widow who lived in his building, and he asked if I might call her to see whether she would be willing to assist him. This shy gentleman had seen the lovely widow numerous times in the building elevator and had chatted with her once or twice about the weather. But he was embarrassed to proceed further 'without a proper introduction.'

"I called the woman and asked if she would oversee twice daily what I was certain was a harmless dosage of a widely advertised memory enhancer. She eagerly agreed 'to do anything to help a needy neighbor.' I was invited to their wedding four months later, where my former patient informed me with a wink that he no longer needed the memory pill."

A Good Ending

When medicine and psychiatry take up arms together, we can work miracles. The accomplishments of biopsychiatry in the treatment of older individuals ranks among the best news of which we have spoken throughout these many pages. After a long, hard-working life, one has the right to hope for peace of mind. Up to 80 percent of depressed, confused, hopeless elderly persons can immediately be treated and returned to dignified existence.

All they need to do is get treatment. For this to happen, word of the advances in diagnosis and care must spread to the suffering individuals and their families, to their physicians, to medical students, to insurance companies, and to helping agencies throughout the community. People who become aware that much of the mental and physical agony of later life is reversible will demand better care for themselves and for members of their family.

The same can be said for mental health care at every age. Demand better for yourselves. The skill and technology is there and you will get it if you insist on it.

We have good reason to expect that given the present rate of advance in biopsychiatric research and understanding, and knowing the potential for rapid developments of psychiatric brain imaging and laboratory technology, we can halt the epidemic of depression that is sweeping our country as we approach the end of the century. Right now biopsychiatrists can identify and treat acute depression in most cases from infancy onward. Steadily we will improve our ability to identify the signs of the disease and develop pharmacological agents that will target precise receptors in the brain without adversely affecting others. Identification of genetic markers will follow; manipulation of affected genes possibly awaits us in the next century. Psychiatrists will become highly skilled physicians, and physicians will become skilled in the recognition of mental disease in their patients. Increasingly we will understand how the mind and brain and body are linked. We will elucidate the biological mechanisms of depression. We will know better how to harness the mind to improve the quality of its own existence. Depression will lose its stigma.

By the time the baby boomers have reached the venerable years, depression, the illness, will cease to be a problem. When sadness comes, it will go away.

BIBLIOGRAPHY

Adler, Stephen N., Mildred Lam, and Alfred F. Connors, Jr. *A Pocket Manual of Differential Diagnosis.* Boston and Toronto: Little, Brown and Co., 1982.

"AIDS." *Newsweek* (August 12, 1985): 20–27.

Akiskal, Hagop Souren. "Dysthymic Disorder: Psychopathology of Proposed Chronic Subtypes." *American Journal of Psychiatry* 140 (January 1983): 11–20.

Alper, Joseph. "Biology and Mental Illness." *The Atlantic Monthly* (December 1983): 70–76.

American Psychiatric Association. *Diagnostic and Statistical Manual of Mental Disorders.* 3rd edition. Washington, D.C.: American Psychiatric Association Press, 1980.

Andreasen, Nancy C. *The Broken Brain: The Biological Revolution in Psychiatry.* New York: Harper and Row, 1984.

Anthony, Catherine Parker, and Gary A. Thibodeau. *Structure and Function of the Body.* 7th edition. St. Louis: Times Mirror/Mosby College Publishing, 1984.

Aschoff, Juergen. "The Circadian System in Man." Chapter 8 in *Neuroendocrinology,* edited by Dorothy T. Krieger and Joan C. Hughes. Sunderland, Massachusetts. A Hospital Practice Book, Sinauer Associates, Inc., 1980.

Ayd, Frank, Jr., ed. *Clinical Depressions: Diagnostic and Therapeutic Challenges.* Baltimore: Ayd Medical Communications, 1980.

Baldessarini, Ross J. *Biomedical Aspects of Depression and Its Treatment.* Washington, D.C.: American Psychiatric Association Press, Inc., 1983.

Barikolate, Gina. "Clinical Trial of Psychotherapies Under Way." *Science* 212 (April 24, 1981): 432–433.

Baxter, Lewis R., Jr., Michael E. Phelps, John C. Mazziotta, et al. "Cerebral Metabolic Rates for Glucose in Mood Disorders." *Archives of General Psychiatry* 42 (May 1985): 441–447.

Beardslee, William R., Gerald L. Klerman, Martin B. Keller, Philip W. Lavori, and Donna L. Podorefsky. "But Are They Cases? Validity of DSM-III. Major Depression in Children Identified in a Family Study." *American Journal of Psychiatry* 142:6 (June 1985): 687–691.

————, Jules Bemporad, Martin B. Keller, and Gerald L. Klerman. "Children of Parents With Major Affective Disorder: A Review." *American Journal of Psychiatry* 140:7 (July 1983): 825–832.

Beck, Aaron T., Robert A. Steer, Maria Kovacs, and Betsy Garrison. "Hopelessness and Eventual Suicide: A 10-Year Prospective Study of Patients Hospitalized With Suicidal Ideation." *American Journal of Psychiatry* 142:5 (May 1985): 559–563.

Belson, Abby Avin. "New Focus on Chemistry of Joylessness." *The New York Times* (March 15, 1983): C1, C8.

Benevenga, N.J., and R. D. Steele. "Adverse Effects of Excessive Consumption of Amino Acids." *Annual Review of Nutrition* 4 (1984): 157–181.

Bernstein, Jerrold G., ed., *Clinical Psychopharmacology.* 2nd edition. Boston, Bristol, and London: John Wright PSG, Inc., 1984.

————. "Neurotransmitters and Receptors in Pharmacopsychiatry." Chapter 4 in Clinical Psychopharmacology, edited by Jerrold G. Bernstein. 2nd edition. Boston, Bristol, and London: John Wright PSG, Inc., 1984.

————. "Pharmacological Management of The Elderly Patient." Chapter 12 in Clinical Psychopharmacology, edited by Jerrold G. Bernstein. 2nd edition. Boston, Bristol, and London: John Wright PSG, Inc., 1984.

Bird, Stephanie J. "Presymptomatic Testing for Huntington's Disease." *Journal of the American Medical Association* 253:22 (June 14, 1985): 3286–3291.

Black, Donald W., Giles Warrack, and George Winokur. "Excess Mortality Among Psychiatric Patients." *Journal of the American Medical Association* 253:1 (January 4, 1985): 58–61.

Bloodworth, Ronald C. Personal communication to Mark Gold, spring 1985.

Boffey, Phillip M. "Rare Disease Proposed as Cause for "Vampires." *The New York Times* (May 31, 1985): A15.

Bommer, M., and D. Naber. "Subclinical Hypothyroidism in Recurrent Mania." *Biological Psychiatry* 31 (1992): 729–734

Boxill, Diana. "Teenage Suicide: Prevalent Problem." *Dispatch* (February 14, 1982).

Brayshaw, N., and M. S. Gold. "Thyroid Dysfunction in Premenstrual Syndrome." *APA Abstract* 102 (1985): 191.

Brody, Jane E. "Personal Health: Detecting Signs and Preventing Teen-Age Suicide." *The New York Times* (March 7, 1984): C7.

Brown, Marvin R., and Laurel A. Fisher. "Brain Peptides as Intercellular Messengers: Implications for Medicine." *Journal of the American Medical Association* 251:10 (March 9, 1984): 1310–1315.

Buchsbaum, Monte S., and Richard J. Haier. "Psychopathology: Biological Approaches." *Annual Review of Psychology* 34 (1983): 401–430.

Burch, E. A., and T. J. Goldschmidt. "Depression in the Elderly: A Beta-Adrenergic Receptor Function." *International Journal of Psychiatry in Medicine* 13:3 (1983–84): 207–213.

Cleghoarn, John M., Sherryl Franco, Barbara Szechtman, Ronald D. Kaplan, Henry Szechtman, Gregory M. Brown, Claude Nahmias, Stephen Garnett. "Toward a Brain Map of Auditory Hallucinations." *American Journal of Psychiatry* 149:8 (August, 1992): 1062–1070.

Cloninger, C. Robert. "Unraveling the Causal Pathway to Major Depression." *American Journal of Psychiatry* 150:8 (August, 1993), 137–138.

"Cognitive Therapy Outperforms Drugs in Certain Cases, Researchers Find." *Psychiatric News* (November 20, 1992): 4.

Cohen, Martin R., David Picker, Irl Extein, et al. "Plasma Cortisol and B-Endorphin Immunoreactivity in Nonmajor and Major Depression." *American Journal of Psychiatry* 141:5 (May 1984): 628–632.

Cohn, Victor. "Gene Defect Linked to Manic-Depression." *Miami Herald* (August 1, 1984): Section F.

"Commission Releases Findings on Unemployment and MH." *Psychiatric News* 20:18 (September 20, 1985): 1.

Consensus Development Panel of the NIMH/NIH Consensus Development Conference. "Mood Disorders: Pharmacologic Prevention of Recurrences." *American Journal of Psychiatry* 142:4 (April 1985): 469–476.

Corfman, Eunice. *National Institute of Mental Health: Science Reports: Depression, Manic-Depression and Biological Rhythms.* U.S. Government Printing Office, Washington, D.C.: National Institute of Mental Health, 1982. 0-377-011.

Coryell, William. "The Organic-Dynamic Continuum in Psychiatry: Trends in Attitudes Among Third-Year Residents." *American Journal of Psychiatry* 139:1 (January 1982): 89–91.

Crayton, John W. "Adverse Reactions to Foods: Relevance to Psychiatric Disorders." *Journal of Clinical Immunology*, in press, 1985.

" 'Creativity and Madness Are Linked,' Study Says." *The New York Times* (September 23, 1984): 63.

Cytryn, Leon, and Donald H. McKnew. "Treatment Issues in Childhood Depression." *Psychiatric Annals* 15:6 (June 1985): 401–403.

Dackis, Charles A., and M. S. Gold. "Bromocriptine as Treatment of Cocaine Abuse." *Lancet* 1:8438 (1985): 1151–1152.

————, M. S. Gold, A. L. C. Pottash, and D. R. Sweeney. "Evaluating Depression in Alcoholics." *Psychiatry Research* 17 (1986): 105–109.

————, and Mark S. Gold. "Opiate Addiction and Depression: Cause or Effect." *Drug and Alcohol Dependence* 2 (1983): 105–109.

————, Joyce Bailey, A. L. C. Pottash, et al. "Specificity of the DST and the TRH Test for Major Depression in Alcoholics." *American Journal of Psychiatry* 141:5 (March 1984): 680–683.

Davidson, Jonathan, Craig Turnbull, Rosemary Strickland, and Michael Belyes. "Comparative Diagnostic Criteria for Melancholia and Endogenous Depression." *Archives of General Psychiatry* 41 (May 1984): 506–511.

DelBello, Alfred B. "Needed: A U.S. Commission on Teen-age Suicide." *The New York Times* (September 12, 1984): A31.

deMilio, Lawrence T., and Lynne Weisberg. "Subclinical Hypothyroidism Presenting as Adolescent Depression." Unpublished manuscript, 1985.

"Depression: A Problem for Learning-Disabled Young." *American Medical News* (March 8, 1985): 35.

"Depression, Violent Suicides Tied to Low Metabolite Level." *Journal of the American Medical Association* 250:23 (December 16, 1983): 3141.

Deptula, Dennis J., Alan Manevitz, and Allen Yozawitz. "Lateralization of Memory Deficits in Depression." Paper presented at American Psychiatric Association, May 1984.

DeVane, C. L. "Pharmacokinetics of the Selective Serotonin Reuptake Inhibitors." *Journal of Clinical Psychiatry* 53 Suppl: (February, 1992): 13–20.

"Diagnostic Tests." *Healthfacts* 9:62 (July 1984): 1–6.

Di Giacomo, Joseph. "Treating the Depressed Hypertensive Patient." *Medicine and Psychiatry* 1:1 (Summer 1983): 3.

"Don't Overlook Homicidal Tendencies in Depressed Patients, Report Warns." *Psychiatric News* (July 5, 1985): 10.

Dorland's Illustrated Medical Dictionary. 26th edition. Philadelphia: W. B. Saunders Company, 1981.

Edwards, Neil. "Mental Disturbances Related to Metals." Chapter 17 in *Psychiatric Presentations in Medical Illness: Somatopsychic Disorders*, edited by Richard C. W. Hall. New York, London: SP Medical and Scientific Books, 1980.

Elsenga, S., and R. VanDenHoofdakker. "Clinical Effects of Sleep Deprivation and Clomipramine in Endogenous Depression." *Journal of Psychiatric Research* 17:4 (1982–83): 361–374.

"Enhanced Sensitivity to Light: A Risk Factor for Depression?" *Currents* 4:8 (August 1985): 14.

Evans, Dwight L., Gail A. Edelsohn, and Robert N. Golden. "Organic Psychosis Without Anemia or Spinal Cord Symptoms in Patients With B12 Deficiency." *American Journal of Psychiatry* 140:2 (February 1983): 218–221.

Extein, Irl, A. L. C. Pottash, M. S. Gold, and R. W. Cowdry. "Changes in TSH Response to TRH in Affective Disorders." In *Neurobiology of Mood Disorders* by Robert M. Post, M.D. and James C. Ballenger, M.D. Volume 1 of *Frontiers of Clinical Neuroscience.* Baltimore, London: Williams and Wilkins, 1984.

————, G. Rosenberg, A. L. C. Pottash, and M. S. Gold. "The DST in Depressed Adolescents." *American Journal of Psychiatry* 139:12 (1982): 1617–1619.

————, and M. S. Gold, eds. *Medical Mimics of Psychiatric Disorders.* Washington, D.C.: American Psychiatric Association Press, 1986.

————, and M. S. Gold. "Psychiatric Applications of Thyroid Tests." *Journal of Clinical Psychiatry* 47:1 (1986): 13–16.

————, M. S. Gold, and A. L. C. Pottash. "Psychopharmacological Treatment of Depression." Psychiatric Clinics of North America 7:3 (1984): 503–517.

————, A. L. C. Pottash, and M. S. Gold. "Thyroid Tests as Predictors of Treatment Response and Prognosis in Psychiatry." *Psychiatric Hospital* 16:3 (1985): 127–160.

————, A. L. C. Pottash, and M. S. Gold. "The TRH Test in Affective Disorders: Experience in a Private Clinical Setting." *Psychosomatics* 25:5 (1984): 379–389.

————. Memo to Mark Gold, March 29, 1985.

"Family Medical and Health Guide." *Consumer Guide Magazine Health/Exercise Bimonthly* 383 (March 1985): 59.

Ferrell, Tom. "Some Sad People, It Seems, Are Unhappy as a Matter of Habit." *The New York Times* (November 15, 1983): C2.

Fieve, Ronald R. *Moodswing.* New York: William Morrow and Co., 1975.

Fishbein, Morris. "Is Affective Illness on the Increase?" *Journal of the American Medical Association* 241:6 (February 9, 1979): 545.

Forester, Bruce, Donald S. Kornfeld, Joseph L. Fleiss, Seth Thompson. "Group Psychotherapy During Radiotherapy: Effects on Emotional Distress." *American Journal of Psychiatry* 150:11 (November 1993): 1700.

Freud, Sigmund. "Analysis Terminable and Interminable." Volume 23, 1937. In standard edition of *The Complete Psychological Works.* London: Hogarth Press, 1953–74.

"From Fluoxetine to Bupropion." *The Harvard Mental Health Letter.* 11:2 (August 1994): 7.

Fulcha, Robert, Joy Stapp, and Marlene Wicherski. "Detailed Statistical Tables: 1979 and 1980 Doctorate Employment Surveys." American Psychological Association report, November 1982.

Gada, M. T. "A Cross Cultural Study of Symptomatology of Depression: Eastern Versus Western Patients." *International Journal of Social Psychiatry* 28:3 (Autumn 1982): 195-202.

Garelik, Glenn, and Gina Maranto. "Multiple Murderers." *Discover* (July 1984): 26-29.

Garvey, M. J., and G. D. Toliefson. "Post-Partum Depression." *Journal of Reproductive Medicine* 29:2 (1984): 113-116.

Geertsma, Robert H., and Donald R. Ginols. "Specialty Choice in Medicine." *Journal of Medical Education* 47 (July 1972): 509-517.

Gehris, Timothy L., Roger Kathol, William H. Meller, Juan F. Lopez, Richard S. Jaeckle. "Multiple Steroid Hormone Levels in Depressed Patients and Normal Controls Before and After Exogenous ACTH." *Psychoneuroendocrinology* 16:6 (1991): 481-497.

"Genetic Link in Suicide Supported by Study of Amish." *Psychiatric News* (September 6, 1985): 20-21.

Gershon, Elliot S., Judith Schreiber, Joel Hamovit, Eleanor Dibble, et al. "Clinical Findings in Patients With Anorexia Nervosa and Affective Illness in Their Relatives." *American Journal of Psychiatry* 141:11 (November 1984): 1419.

Giannini, A. James, William A. Price, and Robert H. Loiselle. "Prevalence of Mitral Valve Prolapse in Bipolar Affective Disorder." *American Journal of Psychiatry* 141:8 (August 1984): 991-992.

————. Personal communication to Mark S. Gold, May 1985.

Gittleman, Rachel, and Andres Kanner. "Overview of Clinical Psychopharmacology in Childhood Disorders." Chapter 10 in *Clinical Psychopharmacology,* edited by Jerrold G. Bernstein. 2nd edition. Boston, Bristol, and London: John Wright PSG, Inc., 1984.

Goggans, Frederick C. "Nutritional Deficiency Syndromes in Clinical Psychiatry." Chapter 9 in *Diagnostic and Laboratory Testing in Psychiatry*, edited by M. S. Gold and A. L. C. Pottash. New York and London: Plenum Publishing Corp., 1986.

————. "Thyroid Disorder in Psychiatric Practice." In *Medical Mimics of Psychiatric Disorders,* edited by Irl Extein and Mark S. Gold. Washington, D.C.: American Psychiatric Association Press, 1986.

Gold, Mark S., R. B. Lydiard, and J. S. Carman, eds. *Advances in Psychopharmacology: Predicting and Improving Treatment Response.* Boca Raton, Florida: CRC Press, Inc., 1984.

————, A. Carter Pottash, Donald Sweeney, et al. "Antimanic Antidepressant, and Antipanic Effects of Opiates: Clinical Neuroanatomical, and Biochemical Evidence." *Annals of The New York Academy of Sciences* (1982): 140-150.

————. "The Challenge of Misdiagnosis." In *Biopsychiatric Insights on Depression: PDLA Depression Monograph* (1985): 14-21.

————, and M. Kronig. "Comprehensive Thyroid Evaluation in Psychiatric Patients." Chapter 1 in *Handbook of Psychiatric Diagnostic Procedures,* edited by R.C.W. Hall and T.P. Beresford. New York: Spectrum Publications, 1984.

————, B. Lydiard, A. L. C. Pottash, and D. M. Martin. "The Contribution of Blood Levels to the Treatment of 'Resistant' Depression." In *Special Treatments of Resistant Depression,* edited by J. Zohar and R. H. Belmaker. Jamaica, N.Y.: Spectrum Publications, 1986 (in press).

————, and H. R. Pearsall. "Depression and Hypothyroidism." *Journal of the American Medical Association* 250:18 (1983): 2470–2471.

————, A. Carter Pottash, Donald Sweeney, et al. "Diagnosis of Depression in the 1980s." *Journal of the American Medical Association* 245:15 (April 17, 1981): 1562–1564.

————, *800-COCAINE.* New York: Bantam Books, 1984.

————, and H. R. Pearsall. "Hypothyroidism or Is It Depression?" *Psychosomatics* 24:7 (1983): 646–657.

————, A. L. C. Pottash, T. W. Estroff, and I. Extein. "Laboratory Evaluation in Treatment Planning." In *The Somatic Therapies,* edited by T. B. Karasu, 31–50. Part I of *The Psychiatric Therapies.* APA Commission on Psychiatric Therapies. Washington, D.C.: American Psychiatric Association Press, 1984.

————, A. L. C. Pottash, A. Stoll, D. M. Martin, L. B. Finn, and I. Extein. "Nortriptyline Plasma Levels and Clinical Response in Patients with Familial Pure Unipolar Depression and Blunted TRH Tests." *International Journal of Psychiatry in Medicine* 13:3 (1983): 215–220.

————, and H. Rowland Pearsall. "Platelet and Trait Markers." Chapter 8 in *Diagnostic and Laboratory Testing in Psychiatry,* edited by M. S. Gold and A. L. C. Pottash. New York and London: Plenum Publishing Corp., 1986.

————, A. L. C. Pottash, and I. Extein. "The Psychiatric Laboratory." In *Clinical Psychopharmacology,* edited by Jerrold G. Berstein, 29–58. Boston, Bristol and London: John Wright PSG, Inc., 1984.

————. "The Risk of Misdiagnosing Physical Illness as Depression." Directions in Psychiatry 4:27 (1984): 1–7.

————. "The Role of the Laboratory." In Biopsychiatric Insights on Depression: PDLA Depression Monograph, (1985): 34–38.

————, A. L. C. Pottash, J. S. Carman, and R. B. Lydiard. "The Role of the Laboratory in Psychiatry." Chapter 12 in *Advances in Psychopharmacology: Predicting and Improving Treatment Response,* edited by M. S. Gold, R. B. Lydiard, and J. S. Carman. Boca Raton, Florida: CRC Press, Inc., 1984.

————. "The Serotonin Subtype." Chapter 5 in *Advances in Psychopharmacology: Predicting and Improving Treatment Response,* edited by M. S. Gold, R. Bruce Lydiard, and John S. Carman. Boca Raton, Florida: CRC Press, Inc., 1984.

————, T. W. Estroff, and A. L. C. Pottash. "Substance Induced Organic Mental Disorders." Chapter 12 in *American Psychiatric Association Annual Review,* Vol. 4, edited by Robert E. Hales and Allen J. Frances. Washington, D.C.: American Psychiatric Association Press, 1985.

————, A. L. C. Pottash, and I. Extein. "The TRH Test in the Diagnosis of Affective Disorders and Schizophrenia." In *Psychoneuroendocrine Dysfunction,* edited by N. S. Shah and A. G. Donald. New York and London: Plenum Publishing Corporation, 1984.

————, and H. Rowland Pearsall. "What's New in Laboratory Testing Procedures For Psychiatrists?" *The Psychiatric Hospital* 15:1 (Winter 1984): 3–9.

Gold, Phillip W., George Chrousos, Charles Kellner, et al. "Psychiatric Implications of Basic and Clinical Studies With Corticotropin-Releasing Factor." *American Journal of Psychiatry* 141:5 (May 1984): 619–627.

Goldsmith, Marsha F. "Psychiatrists Analyze Their Present Problems, Project a Bright Future." *Journal of the American Medical Association* 252:6 (August 10, 1984): 737–740.

_____. "Research on Aging Burgeons As More Americans Grow Older." *Journal of the American Medical Association* 253:10 (March 8, 1985): 1369-1370.

_____. "Steps Toward Staging, Therapy of Dementia." *Journal of the American Medical Association* 251:14 (April 13, 1984): 1812.

Golemann, Daniel. "Clues to Suicide: A Brain Chemical Is Implicated." *The New York Times* (October 8, 1985): C1.

Goodwin, Donald W. "What is Mental Illness?" *American Journal of Psychiatry* 141:8 (August 1984): 1001.

Goodwin, Frederick K. "Epidemiology and Clinical Description of Depression." In *Biopsychiatric Insights on Depression.* Symposium report, Psychiatric Diagnostic Laboratories of America, 1985.

Gore, Mary Jane. "The Psychological Input." *Psychology Today* (August 1984): 17.

Gray, Gregory E., David Baron, and Joseph Herman. "The Importance of Medical Anthropology in Clinical Psychiatry." *American Journal of Psychiatry* 142:2 (February 1985): 275.

Greist, John, and James W. Jefferson. *Depression and Its Treatment.* Washington, D.C.: American Psychiatric Association Press, 1984.

Grinfeld, Michael J. "Health Plan Type Affects Depression Treatment." *Psychiatric Times* X:9 (September 1993): 1.

Gross, David A., Fair Oaks Hospital at Delray Beach, Florida. Personal communication to Mark S. Gold.

Gurpegui, M., I. Extein, M. S. Gold, and D. R. Sweeney. "The Study of the Hypothalamic-Pituitary-Thyroid Axis in the Psychiatric Disorders: A Review." *Archive de Neurobiologie* 46:2 (1983): 79-108.

Haalenar, John F. "Maybe Doctors Aren't Doing Enough Testing." Medical Economics (July 7, 1980): 63-65.

Hall, Richard C. W., Thomas P. Beresford, Earl R. Gardner, and Michael K. Popkin. "The Medical Care of Psychiatric Patients." *Hospital and Community Psychiatry* 33:1 (January 1, 1982): 25-33.

_____, "Psychiatric Effects of Thyroid Hormone Disturbance." *Psychosomatics* 24:1 (January 1983): 7-18.

_____, Thomas P. Beresford, Earl R. Gardner, Michael K. Popkin. "Unrecognized Physical Illness Prompting Psychiatric Admission: A Prospective Study." *American Journal of Psychiatry* 138:5 (May 1981): 629 ff.

Hamilton, Jean A., Barbara L. Parry, Sheryle Alagna, Susan Blumenthal, and Elizabeth Herz. "Premenstrual Mood Changes: A Guide to Evaluation and Treatment." *Psychiatric Annals* 14:6 (June 1984): 426-435.

Hamilton, Max. "The Effect of Treatment on The Melancholias (Depression)." *British Journal of Psychiatry* 140 (1982): 223-230.

Hammer, Signe. "The Mind as Healer." *Science Digest* (April 1984): 47-50, 100.

Harden, Blaine. "Why Psychiatrists Are Blue." *The Washingtonian* (July 1984): 95-97, 136, 137.

Harrison, Wilma M., Judith G. Rabkin, and Jean Endicott. "Psychiatric Evaluation of Premenstrual Changes." *Psychosomatics* 26:10 (October 1985): 789-799.

_____, Thomas B. Cooper, Jonathan W. Stewart, et al. "The Tyramine Challenge Test as a Marker for Melancholia." *Archives of General Psychiatry* 41 (July 1984): 681-685.

Hatsukami, Dorothy, and Roy W. Pickens. "Post-Treatment Depression in an Alcohol and Drug Abuse Population." *American Journal of Psychiatry* 139:12 (December 1982): 1563-1566.

Herbert, Tracy B., Sheldon Cohen. "Depression and Immunity: A Meta-Analytic Review." *Psychological Bulletin* 113 (1993): 472-486.

Hopkins, Joyce, Marsha Marcus, and Susan B. Campbell. "Postpartum Depression: A Critical Review." *Psychological Bulletin* 95:3 (1984): 498-515.

Hudson, James I., Margo S. Hudson, Lillian F. Pliner, et al. "Fibromyalgia and Major Affective Disorder: A Controlled Phenomenology and Family History Study." *American Journal of Psychiatry* 142:4 (April 1985): 441-446.

Hudson, James I., Joseph F. Lipinski, Paul E. Keck, Jr., Harlyn G. Aizley, Scott E. Lukas, Anthony J. Rothschild, Christine Waternaux, David J. Kupfer. "Polysomnographic Characteristics of Young Manic Patients." *Archives of General Psychiatry* 49 (May 1992): 378-395.

Hurst, Daniel L., and Mary Jane Hurst. "Bromide Psychosis: A Literary Case." *Clinical Neuropharmacology* 7:3 (1984): 259-264.

Jamison, Kay R. *Touched With Fire*. New York: Macmillan, Inc., 1993.

Jenkins, Rachel, and Anthony W. Clare. "Women and Mental Illness." *British Medical Journal* 291 (November 30, 1985): 1521-1522.

Kandel, Eric R. "From Metapsychology to Molecular Biology: Explorations Into the Nature of Anxiety." *American Journal of Psychiatry* 140:10 (October 1983): 1277-1293.

Karasu, Toksoz B., ed. *The Psychiatric Therapies*. Washington D.C.: American Psychiatric Association Press, 1984.

Kashani, Javad H., and Marybeth Priesmeyer. "Differences in Depressive Symptoms and Depression Among College Students." *American Journal of Psychiatry* 140:8 (August 1983): 1081-1082.

Katz, Jack L., Avi Kuperberg, Charles P. Pollack, et al. "Is There a Relationship Between Eating Disorder and Affective Disorder? New Evidence From Sleep Recordings." *American Journal of Psychiatry* 141:6 (June 1984): 753-759.

Keller, Martin B., Phillip W. Lavori, Jean Endicott, William Coryell, and Gerald L. Klerman. "'Double Depression': Two-Year Follow-Up." *American Journal of Psychiatry* 140:6 (June 1983): 689-694.

Kendler, Kenneth S., Ronald C. Kessler, Michael C. Neale, Andrew C. Heath, and Lindon J. Eaves. "The Prediction of Major Depression in Women: Toward an Integrated Etiologic Model." *American Journal of Psychiatry* 150:8 (August 1993): 1139-1144.

Kinzie, J. David, Spero M. Manson, Do The Vinh, et al. "Development and Validation of a Vietnamese-Language Depression Rating Scale." *American Journal of Psychiatry* 139:10 (October 1982): 1276-1281.

Klerman, Gerald L., George E. Vaillant, Robert Spitzer, and Robert Michaels. "A Debate on DSM-III." *American Journal of Psychiatry* 141:4 (April 1984): 539 ff.

————. "History and Development of Modern Concepts of Affective Illness." Chapter 1 in *Neurobiology of Mood Disorders* by Robert M. Post, M.D., and James C. Ballenger, M.D. Volume 1 of *Frontiers of Clinical Neuroscience*. Baltimore and London: Williams and Wilkins, 1984.

————. "Psychotherapy and Pharmacotherapy." Chapter 1 in *Clinical Psychopharmacology*, edited by Jerrold G. Bernstein. 2nd edition. Boston, Bristol, and London: John Wright PSG, Inc., 1984.

Kline, Nathan S. *From Sad to Glad.* New York: Ballantine, 1974.

Kolivakis, Thomas, and Jambur Ananth. "Think Depression! The Signs and Symptoms of Primary and Secondary Depression." In *Clinical Depressions: Diagnostic and Therapeutic Challenges,* edited by Frank Ayd, Jr. Washington, D.C.: American Psychiatric Association Press, Inc., 1983.

Konner, Melvin. *The Tangled Wing: Biological Constraints on the Human Spirit.* New York: Holt, Rinehart and Winston, 1982.

Kramer, Peter D. *Listening to Prozac.* New York: Viking Penguin, 1993.

Kreiger, Dorothy T. "The Hypothalamus and Neuroendocrinology." In *Neuroendocrinology,* edited by Dorothy T. Kreiger and Joan C. Hughes. Sunderland, Massachusetts: A Hospital Practice Book, Sinauer Associates, Inc., 1980.

Kreiger, Richard B., Elinor M. Levy, Edgar S. Cathcart, et al. "Lymphocyte Subsets in Patients With Major Depression: Preliminary FIndings." *Advances* 1:1 (Winter 1984): 5-9.

Langsley, Donald G., and Marc H. Hollender. "The Definition of a Psychiatrist." *American Journal of Psychiatry* 139:1 (January 1982): 81-85.

Lehmann, H. E. "Recognition and Treatment of Depression in Geriatric Patients." Chapter 5 in *Clinical Depressions: Diagnostic and Therapeutic Challenges,* edited by Frank Ayd, Jr. Washington, D.C.: American Psychiatric Association Press, Inc., 1983.

Leiber, Arnold L., and Nancy Newburg. "Use of Biological Markers in a General Hospital Affective Disorders Program." Unpublished paper, 1984.

Liebmann-Smith, Joan. "PMS, Insomnia . . . or Thyroid?" *American Health* (September 1985): 76-81.

Leibowitz, Michael R. *The Chemistry of Love.* Boston and Toronto: Little, Brown and Company, 1983.

Leigh, Hoyle. "Comment: The Role of Psychiatry in Medicine." *American Journal of Psychiatry* 139:12 (December 1982): 1581-1586.

Leitner, G. I. "Misdiagnosis of Affective Disorders in Adolescents." *American Journal of Psychiatry* 139:11 (November 1982): 1527.

Leo, John. "The Ups and Downs of Creativity." *Time* (October 8, 1984): 76.

Lesse, Stanley. "Unmasking the Masks of Depression." Chapter 4 in Clinical Depressions: Diagnostic and Therapeutic Challenges, edited by Frank Ayd, Jr. Washington, D.C.: American Psychiatric Association Press, Inc., 1983.

"Let's Talk Facts About Mental Illness: Depression." Washington, DC: American Psychiatric Press, 1989.

Levy, Elinor M., David J. Borrelli, Steven M. Mirin, et al. "Biological Measures and Cellular Immunological Function in Depressed Psychiatric Patients." *Psychiatry Research* 36 (1991): 157-167.

Lipton, Morris A., and Robert N. Golden. "Nutritional Therapies." Chapter 3 in *The Psychiatric Therapies*, edited by Toksoz B. Karasu. Washington, D.C.: American Psychiatric Association Press, 1984.

Lobel, Brana, and Robert M. A. Hirschfeld. Depression: What We Know. Department of Health and Human Services Publication # (ADM) 84-1318. Washington, D.C.: U.S. Government Printing Office, 1984.

MacDonald, Ewen, David Rubinow, and Markku Linnoila. "Sensitivity of RBC Membrane Ca2: Adenosine Triphosphatase to Calmodulin Stimulation." *Archives of General Psychiatry* 4:15 (May 1984): 487-493.

Malcom, Janet. "The Patient Is Always Right." *New York Review of Books* 21:20 (December 20, 1984): 13–14, 16, 18.

Maler, Steven F. "Animal Models of Depression: New Findings." *Psychopharmacology Bulletin* 19:3 (1983): 531–536.

Malesky, Gale. "Troubleshooting Your Thyroid." *Prevention* (June 1985): 112–121.

Maranto, Gina. "The Mind Within the Brain." *Discover* (May 1984): 34–43.

Martin, David M., and Frederick Van Lente. "On the Diagnostic Frontier: The Laboratory in Mental Illness." *Diagnostic Medicine* (May/June 1980): 87.

Martin-Iverson, Mathew T. "An Animal Model of Stimulant Psychoses" in *Neuromethods, Vol. 19: Animal Models in Psychiatry I* Eds.: A. Boulton, G. Baker, and M. Martin-Iverson, The Humana Press Inc., 1991.

Marx, Jean L. "Diabetes: A Possible Autoimmune Disease." *Science* (September 21, 1984): 1381–1383.

McCormick, Richard A., Angel M. Russo, Luis F. Ramirez, et al. "Affective Disorders Among Pathological Gamblers Seeking Treatment." *American Journal of Psychiatry* 141:2 (February 1984): 215–218.

McKnew, Donald H., Jr. Leon Cytryn, and Herbert Yahraes. *Why Isn't Johnny Crying?: Coping With Depression in Children.* New York: W. W. Norton, 1985.

"Melancholic Patients: A New Test to Identify Depression." *Lab World* (September 1981): 25–29.

Melnechuk, Theodore. "Neuroimmunomodulation." *Advances* (1983): 1.

Melvin, Tessa. "Depression in Aged Termed Reversible." *The New York Times,* Section 22 (February 20, 1983): 1–5.

Messisha, F. S. "Fluoxetine: A Spectrum of Clinical Applications and Postulates of Underlying Mechanisms." *Neuroscience and Biobehavioral Reviews* 17: (1993): 385–396.

Mick, Stephen S., and Jacqueline Lowe Worobey. "Foreign Medical Graduates in the 1980s: Trends in Specialization." *American Journal of Public Health* 74:7 (July 1984): 698–703.

Miller, Sigmund S., ed. *Symptoms: The Complete Home Medical Encyclopedia.* New York: Avon Books, 1978.

"Mind-Body Confusion." *Science News* 118 (October 11, 1980): 238.

Montandon, Cleopatra, and Timothy Harding. "The Reliability of Dangerousness Assessments: A Decision-Making Exercise." *British Journal of Psychiatry* 144 (1984): 149–155.

"Mood Disorder Victims Are Undertreated." *American Medical News* 27:18 (May 11, 1984): 24.

Morris, Lois B. "Infants' Emotional Health." *Sunday Woman* (July 4, 1982).

————, et al. *The Little Black Pill Book.* Toronto, New York: London, Sydney: Bantam Books, 1983.

Motto, Jerome A., David C. Heilbron, and Richard P. Juster. "Development of a Clinical Instrument to Estimate Suicide Risk." *American Journal of Psychiatry* 142:6 (June 1985): 684.

Mueller, Peter S., and N. Grace Allen. "Diagnosis and Treatment of Severe Light-Sensitive Seasonal Energy Syndrome (SES) and its Relationship to Melatonin Anabolism." *Fair Oaks Hospital Psychiatry Letter* 2:9 (September 1984).

Nelson, Bryce. "Despite a Blur of Change, Clear Trends Emerging in Psychotherapy." *The New York Times,* (March 1, 1983): C1, C6.

"Neuroscience Targets Manic Depressive Illness." *Brain Work*. 2:1 (Winter/Spring 1992): 1.

Newson, Gary, and Nevill Murray. "Reversal of Dexamethasone Suppression Test Nonsuppression in Alcohol Abusers." *American Journal of Psychiatry* 140:3 (March 1983): 353–354.

Nurnberger, John I., Jr., and Elliot S. Gershon. "Genetics of Affective Disorders." Chapter 5 in *Neurobiology of Mood Disorders* by Robert M. Post and James C. Ballenger. Volume 1 of *Frontiers of Clinical Neuroscience*. Baltimore and London: Williams and Wilkins, 1984.

Ornstein, Robert, and Richard F. Thompson. *The Amazing Brain*. Boston: Houghton Mifflin Company, 1984.

Owens, Michael J., Charles B. Nemeroff. "The Role of Corticotropin-Releasing Factor in the Pathophysiology of Affective and Anxiety Disorders: Laboratory and Clinical Studies." Wiley, Chichester. *Ciba Foundation Symposium 172*. (1993): 296–316.

Pardes, Herbert. "Medical Education and Recruitment in Psychiatry." *American Journal of Psychiatry* 139:8 (August 1982): 1033–1035.

Pearsall, H. R., M. S. Gold, and A. L. C. Pottash. "Hypothyroidism and Depression: The Casual Connection." *Diagnosis* (1983): 77–80.

Perry, Barbara. "Depression and Psychobiology in Women's Life Cycles." Tape of symposium at American Psychiatric Association Annual Meeting, Los Angeles, May 1984.

Perry, Paul. "The Ironic Epidemic." *American Health* (October 1984): 41–43.

Peterson, Linda Gay, and Mark Perl. "Psychiatric Presentations of Cancer." *Psychosomatics* 23:6 (June 1982): 601–604.

Pollner, Fran, Judy Alsofrom, Rochelle Green, and Liz Gonzalez. "Phenylalanine: A Psychoactive Nutrient for Some Depressives?" *Medical World News* 24:20 (October 24, 1983): 21–22.

Pomara, N., and S. Gershon. "Treatment-Resistant Depression in an Elderly Patient with Pancreatic Carcinoma: Case Report." *Journal of Clinical Psychiatry* 45:10 (1984): 439–440.

Post, Robert M., and James C. Ballenger. Neurobiology of Mood Disorders. Volume 1 of *Frontiers of Clinical Neuroscience*. Baltimore and London: Williams and Wilkins, 1984.

Pottash, A. L. C., M.S. Gold, and I. Extein. "The Use of the Clinical Laboratory." In *Inpatient Psychiatry: Diagnosis and Treatment,* edited by Lloyd I. Sederer. Baltimore and London: Williams and Wilkins, 1983.

Poznanski, Elva. "Depression in Children and Adolescents: An Overview." *Psychiatric Annals* 15:6 (June 1985): 365–367.

Prange, Arthur J., Jr. "Depression and Thyroid Function: A Brief Review." *Fair Oaks Hospital Psychiatry Letter* 1:3 (March 1983).

Prasad, Ananda S. "Clinical, Biochemical and Nutritional Spectrum of Zinc Deficiency in Human Subjects: An Update." *Nutrition Reviews* 41:7 (July 1983): 197–208.

"Preventing Affective Recurrence: An Interview with Robert F. Prien, Ph.D." *Currents* (1985): 5–9.

Prose, Mel, David C. Clark, Martin Harrow, and Jen Fawcett. "Guilt and Conscience in Major Depressive Disorders." *American Journal of Psychiatry* 140 (July 1983): 839–884.

"Psychiatric Diagnosis: Off the Mark." *Science News* 122 (September 11, 1982): 168.

Puig-Antich, Joaquim. "Affective Disorders in Childhood: A Review and Perspective." *Psychiatric Clinics of North America* 3:3 (December 1980): 417.

Rabkin, Judith G., Edward Charles, and Frederick Kass. "Hypertension and DSM-III Depression in Psychiatric Outpatients." *American Journal of Psychiatry* 140:8 (August 1983): 1072–1074.

Rabkin, J. "Therapeutic Attitudes Towards Mental Illness and Health." In *Effective Psychotherapy: A Handbook of Research,* edited by A. S. Gurman and A. M. Razin. Oxford: Pergamon, 1977.

Rafuls, W. A., I. Extein, M. S. Gold, and F. C. Goggans. "Neuropsychiatric Manifestations of Endocrine Disorders." In *Textbook of Neuropsychiatry,* edited by R. E. Hales and S. C. Yudofsky. Washington, D.C.: American Psychiatric Association Press, 1986 (in press).

Ray, Richard A., and Peter Howanitz. "RIA in Thyroid Function Testing." *Diagnostic Medicine* (May 1984): 55–70.

"A Recovering Patient: 'Can We Talk?' The Schizophrenic Patient in Psychotherapy." *American Journal of Psychiatry* 143:1 (January 1986): 68–70.

Reus, Victor I., and Jeffrey R. Berlant. "Pituitary-Adrenal Dysfunction in Psychiatric Illness." In *Medical Mimics of Psychiatric Disorders,* edited by Irl Extein and Mark S. Gold. Washington, D.C.: American Psychiatric Association Press, 1986.

Rickels, Karl. "Premenstrual Syndrome, Introduction." *Psychosomatics* 26:10 (October 1985): 785.

Rivinus, Timothy M., Joseph Biederman, David B. Herzog, et al. "Anorexia Nervosa and Affective Disorders: A Controlled Family History Study." *American Journal of Psychiatry* 141:11 (November 1984): 1414.

Rogers, June. "Psychiatry Puts Itself on the Couch." *MacLeans* 95 (November 27, 1982): 57–58.

Rogoff, Jerome. "Individual Psychotherapy." Chapter 12 in *Inpatient Diagnosis and Treatment,* edited by Lloyd I. Sederer, M.D. Baltimore and London: Williams and Wilkins, 1983.

Ross, C. A. "Biological Tests for Mental Illness: Their Use and Misuse." *Biological Psychiatry* 21 (1986): 431–435.

Rouner, Sandy. "Healthtalk: Shedding Light on Moods." *Washington Post* (June 24, 1983): C-5.

Rubinow, David R., and Robert M. Post. "Impaired Recognition of Affect in Facial Expression in Depressed Patients." *Biological Psychiatry* 31 (1992): 947–953.

Rubinow, David, Robert Post, Robert Savard, and Philip W. Gold. "Cortisol Hypersecretion and Cognitive Impairment in Depression." *Archives of General Psychiatry* 41 (March 1984): 279–283.

Rush, A. John, Michael A. Schlesser, Carl Fulton, and Michael A. Allen. "Biological Basis of Psychiatric Disorders." Chapter in *Clinical Neurosciences,* Vol. 1, edited by R. Rosenberg. London: Churchill-Livingston, 1983: I679–720.

Sabelli, H., J. Fawcett, P. Epstein, et al. "PAA, MHPG, DST and Methylphenidate Test in Depression." Unpublished paper.

Schatzberg, Alan F., Paul J. Orsulak, Alan H. Rosenbaum, et al. "Catecholamine Measures for Diagnosis and Treatment of Patients with Depressive Disorders." *Journal of Clinical Psychiatry* 4:12 (December 1980): Section 2, 35–38.

————. "Clinical Diagnosis and Classification of Affective Disorders." In *The Brain, Biochemistry, and Behavior: Proceedings of the Sixth Arnold O. Beckman Conference in Clinical Chemistry*, edited by Robert L. Habig. Washington, D.C.: The American Association for Clinical Chemistry (1984): 29–46.

————, "Evaluation and Treatment of the Refractory Depressed Patient." Chapter 5 in *Clinical Psychopharmacology*, edited by Jerrold G. Bernstein. 2nd edition. Boston, Bristol, and London: John Wright PSG, Inc., 1984.

————, Paul J. Orsulak, Anthony J. Rothschild, et al. "Platelet MAO Activity and The Dexamethasone Suppression Test in Depressed Patients." *American Journal of Psychiatry* 140:9 (September 1983): 1231–1233.

Schleifer, Steven J., Steven E. Keller, Arthur T. Meyerson, et al. "Lymphocyte Function in Major Depressive Disorder." *Archives of General Psychiatry* 41 (May 1984): 484–486.

Schmeck, Harold M., Jr. "Addict's Brain: Chemistry Holds Hope for Answers." *The New York Times* (January 25, 1983): C1, C4.

————. "Domination Is Linked to Chemical in the Brain." *The New York Times* (September 27, 1983): C3.

————. "Grim New Ravage of AIDS: Brain Damage." *The New York Times* (October 15, 1985): C1.

Schottenfeld, Richard, and Mark Cullen. "Organic Affective Illness Associated with Lead Intoxication." *American Journal of Psychiatry* 141:11 (1984): 1423–1426.

Schuckit, Marc A. "Prevalence of Affective Disorder in a Sample of Young Men." *American Journal of Psychiatry* 139:11 (November 1982): 1431–1436.

Schuster, Joseph. "At Last, a Proven, Drug-Free Treatment for Depression." *Washington University Magazine* 54(2): 27–29.

Schwartz, Richard H. "Suicide: A Pediatrician's View." *Epidemic . . .* Number 6. Straight, Inc., St. Petersburg, Florida.

Sederer, Lloyd I., ed. *Inpatient Psychiatry: Diagnosis and Treatment.* Baltimore and London: Williams and Wilkins, 1983.

Shamberger, Raymond J. "The Subtle Signs of Chronic Vitamin Undernutrition." *Diagnostic Medicine* (April 1984): 61–70.

Shapiro, Robert W., Martin R. Keller. "Initial Six-Month Follow-Up of Patient with Major Depressive Disorder." *Journal of Affective Disorders* 3 (1981): 206–220.

Shemo, John, et al. "A Conjoint Psychiatry-Internal Medicine Program: Development of a Teaching and Clinical Model." *American Journal of Psychiatry* 139:11 (November 1982): 1437–1442.

Sherman, A. D., and F. Petty. "Learned Helplessness Decreases (3H) Imipramine Binding in Rat Cortex." *Journal of Affective Disorders* 6:1 (February 1984): 25–32.

Siever, Larry J., Thomas W. Uhde, David C. Jimerson, et al. "Differential Inhibitory Noradrenergic Responses to Clonidine in 25 Depressed Patients and 25 Normal Control Subjects." *American Journal of Psychiatry* 141:6 (June 1984): 733–741.

Silverman, Harold M., and Gilbert I. Simon. *The Pill Book.* 2nd edition. New York: Bantam Books, 1982.

Silverman, Joseph Shepsel, Julia Ann Silverman, and David A. Eardley. "Do Maladaptive Attitudes Cause Depression?" *Archives of General Psychiatry* 41 (January 1984): 28–30.

Sim, Myre. "What It Means to Be Depressed: Its Primary and Secondary Effects." Chapter 7 in *Clinical Depressions: Diagnostic and Therapeutic Challenges,* edited by Frank Ayd, Jr. Baltimore: Ayd Medical Communications, 1980.

Simons, Anne D., et al. "Cognitive and/or Pharmacotherapy: One Year Later." Paper delivered at American Psychiatric Association annual meeting May 9, 1984, Los Angeles.

Sinyor, D., S. G. Schwartz, F. Peonnet, et al. "Aerobic Fitness Level and Reactivity to Psychosocial Stress: Physiological, Biochemical, and Subjective Measures." *Psychosomatic Medicine* 45:3 (June 1983): 205–216.

Slaby, Andrew E., and Barry S. Fogel. "Identifying Occult Neurological Illness on a Psychiatric Service." *Fair Oaks Hospital Psychiatry Letter* 2:8 (August 1984).

Slawson, Paul Fredric. "Psychiatric Malpractice: The California Experience." *American Journal of Psychiatry* 136:5 (May 1979): 650–654.

―――――, and Frederick G. Guggenheim. "Psychiatric Malpractice: A Review of the National Loss Experience." *American Journal of Psychiatry* 141:8 (August 1984): 979–981.

"Somatic Disease Rate Found High in Psychiatric Patients." *Psychiatric News* (March 1, 1985): 17–20.

Sondheimer, Steven J., Ellen W. Freeman, Beth Scharlop, and Karl Rickels. "Hormonal Changes in Premenstrual Syndrome." *Psychosomatics* 26:10 (October 1985): 803–809.

Stern, Theodore A., Albert Mulley, and George E. Thibault. "Life-Threatening Drug Overdose: Precipitants and Prognosis." *Journal of the American Medical Association* 251:15 (April 20, 1984): 1983–1985.

Sternbach, H. A., I. Extein, D. R. Sweeney, M. S. Gold, and A. L. C. Pottash. "Cortisol Secretion and Urinary MHPG in Unipolar Depression." *International Journal of Psychiatric Medicine* 13:4 (1984): 261–266.

―――――, L. Kirstein, A. L. C. Pottash, M. S. Gold, I. Extein, and D. R. Sweeney. "The TRH Test and Urinary MHPG in Unipolar Depression." *Journal of Affective Disorders* 5:3 (1983): 233–237.

Stone, Alan A. "The New Paradox of Psychiatric Malpractice." *New England Journal of Medicine* 311:21 (November 22, 1984): 1384–1387.

Strauss, Gordon D., et al. "The Cutting Edge in Psychiatry." *American Journal of Psychiatry* 141:1 (January 1984): 38–43.

Sturgeon, Wina. *Depression: How to Recognize It, How to Treat It, and How to Grow From It.* Englewood Cliffs, New Jersey: Prentice-Hall, Inc., 1979.

Talbott, John A. "Psychiatry's Agenda for the '80s." *Journal of the American Medical Association* 251:17 (May 4, 1984): 2250.

―――――. "Psychiatry's Unfinished Business in the 20th Century." Address presented by new president of the American Psychiatric Association at annual meeting, May 1984.

Talley, Joseph H. "When Antidepressants Don't Work." Chapter 13 in *Clinical Depressions: Diagnostic and Therapeutic Challenges,* edited by Frank Ayd, Jr. Baltimore: Ayd Medical Communications, 1980.

Thompson, James W., et al. "The Decline of State Mental Hospitals as Training Sites for Psychiatric Residents." *American Journal of Psychiatry* 140:6 (June 1983): 704–707.

Topping, Robin. "Handicapped by a Misdiagnosis." *Newsday* (January 13, 1985): 6, 23–24.

Torrey, E. Fuller. "The Death of Psychiatry: A Progress Report." Paper presented at annual meeting of American Psychiatric Association, May 1984.

————, "Hollywood's Pique at Psychiatry." *Psychology Today* 5 (July 1981): 74–79.

"Treating Depression with Light: An Interview with Daniel F. Kripke, M.D." *Currents* 4:5 (May 1985): 5–8.

"Treatment of the Winter Blues?" *Medical World News for Psychiatrists* (January 1985): 7.

Tueting, Patricia. *National Institute of Mental Health Sciences Report: Special Report on Depression Research.* Washington D.C.: U.S. Government Printing Office, 1983. 0-418-733.

"Two-Year Follow-Up of Subjects and Their Families Defined as at Risk for Psychopathology on the Basis of Platelet MAO Activities." *Neuropsychobiology* 8 (1982): 51–56.

Udelman, Donna. "Hope and the Immune System." Paper delivered at annual meeting of American Psychiatric Association, May 1984.

van Praag, H. M. "A Transatlantic View of the Diagnosis of Depressions According to DSM-III: Did the DSM-III Solve the Problem of Depression Diagnosis?" *Comprehensive Psychiatry* 23:4 (July/August 1982): 315–329.

Vaughn, Lewis. "The 'Secret Threat' of Marginal Deficiencies." *Prevention* (August 1984): 122.

von Zerssen, Detlev, Mathias Berger, and Peter Doerr. "Neuroendocrine Dysfunction in Subtypes of Depression." Chapter 19 in *Psychoneuroendocrine Dysfunction,* edited by Nandkumer S. Shah and Alexander G. Donald. New York and London: Plenum Medical Book Company, 1984.

Wanbolt, Marianne Z., Ned H. Kalin, and Stephen J. Weiler. "Consistent Reversal of Abnormal DSTs After Different Antidepressant Therapies in a Patient With Dementia." *American Journal of Psychiatry* 142:1 (January 1985): 100–103.

Ward, N. G., H. O. Doerr, and M. C. Storrie. "Skin Conductance: A Potentially Sensitive Test for Depression." *Psychiatry Research* 10:4 (December 1983): 295–302.

Weisse, Carol S. "Depression and Immunocompetence: A Review of the Literature." *Psychological Bulletin* 111 (1992): 475–489.

Weissman, Myrna M., et al. "The Efficacy of Drugs and Psychotherapy in the Treatment of Acute Depressive Episodes." *American Journal of Psychiatry* 136:4B (April 1979): 555–558.

————, and Jeffrey H. Boyd. "The Epidemiology of Affective Disorders." Chapter 4 in *Neurobiology of Mood Disorders,* by Robert M. Post and James C. Ballenger. Volume 1 of *Frontiers of Clinical Neuroscience.* Baltimore and London: Williams and Wilkins, 1984.

————, Priya Wickramaratne, Kathleen R. Merikangas, et al. "Onset of Major Depression in Early Adulthood: Increased Familial Loading and Specificity." *Archives of General Psychiatry* 41 (December 1984): 1136–1143.

————, Elliot S. Gershon, Kenneth K. Kidd, et al. "Psychiatric Disorders in the

Relatives of Probands with Affective Disorders." *Archives of General Psychiatry* 41 (January 1984): 13–21.

————. Psychotherapy in Comparison and in Combination with Pharmacotherapy for the Depressed Outpatient." Chapter 31 in *The Affective Disorders,* edited by John M. Davis and James W. Maas. Washington, D.C.: American Psychiatric Association Press, 1983.

Wender, Paul H., and Donald F. Klein. *Mind, Mood, and Medicine: A Guide to the New Biopsychiatry.* New York: New American Library (A Meridian Book), 1981.

————, et al. "Prevalence of Attention Deficit Disorder, Residual Type, and Other Psychiatric Disorders in Patients with Irritable Colon Syndrome." *American Journal of Psychiatry* 140:12 (December 1983): 1579–1582.

Wilford, Bonnie Baird. *Drug Abuse, A Guide for the Primary Care Physician.* Chicago: American Medical Association, 1981.

Winokur, George, William Coryell, Jean Endicott, and Hagop Akiskal. "Further Distinctions Between Manic-Depressive Illness (Bipolar Disorder) and Primary Depressive Disorder (Unipolar Depression)." *American Journal of Psychiatry* 150:8 (August 1993): 1176–1180.

Winokur, George, Mong T. Tsuang, and Raymond R. Crowe. "The Iowa 500: Affective Disorder in Relatives of Manic and Depressed Patients." *American Journal of Psychiatry* 139:2 (February 1982): 209–212.

"Women's Mental Health Needs Are Not Met: Panel Report." *International Medical Tribune News* (April 1985): 8.

Woo, Olga F. "Toxic Time Bombs: Understanding the Actions of Slow Poisons." *Diagnostic Medicine* (June 1984): 57–62.

Yager, Joel, Katherine LaMotte, and Lynn Fairbanks. "Medical Student Attitudes Toward Psychiatry in Relation to Psychiatric Career Choice." *Journal of Medical Education* 57 (December 1982): 949–951.

————, et al. "Medical Students' Evaluation of Psychiatry: A Cross-Country Comparison." *American Journal of Psychiatry* 139:8 (August 1982): 1003–1009.

Yahraes, Herbert. National Institute of Mental Health Science Reports: "Genes and Mental Health: The Mechanisms of Heredity in Major Mental Illnesses." Washington, D.C.: U.S. Government Printing Office, 1978. 0-274-688 (ADM) 78–640.

Yudofsky, Stuart C., Robert E. Hales, Tom Ferguson. *What You Need to Know About Psychiatric Drugs.* New York: Ballantine Books, 1992.

Zarrow, Susan. "Out of Your Mind . . . Or Out of B_{12}?" *Prevention* (September 1984): 22–26.

Ziporyn, Terra. "Rare Hyper-, Hypothyroid States Require Unconventional Therapies." *Journal of the American Medical Association* 253:6 (February 8, 1985): 737–739, 743.

————. " 'Rip van Winkle Period' Ends for Puerperal Psychiatric Problems." *Journal of the American Medical Association* 251:16 (April 27, 1984): 2061–2064, 2067.

INDEX

ABOUT THE AUTHOR

Mark S. Gold, M.D., is a Professor in the departments of Neuroscience, Psychiatry, and Community Health and Family Medicine at the University of Florida College of Medicine. One of the nation's leading scientific researchers and inventors, he is the author of hundreds of scientific papers, ten medical textbooks, and several bestselling consumer books, including *The Good News About Panic, Anxiety and Phobias.*

He is active in drug education and prevention both nationally and internationally, and currently serves on the Board of Directors of four of America's major drug education and prevention organizations. Dr. Gold has been a two-time Presidential Appointee and Consultant to numerous governmental organizations as well as a drug prevention consultant to private industry, professional sports, and state government. In 1993, he was given a "special agent" award by the Drug Enforcement Administration for a decade of service.

A Fellow in the American College of Clinical Pharmacology and the American Psychiatric Association, Dr. Gold was chosen by his peers as one of the Best Doctors in America in 1992, 1993, 1994, and 1995.